What's
What

What's What

A Visual Glossary of the Physical World

Reginald Bragonier Jr.

and

David Fisher

HAMMOND®

INCORPORATED

MAPLEWOOD, NEW JERSEY

Library of Congress Cataloging in Publication Data

Bragonier, Reginald.
   What's what, a visual glossary of the physical world.

  Includes index.
  Summary: Pictures of common objects and the parts of which they are composed, classed under general categories such as living things, transportation, and personal items, are identified by name.
   1. Picture dictionaries, English. [1. Picture dictionaries. 2. Vocabulary. 3. English language—Terms and phrases] I. Fisher, David, 1946-   . II. Title.
AG250.B7   031'.02   81-7149
ISBN 0-8437-3329-2   AACR2

Editors
Reginald Bragonier Jr., David Fisher

Senior Research Editors
Stephanie Bernardo, Denise Demong,
Sandy Dorfman, Barbara Lefferts

Associate Research Editors
Susan Baran, Dina Boogaard, Edith Hathaway,
Howard Leib, Barry O'Donnell, Patricia Schulman,
Lita Telerico, Carol Tormey, Beverly Weintraub

Assistant Research Editors
Reginald Bragonier III, Brooke Nelson, Tina Oxenberg

Graphics Staff
Peter Kleinman, Donald J. Murphy
Michael Renchiwich – *Art Associate*

Contributing Artists
Neal Adams, Charles Addams, John Hill,
Calvin Klein, Jan Leighton, Dee Molenaar,
The Schechter Group, Dr. Seuss, Mort Walker,
Jo Ann Wanamaker, Andy Warhol, Mike Witte

Contributing Photographers
Bill Ashe, John Barrett, BODI,
David Burnett, Phil Koenig, Michael Weiss

Indexing
Dorothy Macdonald
Annamaria Bouza, Marion D. S. Dreyfus, Andrea Immel

Thumbnail Group
Melissa Ayers – *Production Manager*
Gary Bralow – *Art Director*
Eric Kibble – *Typesetter*
Mark Mugrage – *Mechanical Artist*

Hammond Incorporated
Hugh Johnson – *Publisher*
Warren Cox – *Editorial Director, Trade*
Dwight Dobbins – *Art Director*
Dorothy Bacheller – *Editor*
Maria Maggi – *Copy Editor*
Herb Pierce – *Technical Director*

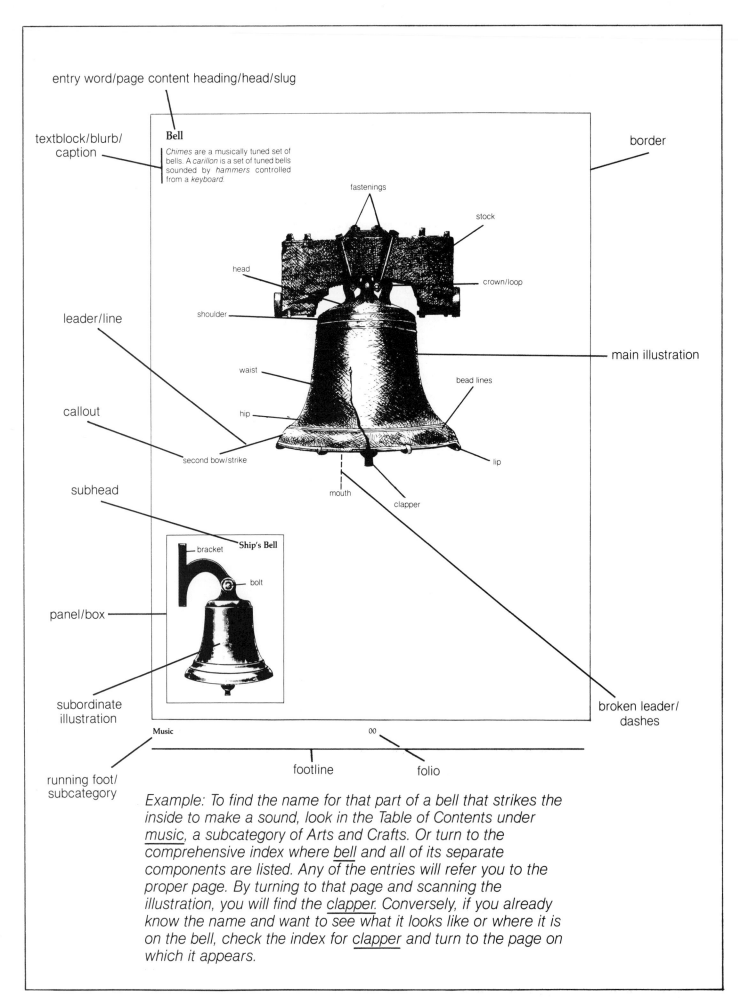

entry word/page content heading/head/slug

textblock/blurb/caption

border

Bell

Chimes are a musically tuned set of bells. A *carillon* is a set of tuned bells sounded by *hammers* controlled from a *keyboard*.

fastenings

stock

head

crown/loop

shoulder

leader/line

main illustration

waist

bead lines

callout

hip

second bow/strike

lip

mouth

clapper

subhead

Ship's Bell

bracket

bolt

panel/box

broken leader/dashes

subordinate illustration

footline

folio

running foot/subcategory

Example: To find the name for that part of a bell that strikes the inside to make a sound, look in the Table of Contents under music, a subcategory of Arts and Crafts. Or turn to the comprehensive index where bell and all of its separate components are listed. Any of the entries will refer you to the proper page. By turning to that page and scanning the illustration, you will find the clapper. Conversely, if you already know the name and want to see what it looks like or where it is on the bell, check the index for clapper and turn to the page on which it appears.

What It Is

Until now, it has been all but impossible to find words you've forgotten or never knew to begin with. The reason for this is obvious: to use a dictionary you need to know the word in order to find it. WHAT'S WHAT provides access to words in an entirely new way—*visually.* Readers can now find words they are seeking by turning to detailed illustrations in which all the visible parts are identified and labeled. This system of visual classification puts within verbal reach of everyone, for the first time, the words used to describe the myriad objects in our everyday world.

The objects chosen for inclusion in WHAT'S WHAT have been selected on the basis of their usefulness to contemporary readers; and although no single volume of this kind can be encyclopedic in its coverage, WHAT'S WHAT is both comprehensive in its scope and practical in its treatment of individual items. Thus, illustrations generally include only the visible parts of objects. However, when it is necessary or desirable to identify part of an item not actually shown, its location is indicated by a broken line. Variations and styles of objects have been presented only when the object's parts make it so distinctive that the item itself has a unique name—lorgnette, for example, which appears on the eyeglasses page. In addition, considerable use has been made of composite illustrations—nonliteral representations combining diverse elements found among similar objects.

How It Works

The book's system of classification is simple and straightforward. Since every object in the physical world is part of a larger whole, the reader can find any detail by locating the larger item. All objects fall naturally into one of the following twelve categories: *The Earth; Living Things; Shelters and Structures; Transportation; Communications; Personal Items; The Home; Sports and Recreation; Arts and Crafts; Machinery, Tools and Weapons; Uniforms, Costumes and Ceremonial Attire;* and *Signs and Symbols.*

To locate an item, turn first to the Table of Contents, where each entry is arranged by category and subcategory according to the object's nature and use. There you will readily determine in what part of the book the item is located. An automobile, for example, is listed under Transportation. An object, or the name of a part, can also be found by consulting the all-inclusive index at the back of the book. A collar stay, for example, can be located by looking under "shirt," "collar," or any other part of a shirt known to the reader, since all these entries will refer to the page on which a shirt is illustrated and all its parts are identified. Rigorous cross-referencing makes the task of finding any item or detail in the book even simpler.

And Why

WHAT'S WHAT is far more than an ordinary reference book. Aided by well-known artists and experts in the visual-arts fields, the editors have made every effort to produce a book that is as engaging as it is informative. Its use, it is hoped, will entertain as well as enlighten.

TABLE OF CONTENTS

TABLE OF CONTENTS *(Continued)*

TABLE OF CONTENTS *(Continued)*

The Earth

This section offers various ways of looking at the earth, ranging from showing the earth as a small planet in the larger space it shares with other heavenly bodies to physical features and symbolic depictions illustrating aspects and details of the earth's surface.

Nonliteral renditions, such as the illustration of the universe, condense information visually by pulling together disparate elements for labeling. Cutaway illustrations like the one of the earth's inner layers are used only when elements considered essential to show and identify are not readily visible. The cave illustration, on the other hand, is rendered in cross section in order to show parts and details which might not be apparent in a traditional illustration.

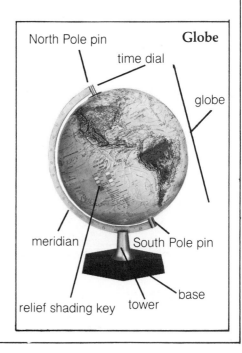

Globe

North Pole pin

time dial

globe

meridian

South Pole pin

relief shading key

tower

base

The Universe

This whimsical creation of the universe includes such bits and pieces of the entire *cosmic mass* as the *solar system*, *local galaxies* and *external galaxies*. Observable *planets* are illuminated by the light of our sun. *Meteors*, or *shooting stars*, are seen as streaks of light in the *sky* as they are vaporized on entering earth's atmosphere.

spiral galaxy

red supergiant star

side

elliptical galaxies

full face

common spiral galaxi

black hole

irregular galaxies

barrel spiral galaxy

asteroids/planetoids

Pluto

nebula/interstellar cloud

Neptune

stars

Uranus

doppler shift

constellation

mystery gas cloud

pulsar

quark

quasar

radiation belt

tail

comet

head/coma

white dwarf star

binary stars/double stars

ion particle cloud

radio waves

supernova

satellite

Cassini division

rings

Saturn

solar flare/solar prominence

Jupiter

Titan

Mars

Earth

Venus

Mercury

moon/satellite

Milky Way Galaxy

Sun

Sun spots

cosmic rays

The Planetary System

Earth Core

Geologists divide the earth into three zones: the lithosphere, containing all solids from the land surface to the earth's center; the hydrosphere, all surface water areas; and the atmosphere, the layered gaseous envelope surrounding the earth's surface. The moon goes through eight phases every 29.5 days, called a synodic period, or lunar month, in which parts of it are in dark shadow and not visible from earth.

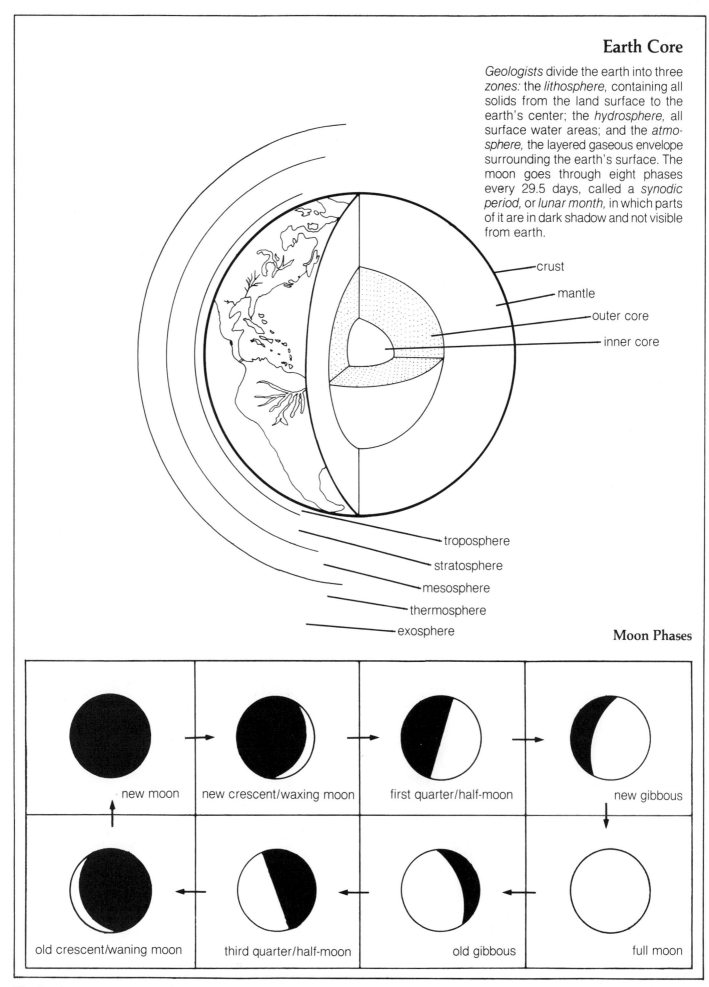

crust
mantle
outer core
inner core

troposphere
stratosphere
mesosphere
thermosphere
exosphere

Moon Phases

new moon	new crescent/waxing moon	first quarter/half-moon	new gibbous
old crescent/waning moon	third quarter/half-moon	old gibbous	full moon

Cartographer's World

Position on the earth's *grid* can be determined by finding exact *latitude, north* or *south* of the equator, and *longitude, east* or *west* of the prime meridian. As the earth makes its daily rotation, the sun crosses every meridian once each day. When this occurs, all points on the meridian experience *noon* at the same instant. At the same time on the opposite side of the earth it is *midnight* and a new *calendar day* is beginning. There is a difference of one hour in *solar time* every 15 *degrees*. The world time zone map shows how the theoretical division of the world into 24 equal *time belts* has been modified to follow *political* or *geographical boundaries*.

pole

rhumb line

parallels of latitude/
latitude lines

meridians/
longitude lines

prime meridian/
first meridian

equator

Central
Standard Time

Greenwich
Mean Time

Mountain
Standard Time

Eastern
Standard Time

Pacific
Standard Time

Time Zones

International
Date Line

EQUATOR

PRIME
MERIDIAN
(GREENWICH)

The Earth

Wind and Ocean Currents

The *zonal patterns* of wind are displaced northward and southward seasonally. Those shown here prevail in winter. *Seasonal currents* change speed and direction due to seasonal winds, whereas *permanent currents* experience relatively little change.

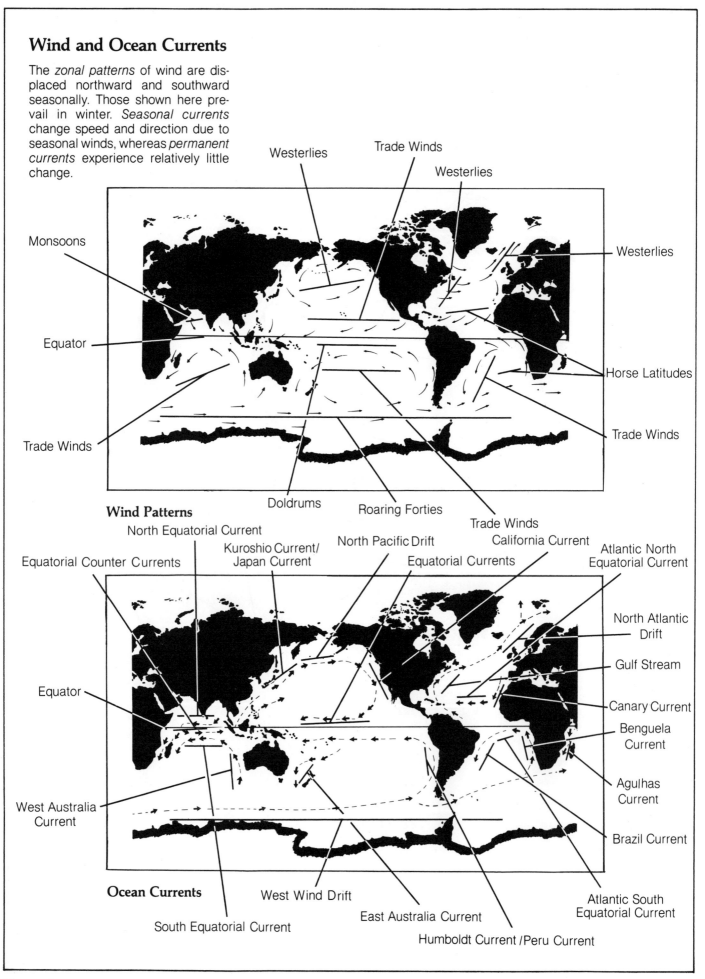

Westerlies

Trade Winds

Westerlies

Westerlies

Monsoons

Equator

Horse Latitudes

Trade Winds

Trade Winds

Wind Patterns

Doldrums

Roaring Forties

Trade Winds

North Equatorial Current

North Pacific Drift

California Current

Equatorial Counter Currents

Kuroshio Current/ Japan Current

Equatorial Currents

Atlantic North Equatorial Current

North Atlantic Drift

Gulf Stream

Equator

Canary Current

Benguela Current

Agulhas Current

West Australia Current

Brazil Current

Ocean Currents

West Wind Drift

South Equatorial Current

East Australia Current

Humboldt Current / Peru Current

Atlantic South Equatorial Current

Land Features

A part of an *ocean* or *sea* extending into the land is a *gulf*. A narrow finger of land extending into the water is a *spit*. A sand or gravel bar connecting an island with the *mainland* or another island is a *tombolo*.

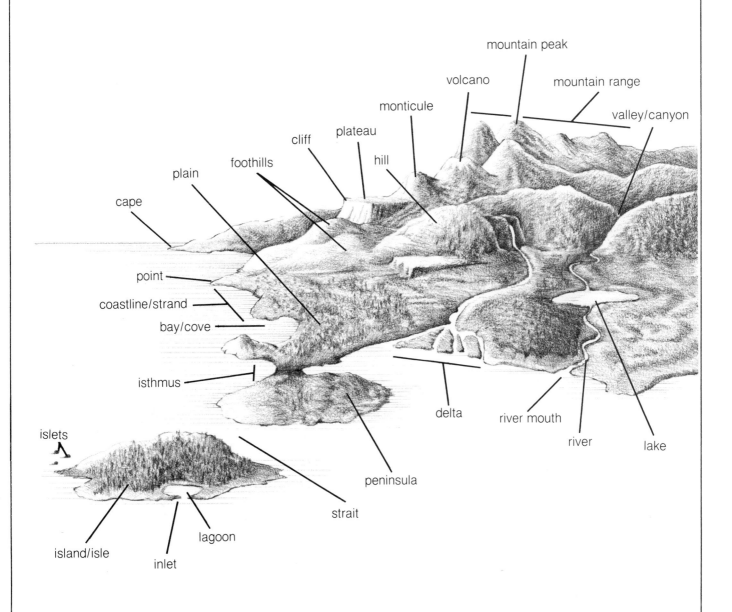

mountain peak

volcano

mountain range

monticule

valley/canyon

plateau

cliff

hill

foothills

plain

cape

point

coastline/strand

bay/cove

isthmus

delta

river mouth

river

lake

islets

peninsula

strait

lagoon

island/isle

inlet

Mountains

A series of mountains, such as the Alpine mountains shown here, is a *range*. A circular space in mountains is a *cirque,* or *cwm*. A *kame* is a ridge or material left by a retreating *ice sheet*. An isolated hill or mountain rising abruptly from the surrounding land is a *butte*.

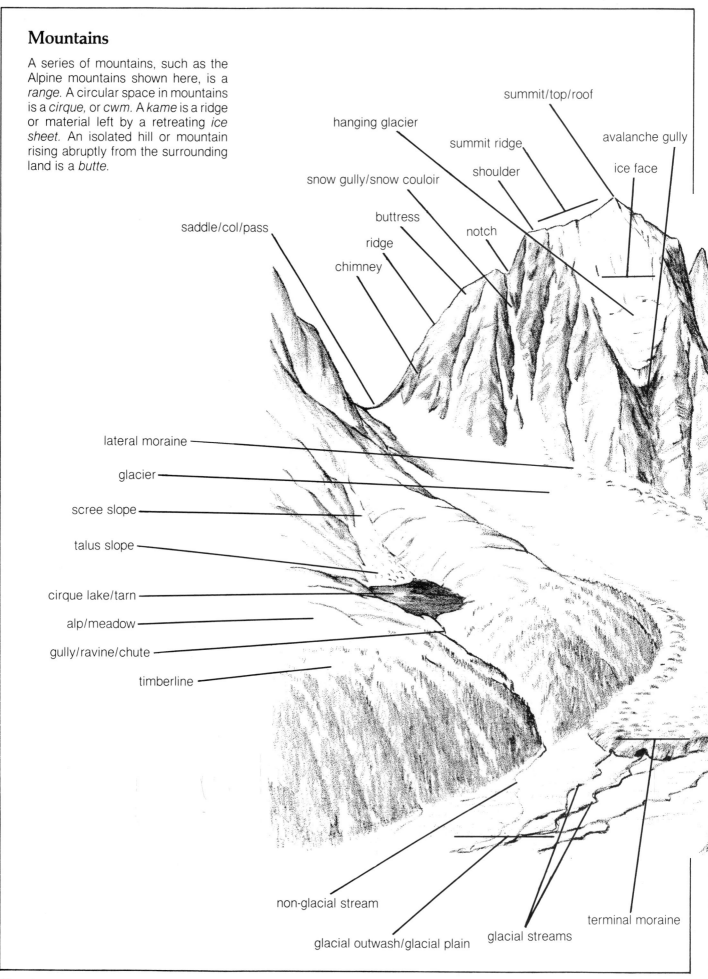

summit/top/roof

hanging glacier

avalanche gully

summit ridge

shoulder

ice face

snow gully/snow couloir

buttress

notch

ridge

saddle/col/pass

chimney

lateral moraine

glacier

scree slope

talus slope

cirque lake/tarn

alp/meadow

gully/ravine/chute

timberline

non-glacial stream

glacial outwash/glacial plain

glacial streams

terminal moraine

ridge/arete

bergschrund

cirque headwall

cirque glacier

tower/pinnacle/spire/ gendarme/needle/pillar

crest

ice field/snowfield/ névé/firn

cliff/wall/face

rib

moat

crevasse

ice cliff

icefall

seracs

avalanche area

lateral moraine

medial moraine

ledge

crevice

overhang

9

Terrains

Volcano

In *central-vent volcanoes*, such as the one shown here, material erupts from a single pipe. *Fissure volcanoes* extrude material along extensive *fractures*.

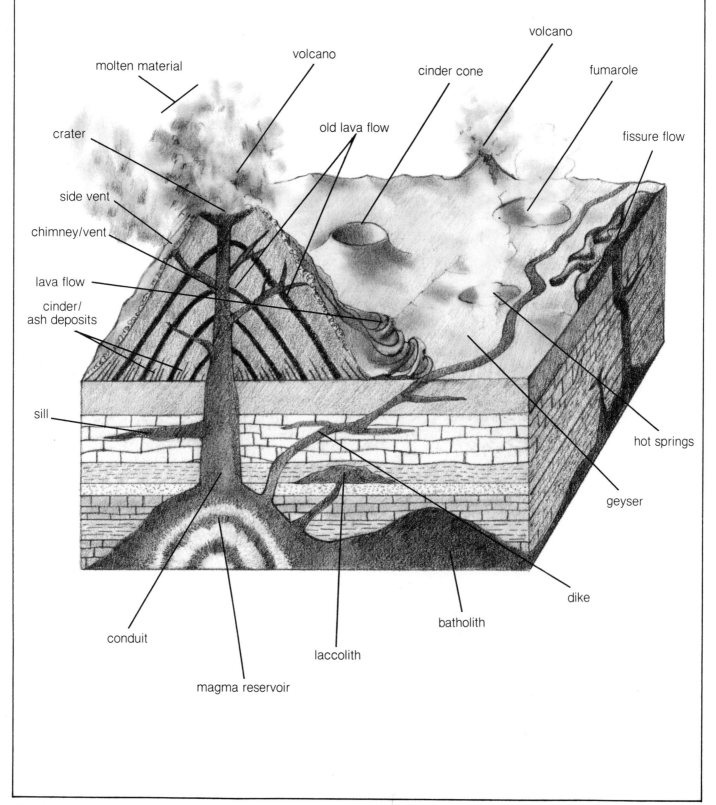

molten material

volcano

volcano

cinder cone

fumarole

crater

old lava flow

fissure flow

side vent

chimney/vent

lava flow

cinder/ ash deposits

sill

hot springs

geyser

dike

conduit

batholith

laccolith

magma reservoir

Cave Cross Section

The exploration of caves, or *caverns,* is called *spelunking* or *caving.* The area lighted by daylight just inside a cave entrance is the *twilight zone.* An underground structure containing many *galleries, chambers* or *rooms* is a *cave system.* Anything formed inside a cave, *cavern* or *grotto,* by dripping water is *dripstone.* Knobby calcite growths often found on *walls* and *floors* of once-submerged caves are called *cave coral* or *cave popcorn.*

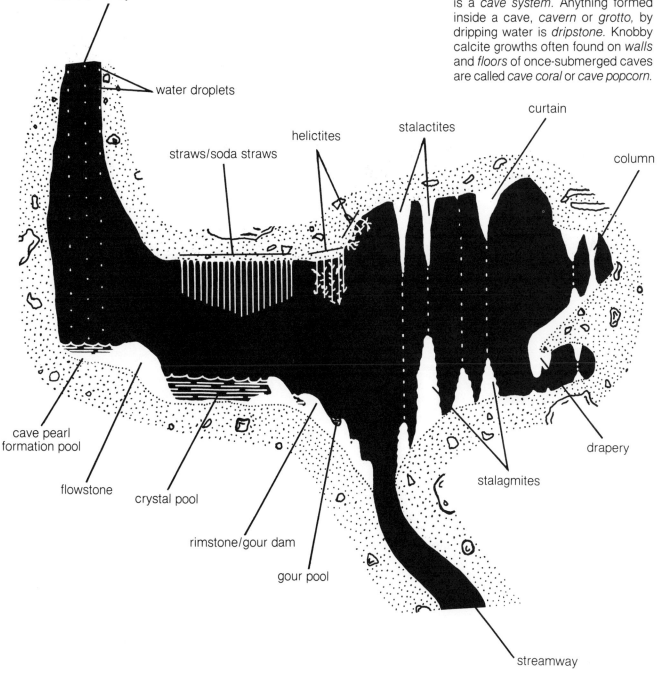

shaft/chimney/aven

water droplets

straws/soda straws

helictites

stalactites

curtain

column

cave pearl
formation pool

flowstone

crystal pool

rimstone/gour dam

gour pool

stalagmites

drapery

streamway

11

Glacier

When a glacier terminates at the water's edge, sections break off, or *calve,* to form icebergs. Icebergs often break apart to form smaller, separate *bergs, bergy bits* or *bitty bergs.* Even smaller sections are called *growlers. Ice packs,* formed when the water surface between floating ice freezes, are called *floes.* Sections that break off are called *floebergs.*

horn/spitz/peak

accumulation zone

arête

cirque glacier

snowfield

non-glaciated valley

valley glacier

lateral moraine

drumlin

medial moraine

ablation zone

terminal moraine/
front/terminus/snout

Glacier

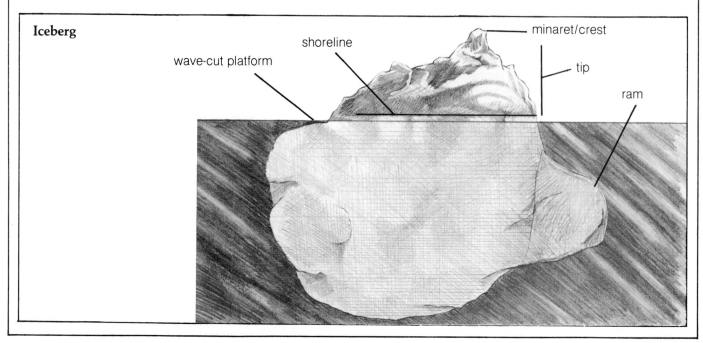

Iceberg

minaret/crest

shoreline

wave-cut platform

tip

ram

River

A *river system* consists of the main river and its tributaries or branches. It drains from a *river basin*, and flows along a *course*, or *watercourse*, cutting a *channel* through the land. A *flood* occurs when it overflows its banks.

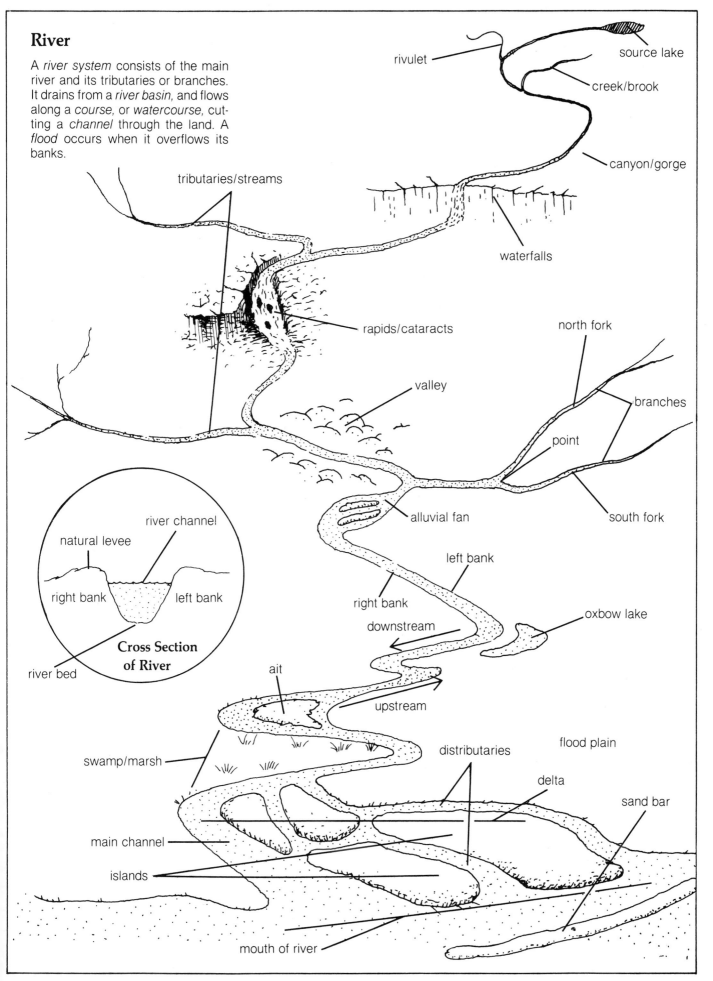

rivulet

source lake

creek/brook

canyon/gorge

tributaries/streams

waterfalls

rapids/cataracts

north fork

branches

valley

point

south fork

alluvial fan

left bank

river channel

natural levee

right bank

left bank

right bank

oxbow lake

river bed

downstream

Cross Section of River

ait

upstream

flood plain

swamp/marsh

distributaries

delta

sand bar

main channel

islands

mouth of river

Water Systems

Wave and Shoreline

Wavelength is the linear distance between two wave crests, *period* is the time it takes two crests to pass a given point, and *wave height* is the vertical distance measured from the trough to the crest of a wave. There are *surface waves*, *tidal waves*, *internal waves*, *tsunamis*, *storm surges* and *seiches*. Long, crestless waves are *swells*. The rapid flow of water up onto the *beach face* following the breaking of *surf* is the *uprush* or *swash*.

crest

whitecap/spindrift

scend

curl/tunnel/
tube/pipeline

back

shoulder/wall

trough

Shoreline Profile

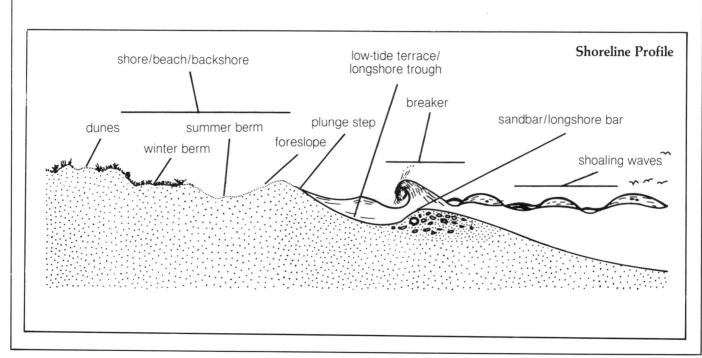

shore/beach/backshore

low-tide terrace/
longshore trough

breaker

dunes

summer berm

plunge step

sandbar/longshore bar

winter berm

foreslope

shoaling waves

Coastline and Continental Margin

The *littoral zone* is that part of the shoreline that lies between *high* and *low tides.* The continental shelf is the submerged border of *landmasses* extending into the *ocean basin.* The *100-fathom curve* has long been used as the outer limit of the continental shelf.

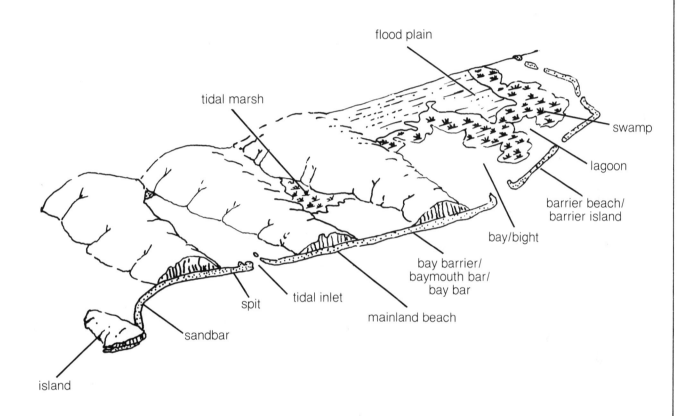

flood plain

tidal marsh

swamp

lagoon

barrier beach/
barrier island

bay/bight

bay barrier/
baymouth bar/
bay bar

mainland beach

spit

tidal inlet

sandbar

island

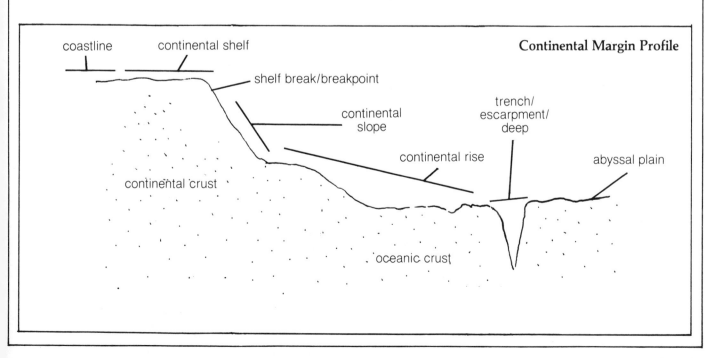

Continental Margin Profile

coastline

continental shelf

shelf break/breakpoint

continental
slope

trench/
escarpment/
deep

continental rise

abyssal plain

continental crust

oceanic crust

Clouds

The name of a cloud describes both its appearance and its height above the ground. Clouds are formed from tiny droplets of water or *ice crystals* and continually change shape due to evaporation, wind and *air movements.*

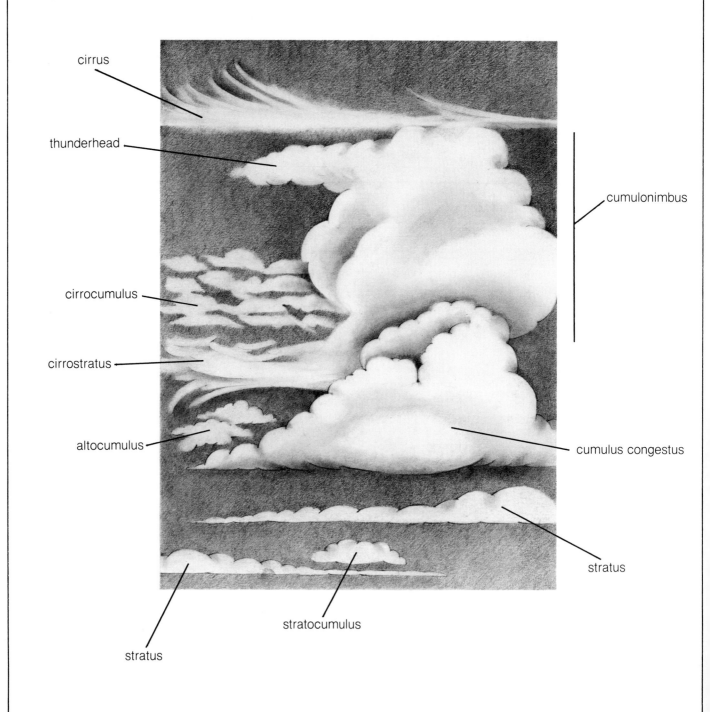

cirrus

thunderhead

cirrocumulus

cirrostratus

altocumulus

cumulonimbus

cumulus congestus

stratus

stratus

stratocumulus

Storm Systems

Thunderstorms carry the same general features: lightning, *thunder,* strong gusts of *wind,* heavy *showers,* and occasionally *hailstones.* When hurricanes occur in the Pacific, they are called *typhoons.* Tornados are also known as *twisters.*

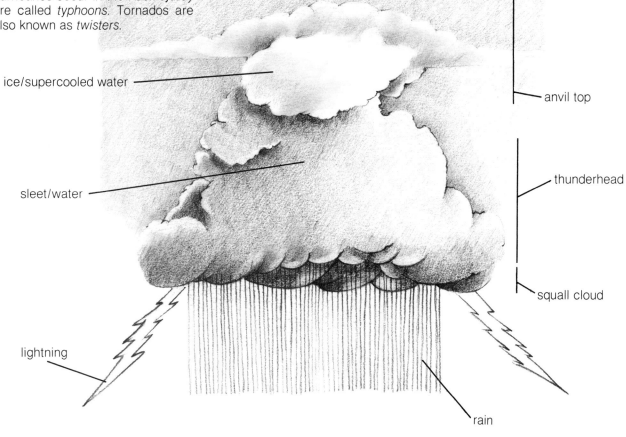

ice/supercooled water

anvil top

sleet/water

thunderhead

squall cloud

lightning

rain

Thunderstorm

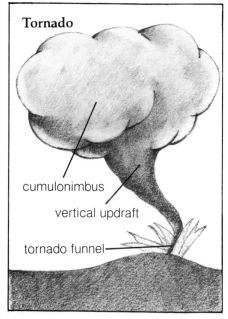

Tornado

cumulonimbus

vertical updraft

tornado funnel

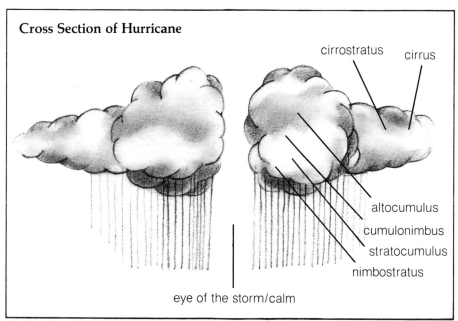

Cross Section of Hurricane

cirrostratus

cirrus

altocumulus

cumulonimbus

stratocumulus

nimbostratus

eye of the storm/calm

Weather

Weather Monitoring Equipment

Equipment, such as that shown here, helps a *meteorologist* predict weather and make *weather forecasts*.

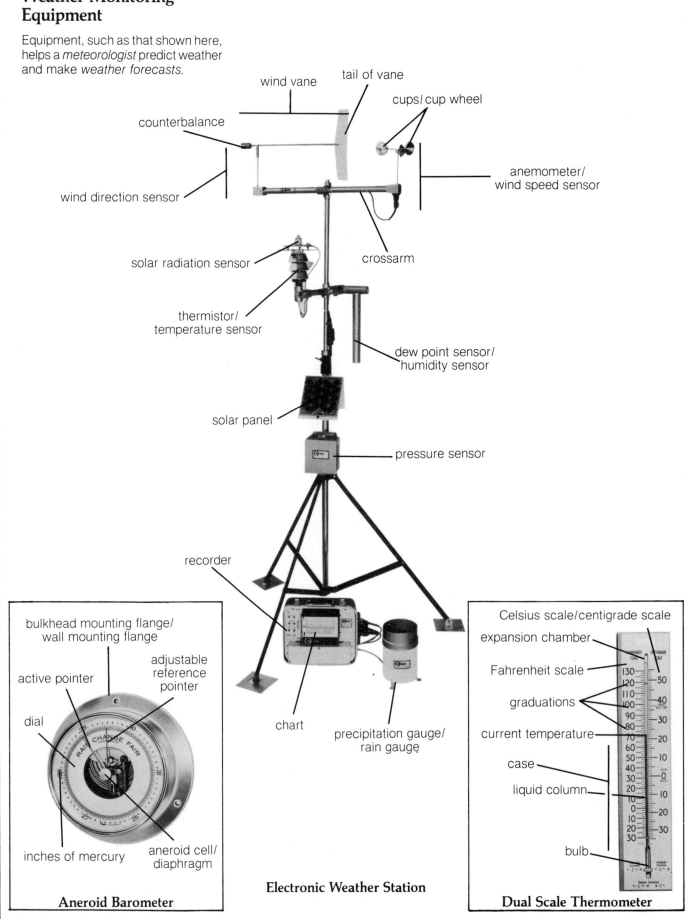

wind vane

tail of vane

cups/cup wheel

counterbalance

anemometer/ wind speed sensor

wind direction sensor

solar radiation sensor

crossarm

thermistor/ temperature sensor

dew point sensor/ humidity sensor

solar panel

pressure sensor

recorder

bulkhead mounting flange/ wall mounting flange

adjustable reference pointer

active pointer

dial

chart

precipitation gauge/ rain gauge

inches of mercury

aneroid cell/ diaphragm

Aneroid Barometer

Electronic Weather Station

Celsius scale/centigrade scale

expansion chamber

Fahrenheit scale

graduations

current temperature

case

liquid column

bulb

Dual Scale Thermometer

Weather Map

This composite weather map, or *synoptic chart,* displays conditions over a broad area. The numbers around the station model indicate *temperature, barometric pressure* and *pressure change.*

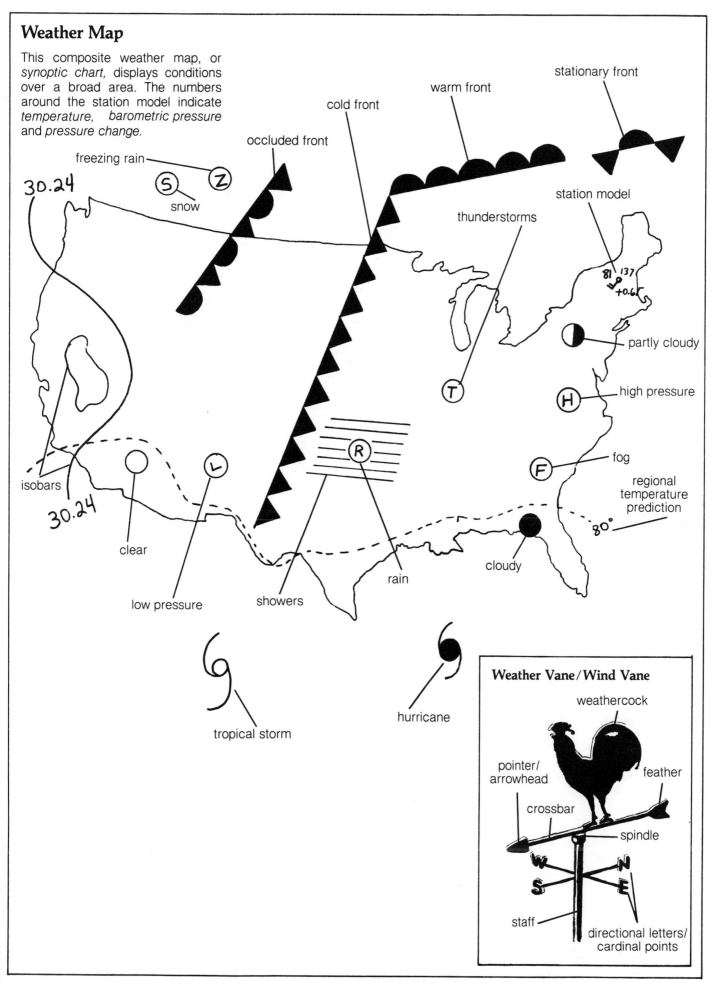

freezing rain

occluded front

cold front

warm front

stationary front

snow

thunderstorms

station model

81 137
9
+0.6

partly cloudy

high pressure

fog

regional temperature prediction

80°

isobars

clear

low pressure

showers

rain

cloudy

tropical storm

hurricane

Weather Vane/Wind Vane

weathercock

pointer/ arrowhead

feather

crossbar

spindle

staff

directional letters/ cardinal points

Map

The science of *mapmaking* is also known as *cartography*. The *projection* of a map is the framework on which its main components, *linework,* point or area symbols and type are placed.

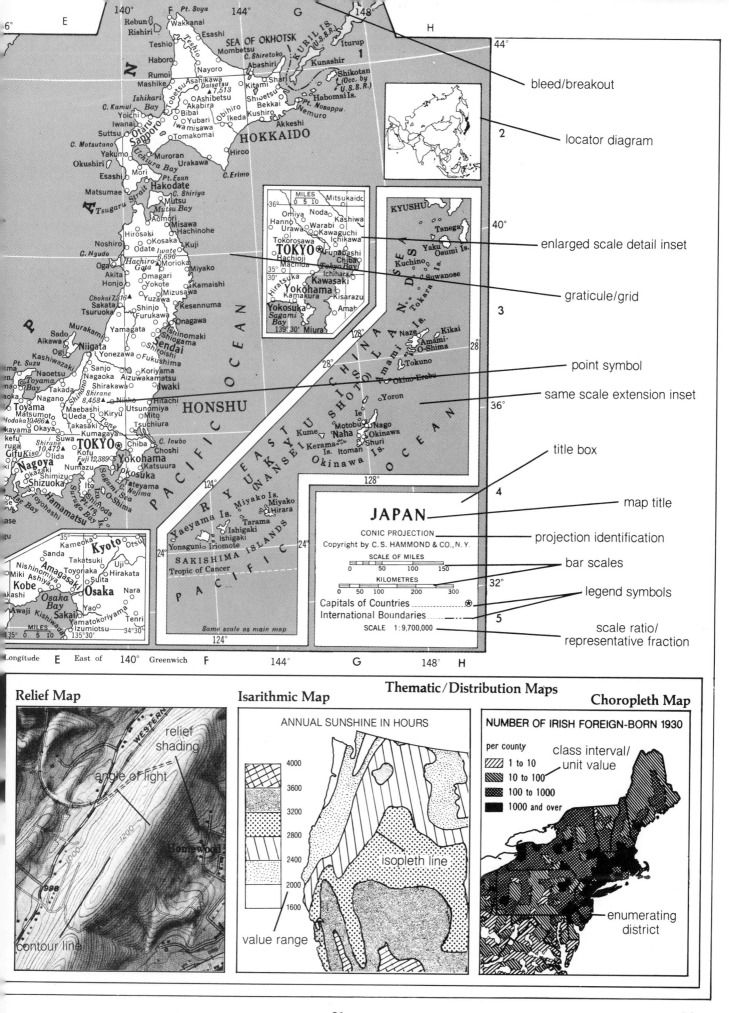

bleed/breakout

locator diagram

enlarged scale detail inset

graticule/grid

point symbol

same scale extension inset

title box

map title

projection identification

bar scales

legend symbols

scale ratio/
representative fraction

JAPAN

CONIC PROJECTION
Copyright by C.S. HAMMOND & CO., N.Y.

SCALE OF MILES
0   50   100   150

KILOMETRES
0   50   100   200   300

Capitals of Countries .... ⊛
International Boundaries ....
SCALE   1:9,700,000

Longitude   East of   140° Greenwich

Thematic/Distribution Maps

Relief Map

relief shading

angle of light

contour line

Isarithmic Map

ANNUAL SUNSHINE IN HOURS

4000
3600
3200
2800
2400
2000
1600

isopleth line

value range

Choropleth Map

NUMBER OF IRISH FOREIGN-BORN 1930

per county
1 to 10
10 to 100
100 to 1000
1000 and over

class interval/
unit value

enumerating
district

Nautical Chart and Topographic Map

On nautical charts, *sounding datum reference* is stated in the *chart title*. *Depth conversion scales* are provided to enable the mariner to work in *meters, fathoms,* or *feet*. The space outside a chart or map, used to identify and explain the map, is the *map margin*.

light-horn
mud
spit
can/cylindrical buoy
wreck
rocks
submerged rock
midchannel bell buoy
channel
nun/conical buoy
jetty
Coast Guard station
pier
anchorage
soundings
flat coast
true north
magnetic north
compass rose
light/lighthouse
bluff
town
water tower
towers
shoreline
aeronautical light
depth contours
sandhills/dunes

Nautical Chart

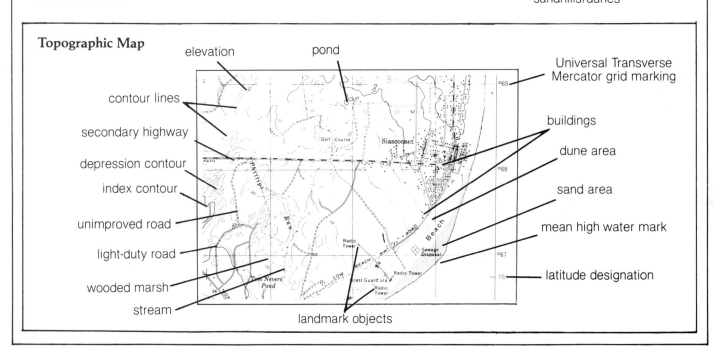

Topographic Map

elevation
pond
contour lines
secondary highway
depression contour
index contour
unimproved road
light-duty road
wooded marsh
stream
landmark objects
Universal Transverse Mercator grid marking
buildings
dune area
sand area
mean high water mark
latitude designation

Living Things

For ease of reference, this section has been divided into five subcategories: man, edible animals, domestic animals, wild animals, and plants. The animals and plants selected for inclusion within each subsection contain most of the parts common to all members of the major families they represent.

With the exception of man, examined more closely than any other subject in this section because of his obvious importance to us, only the external parts of living things have been identified. However, edible animals have been illustrated in such a way as to show those parts which supply our daily food. Domestic and wild animals, some of them grouped by habitat, are represented by single members of a species. But because there are parts which are unique to certain animals, a composite "beast" has been created to illustrate some of them.

The plant kingdom is represented from the roots up, literally, including coverage of parts of a flower, special plants, and edible portions called fruits and vegetables.

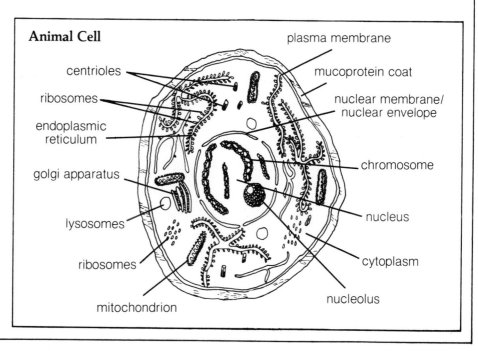

Animal Cell

- plasma membrane
- centrioles
- mucoprotein coat
- ribosomes
- nuclear membrane/ nuclear envelope
- endoplasmic reticulum
- chromosome
- golgi apparatus
- nucleus
- lysosomes
- ribosomes
- cytoplasm
- nucleolus
- mitochondrion

The Human Body

The body, less the *head* and *limbs,* is referred to as the *trunk* or *torso.*

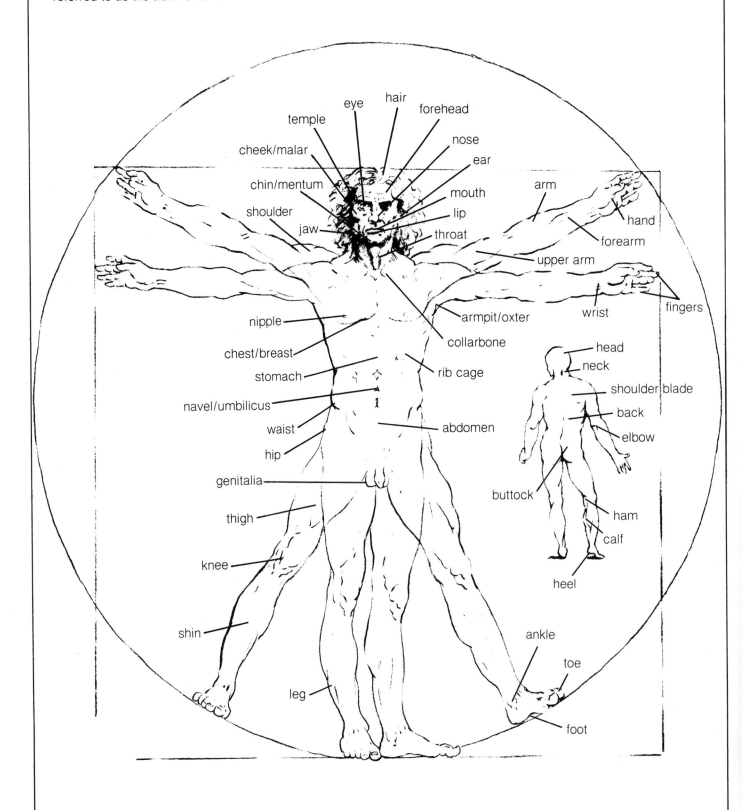

temple
eye
hair
forehead
cheek/malar
nose
ear
chin/mentum
mouth
shoulder
lip
jaw
throat
arm
hand
forearm
upper arm
nipple
armpit/oxter
wrist
fingers
chest/breast
collarbone
stomach
rib cage
navel/umbilicus
head
neck
waist
shoulder blade
hip
abdomen
back
genitalia
elbow
thigh
buttock
knee
ham
calf
shin
heel
leg
ankle
toe
foot

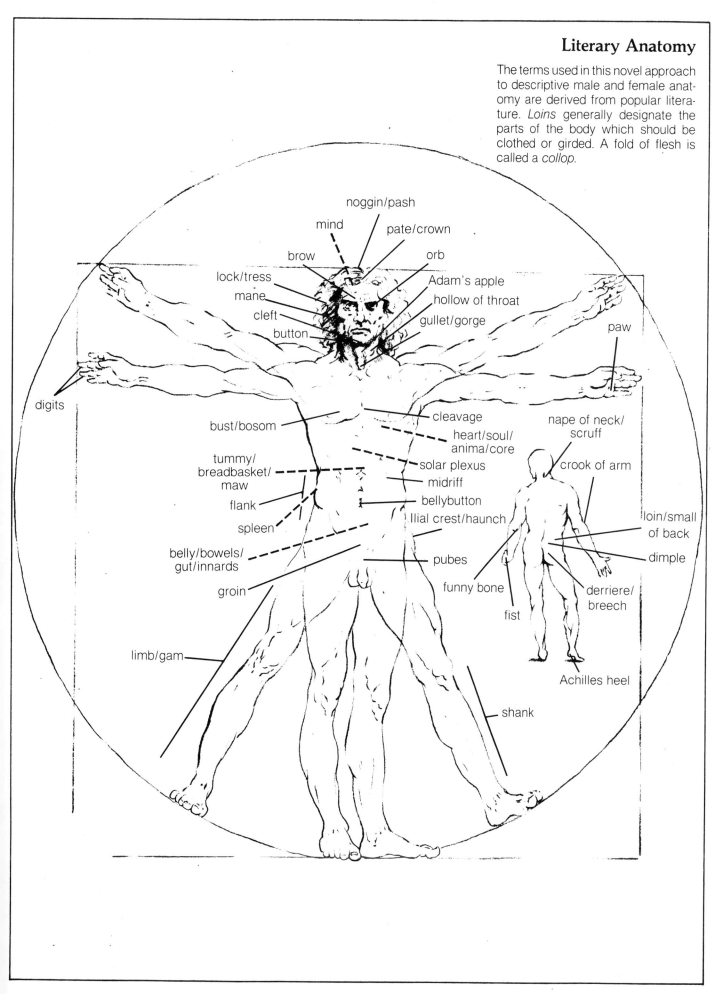

Literary Anatomy

The terms used in this novel approach to descriptive male and female anatomy are derived from popular literature. *Loins* generally designate the parts of the body which should be clothed or girded. A fold of flesh is called a *collop*.

noggin/pash

mind

pate/crown

brow

orb

lock/tress

Adam's apple

mane

hollow of throat

cleft

gullet/gorge

button

paw

digits

cleavage

bust/bosom

nape of neck/ scruff

heart/soul/ anima/core

tummy/ breadbasket/ maw

crook of arm

solar plexus

midriff

flank

bellybutton

loin/small of back

spleen

Ilial crest/haunch

dimple

belly/bowels/ gut/innards

pubes

derriere/ breech

funny bone

groin

fist

limb/gam

Achilles heel

shank

Man

Skeletal and Muscular System

Voluntary muscles are subject to or controlled by will, pulling on *bones* of the *skeleton* to produce movement. *Involuntary muscles,* like the heart, act independently of volition. Where one bone meets another is a *joint.* *Cartilage,* or *gristle,* is a flexible type of connective tissue. The bony structure in which the brain is housed is the *cranium.*

frontal

sternocleidomastoid

maxilla

skull

trapezius

malar

mandible

deltoid

cervical vertebrae

pectoralis major

clavicle

scapula

latissimus dorsi

sternum

triceps

ribs

humerus

biceps

vertebral column

brachioradialis

ilium

flexor carpi radialis

pubis

radius

adductor policis

ulna

gluteus medius

sartorius

ischium

carpal

adductor longus

sacrum

intercarpal

rectus

femur

phalanges

gracilis

patella

vastus medialis

tibialis anterior

fibula

gastrocnemius

tibia

soleus

calcaneus

tarsals

metatarsals

tibialis posterior

phalanges

Internal Organs

The stomach and intestines are the principal organs of the *digestive system*, or *alimentary canal*, and the *pancreas*, liver and *gall bladder* all aid in the nutrition process and the elimination of wastes. The heart is the pump of the *circulatory system*, sending blood through *arteries*, *veins* and *capillaries*. The lungs are the center of the *respiratory system*.

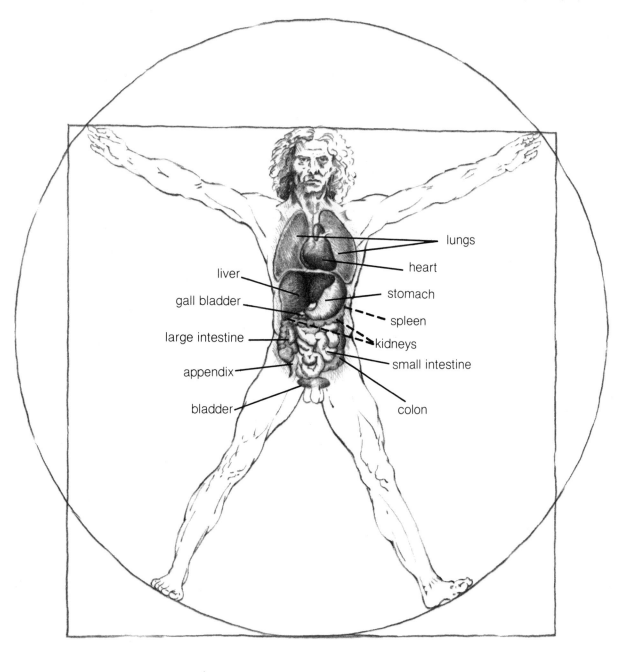

lungs

heart

liver

stomach

gall bladder

spleen

large intestine

kidneys

small intestine

appendix

bladder

colon

Man

Sense Organs

The eye, which is located in an *eye socket*, or *orbit*, is covered with a transparent layer called the *cornea*. The angle formed where upper and lower eyelids come together is called the *cantus*. The junction nearest the nose is the *inner cantus*, the other is the *outer cantus*. The tongue rubs against the *palate* at the top of the mouth. The *pharynx* is the beginning of the *throat*, or *gullet*.

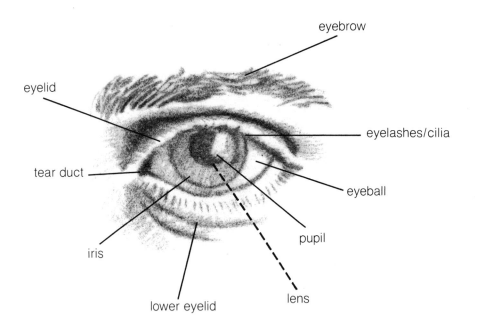

eyebrow
eyelid
eyelashes/cilia
tear duct
eyeball
iris
pupil
lower eyelid
lens

Eye

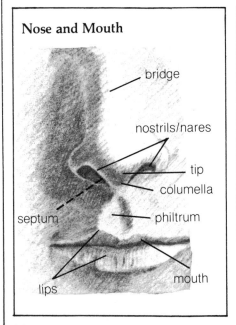

Nose and Mouth

bridge
nostrils/nares
tip
columella
septum
philtrum
lips
mouth

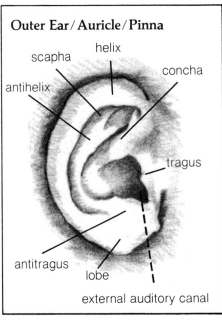

Outer Ear / Auricle / Pinna

scapha
helix
concha
antihelix
tragus
antitragus
lobe
external auditory canal

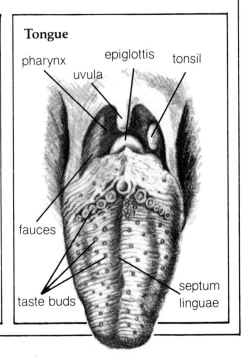

Tongue

pharynx
uvula
epiglottis
tonsil
fauces
taste buds
septum linguae

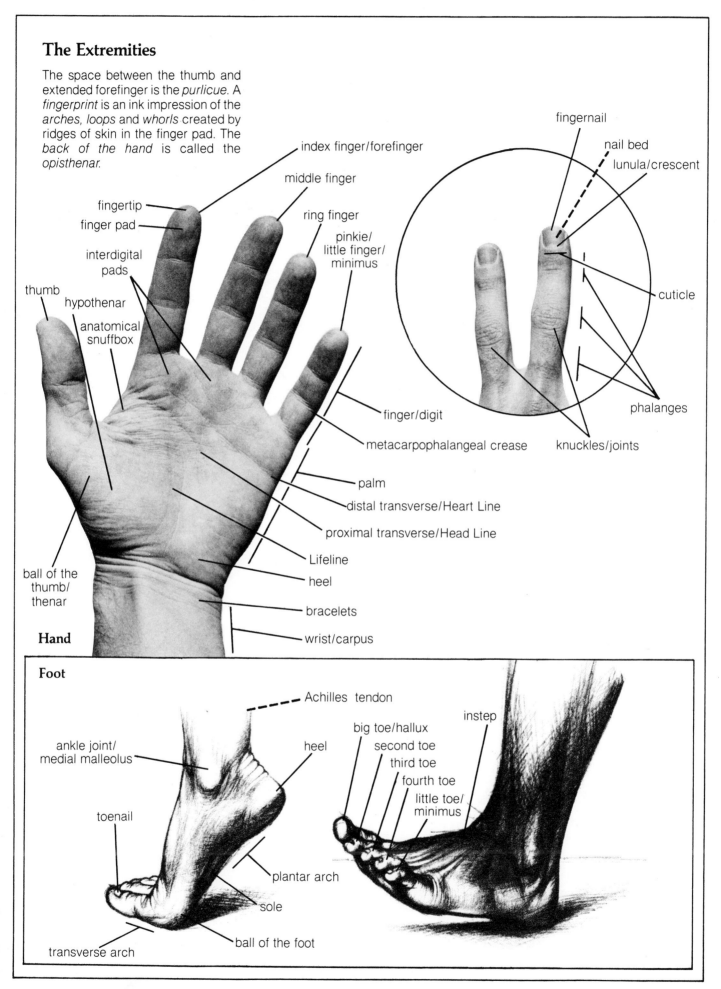

The Extremities

The space between the thumb and extended forefinger is the *purlicue*. A *fingerprint* is an ink impression of the *arches, loops* and *whorls* created by ridges of skin in the finger pad. The *back of the hand* is called the *opisthenar*.

Hand

index finger/forefinger

middle finger

ring finger

pinkie/
little finger/
minimus

fingertip

finger pad

interdigital
pads

thumb

hypothenar

anatomical
snuffbox

ball of the
thumb/
thenar

finger/digit

metacarpophalangeal crease

palm

distal transverse/Heart Line

proximal transverse/Head Line

Lifeline

heel

bracelets

wrist/carpus

fingernail

nail bed

lunula/crescent

cuticle

phalanges

knuckles/joints

Foot

Achilles tendon

ankle joint/
medial malleolus

heel

big toe/hallux

second toe

third toe

fourth toe

little toe/
minimus

instep

toenail

plantar arch

sole

ball of the foot

transverse arch

Cow

Young *cattle* are *calves;* females are *heifers* until they give birth and are then cows; males are *bulls.* Castrated males, raised for *beef,* are *steers.* Castrated males, raised as draft animals, are *oxen.* The body, or *torso,* of a cow is known as the *barrel.*

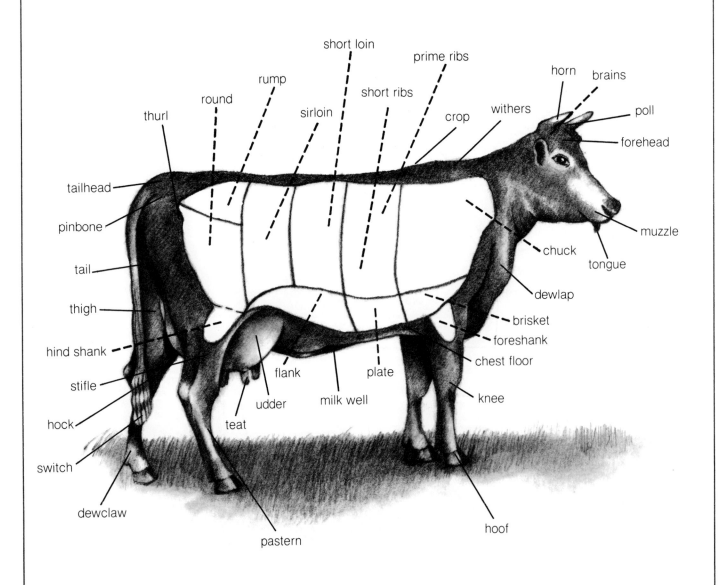

Sheep

A young sheep is called a *lamb*. An adult male is a *ram;* an adult female is a *ewe*. The meat of a young sheep is called *lamb,* while that of an animal over eighteen months old is called *mutton.*

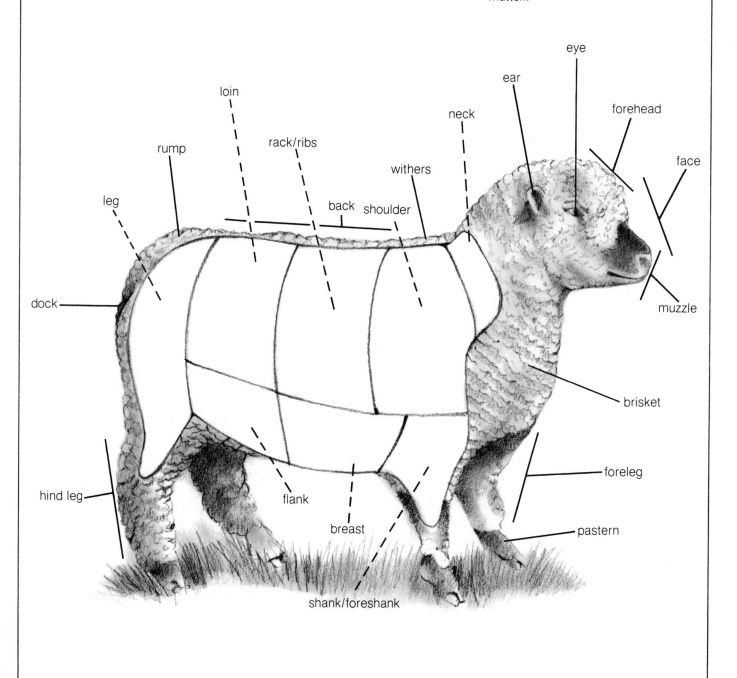

eye

ear

forehead

neck

face

loin

rack/ribs

withers

rump

back   shoulder

leg

muzzle

dock

brisket

foreleg

hind leg

flank

pastern

breast

shank/foreshank

Edible Animals

Pig

Young pigs are called *shoats*. Small or sub-adult domestic animals are *pigs* or *gruntlings*. If they weigh over 120 pounds, they are called *hogs*. Adult males are *boars*. Adult females are *sows*. Pigs, hogs, boars and sows are referred to as *swine*. Pig meat is called *pork*.

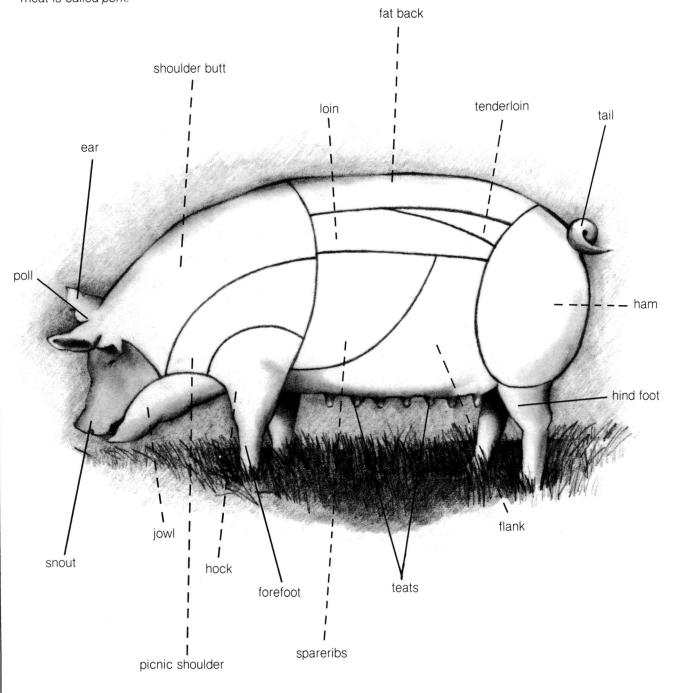

fat back

shoulder butt

loin

tenderloin

tail

ear

poll

ham

snout

jowl

hock

forefoot

teats

flank

hind foot

picnic shoulder

spareribs

Poultry

Chickens, turkeys, *ducks, geese* and *pheasants* are known collectively as *fowl* in the wild, as *poultry* if domesticated. A male chicken is a *rooster;* a female is a *hen.* A male turkey is a *tom.* Young chickens are *chicks;* young turkeys are *poults.* A *capon* is a male chicken that has been castrated before sexual maturity. Unlike other poultry, ducks have *webbed feet* and broad, flat *bills* with small *teeth.* Among the *entrails* of a fowl, the most edible are the *giblets,* the *heart,* the *liver* and the *gizzard.*

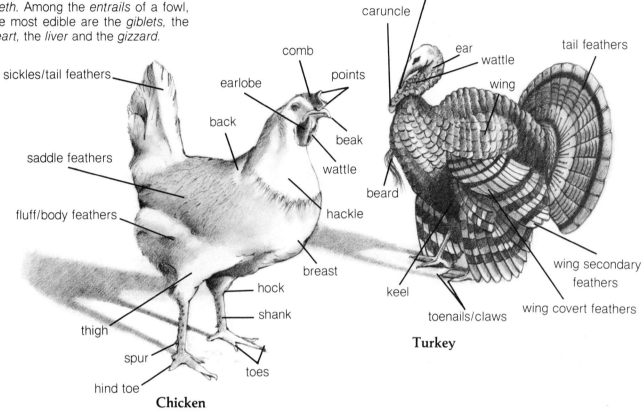

comb
earlobe
back
points
beak
wattle
hackle
sickles/tail feathers
saddle feathers
fluff/body feathers
breast
thigh
hock
shank
spur
hind toe
toes

Chicken

snood/dewbill
caruncle
ear
wattle
wing
tail feathers
beard
keel
toenails/claws
wing secondary feathers
wing covert feathers

Turkey

Poultry Parts

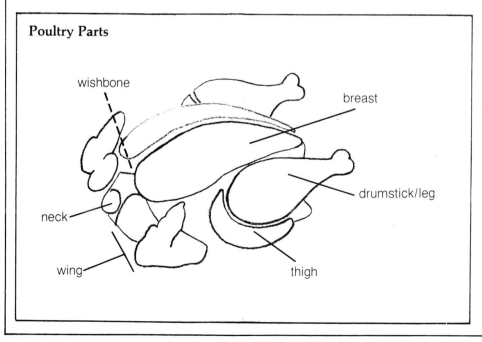

wishbone
breast
neck
drumstick/leg
wing
thigh

Edible Animals

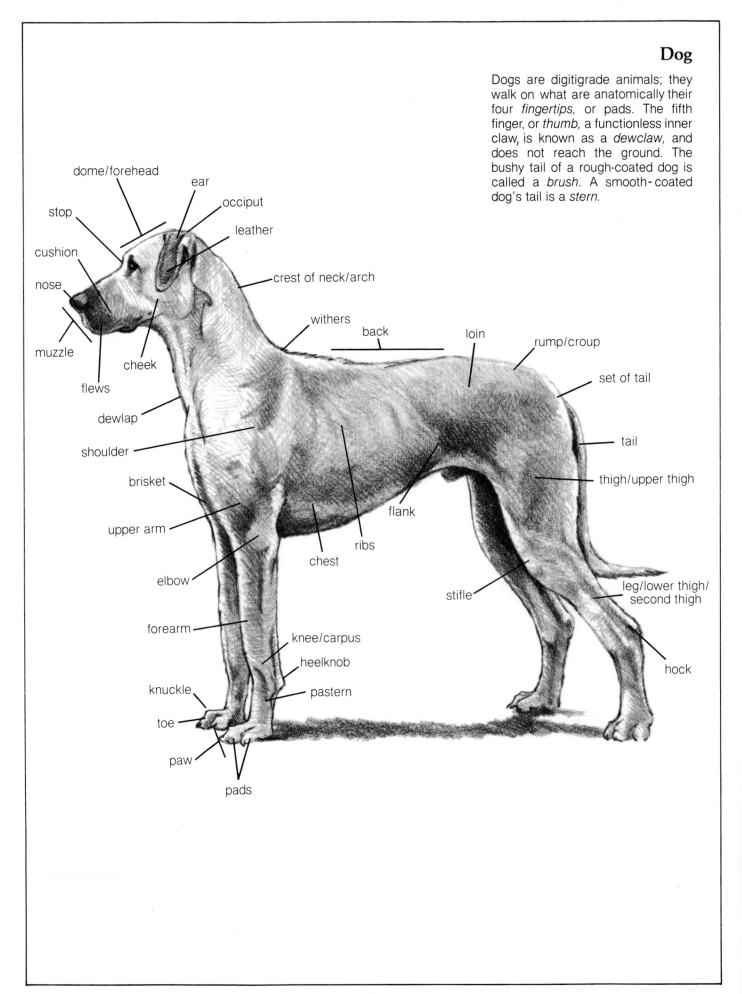

Dog

Dogs are digitigrade animals; they walk on what are anatomically their four *fingertips*, or pads. The fifth finger, or *thumb*, a functionless inner claw, is known as a *dewclaw*, and does not reach the ground. The bushy tail of a rough-coated dog is called a *brush*. A smooth-coated dog's tail is a *stern*.

dome/forehead

ear

occiput

stop

leather

cushion

crest of neck/arch

nose

withers

back

loin

rump/croup

muzzle

set of tail

flews

cheek

tail

dewlap

thigh/upper thigh

shoulder

brisket

flank

upper arm

ribs

elbow

chest

stifle

leg/lower thigh/ second thigh

forearm

knee/carpus

hock

heelknob

knuckle

pastern

toe

paw

pads

Cat

Newborn cats are called *kittens*, adult males are *tomcats*, and adult females are *cattas*. Cats are capable of drawing their *toenails*, or *claws*, into *sheaths* located above the *pads* of their feet. A cat's *muzzle* consists of the *nose* and *jaw* sections of its face.

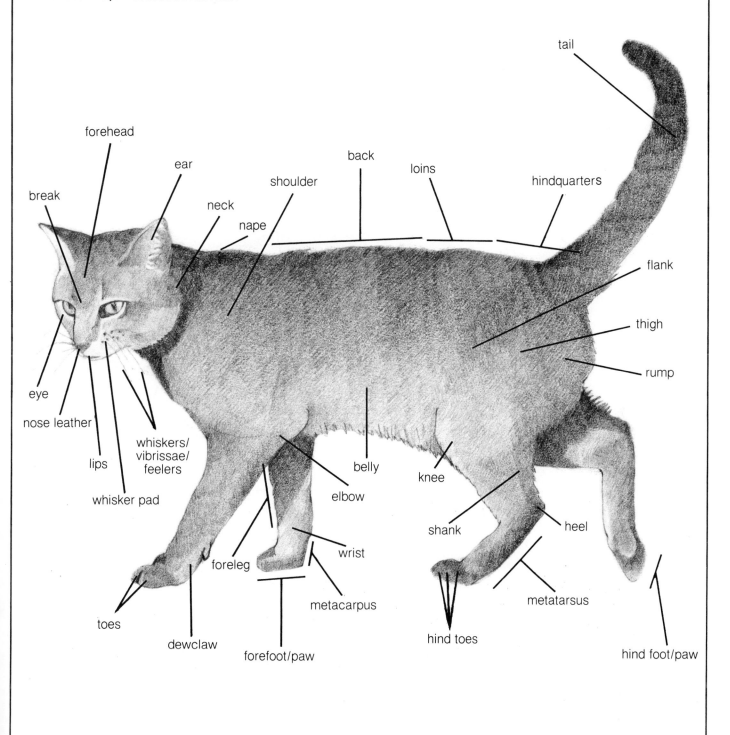

tail

forehead

back

loins

hindquarters

ear

shoulder

neck

break

nape

flank

thigh

rump

eye

nose leather

whiskers/
vibrissae/
feelers

lips

whisker pad

belly

knee

elbow

shank

heel

wrist

foreleg

metacarpus

metatarsus

toes

dewclaw

hind toes

forefoot/paw

hind foot/paw

Domestic Animals

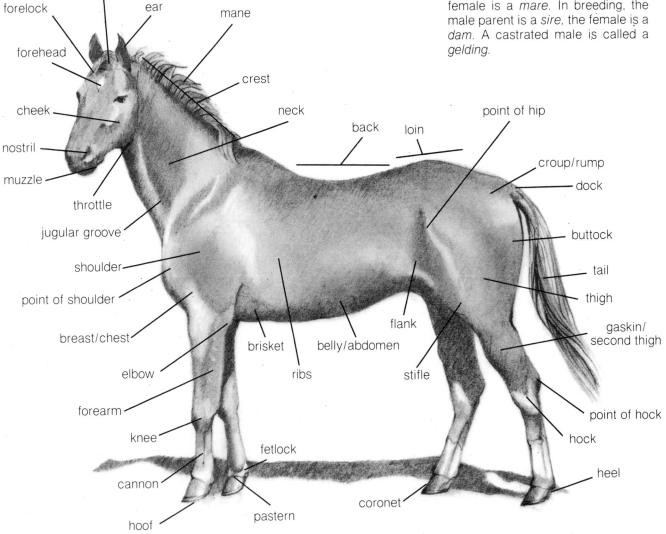

Horse

A horse less than a year old is a *foal*. Male foals are *colts*, females are *fillies*. A mature male is a *stallion*, a female is a *mare*. In breeding, the male parent is a *sire*, the female is a *dam*. A castrated male is called a *gelding*.

poll

forelock

ear

mane

forehead

crest

cheek

neck

nostril

muzzle

throttle

jugular groove

shoulder

point of shoulder

breast/chest

elbow

forearm

knee

cannon

hoof

pastern

fetlock

brisket

ribs

belly/abdomen

flank

stifle

back

loin

point of hip

croup/rump

dock

buttock

tail

thigh

gaskin/second thigh

point of hock

hock

heel

coronet

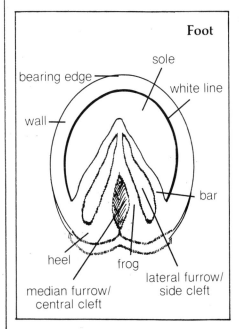

Foot

sole

bearing edge

white line

wall

bar

heel

frog

median furrow/central cleft

lateral furrow/side cleft

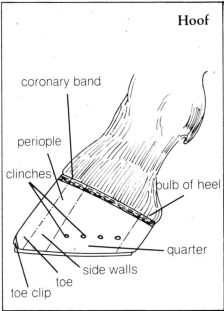

Hoof

coronary band

periople

clinches

bulb of heel

quarter

side walls

toe

toe clip

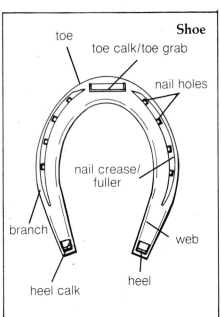

Shoe

toe

toe calk/toe grab

nail holes

nail crease/fuller

branch

web

heel calk

heel

Bird

A *flight feather* consists of tightly meshed *barbs* along the vane. *Contour feathers* and an *undercoat* of fine *down* cover the bird's body. A featherless portion of a bird's skin is called an *apterium*.

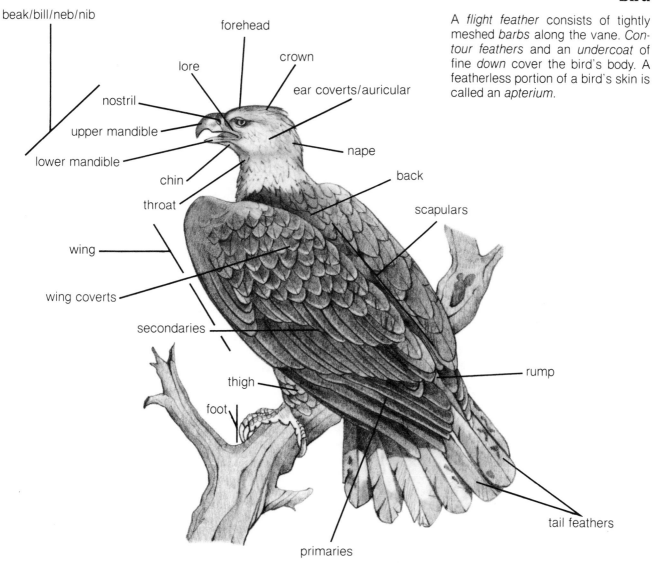

beak/bill/neb/nib
forehead
crown
lore
ear coverts/auricular
nostril
upper mandible
lower mandible
nape
chin
throat
back
scapulars
wing
wing coverts
secondaries
thigh
foot
rump
primaries
tail feathers

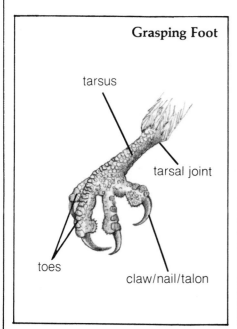

Grasping Foot

tarsus
tarsal joint
toes
claw/nail/talon

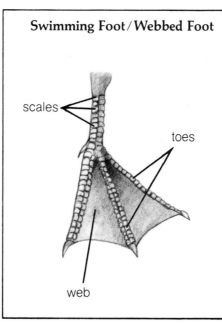

Swimming Foot / Webbed Foot

scales
toes
web

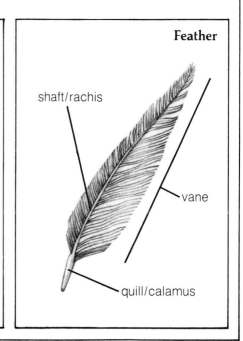

Feather

shaft/rachis
vane
quill/calamus

Wild Animals

Spider

Spiders produce *silk threads* which they use to make webs, *nests* or *parachutes* that allow the wind to carry them from one location to another. When a spider spins a web, it first constructs a *bridge* between two supports and fashions an *orb* beneath. A *scaffolding web* of dry thread is then used to lay down a *viscid spiral* of sticky thread.

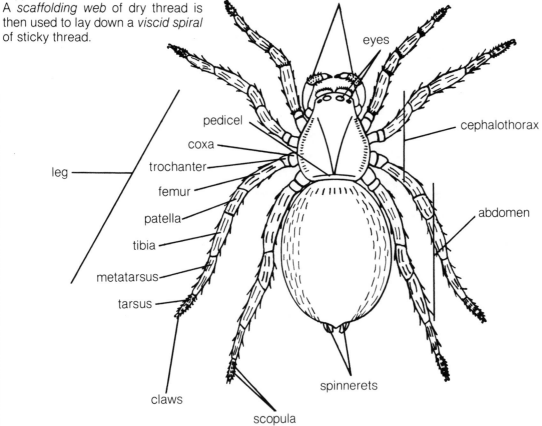

pedipalpi

eyes

cephalothorax

pedicel

coxa

trochanter

femur

patella

tibia

metatarsus

tarsus

leg

claws

scopula

spinnerets

abdomen

Face

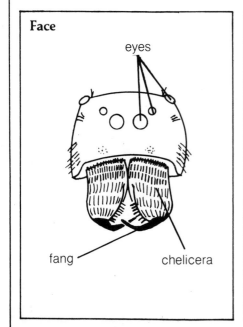

eyes

fang

chelicera

Web

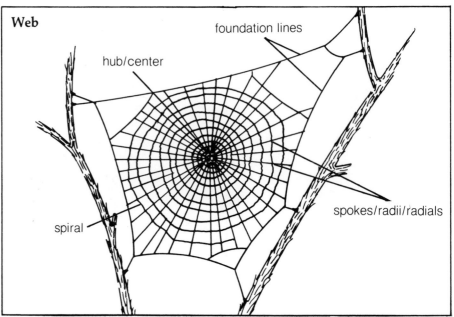

foundation lines

hub/center

spokes/radii/radials

spiral

Insects

Insects have shell-like outer coverings called *exoskeletons*. Most undergo four stages during *metamorphosis*: the *egg*, the *larva*, the *pupa*, and the *adult*.

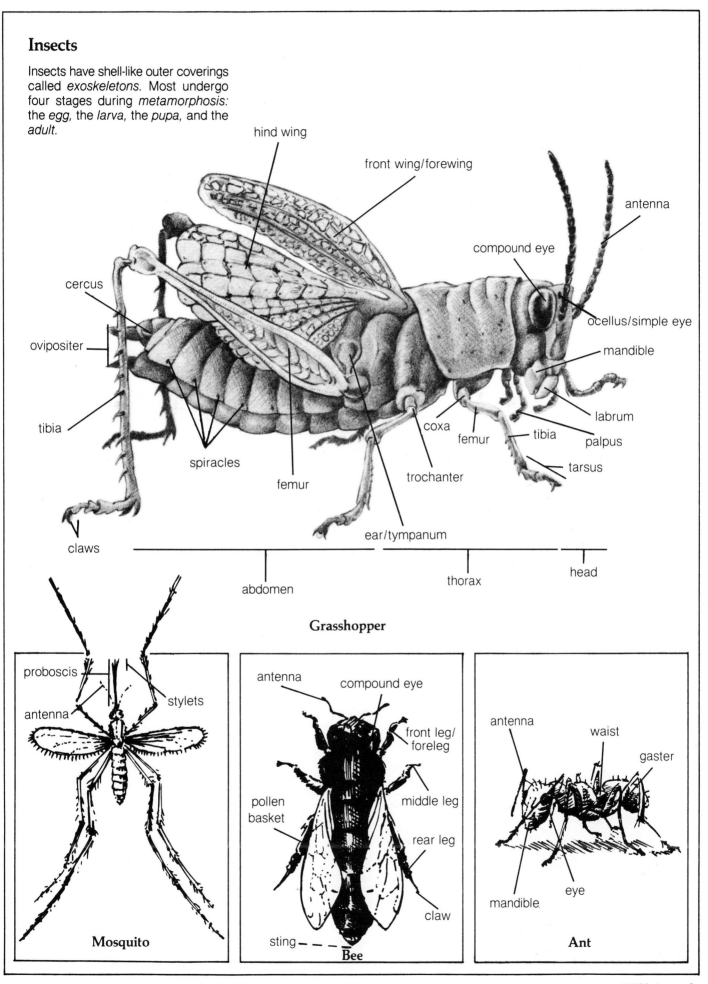

hind wing

front wing/forewing

antenna

compound eye

ocellus/simple eye

cercus

mandible

ovipositer

labrum

tibia

femur

palpus

spiracles

tibia

tarsus

femur

coxa

claws

trochanter

ear/tympanum

abdomen

thorax

head

Grasshopper

proboscis

antenna

compound eye

stylets

antenna

front leg/foreleg

waist

gaster

middle leg

pollen basket

rear leg

mandible

eye

claw

sting

Mosquito

Bee

Ant

Reptiles

In addition to the reptile families represented here, there is the lizard-like *tuatara,* a leftover from the days of the *dinosaurs,* with a vestigial *third eye* on the top of its head. All *poisonous snakes* inject their prey with *venom* through fangs, but not all venomous snakes have *"hypodermic fangs,"* like the rattler shown here. The flattened swelling below a cobra's head is called the *hood.* Most land-living turtles are called *tortoises.* Turtles that live in the sea have *flippers.* Many *skinks,* which are lizards, have no legs or eyelids.

button

rattle/segments

Snake

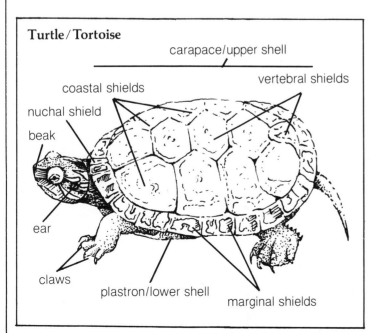

Turtle / Tortoise

carapace/upper shell

coastal shields

vertebral shields

nuchal shield

beak

ear

claws

plastron/lower shell

marginal shields

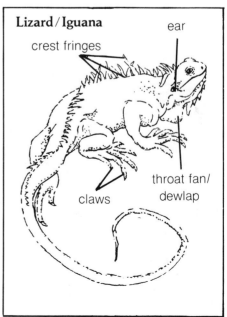

Lizard / Iguana

ear

crest fringes

claws

throat fan/ dewlap

poison fang sheaths

fangs

pit

eye

tongue

teeth

lower jaw

anal shield

dorsal scales

ventral scales

body

Crocodilians

nostril

horny scales

hump

Alligator

snout

Crocodile

fourth tooth

41

Wild Animals

Amphibians

Frogs and toads resemble one another closely, but toads are charac-
teristically more terrestrial and have
rougher, drier skin.

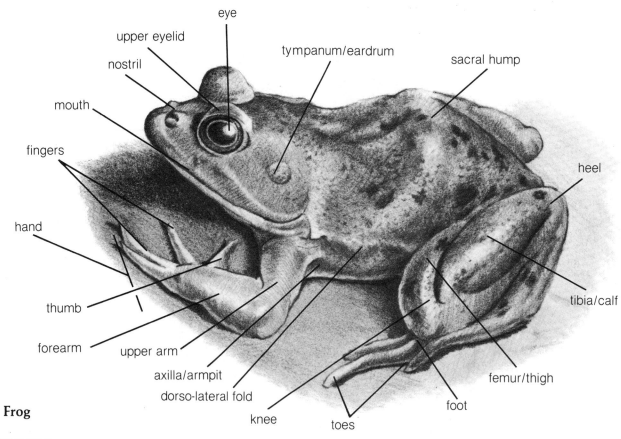

eye

upper eyelid

nostril

tympanum/eardrum

sacral hump

mouth

fingers

heel

hand

thumb

tibia/calf

forearm

upper arm

axilla/armpit

femur/thigh

dorso-lateral fold

foot

Frog

knee

toes

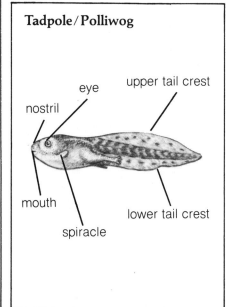

Tadpole / Polliwog

eye

upper tail crest

nostril

mouth

lower tail crest

spiracle

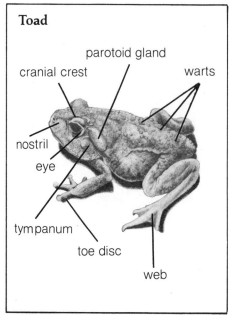

Toad

parotoid gland

cranial crest

warts

nostril

eye

tympanum

toe disc

web

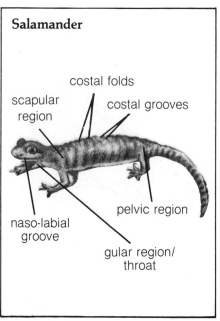

Salamander

costal folds

scapular
region

costal grooves

naso-labial
groove

pelvic region

gular region/
throat

Marine Life

Fish often swim in groups, called *schools*, and reproduce by depositing eggs, or *spawning*. Recently hatched or small adult fish are called *fry*.

spiny rays

dorsal fin/spiny dorsal fin

adipose fin/soft dorsal fin

soft rays

nostril

upper jaw

snout

eye

lateral line

tail fin/caudal fin

mouth

mandible

maxilla

preopercle

gill opening

gill cover/operculum

pectoral fin

scales

pelvic fin/ventral fin

caudal peduncle

anal fin

tail

head

trunk

Fish

Dolphin

dorsal fin

flukes

blowhole

flipper

beak

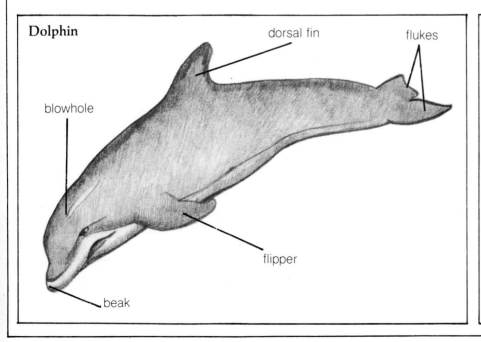

Stingray

sting/spine

tail

disk

tubercles

snout

pectoral fin

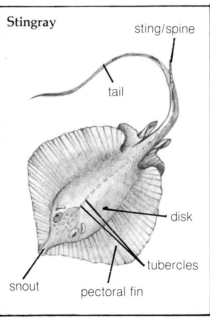

Wild Animals

Marine Life

The *mantle* of an octopus is the tough protective wrapper that covers the body and gives it shape. Octopuses and squid have *chromatophores*, or *pigment cells*, which enable them to change color, as well as *ink glands*, or *sacs*, that secrete protective *"ink."* Starfish have *mouths* on their *oral surfaces*. Coral polyps live within limestone *skeletons*, which form the basis for *coral reefs*.

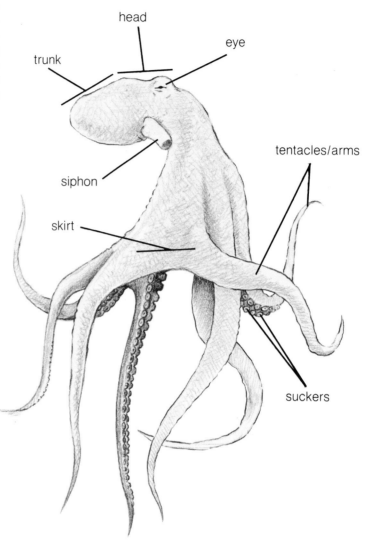

head

eye

trunk

tentacles/arms

siphon

skirt

suckers

Octopus/Devilfish

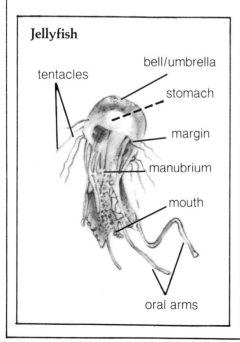

Jellyfish

tentacles

bell/umbrella

stomach

margin

manubrium

mouth

oral arms

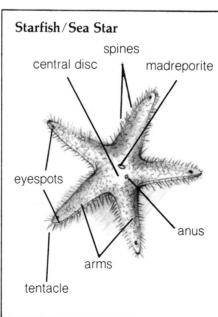

Starfish/Sea Star

spines

central disc

madreporite

eyespots

anus

arms

tentacle

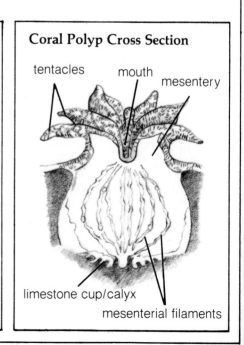

Coral Polyp Cross Section

tentacles

mouth

mesentery

limestone cup/calyx

mesenterial filaments

Shellfish

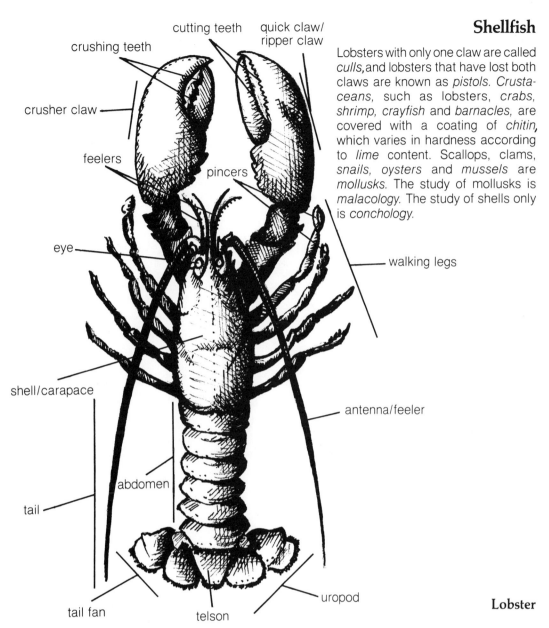

Lobsters with only one claw are called *culls*, and lobsters that have lost both claws are known as *pistols*. *Crustaceans*, such as lobsters, *crabs*, *shrimp*, *crayfish* and *barnacles*, are covered with a coating of *chitin*, which varies in hardness according to *lime* content. Scallops, clams, *snails*, *oysters* and *mussels* are *mollusks*. The study of mollusks is *malacology*. The study of shells only is *conchology*.

crushing teeth
cutting teeth
quick claw/ ripper claw
crusher claw
feelers
pincers
eye
walking legs
shell/carapace
antenna/feeler
abdomen
tail
tail fan
telson
uropod

Lobster

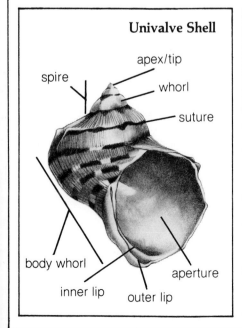

Univalve Shell

apex/tip
spire
whorl
suture
body whorl
inner lip
outer lip
aperture

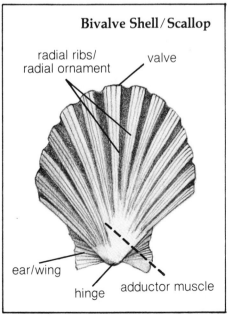

Bivalve Shell / Scallop

radial ribs/ radial ornament
valve
ear/wing
hinge
adductor muscle

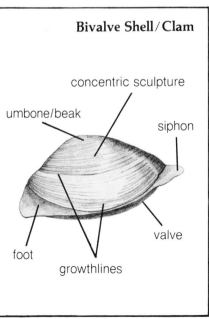

Bivalve Shell / Clam

concentric sculpture
umbone/beak
siphon
foot
growthlines
valve

Ultimate Beast

This remarkable *creature* calls attention to those parts of animals which are distinctive to particular species. Missing are posterior extensions, or *tails,* which vary from long, thin tails that end in a *brush* and have a horny appendage called a *thorn* in the middle, such as a lion's, to brushy fox tails and stubby boar tails. Another composite animal is the legendary *manticore,* which combined the head of a man, the body of a lion, and the tail of a *dragon* or *scorpion.*

giraffe horn

moose antlers

porcupine quills

kudu horn

monkey ear

deer ear

whiskers/vibrissae

lion mane

jaguar, or leopard, coat

giraffe coat

kangaroo, or wallaby, pouch

lion paw

claw

dewclaw

cow hoof/cloven hoof

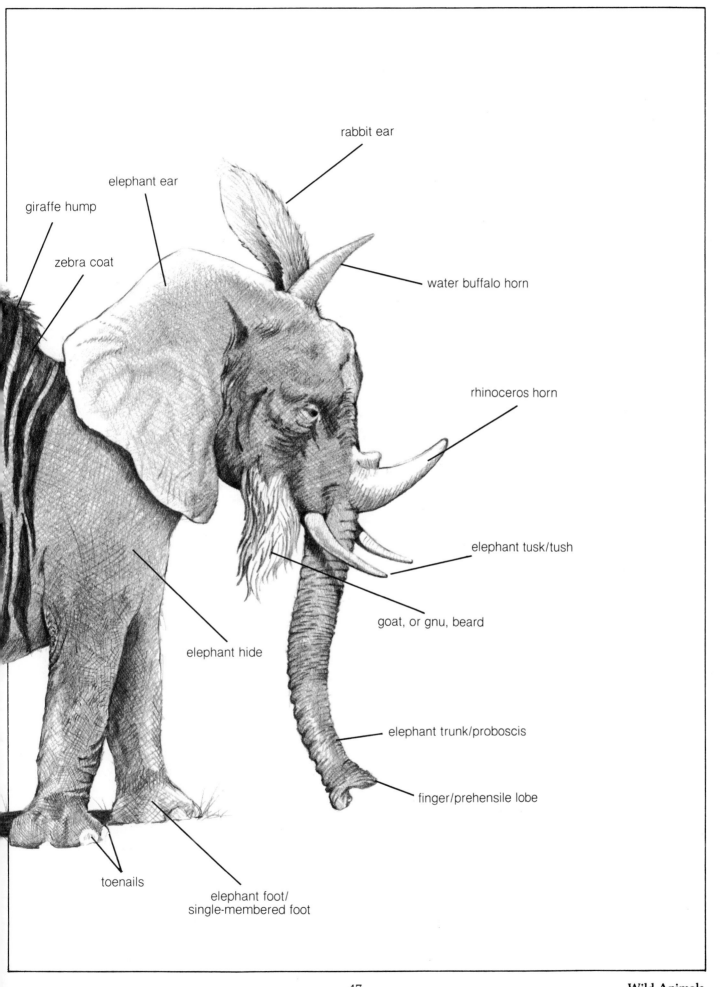

rabbit ear

elephant ear

giraffe hump

zebra coat

water buffalo horn

rhinoceros horn

elephant tusk/tush

goat, or gnu, beard

elephant hide

elephant trunk/proboscis

finger/prehensile lobe

toenails

elephant foot/
single-membered foot

Wild Animals

Tree

When a tree is cut down, what remains attached to the *root* is called a *stump*.

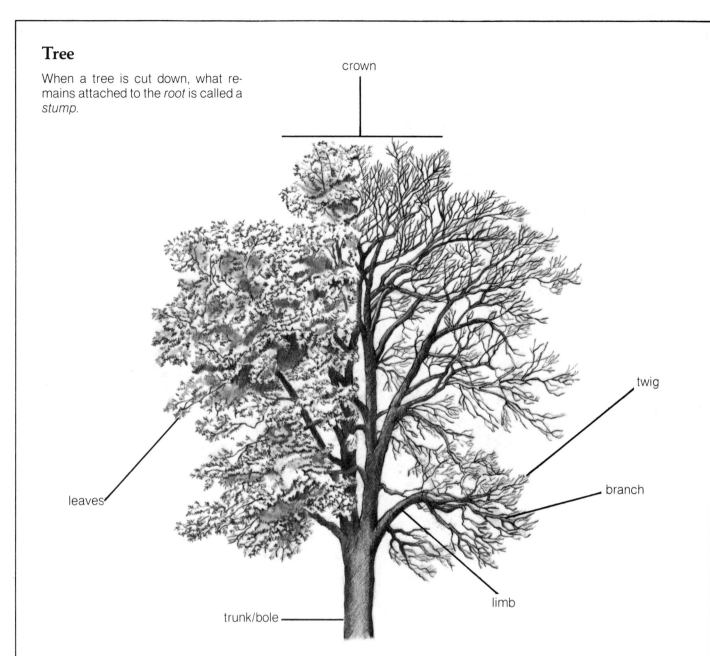

crown

twig

branch

leaves

limb

trunk/bole

Tree Trunk Cross Section

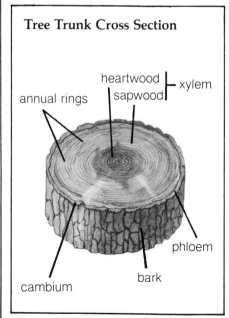

annual rings

heartwood
sapwood

xylem

phloem

cambium

bark

Twig

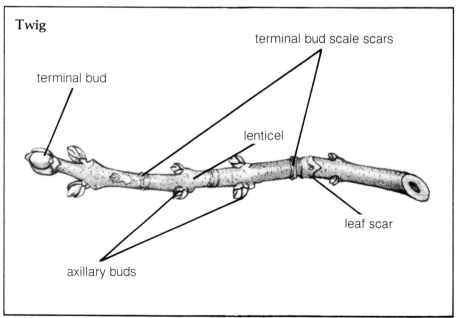

terminal bud scale scars

terminal bud

lenticel

axillary buds

leaf scar

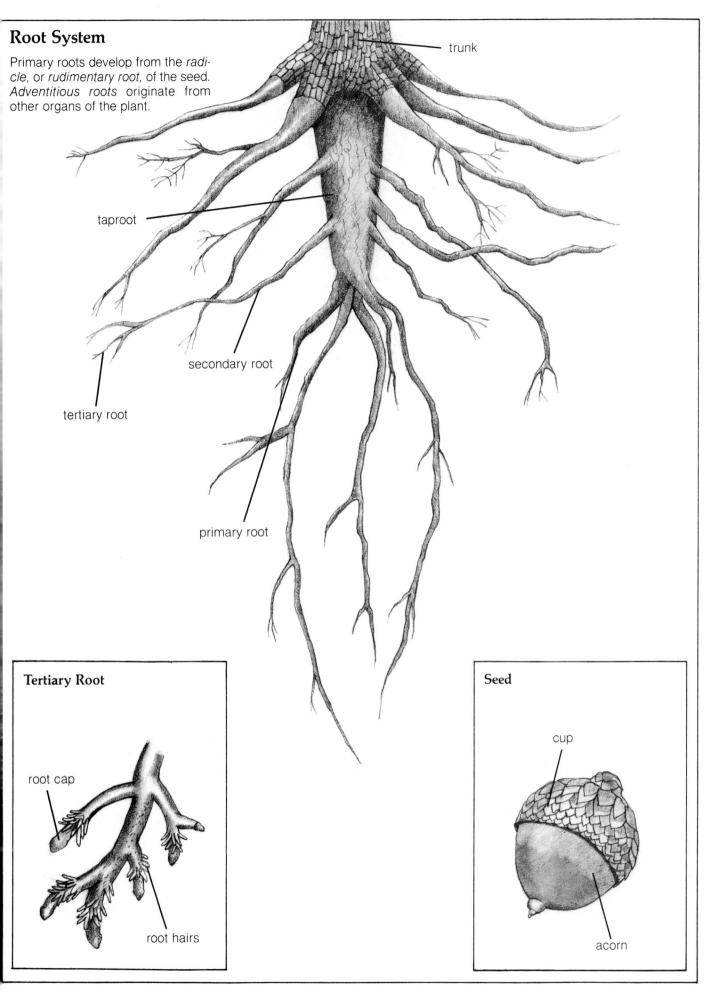

Root System

Primary roots develop from the *radicle*, or *rudimentary root*, of the seed. *Adventitious roots* originate from other organs of the plant.

trunk

taproot

secondary root

tertiary root

primary root

Tertiary Root

root cap

root hairs

Seed

cup

acorn

Plants

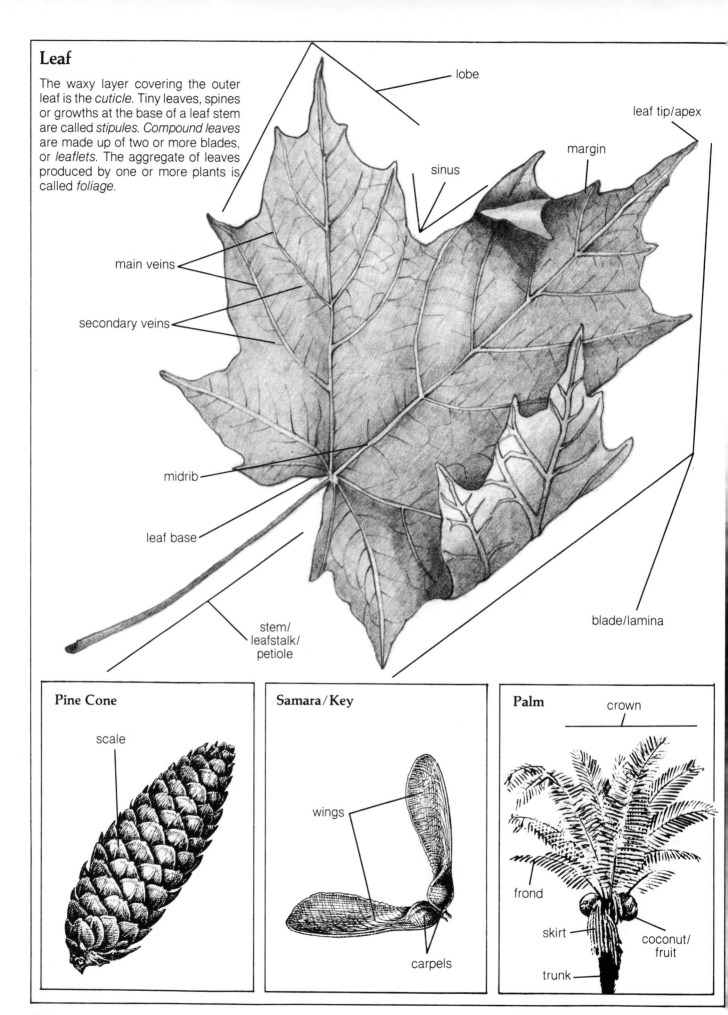

Leaf

The waxy layer covering the outer leaf is the *cuticle.* Tiny leaves, spines or growths at the base of a leaf stem are called *stipules. Compound leaves* are made up of two or more blades, or *leaflets.* The aggregate of leaves produced by one or more plants is called *foliage.*

lobe

leaf tip/apex

margin

sinus

main veins

secondary veins

midrib

leaf base

stem/
leafstalk/
petiole

blade/lamina

Pine Cone

scale

Samara/Key

wings

carpels

Palm

crown

frond

skirt

coconut/
fruit

trunk

Flower

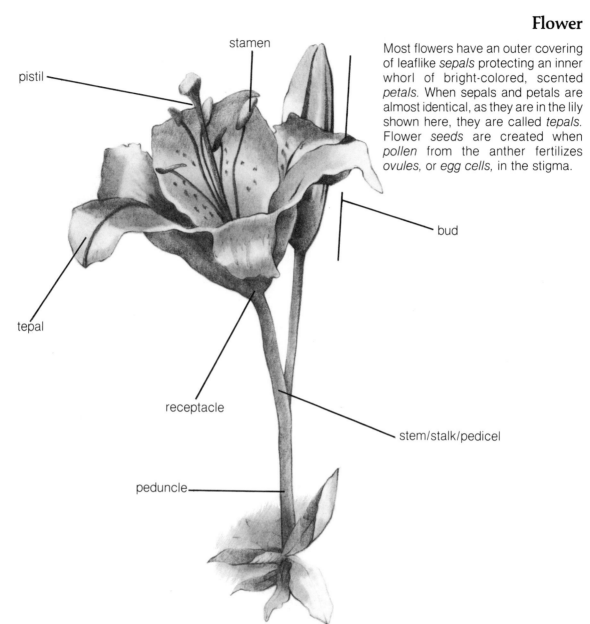

pistil

stamen

Most flowers have an outer covering of leaflike *sepals* protecting an inner whorl of bright-colored, scented *petals*. When sepals and petals are almost identical, as they are in the lily shown here, they are called *tepals*. Flower *seeds* are created when *pollen* from the anther fertilizes *ovules*, or *egg cells,* in the stigma.

bud

tepal

receptacle

stem/stalk/pedicel

peduncle

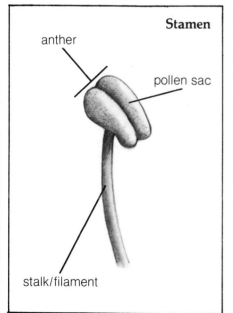

Stamen

anther

pollen sac

stalk/filament

Petal

blade

claw

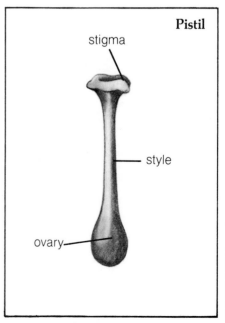

Pistil

stigma

style

ovary

Plants

Vegetables

A vegetable is that part of a plant that can be eaten. The roots of carrots, beets and turnips are edible, as are asparagus stems, potato tubers, leek and onion leaf bases, cabbage, lettuce and spinach leaves, the *immature fruit,* or *ovary,* of cucumbers, peas and summer squash, and the *mature fruit* of tomatoes and winter squash.

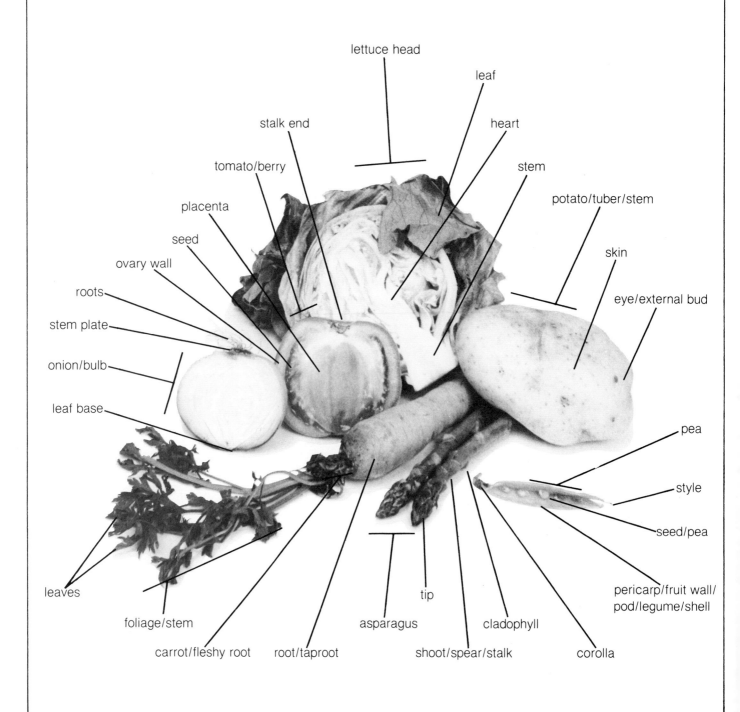

lettuce head

leaf

stalk end

heart

tomato/berry

stem

placenta

potato/tuber/stem

seed

skin

ovary wall

eye/external bud

roots

stem plate

onion/bulb

leaf base

pea

style

seed/pea

pericarp/fruit wall/ pod/legume/shell

leaves

tip

foliage/stem

asparagus

cladophyll

carrot/fleshy root

root/taproot

shoot/spear/stalk

corolla

Fruits

Nuts and crops commonly referred to as vegetables, such as tomatoes and melons, are actually *vegetable fruits.* Fruits are classed according to the number of ovaries they have: They range from simple fruits, such as peaches, to aggregate fruits, such as strawberries. Each segment of *multiple fruits,* such as pineapples and figs, is edible.

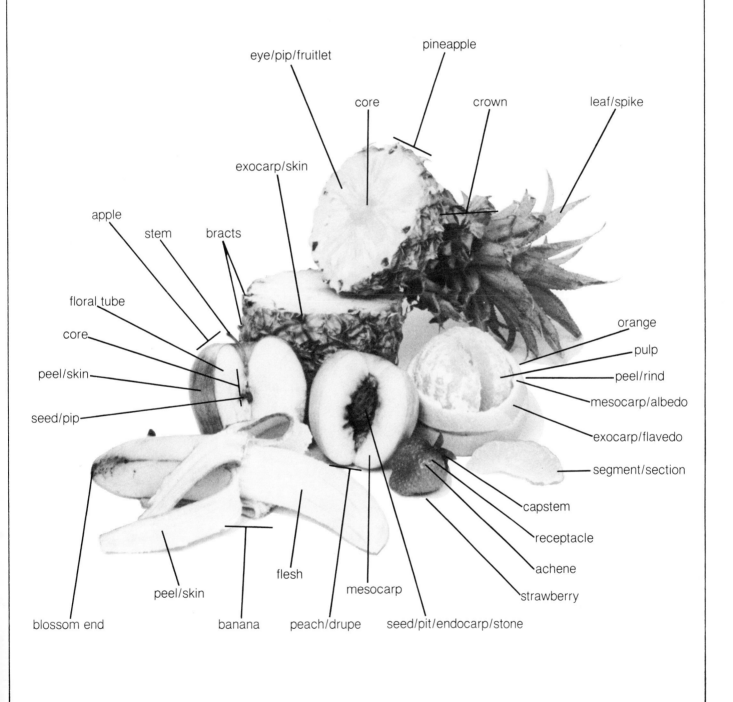

eye/pip/fruitlet

pineapple

core

crown

leaf/spike

exocarp/skin

apple

stem

bracts

floral tube

core

peel/skin

seed/pip

orange

pulp

peel/rind

mesocarp/albedo

exocarp/flavedo

segment/section

capstem

receptacle

achene

strawberry

flesh

peel/skin

mesocarp

blossom end

banana

peach/drupe

seed/pit/endocarp/stone

Succulents

Succulents are plants with *fleshy tissue* that have the ability to store moisture for long periods of time in their stem. Some cacti have protective *glochidia,* razor-sharp hairlike bristles, in addition to spines and flowers.

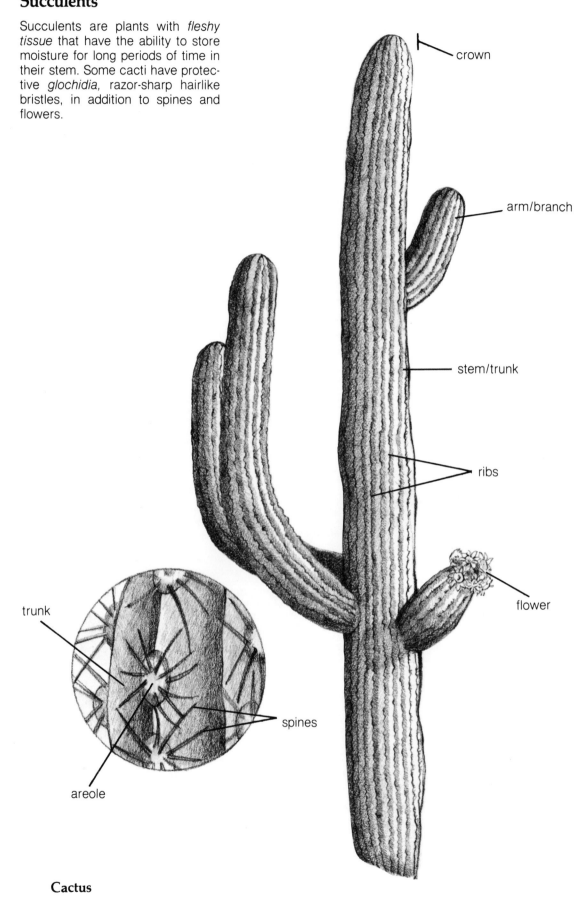

crown

arm/branch

stem/trunk

ribs

flower

trunk

spines

areole

Cactus

remnants of universal veil

gills

ring/annulus

cap/pileus

stem/stalk/stipe

volva

mycelium

Mushroom

Special Plants

Toadstools are inedible mushrooms, or *fungi*. Flowerless, seedless ferns reproduce by means of *spores* carried in spore cases on the underside of the leaves. Seaweed, such as the *marine algae* shown here, attaches itself to the ocean floor by means of a *holdfast*.

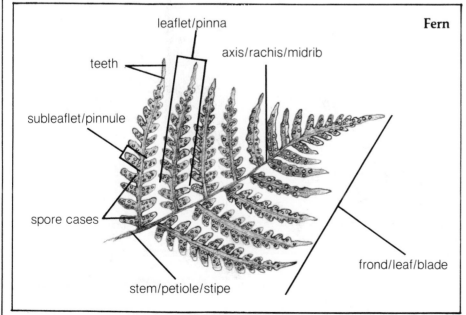

Fern

leaflet/pinna

axis/rachis/midrib

teeth

subleaflet/pinnule

spore cases

stem/petiole/stipe

frond/leaf/blade

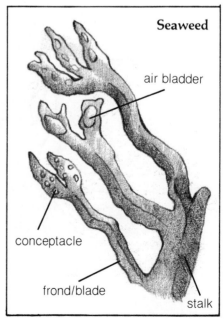

Seaweed

air bladder

conceptacle

frond/blade

stalk

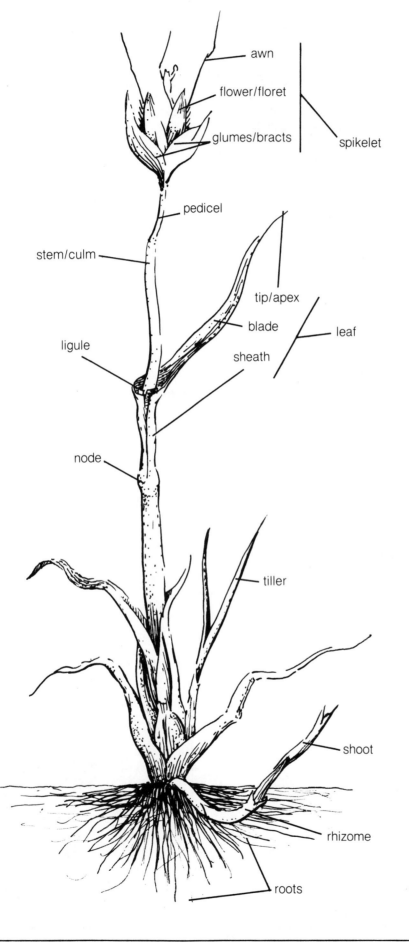

awn

flower/floret

glumes/bracts

spikelet

pedicel

stem/culm

tip/apex

blade

leaf

sheath

ligule

node

tiller

shoot

rhizome

roots

Grass

There are two parts to grass plants, the *vegetable organs* and the *floral organs. Cereal grasses,* such as *wheat, oat, barley* and corn, produce edible *fruit, seed* or *kernels.* Rhizomes and *stolons,* or *runners*—above-ground stems—spread out from grass plants to produce new plants. The *inflorescence,* or *flower cluster,* of grasses consists of many spikelets. Grass leaves are *parallel-veined.*

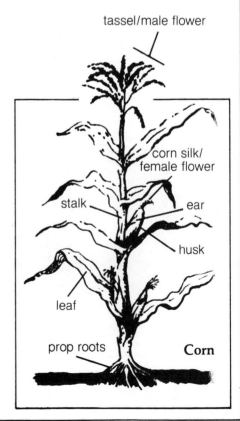

tassel/male flower

corn silk/female flower

stalk

ear

husk

leaf

prop roots

Corn

Shelters and Structures

Since man's most basic shelter is a house, it is illustrated in a variety of ways, from foundation and frame to windows and walls.

The shelters and structures in the rest of the section are grouped in three subcategories: designs from other lands, which range from pagodas to pyramids; special-purpose buildings such as the Capitol and the White House, skyscrapers and prisons, amusement parks and airports; and other structures which bear on our everyday lives—bridges, tunnels, canals and dams.

The terms for the parts of objects found in most shelter interiors are the same as those found in a house, all of which have been illustrated. But those of a courtroom are sufficiently different to merit coverage, as are the parts of a skyscraper's elevator and escalator. In some cases floor plans and cross-section illustrations have been used to facilitate the reader's access to terms which are unique to a particular structure.

Building Connections

gas shut-off valve

siamese pipe

fresh air plate

cap

sill cock

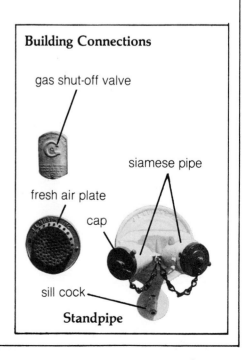

Standpipe

Foundation

Some houses are built on sunken *posts,* or *piers.* Others are built on concrete floors, or *slabs.* The area of a house built below ground level is the *basement.* Houses without basements usually have an area between the floor joists and the ground called a *crawl space,* through which access is gained to inspect pipes.

roof sheathing

fascia

partition wall

outside load bearing wall/ center bearing wall

subflooring

sheathing

header

fire stop

floor joists

post footing

concrete block foundation

lumber post

anchor bolt

lumber girder

footing

sill

Frame

Any diagonally placed piece of timber in a frame is a *brace*. A *cat* is a small piece of lumber nailed between studs for reinforcement. *Beams* are squared off pieces of timber, such as *joists*, used to support *floor* or *ceiling*, or *lintels*, horizontal *members* designed to carry loads above openings such as doors and windows.

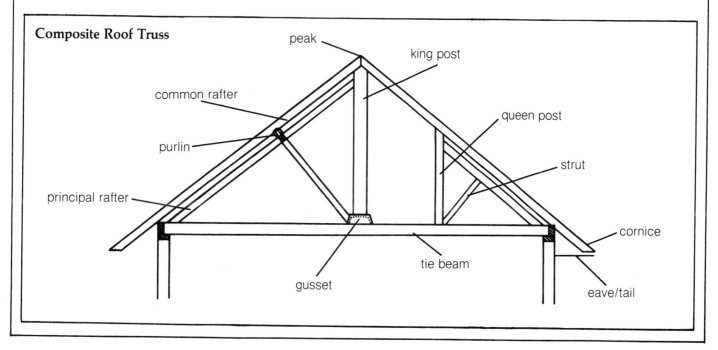

ridgepole/ridgeboard

wood splice

collar beam

roof rafter

ceiling joist

fascia rafter

top plate

cripples

jack stud

fascia

outrigger

door bucks

header joist

header

bottom plate/sole plate

stud

anchor bolt

sill plate

corner post

doubling

rough sill

Composite Roof Truss

peak

king post

common rafter

queen post

purlin

strut

principal rafter

cornice

gusset

tie beam

eave/tail

House Exterior

oculus window

door casing

cornice

roof cresting

flues

chimney

garret/ attic story

frieze

vent pipe

bracket

keystone

corner board

drip edge

bay window/ bow window

sidelight

threshold

A flat observation platform with railings on the roof of a house is a *widow's walk*. An underground passageway or group of passageways is a *catacomb*. A drawing of one floor or level of a building, as seen from above, is a *floor plan*. Together with a *foundation plan* and *elevations,* a floor plan shows the builder what to build.

parapet

sloping dormer

sill

shutters

wooden siding

front yard

pilaster/pillar

arched doorway

Working Drawing/ Blueprint

French doors

wall

stairs

room identification

detail description

cabinetwork

graphic scale

project name

title block

architect's name

FIRST FLOOR PLAN

Addams Family Residence
Carl Hribar Architect
New York City

DATE: 15 MAY 1981   DRAWN BY: K.A.

sink

dimension line

dimension

door swing

material identification/ flooring

kitchen range

window

draftsman

registered architect seal/stamp

drawing number

House Exterior

The room or space under the roof is the *attic*. The lowest story of a house is called the *basement* if it is at least partly below ground or street level. A part of a house projecting on one side or subordinate to the main structure is called a *wing*. *Patios, terraces, decks* and *porches* adjoin a house and are used for play or relaxation. An open *gallery* alongside a house with its own roof is a *veranda*. The trees, shrubs, paths and gardens around a house are called *landscaping*.

television antenna
dormer
ridgeline/peak
chimney cap
roof
gable vent
corner board
chimney
bargeboard/ gableboard/ vergeboard
valley
gable/gable end
downspout/ downpipe/ leader
garage
gutter/drainpipe

overhang
stoop/steps
porch light
electric meter
post lamp
eave
bay window
shutter
swan neck
picket fence
storm door
clapboard siding
garage door
double-hung window
driveway apron

House

Door

The *sill, threshold,* or *saddle* is that part directly beneath the door. Entrance doors are often covered by *screendoors.* A door cut in half horizontally whose two parts can be used independently is called a *Dutch door.* A door having glass panes throughout or nearly throughout its length is a *French door.* The rubber-tipped projection attached to the wall behind an opening door to protect it from the impact is a *doorstop.*

fanlight

keystone

transom

sidelight

casing trim

sidelight sash

butte stile

mail drop

lintel

top rail

doorjamb

light fixture

peephole

doorbell

door knocker

lock stile

keyhole

doorknob

panel

bottom rail

stoop

doormat

center stile

doorstep

Window

head jamb/yoke

exterior

meeting rails

interior

A windowsill refers to the bottom part of a window opening, both inside and outside. A *double-hung window*, shown here, allows the inner and outer sashes to move up and down freely. A *casement window* operates on hinges. A *jalousie window* has adjustable glass louvers called *slats*. A *fixed window* does not open. *Window frame* can mean either the casing, in which the window sash is hung, or the sash itself.

outer sash/upper sash

parting strip

counterweight channel

jamb

stop

rail/top rail

lock

brickmold

casing/interior casing

stile

side jamb

muntins/sash bars

inner sash/lower sash

stool

apron/skirt

bottom rail

pane/windowpane

Insulated Window Cross-Section

glazing/insulating glass

frame

glazing bead

weather stripping

sash

Staircase

A tread and riser comprise a *step*. A tread's depth is its *run*. A step in a straight *flight*, or series of steps, is called a *flier*. A series of flights connecting landings is a *stairway*. The vertical space occupied by stairs is called a *stairwell*. An entrance stairway to a building is a *stoop*.

balustrade

baluster

tread

banister/handrail/top rail

landing

newel cap

nosing

newel post

bottom rail

cove mold

riser

Fence

A solid fence can be called a *screen*. If it holds back a slope of ground it is a *retaining wall. Supporting members,* or *fence posts,* are anchored in foundation *postholes.* Any material used between posts is *infill.* A *weep hole* in a retaining wall allows water to seep through.

crop

cap/finial/acroterion

terminal cap/gatepost cap

scroll work/scroll

rail end/brace

spike/spear point

pipe/
endpost/
gatepost

capstone

picket

top rail

rail/fencing strip

elbow

coping

chain link fabric/
woven wire fabric

post

scroll/torsade

tension bar

picket/slat/pale

quoin

tension bar band

rail

brace band

Wood Fence   **Masonry Gate Post/**   **Wrought Iron Fence**   **Steel Chain Gate**
                     Gate Pier

House

Building Materials

Boards are *timber*, or lumber, cut in long, flat *slabs*. When used in construction, boards are referred to as *beams*, or *balks*. When they are used to support a pitched roof, they are called *rafters*. A *plank* is thicker than a board. *Shakes* are *wooden shingles*, but cracks in wood caused by wind or frost are also called shakes. A *spall* is a chip or flaking of brick.

knothole

grain

face/tangential section

side/radial section

end grain/cross section

growth rings/annual rings

knot

seasoning checks

Lumber

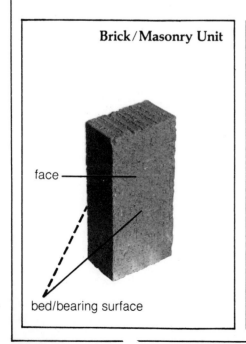

Brick/Masonry Unit

face

bed/bearing surface

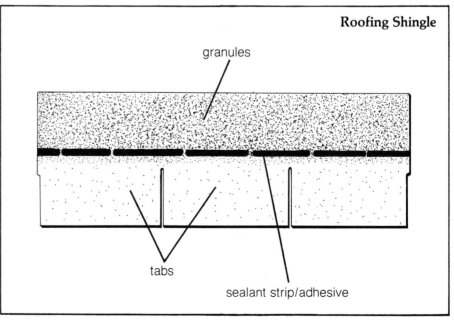

Roofing Shingle

granules

tabs

sealant strip/adhesive

Brick Wall

Bricks and brick faces take on different names, depending on where and how they are used or exposed. Structures built of *stone* or brick are called *masonry*. The pattern in which a wall is laid is its *bond*. The exposed surface is the *face*. A piece of iron or steel used to brace a wall is a *cramp*, while a recess left within for pipes or ducts is a *chase*. A *tie* is any material that holds masonry together.

soldier

shiner

head joint/
cross joint/
mortar joint

bed joint/mortar joint

header

stretchers

closers

bat

bat

weep hole

dog's tooth/stretcher

course

quoin/corner

International Architecture

The Japanese developed the *whole-timbered building*, with *interlocking timbered joints.* Minarets, from which *criers,* or *muezzins,* call people to prayer, are normally attached or annexed to a mosque. Obelisks were often surrounded by *pillars,* or stelae, erected in honor of gods. Pyramids, *quadrilateral structures,* were used as tombs or temples. Flat-topped pyramids called *mastabas* were strictly *funerary structures,* while *ziggurats,* stepped pyramids supporting a *shrine,* were used for worship.

Torii/Shinto Temple Gateway

crowning pavilion

cornice/collar

Kokoshniki

balconies

cupola

cupola

neck

corbeled arches

dome

cornice

story

ring molding

polygonal base

fluted spire

Minarets/Manaras

skins

framework

Yurt

cloisters/riwaq

lintel/kasagi

shimagi

gakuzuka

daiwa

kusabi

crosspiece/nyki

cupola

dome

pendentives

spandrel

pillar

Obelisk/Stela

pyramidion

hieroglyphs

Pagoda/Polygonal Tower

face

shaft

tee/finial

stupa/tope

pent roof

balcony

Pyramid

apex/vertex

mantle/casing

base

pedestal

Mosque/Muslim Temple

prayer hall/liwan/
main sanctuary

Arch

The distance between the imposts is called the *span*. The *rise* is the distance between the top of the imposts and the highest point of the intrados. The *crown* is the highest point of the extrados. The area of an arch extending from the crown to the impost is the *haunch*, or *hance*.

spandrel

voussoir/arch-stones

keystone

extrados

intrados

impost

abutment

springer/skewback

pier/pillar

Column

The clear space between two columns is *intercolumniation*.

cymatium

cornice

corona

bed mold

entablature

frieze

taenia

architrave

abacus

echinus

capital

cincture

neck

astragal

shaft

fluting

upper rail

sleeve

baluster

scotia

cincture

base

torus

belly

plinth

surbase

pedestal

dado

lower rail

base

Balustrade

Architectural Designs from Other Lands

Capitol

The first floor of the Capitol contains the *Hall of Columns, House* and *Senate corridors, committee rooms, restaurants, transportation offices* and a *post office.* When the House is called to order, the *Mace of the House of Representatives* is placed on a cylindrical *pedestal* to the right of the Speaker's desk. On the Senate side is a *chandelier* with two bulbs below it. The red one indicates an executive session; the white, a regular session. Visitors to the chambers of Congress sit in *galleries.*

House of Representatives Chamber

floor leaders
"the aisle"
Republicans
Democrats
official reporters
speaker
parliamentarian
timekeeper
journal clerk, tally clerk, reading clerk

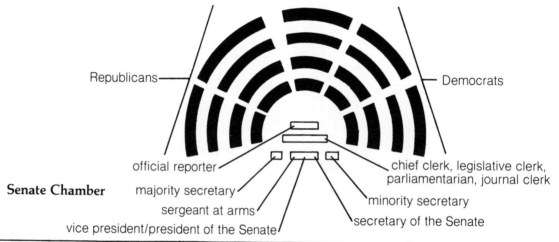

Senate Chamber

Republicans
Democrats
official reporter
chief clerk, legislative clerk, parliamentarian, journal clerk
majority secretary
minority secretary
sergeant at arms
secretary of the Senate
vice president/president of the Senate

Capitol Building

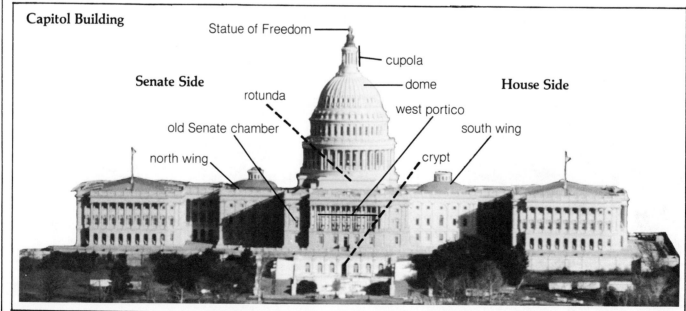

Statue of Freedom
cupola
dome
Senate Side
House Side
rotunda
west portico
old Senate chamber
south wing
north wing
crypt

White House

The White House, a historic *mansion* that serves as the President's *home* and *office*, contains *portraits, antiques* and *memorabilia*. In addition to the rooms and offices shown here, there is a bombproof *command post* in the cellar and a *helipad* on the south lawn.

Second Floor

President's living quarters
Monroe Room
Lincoln Suite
Rose Room
entrance hall

First Floor

Red Room
State dining room
Blue Room
Green Room
East Room
library

Ground Floor

President's executive offices
physician's room, clinic & housekeeper's room
diplomatic reception room
China Room
Vermeil Room
First Lady's offices

House Plan

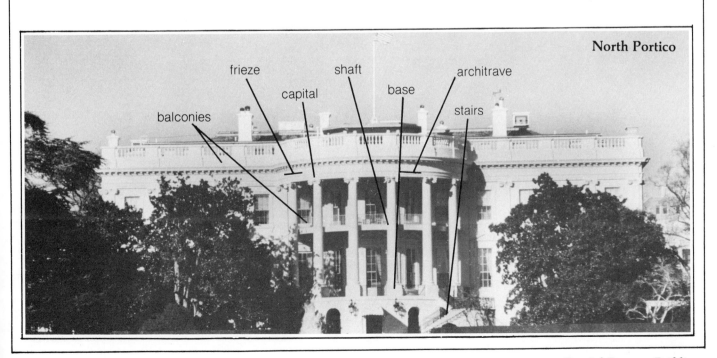

North Portico

frieze
shaft
architrave
capital
base
stairs
balconies

Special Purpose Buildings

Prison

Maximum security prisons, such as the one seen here, are characterized by high *walls, armed guards* and *security checkpoints. Minimum security prisons* may be surrounded by *chainlink fences* and have *security systems* that are largely electronic, with *doors, alarms, TV monitors* and *intercoms* monitored by *central computers. Prisoners,* or *inmates,* in all *correctional facilities,* including *jails,* live in *cells* with *barred doors.*

"E" cell block/ vocational rehabilitation

commissary & garage

laundry

"D" recreation yard

mess halls

shoe & tailor shops

"B" recreation yard

power house

"D" cell block

kitchen/bakery

metal shops

"B" cell block

exercise yard

auditorium/ chapel

hospital

"C" cell block

"A" cell block

school

reception center

Times Square

guard tower

solitary confinement/ "the box"

catwalk & tunnel

front gate

"A" recreation yard

"C" recreation yard

administration building

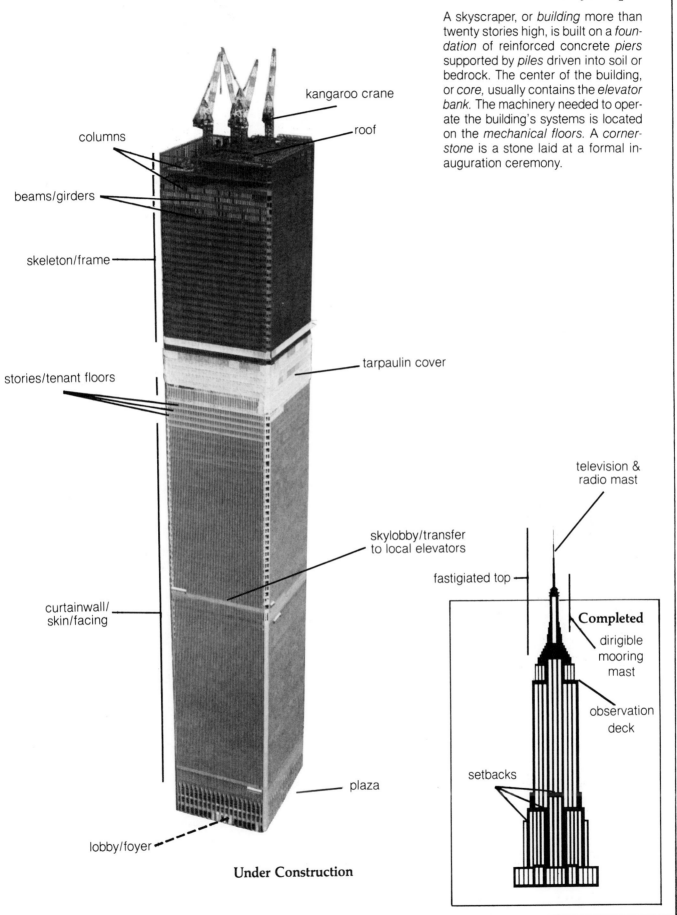

Skyscraper

A skyscraper, or *building* more than twenty stories high, is built on a *foundation* of reinforced concrete *piers* supported by *piles* driven into soil or bedrock. The center of the building, or *core,* usually contains the *elevator bank.* The machinery needed to operate the building's systems is located on the *mechanical floors.* A *cornerstone* is a stone laid at a formal inauguration ceremony.

kangaroo crane

roof

columns

beams/girders

skeleton/frame

tarpaulin cover

stories/tenant floors

television & radio mast

skylobby/transfer to local elevators

fastigiated top

Completed

dirigible mooring mast

curtainwall/ skin/facing

observation deck

setbacks

plaza

lobby/foyer

Under Construction

Special Purpose Buildings

Elevator

There is padding which makes up the *safety edges* on the *shafts*, or inner-most sides, of elevator doors. Most elevator cars have *emergency top exits* in the *canopy* or real ceiling as well as *service cabinets* which contain *fan switches, light* and *start switches.* An individual who directs people to the next available car in a *bank* of elevators is called a *starter.*

suspended ceiling/hung ceiling

light-diffuser panel

position indicator/directory

transom

special instructions card holder

certificate holder

wall

alarm button

door open & close

emergency stop

car-station panel/ floor selector

handrail

auxiliary car-station panel

base

floor

return panel   door

Car/Cab

safety-cable

counterweight

limit switches

roller guide shoe

hoist cables

sling

door operator

emergency exit

inductor

landing-zone detector

car/cab

platform

toe guard

safety

oil buffer

guide rails

buffer footing

compensator sheave

safety-cable tension sheave

Shaft

Escalator

This composite escalator includes both *opaque* and *transparent balustrades*. *Demarcation grooves* on each treadboard call riders' attention to the end of steps. *Emergency-stop buttons* are located at top and bottom newels. *People-movers*, or *moving sidewalks*, are similar to escalators but move horizontally rather than vertically.

newel area

inner deck

molding

handrail

balustrade

deckboard

floor plate

comb

skirt

newel skirt

riding instructions

treadboards/steps

Special Purpose Buildings

Castle

A castle was protected by a moat which could be crossed by a lowered *drawbridge*. Narrow openings in turret or tower floors, used to drop boiling liquids or stones on attackers, were called *machicolations*.

casemates

bastion/mount

turret

rampart/bulwark

battlements

fortress/keep/donjon

tower

wharf

bridge

inner ward/inner bailey

moat

outer ward/ outer bailey

outwork

gatehouse/barbican

Embattled Parapet

loophole/arrow loop/balistraria

crenel/embrasure

merlon

rampart

battlement

Bartizan / Turret

crenel/embrasure

merlon

corbel

loophole/arrow loop/balistraria

bastion/mount

moat/ditch

outer curtain wall

casemates

outer ward/outer bailey

parapet

rampart/bulwark

armory

barracks

chapel

towers

inner ward/inner bailey

bridge

wharf

watergate

gatehouse/barbican

Portcullis/ Gateway

pulley chains

timber

jamb

grating

spikes

79

Special Purpose Buildings

Fortifications

This *field fortification* or *trading post* was protected by wooden walls from behind which soldiers could fire on attackers from raised *parapets*. *Powder* and *ammunition* were stored in a building called a *magazine*.

bakery

band

sutler

office

parade ground

stockade/
stockade fencing/
palisade

company quarters/
barracks

guard house/
stockade

main gate/sally port

gate

laundry

assistant quartermaster

cavalry yard

chapel

guard tower

wagon masters'
quarters

teamsters' quarters

headquarters

officers' quarters

stables

hospital

office

teamsters' mess

hay scale

hay yard

Frontier Fort

creek

mechanics' shops

water gate

woodyard

Fortifications

Permanent fortifications, such as the *point* of the star fort illustrated here, had *walls* and *slopes* made of *masonry* and earth. They often had *casemates; bombproofs,* walls impervious to explosives; *drawbridges* and *earthen breastworks,* breast-high protection for soldiers.

curtain

parade/
parade ground

gorge

interior slope

bastion

glacis

banquette

covered way/
covert/close way

counterscarp

ditch/moat

scarp/escarp

berm

salient angle

parapet

rampart

terreplein

flank

interior slope

banquette

superior slope

interior slope

exterior slope

Permanent Fort / Star Fort Detail

Cross Section

parade/
parade ground

banquette/
infantry banquette

interior slope

terreplein

superior slope

exterior slope

berm

scarp/escarp

covered way/
covert/close way

counterscarp

banquette/
infantry banquette

glacis

ditch/moat

parapet

rampart

Special Purpose Buildings

Tepee / Teepee / Tipi

The *pole frame* of an Indian tepee was held together at the top by a *hide rope*. It was covered with dressed buffalo *skins* and had a *fire pit* on the floor within. Other Indian dwellings included *wigwams*, rounded or oval-shaped lodges formed by poles overlaid with *bark, mats* or skins; *wickiups*, huts made of *brushwood* or covered with mats; and *hogans*, dwellings constructed of *earth* and *branches* and covered with *mud* or *sod*.

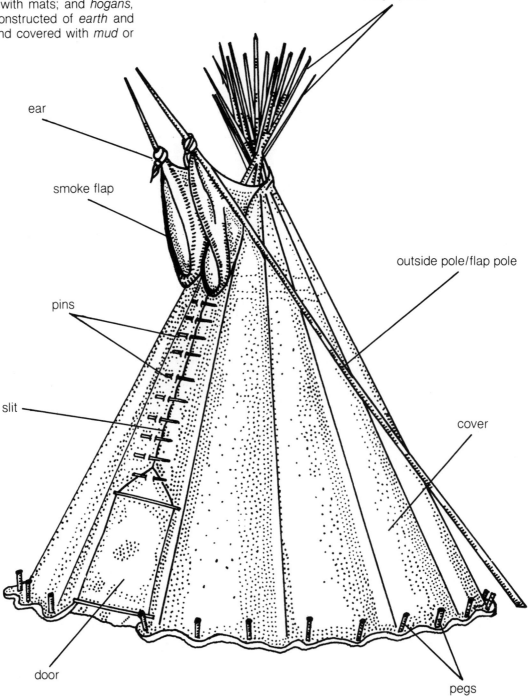

lodge poles

ear

smoke flap

outside pole/flap pole

pins

cover

slit

door

pegs

Domed Structures

Traditionally, a dome is a circular *vault* whose walls exert equal thrust in all directions, resisted by a *tension ring.* The geodesic dome consists of a *grid* of *compression* or *tension members* lying upon *great circles* running in three directions in any given area.

Igloo/Iglu

king block

snow blocks

ice window

storm igloo

air hole

tunnel/tossut

entrance

animal skin

sleeping shelf   entrance

Interior

Geodesic Dome

hubs

spoke/strut

skin/face

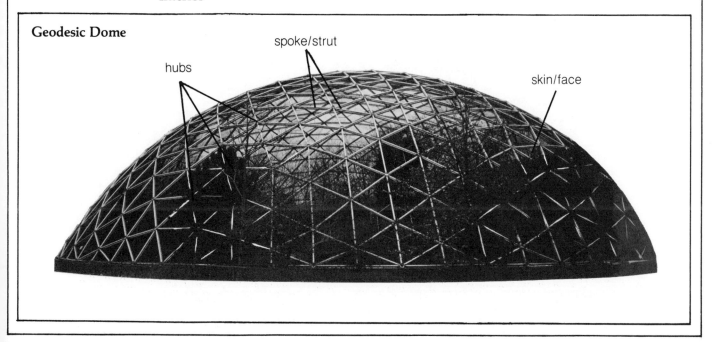

Special Purpose Buildings

Church / Cathedral

A small building used for worship is called a *chapel*. Living quarters used by church clergy are the *rectory*. The office in which church business is conducted is the *chancellery*.

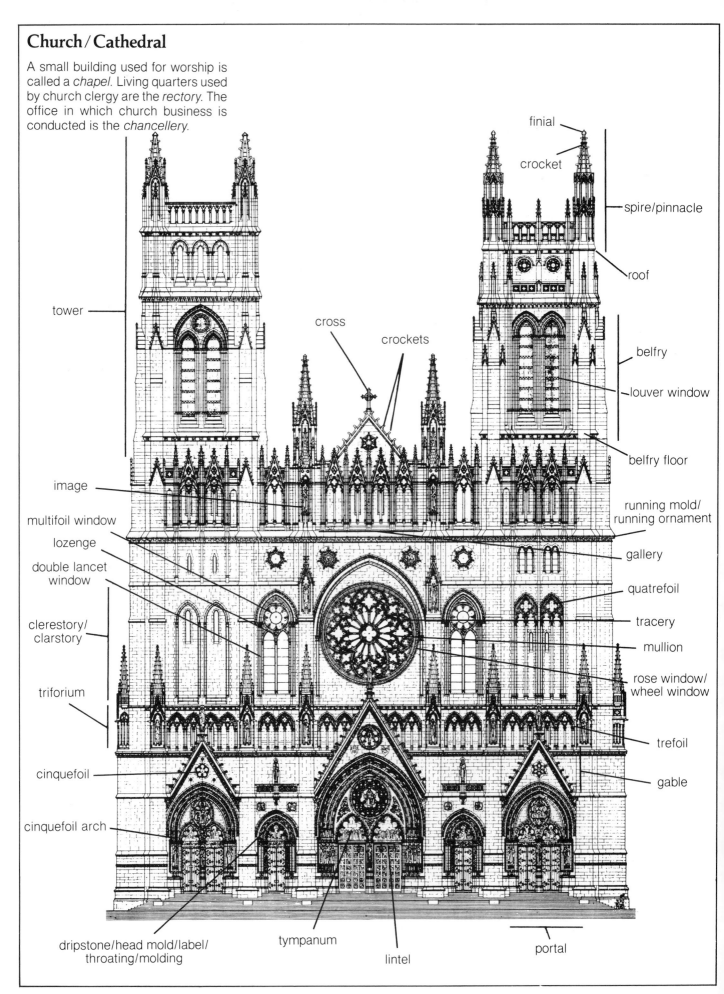

finial

crocket

spire/pinnacle

roof

cross

crockets

belfry

louver window

tower

belfry floor

image

running mold/ running ornament

multifoil window

gallery

lozenge

quatrefoil

double lancet window

tracery

clerestory/ clarstory

mullion

rose window/ wheel window

triforium

trefoil

cinquefoil

gable

cinquefoil arch

dripstone/head mold/label/ throating/molding

tympanum

lintel

portal

Church Interior

That part of a church containing the altar and seats for the clergy and choir is called the *chancel*. A *pulpit* is an elevated platform used in preaching or conducting a worship service. The *tabernacle* is a receptacle for consecrated elements of the Eucharist: the *pix,* the container in which Communion *wafers* are kept; the *paten,* a plate used to hold *Communion bread;* and the *chalice,* or *Communion cup,* used to dispense consecrated *wine.*

north transept

north porch

columbarium

chancel/sanctuary

crossing

north tower

baptistery

north portal

narthex

nave

aisle

chapels/ apsidal chapels

high altar

presbytery

great choir

central portal/ principal doorway

chancel rail

ambulatory

west front

rood screens & organ

sacristies/vestries

exhibit hall

Floor Plan

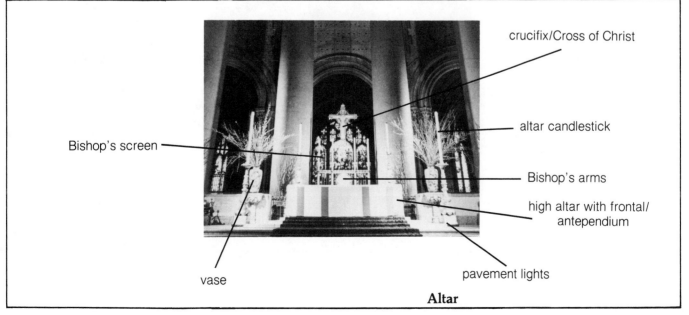

crucifix/Cross of Christ

altar candlestick

Bishop's screen

Bishop's arms

high altar with frontal/ antependium

pavement lights

vase

Altar

Special Purpose Buildings

Synagogue / Temple

The Torah is a parchment or leather *scroll* containing the first five books of the *Scriptures*, or *Pentateuch*, written in Hebrew. It is tied closed with a beltlike *wrapper*.

eternal light/Ner Tamid

Star of David/
Magen David/
Shield of David

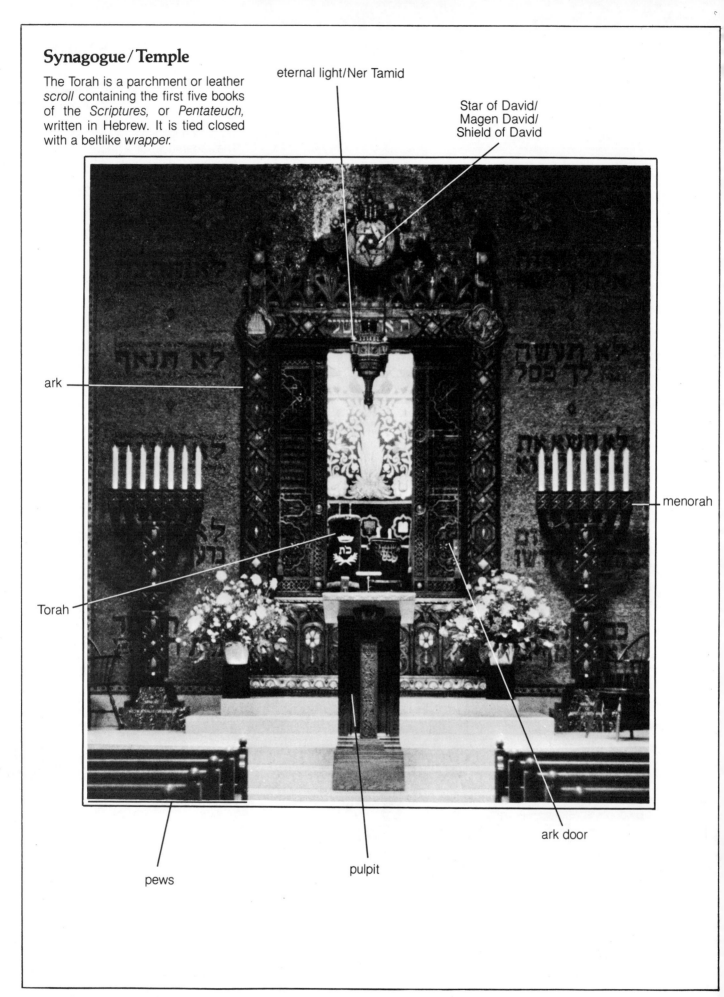

ark

menorah

Torah

ark door

pews

pulpit

Courtroom

The small anteroom off the courtroom in which the *judge* changes into his *robes* and holds conferences is called the *judge's chambers*. After a *jury* has heard a case, it deliberates in a *jury room*. A judge may sometimes use a malletlike *gavel* during proceedings.

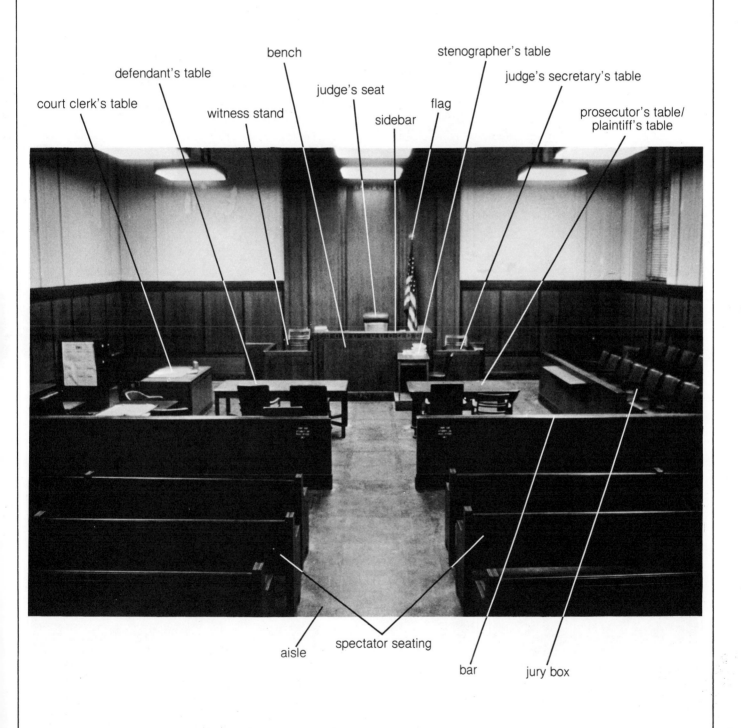

court clerk's table

defendant's table

witness stand

bench

judge's seat

sidebar

flag

stenographer's table

judge's secretary's table

prosecutor's table/ plaintiff's table

aisle

spectator seating

bar

jury box

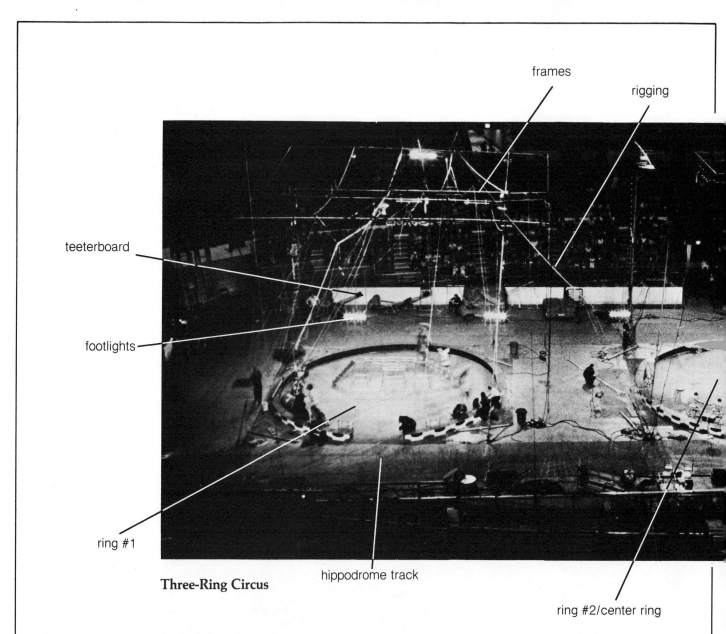

frames

rigging

teeterboard

footlights

ring #1

Three-Ring Circus

hippodrome track

ring #2/center ring

Aerialists/Flyers/Trapeze Artists

platforms

safety loop

safety-net apron

web

rope ladder

Animal Tamer

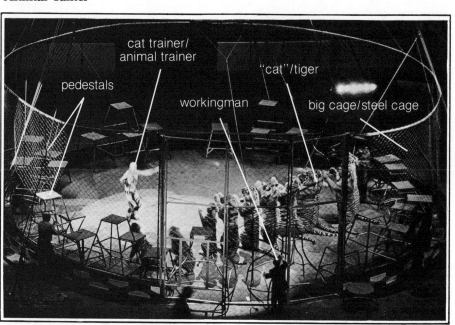

cat trainer/
animal trainer

"cat"/tiger

pedestals

workingman

big cage/steel cage

Circus

Circuses traditionally take place in tents erected by *roustabouts* and begin with a *parade* in which all the performers enter the *arena*. A *ringmaster*, usually clad in *top hat* and *tails*, announces acts, including *animal* and *clown acts; tightrope*, or *high-wire acts;* and *jugglers*. In the past, *sideshows*, which took place in an adjoining tent, featured *tattooed ladies, giants, midgets, swordswallowers* and *fire-eaters*.

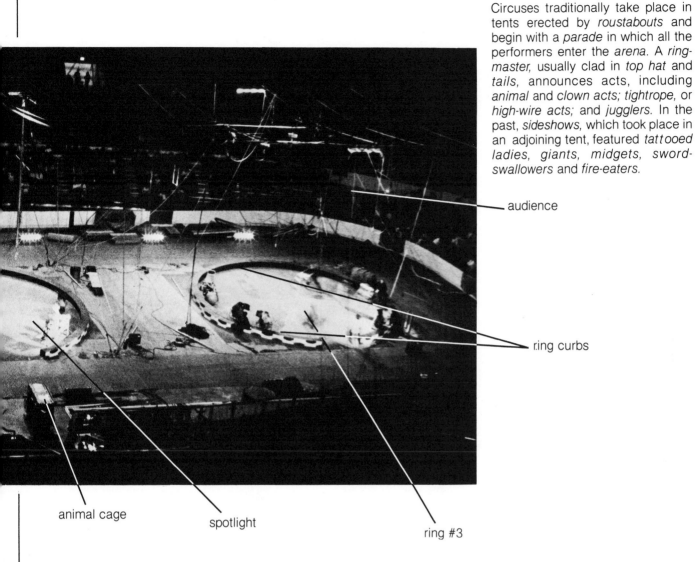

audience

ring curbs

animal cage

spotlight

ring #3

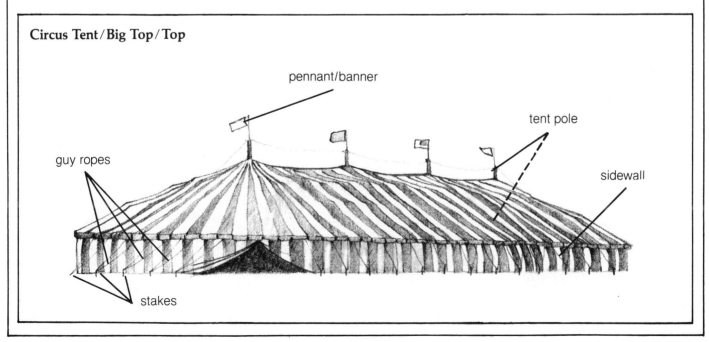

Circus Tent/Big Top/Top

pennant/banner

tent pole

guy ropes

sidewall

stakes

Special Purpose Buildings

Amusement Park

A roller coaster consists of *hills, straightaways* and *loops. Upstop wheels* lock roller-coaster cars to the track, *guide wheels* are used for turns, and tractor wheels are used for gliding.

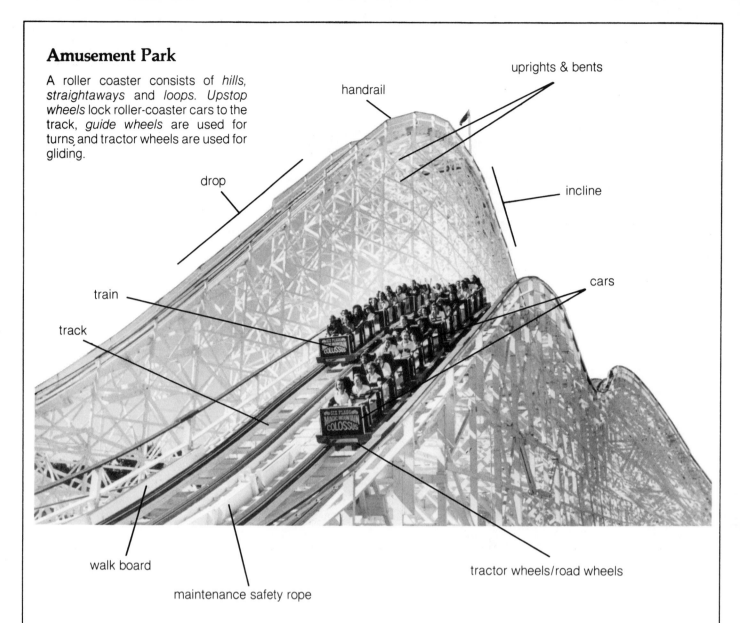

uprights & bents

handrail

drop

incline

cars

train

track

walk board

maintenance safety rope

tractor wheels/road wheels

Roller Coaster

Bumper Car/Scooter Car

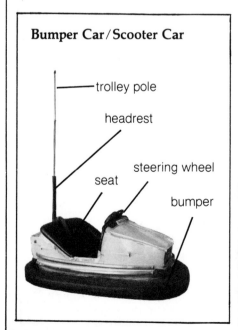

trolley pole

headrest

steering wheel

seat

bumper

Incline Track

tie beams

crown

chain

guide

anti-rollback/
ratchet angle

ledger

Amusement Park

Immobile carousel horses are called *gallopers*. *Jumpers* move up and down on horse rods. *Flying horses* tilt outward as the carousel picks up speed. Merry-go-round music is traditionally provided by a mechanical *band organ*, often referred to as a *calliope*.

outer wheel/outer rim

inner wheel

spokes

car/seat/gondola

axle

safety bar

unistrut/A-frame

tower/leg

safety ladder

support

Ferris Wheel

Merry-Go-Round / Carousel

panel painting

rim/rounding board/
cornice/shield

rotating frame

inner cornice

horse rod

horse

gondola/chariot

platform

inside drive

Special Purpose Buildings

airline identification
location marker

hotel

airport heating &
cooling system

air traffic
control tower

entrance road

long-term
parking lot

gate

ramp

jet bridges/
nose bridges/
passenger loading bridges

passenger concourse

Runway

visual-approach slope
indicator lights/
VASI/glide slope indicators

centerline stripe

runway edge marking

precision approach markings/
instrument approach

runway number/
compass bearing

landing threshold

nonprecision
approach
markings

chevrons/overrun area

threshold lights

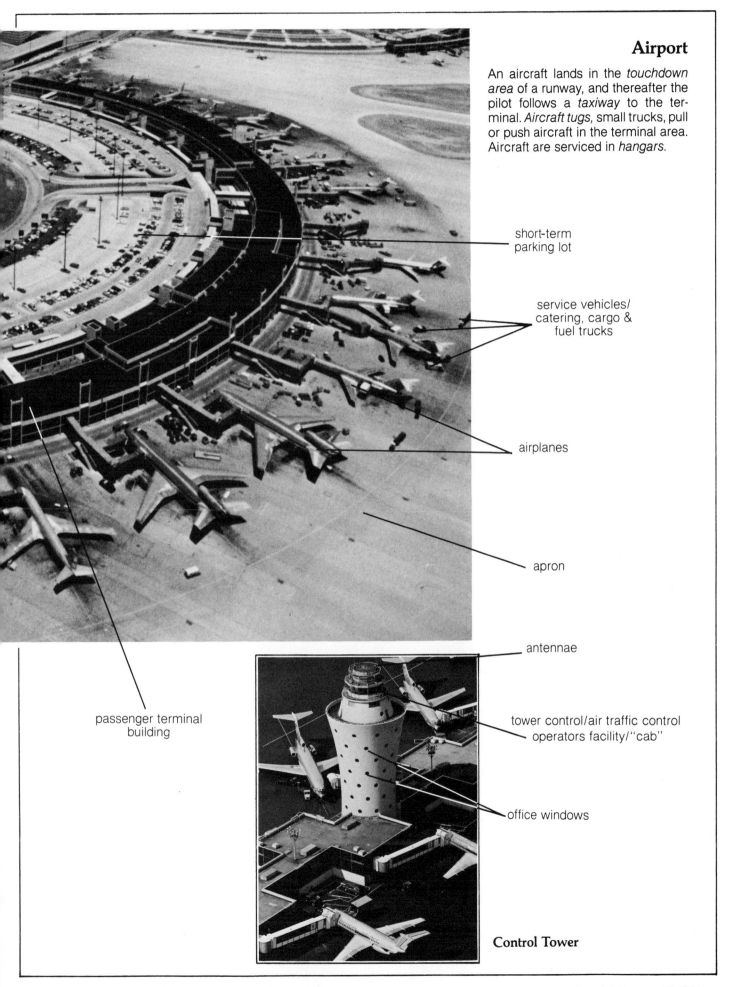

Airport

An aircraft lands in the *touchdown area* of a runway, and thereafter the pilot follows a *taxiway* to the terminal. *Aircraft tugs,* small trucks, pull or push aircraft in the terminal area. Aircraft are serviced in *hangars.*

short-term parking lot

service vehicles/ catering, cargo & fuel trucks

airplanes

apron

passenger terminal building

antennae

tower control/air traffic control operators facility/"cab"

office windows

Control Tower

Special Purpose Buildings

Railroad Yard

A railroad yard, or *marshalling yard,* consists of a system of *parallel tracks, crossovers* and *switches* where *cars* are formed into *trains* and where cars, *locomotives* and other *rolling stock* are kept when not in use or awaiting repair. In *hump yards,* freight cars are pushed down a *hump* onto a *siding,* determined by a *yardmaster,* to be coupled to a forming train. *Electropneumatic retarders* control the speed of the cars as they move along the tracks.

receiving tracks

main line

car service area

stalls

roundhouse/ engine terminal

turntable

lead tracks/ engine terminal tracks

water tanks

classification tracks/ "bowl" tracks

freight cars

sand tower

locomotive shop

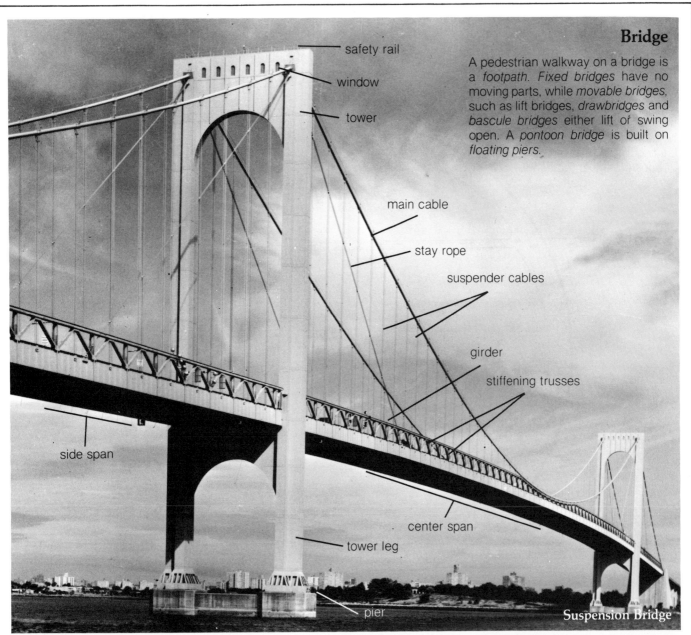

Bridge

A pedestrian walkway on a bridge is a *footpath. Fixed bridges* have no moving parts, while *movable bridges,* such as lift bridges, *drawbridges* and *bascule bridges* either lift or swing open. A *pontoon bridge* is built on *floating piers.*

safety rail

window

tower

main cable

stay rope

suspender cables

girder

stiffening trusses

side span

center span

tower leg

pier

Suspension Bridge

span guide

machinery tower

main counterweight

elevator shaft

auxiliary counterweight

lift span

Lift Bridge

vertical brace

tie brace

aviation light

upper chord

lower chord

roadway

span lock

shoes

gatehouse

fenders

Other Structures

Tunnel

Tunnels that take water to hydroelectric plants or to municipal waterworks and those that remove storm water and sewage are called *conduits*. Tunnels cut through rock frequently require no *lining*. Underwater tunnels can be ventilated by *shafts* leading to the surface or by *exhaust* or *booster fans* at the ends.

exhaust air ducts

grout

steel shield

railing

catwalk

roadway

fresh-air supply duct

Cross Section

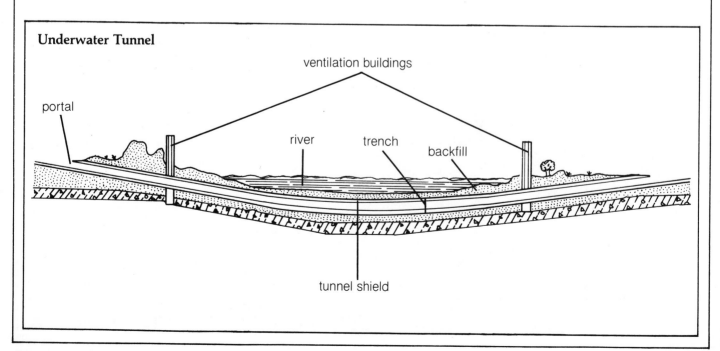

Underwater Tunnel

ventilation buildings

portal

river

trench

backfill

tunnel shield

Canal Lock

The water level in a canal lock is raised or lowered through *sluice gates* in the lock wall or *floor. Shipboard lines* or *hawsers* secured to *bollards* along the lockside hold the vessel steady while the lock is in operation. Before *electric locomotives* were used, animals would haul boats through locks following a *towpath*.

softnose

forebay

upper pool

upper gate/
upstream gate

control cabins

lockside

lock wall/revetment

lock/pound lock/
lock chamber

leaf

catwalk

lower gate/
downstream gate

channel

lower pool

tracks

locomotive/"mule"

forebay

Dam

Many dams have steep channels divided by partitions into pools, called *fishways* or *fish ladders*, that enable fish to swim upriver. Other dams have *log chutes* designed to allow logs to pass through. A *dike*, or *levee*, is an earthwork construction built to block water rather than to regulate its flow.

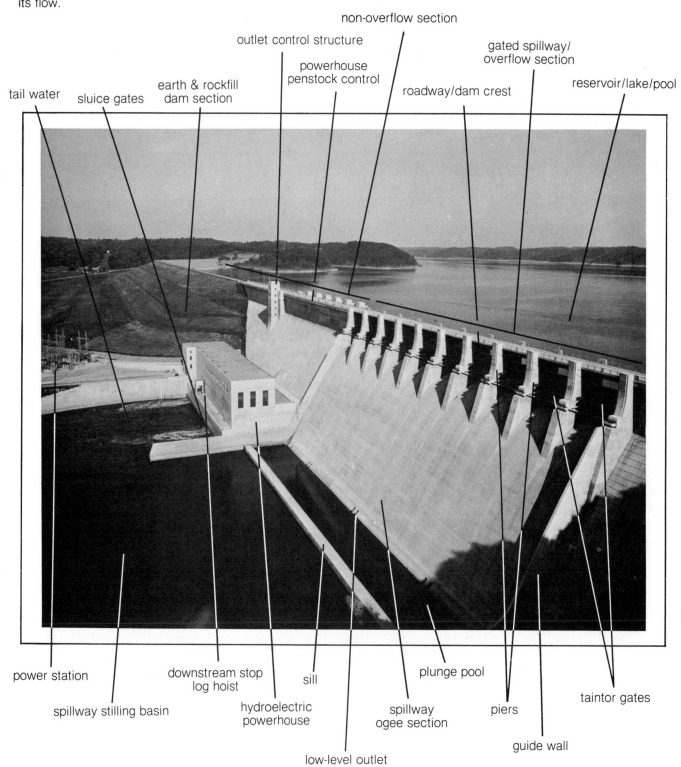

non-overflow section

outlet control structure

powerhouse penstock control

gated spillway/ overflow section

roadway/dam crest

reservoir/lake/pool

tail water

sluice gates

earth & rockfill dam section

power station

downstream stop log hoist

sill

plunge pool

taintor gates

spillway stilling basin

hydroelectric powerhouse

spillway ogee section

piers

guide wall

low-level outlet

Oil Drilling Platform/
Offshore Rig

In shallow water this *semisubmersible* rig drills in the floating position. When drilling at greater depths the motion compensator, a *hydraulic-pneumatic device,* moves up and down as the rig does in the sea to keep the *pipe* stationary in the *hole.* The "driller" controls the *drill, bit* changes and large hydraulic valves, or *blowout preventors.*

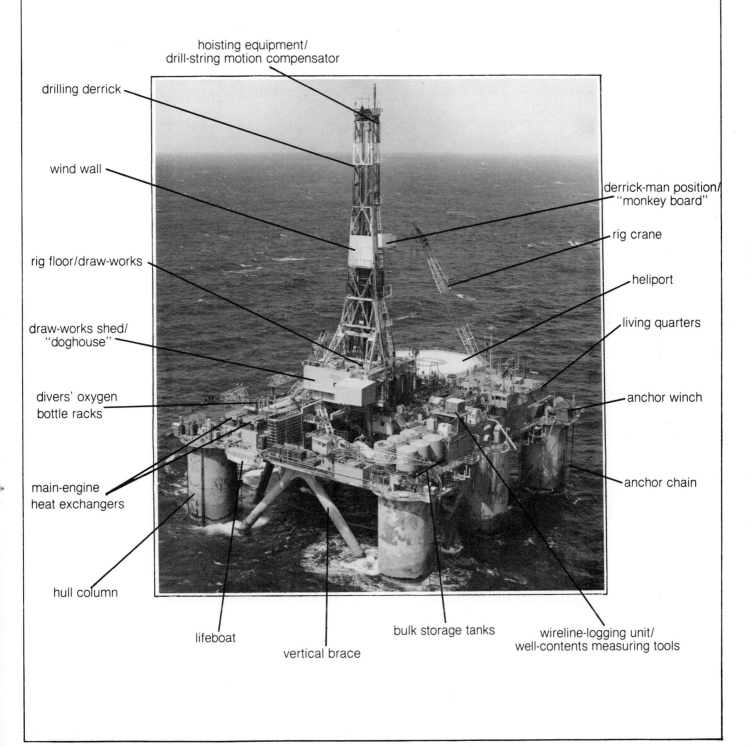

hoisting equipment/
drill-string motion compensator

drilling derrick

wind wall

rig floor/draw-works

draw-works shed/
"doghouse"

divers' oxygen
bottle racks

main-engine
heat exchangers

hull column

derrick-man position/
"monkey board"

rig crane

heliport

living quarters

anchor winch

anchor chain

lifeboat

vertical brace

bulk storage tanks

wireline-logging unit/
well-contents measuring tools

Other Structures

Barn and Silo

A barn *floor* is divided in the center by a *feed passage* that may be lined with *stanchions* to hold cows. On either side are *manure gutters,* and on each side of these are *mangers, boxes* or *troughs,* from which horses or cattle eat. Hay is stored in a *loft,* a storage room next to the roof. Surrounding a barn is a *yard* with a *manure pit* large enough to back a wagon into. Other barnyard structures, adjoining the main barn or built nearby, include *grain pits,* or *bins; springhouses; smokehouses,* and *pigpens.*

intake

dome/umbrella/parachute/ pumpkin/melon

gable/penthouse/door hood

weather vane

tower bin/ tower tank

ridge

cupola/ventilator

verge

hip

ladder

hay doors

dormer

gable wall/ weatherboarding

sliding doors

eave

silo pipe

service court

apron

great door

awning

feeding pen

extended bay

split-rail fencing

Barn

Silo

Transportation

All the major forms of transportation are incorporated in this section, beginning with the most ubiquitous mode of everyday travel—the automobile. Coverage of the car begins with an illustration of a specially built model displaying all the exterior parts that appear or have appeared on recent designs. Also included is a cutaway drawing that shows the major but often unseen interior components of a car as well as illustrations of a car engine, interior dash and traffic control devices.

The other major subcategories cover public conveyances; emergency, public service and recreational vehicles; boats and ships; aircraft and spacecraft. Vehicles used for military purposes, such as fighting ships and aircraft, are included in this section as well.

Cutaway illustrations have been used to show the reader the interior parts of an ocean liner and the cockpits of a jumbo jet, military fighter and space shuttle.

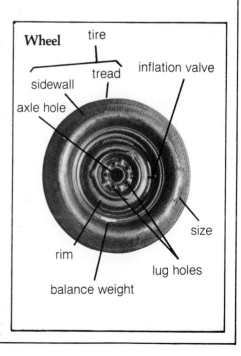

Wheel
tire
tread
inflation valve
sidewall
axle hole
size
rim
lug holes
balance weight

Automobile/Car Exterior

The *body* of this specially designed car, or *customized automobile*, rests on a *chassis* consisting of a *frame* and wheels. Older cars often had *rumble seats* instead of trunks. On *convertibles*, the entire top folds into a compartment called the *boot*. Many contemporary cars have sliding *sun roofs* or *moon roofs*. A *sedan* usually has four doors and full-width front and rear seats. A *coupe* is a smaller version of a sedan, having only two doors. A *station wagon* is a boxlike car with storage space behind the rear seat, which may have *fold-down seats* for additional passenger seating. A high-performance car with a low-slung body is a *sports car*.

front window/front door window

front door

sideview mirrors

air scoop

spare tire

hood

AnyCar II

Manufacturers Hanover

fender/front quarter panel

signal light/cornering lamp

tire/wheel

mag wheel

lug nuts

tire well

rocker panel

roof panel

windshield

windshield molding

windshield wiper arm

antenna

passenger sideview mirror

hood ornament

high-low combination headlamp

driver sideview mirror

hood

grille frame

sidemarker lamp

high beam

headlights

directional signal/turning signal/blinker

low beam

headlamp door

front bumper

930·UOD

NEW YORK

directional light & lens/turning signal/blinker

bumper bolt

grille

license plate

bumper guard

license plate housing

roof

door handle

seat

rear window/
rear door window

rear-quarter glass

antenna

trunk lid

running board

rear door

hubcap/wheel cover

rear quarter panel

windbreaker

convertible top

drip molding

rear windshield

fender blister

air vent

tail fin/rear quarter panel

nameplate

whitewall tire

side body molding/trim/chrome

gas tank door

taillight

reverse light

license plate light

license plate

rear bumper

Automobile Cutaway

Various systems are incorporated in a car: a *power train,* which consists of *clutch,* transmission, driveshaft and rear axle; a *cooling system* designed to control engine temperature; an *electrical system* to power the engine *starter motor,* accessories and lights; a *suspension system* to provide a smooth ride; and a *braking system.*

steering column

front intermediate pipe

master cylinder

engine/motor

expansion tank

battery

radiator

bumper energy absorber

fan

steering gear box

upper control arm bushings

upper ball joint

upper control arm

tie rod end

lower control arm

disc brake caliper

disc brake rotor

front hub

windshield pillar

roof rack

rear axle

gas tank

gas tank filler neck

wheel well

brake drum

rear coil spring

rear shock absorber

differential/rear end

driveshaft

floor pan

muffler

frame

rocker panel

universal joint

transmission

Automobile Interior

In addition to parts shown on this *dash*, or *dashboard*, are *headlight* and *warning light controls*, *hood release*, *engine choke* and *hand throttle*, *windshield wiper speed control* and *directional signal switch*. Above the dash, there is usually a *rearview mirror*. Flip-down *sun visors* are located above the windshield. Car seats are equipped with *seat belts* or *safety belts*.

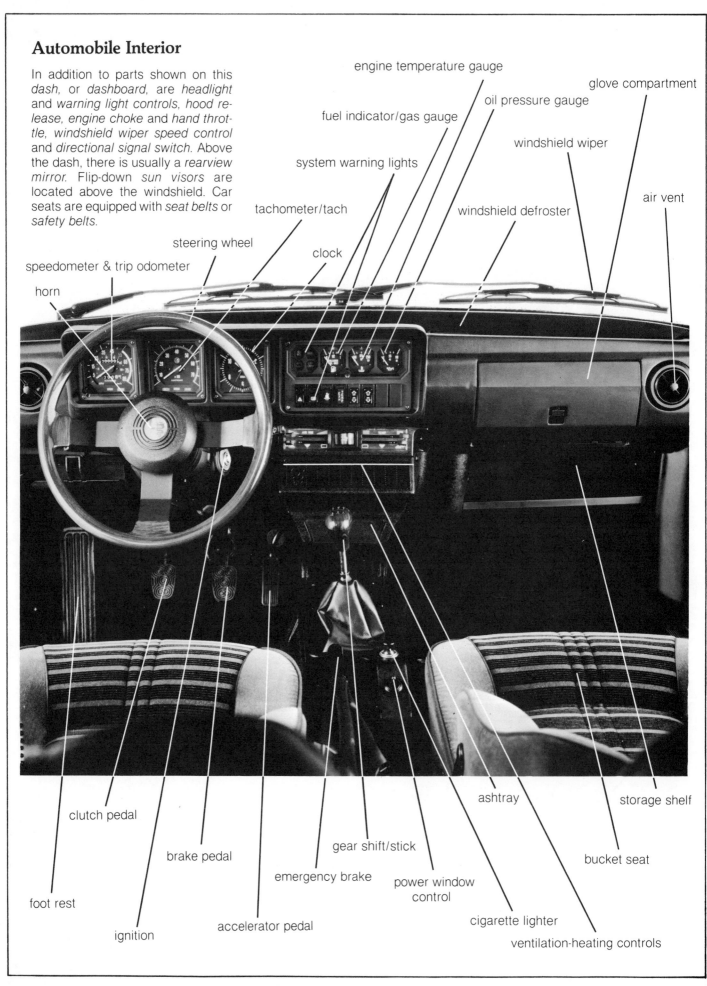

engine temperature gauge

glove compartment

oil pressure gauge

fuel indicator/gas gauge

windshield wiper

system warning lights

air vent

windshield defroster

tachometer/tach

steering wheel

clock

speedometer & trip odometer

horn

clutch pedal

foot rest

brake pedal

ignition

accelerator pedal

emergency brake

gear shift/stick

power window control

cigarette lighter

ashtray

bucket seat

storage shelf

ventilation-heating controls

Automobile Engine

The parts of an engine are fitted into or on the *engine block* or within the *head.* Common engine configurations include the *horizontally opposed,* or *flat four-cylinder;* the *in-line six;* and the *V-8.*

vacuum hose

distributor cap

alternator

distributor vacuum advance

air conditioner compressor

fan belt

distributor wire

cooling fan clutch

fan

vibration damper pulley

power-steering fan belt

fuel-line hose

power-steering pump

oil pan

flywheel

heat-riser valve

power-steering filler tube

spark plugs

spark-plug boots

ignition wire

valve cover

oil cap

oil dipstick

exhaust recirculating valve

idle-speed solenoid

carburetor

air cleaner/"hat"

pollution control valve

automatic choke

valve-distributor cover

alternator

preheater hose

spark plug

water pump

timing case cover

oil filter

motor mount

exhaust manifold

oil pan

starter motor

Automobile

Gasoline Pump

Service station islands can be *self-service* or *full-service.* Gas pumps draw supplies from underground *storage tanks.* Gasoline is purchased in different *grades* determined by *octane number.*

anchor springs

spout

fender guard

trigger

guard

regulator clip

Automatic Nozzle

weights & measures certification

price-poster arm

advertising panel

brand

dial face

money totalizer

gallon totalizer

price per gallon

gas type

coupling

front service door

skirt

nozzle boot

nozzle

reset/ on & off lever

hose

retrieving cable

manufacturer's label

Gas Pump / Island Dispenser

Traffic Control Devices

Four-face traffic signals, or lights, are operated manually by a traffic-control official or run automatically by an electric *timer.* Parking meters, set atop *pipe standards,* contain *self-starting timers.* Jammed meters activate a *slot closer* so that additional coins cannot be inserted in the *slot block.* Some meters have a *washer detector* that allows *washers* and *slugs* to pass through without registering time on the *dial.*

span wire

upper arm

universal cross connection

tunnel visor

face

body

span-wire hanger assembly

rosette cap

lens/red light/ stop signal

yellow light/ caution signal

green light/ proceed signal

Traffic Light

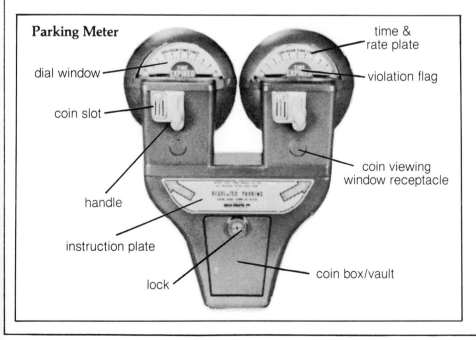

Parking Meter

dial window

coin slot

handle

instruction plate

lock

time & rate plate

violation flag

coin viewing window receptacle

coin box/vault

REGULATED PARKING

Highway

Energy absorbing barriers, or *impact attenuation devices,* are positioned in gore areas to reduce accidents. Some roads are lined with *guardrails,* or *railings. Milestones,* or *mile markers,* provide distance information between specific points. Many *expressways, freeways* and *thruways* have *rest areas, scenic overlooks* and *service areas.*

entrance ramp

gore area

service road

exit ramp

road divider

minor road/
subsidiary road

intersection/junction

major road

shoulder

lane/roadway

overpass/bridge

entrance lane

underpass

loop ramp

roadbed/
divided highway

median/island

access road

Cloverleaf / Interchange

Toll Booth

canopy

lane open &
closed indication

lights

informational signs

toll booth

fee indicator

gate arm

auto gate/barrier gate

island

toll lane

caution stripes

cone/temporary traffic-control device

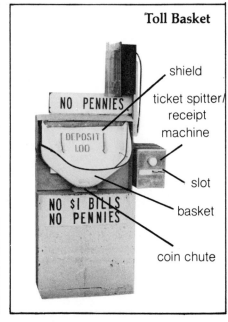

Toll Basket

shield

ticket spitter/
receipt
machine

slot

basket

coin chute

Railroad Crossing

A railroad *roadway* consists of two rails, or tracks, and all their supporting elements, including *railroad bridges, tunnels* and *embankments*. The roadway follows the *right of way*. The distance between rails is the *gauge,* while the degree of rise or fall in a *roadbed* is the *grade*. The top of a rail is the *railhead*. The bottom is the *rail foot*.

bracket

warning lights

crossarm/gate

reflector

post cap

RAIL CROSSING ROAD

crossbucks

2 TRACKS

light

target

bracket

electric wire

post

hinge assembly

bolt

ballast/bed

fishplate/joint bar

rail/track

spike

tie plate/baseplate

crosstie/tie/sleeper

Railroad Track

electrical conduit

control box

counterweight

Crossing Signal

111

Railroad

In addition to the locomotives shown here, there are *diesel* and *electric locomotives. Open-top cars,* boxcars and flatcars are the main types of *freight cars,* while *passenger trains* consist of *dining cars, sleeping cars, lounge* or *observation cars* and *baggage cars.*

boiler plate/jacket

boiler washout plug

smokestack

bell

sandbox

boiler front

sandpipes

whistle

marker lamp

boiler

headlight

injector pipe

steam dome

handrail

hinge

cab

steps

coal tender

coupler

6615

tender trucks

trailing truck

driving wheel

main rod

cylinder

deck brace

Steam Locomotive

reverse

connecting rod

air reservoir

handrail

air brake hose

cow catcher/pilot

Train / Rolling Stock

safety dome

bumper/buffer

hopper car

tank car

locomotive/engine

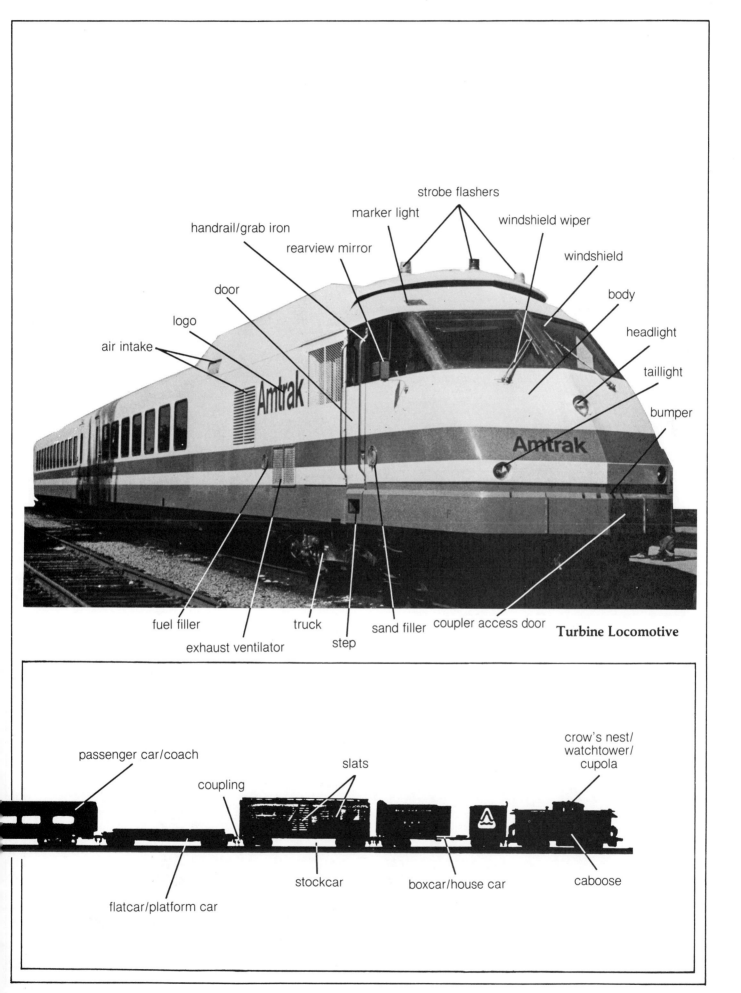

strobe flashers

marker light

handrail/grab iron

windshield wiper

rearview mirror

windshield

door

body

logo

headlight

air intake

taillight

bumper

Amtrak

Amtrak

fuel filler

truck

sand filler

coupler access door

Turbine Locomotive

exhaust ventilator

step

crow's nest/
watchtower/
cupola

passenger car/coach

slats

coupling

stockcar

boxcar/house car

caboose

flatcar/platform car

Public Transportation

Bus

Long-distance coaches have airplanelike *reclining seats* with *overhead baggage racks* and *reading lights*. They may also have *lavatories* and *roof ventilation hatches*. *Sightseeing buses* have *transparent roofs*, at least in part, to increase the viewing area.

"Michigan" marker lights
clearance light
entrance door window
upper windshield
destination sign
hood
side window
windshield
side panel
turn signal light
emergency air vent
logo
air-conditioning intake
headlights
battery compartment
front bumper
rear tires/ drive axle tires
lock
baggage compartments
rearview mirror
front tire/ push axle tire/ bogie
reflectors
curb window
side marker lights
entrance door
windshield wiper

Coach/Intercity Bus

Commuter Bus Interior

handrail
handstrap
bus number
door mirror
exit mirror
front door
advertising panel
exit signal
support beam
side sign
standee window
exit door
bell cord/ signal cord
step well
side window
exit bar
driver's seat
panel
armrail
rearview mirror
fare box
route number/ run number
seats

A subway, or *rapid transit system*, usually consists of a *train* which derives its power from a *third rail;* subterranean *tunnels*, or *tubes; elevated tracks;* and *subway stations*, or *stops*, along each *route.*

window
ventilator
fan
light
emergency brake
advertising panels
handstraps
subway map
door panels
side handrail
seat
handrail/support beam
storm door
destination sign/ side sign

Taxi Roof Light

off-duty sign
medallion number
signal light

OFF 9F8I DUTY

Motorman's Cab

whistle/horn
air valve
indicator light
air gauge
windshield-wiper control
exterior panagraph gate
controller/ dead man's stick
brake-handle box

A *rig* consists of a tractor *coupled* with or *hooked up* to a trailer. A cab may have a partitioned section within, called a *sleeping box,* for the driver, and a *varashield,* a capelike device designed to deflect air and reduce resistance on the trailer, mounted on the roof. The *refrigeration van,* or *reefer,* shown on the opposite page, is a semi, meaning that the tractor bears some of its weight. A true trailer rests and rides on its own wheels.

vertical exhaust

windshield

cab lights

hood

air horn

parking light/turn signal

rearview mirror

assist handle

grille

mud flap/splash guard

fuel tank

tire

step

wheel

bumper step

battery box

air compressor

driving light

lug

headlight

compressed air tanks

Tractor/Cab

air cleaner

air intake

trailer air & electrical connect lines

fifth wheel/trailer connection

frame rail

rearview mirror/ "West Coast" mirror

cab tilting instructions

engine rear

leaf springs

rear axle carrier

spare wheel

fuel tank

refrigeration unit

clearance light

curbside sidewall

vent door

roadside sidewall

upper side-rail

front wall

lower
side-rail

battery box

red marker
light

certification plate

reflector

sliding tandem wheels

mud flap/splash guard

gladhands &
electrical
connection

kingpin

support leg

sand shoe

auxiliary tank

marker light

support leg crank

Semitrailer/Van

Platform/Flat Bed

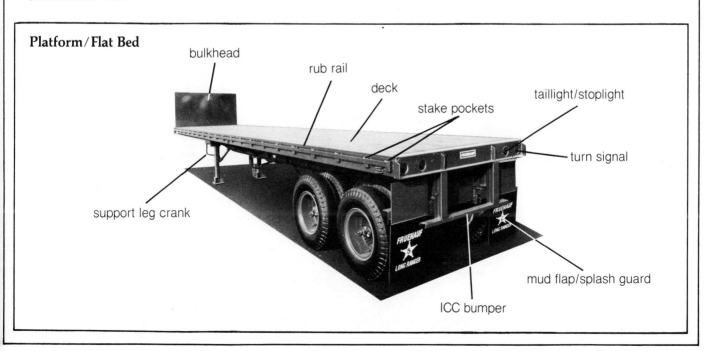

bulkhead

rub rail

deck

stake pockets

taillight/stoplight

turn signal

support leg crank

mud flap/splash guard

ICC bumper

Carriers

Police Car

Many police cars have *alley lights*, strong floodlights at either end of the light bar on the roof. A wire screen between the driver's seat and the back seat of the car is called the *cage*. Contained in the trunk of many police cars are a *hurst tool*, or *jaws of life*, a *haligan tool*, an *oxygen unit*, *flares*, a *fire extinguisher*, a *riot gun*, a *first-aid kit*, *blankets* and a *pillow*.

radar unit

speed selection
on-off test button

audio control
range control

mode selection controls

digital speed readout

antenna cable

microphone

power cable

frequency selectors

CB radio
police radio

emergency light selector

emergency channel

outside speaker selector

trunk opener

volume control

Interior

Exterior

police radio antenna

CB antenna

siren-bullhorn

rotating beacon/cherry

light bar

cone
bracket

radar antenna

STATE ● POLICE

DODGE

Ambulance

Additional equipment carried inside *advanced life-support units*, such as the one shown here, are *burn sheets*, *gauze*, *emesis basins*, *cervical collars*, *neck rolls*, *bitee sticks*, *tongue blades*, *peroxide* and *alcohol*, *extension tubes*, additional *oxygen tanks*, *splints*, *sandbags* (for traction), *linens*, a *scoop stretcher* and a *carrying chair*.

inflatable anti-shock trousers

foot pump

oxygen cylinder

drug box/bandages, syringes, pain-killers, tranquilizers

trauma box

gauge needles

bandages & saline

hare traction splint

blood-pressure cuff

tension screw

defibrillator

portable telemetry radio

portable electrocardiogram/lifepack

intubation box/breathing aid

suction unit/throat pump

Paramedic Equipment

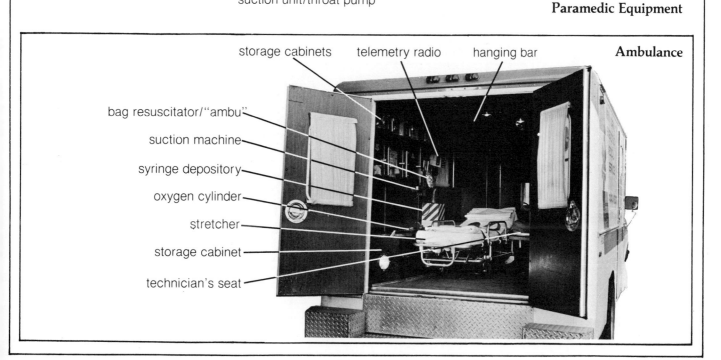

Ambulance

storage cabinets

telemetry radio

hanging bar

bag resuscitator/"ambu"

suction machine

syringe depository

oxygen cylinder

stretcher

storage cabinet

technician's seat

Emergency Vehicles

Fire Engine

On a fire truck, the entire tower ladder and control platform revolve on a *turntable.* Contained within a pumper is a water *booster tank* for fighting small fires, a *booster hose-reel,* for letting out hose line, and an *extension ladder.* Most fire fighting *apparatus* also carry *air tanks, lift-nets, EMT,* or *first aid boxes,* and *smoke ejectors.*

bucket/aerial platform/cherry picker

ladder pipe nozzle/stang

tower ladder

loudspeaker wire

pads

mars lights/marker lights

boom

horn

hydraulic lifter

bell

ladder control platform

bed

chauffeur's cab

stretchers

mount

warning light

ladder

steps

storage compartments

tow hook/tow ring

storage compartment

tormentor controls

siren and loudspeaker

tormentor/stabilizer/outrigger

Tower Ladder / Truck

company logo

bell

horn

mars light

spotlight

mirror

tow hook/tow ring

hydrant intake

siren and loudspeaker

engine company number

chauffeur's cab

stang/deluge gun

nozzle

riding compartment

outlet

stang hose

water pressure gauges

fitting/handle

clamp holder

control wheel/
steering wheel

hose bed tarp/hose cover

soft suction
connection hose

hard suction
connection hose

warning lights

spotlight

hydrant intake

storage compartments

backstep

Fire Hydrant / Fire Plug

bonnet

operating nut

hose nozzle cap

barrel/standpipe

cap chain

steamer connection cap/steamer nozzle cap

Pumper/Engine

Emergency Vehicles

Tow Truck/Wrecker

Tow trucks, or *rigs*, that respond to accident reports are called "chasers." A fully-equipped tow truck carries *fire extinguishers, battery charger, battery jumper cables,* and a two-pronged *lockout tool* which enables the operator to open locked car doors.

upright/stanchion

cable pulley

cable

tow-cable pulley

winch

boom

running lights

winch controls

guardrail

side marker

tailpipe

front push plate

split-rim wheel

step

tool-storage box

inverted hub/ dual wheel·hub

mud flap/splash guard

dual rear wheels

Truck Bed

boom

tow-cable pulley

j-hooks

boom light

light bracket

work spotlights

tail- & stoplight

license plate

winch

tow chain

wooden beam/ undercarriage protector

recessed taillight

safety-chain hole

rear push plate

tailpipe

recessed back-up light

t-bar/towing bar/Ortez bar

chain hook

Sanitation Vehicles

Garbage collectors, sanitation men, or "sanmen," also use a large, water-carrying truck called a *flusher* to wet down and clean streets.

side-view mirror

air cleaner

engine cover

pedestrian safety mirror

sanitation

signal lights

20L·043

D 2

City of New York
Department of Sanitation

reflector

bumper

hopper door

water spray bar

gutter broom head

side broom balance assembly

gutter broom

pivot gear housing

dirt shoe

pick-up broom

Mechanical Sweeper / Street Cleaner

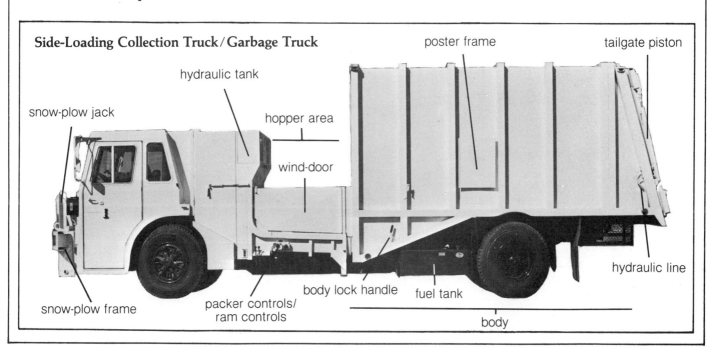

Side-Loading Collection Truck / Garbage Truck

poster frame

tailgate piston

hydraulic tank

snow-plow jack

hopper area

wind-door

snow-plow frame

packer controls/ ram controls

body lock handle

fuel tank

body

hydraulic line

Bicycle

This illustration combines elements from the most popular bicycle styles. The *frame* is the skeleton to which the *wheels* and all other components are attached. A one-wheel cycle is called a *unicycle*. A three-wheeler is a *tricycle*.

saddle/seat

upright handlebar

front brake cable

racing handlebar/ dropped handlebar

stem

seat post

cross bar/top tube

head lug

headset

brake hanger

seat tube

seat lug

brake lever

rack

rear brake

reflectors

cable clip

shifters

head tube

tire pump/ air pump

downtube

front brake

reflector

crank arm

valve

seat stay

fork/ fork blade

front-wheel quick release

derailleur cable

chain guard

cable

chain stay

fork tip

front hub

rear derailleur

fender

rim

tire

spokes

drive chain

chain ring

pedal

chainwheels

toe clip

toe strap

Rear Section

freewheel/ gear cluster

spoke protector

rear drop-out

tension wheel

jockey wheels

Crankset

front derailleur

chain ring

crank axle

chain

pedal

Caliper Brake

yoke cable

mounting plate

pivot point

pivot bolt

brake calipers

brake pad/ brake block

Motorcycle

Motorcycle accessories include *faring*, a molded wind deflector, *sissy bar*, a passenger backrest, and storage containers called *saddlebags*, or *panier cases*. A motorcycle for off-the-road use is called a *trail bike* or *dirt bike*. A *sidestand*, *kickstand* or *centerstand* holds the motorcycle upright when not in use.

handgrip

brake lever

clutch lever

throttle

speedometer & tachometer

headlight

fuel tank cap

brake line

passenger grab strap/c-strap

saddle/seat

rear shock absorber

signal light

rear fender

taillight

fuel tank cover

tachometer cable

front hydraulic fork

front fender

carburetor

frame cover/tool box

horn

air valve

brake caliper

engine

cam chain tensioner

footpeg

drive chain

front disc brake

gearshift lever

muffler

tire

mag wheel/solid spoke wheel

rear drive sprocket

chain guard

cam cover

exhaust pipe

rear drum brake

Recreational Vehicles

The *heating* and *cooking units* in the rear *coach* of a camper run on *propane gas.* Unlike campers, which run under their own power, *trailers* are hitched behind a vehicle and towed. Other *off-the-road vehicles* include *four-wheel drive jeeps* and *dune buggies.*

running lights

side window

roof air conditioner

luggage rack

side window

front window

water fill

road light

sewer valve

fuel tank

power-cord compartment

hot water heater

storage compartment

Camper/Motor Home

Snowmobile

instrument panel

handlebars

windshield

headlight

tail section

nose cone/wedge

seat

bumper

snow spoiler

suspension wheel

cleats

slide rail

track

shock absorber

steering link

skis

shock absorber

Horse-drawn Carriages

Stagecoaches were drawn by teams of horses and commanded by a *driver* called the *whip, Charlie* or *Jehu*. Protection was provided by a *guard*, or *shotgun*. A *buggy* was four-wheeled. A *gig* had two wheels. A *buckboard* had a spring-supported seat attached to a board directly connected to the axles. A *cabriolet* was a *hackney carriage*, or *cab*, with only two wheels and a folding top.

coach body panels

curtain/shade

lamp/sidelight

luggage rack

driver's box/seat

front boot

treasure box/ strongbox storage

rear boot

footboard

thoroughbrace

brake lever

rod/shaft

tire/wheel

wheel rim/felloe

brake shoe

brace

spoke

hub

undercarriage

wagon pole

carriage bolsters/ top & bottom pillows

mortice holes

Stagecoach

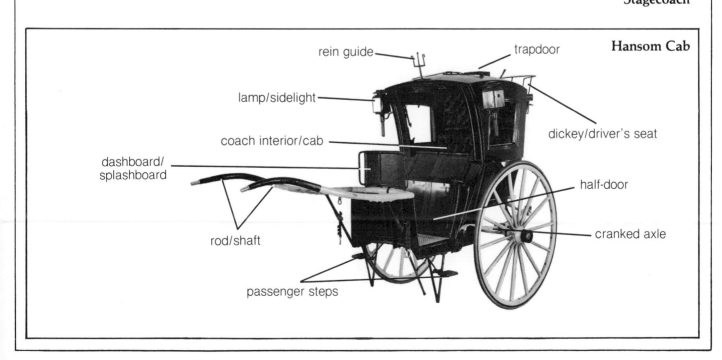

Hansom Cab

rein guide

trapdoor

lamp/sidelight

coach interior/cab

dickey/driver's seat

dashboard/ splashboard

half-door

rod/shaft

cranked axle

passenger steps

Carriages

Nautical Terminology

The outer shell of a boat is the *hull*. A hull's greatest width is the *beam*. Any line running from one side of a boat to the other is said to run *athwartships*. That part of a boat facing the direction from which the wind is blowing is called the *windward* side. The opposite side is called the *leeward* side.

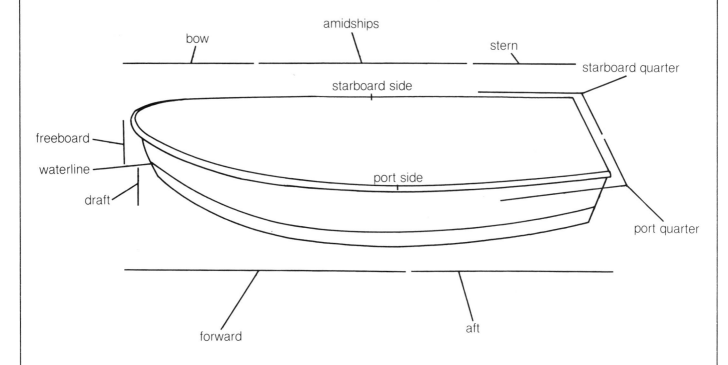

amidships

bow

stern

starboard quarter

starboard side

freeboard

waterline

port side

draft

port quarter

forward

aft

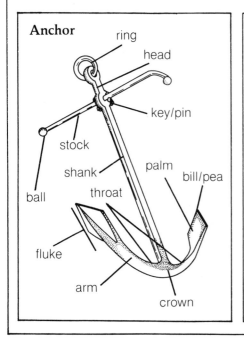

Anchor

ring

head

key/pin

stock

shank

palm

bill/pea

throat

ball

fluke

arm

crown

Rope/Line

yarns

fibers

strands

Buoy

buoy number/ reflective identification

light

clapper/ tapper

radar reflector

skeleton tower/ cage

inspection plate

bell

battery storage compartment

float

lifting eye

Rowboat

Any small *craft*, either *decked* or *open* and propelled by oars, is a rowboat, or *skiff*. If it is used to service a *yacht* or *motor cruiser*, it is called a *dinghy*, *dink* or *tender*.

sailing thwart

rowing thwart

oarlock socket/ rowlock socket

oarlocks/rowlocks

lifting ring

seat

transom

bow eye

painter

stem

grip   loom   shaft   blade

seat

gunwale

oar

Inflatable

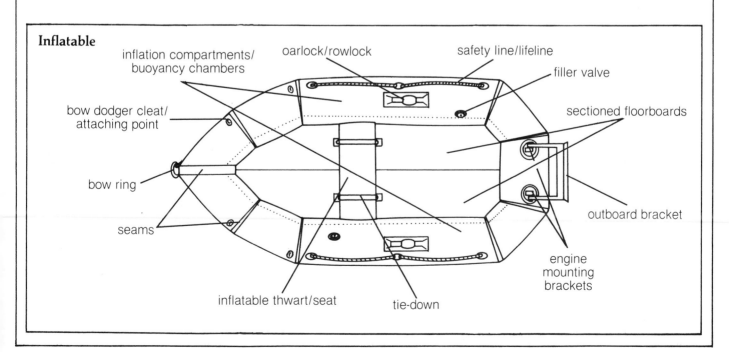

inflation compartments/ buoyancy chambers

oarlock/rowlock

safety line/lifeline

filler valve

bow dodger cleat/ attaching point

sectioned floorboards

bow ring

outboard bracket

seams

engine mounting brackets

inflatable thwart/seat

tie-down

Sailboat

Standing rigging, shrouds and stays, keep a sailing vessel's mast, or *spar*, upright. *Halyards* are used to hoist sails and *running rigging*, lines and *sheets*, control them. On some boats a *tiller* is used instead of a wheel to steer.

masthead

mast

backstay

mainsail

forestay

headstay

spreader

shroud

jib/jib topsail/
yankee/jibtop

staysail/club-footed
forestaysail

boom gallows/gallows frame

traveler

gate

companionway

staysail boom

winch

boom

cockpit

toe rail

stern pulpit/
pushpit

bow pulpit

foredeck

taffrail

wheel/helm

plow anchor

counter

rudder

bowsprit

rudder skeg

windlass

hatches

companionway hatch

forefoot

boot top

keel

stanchion

ports/portlights

lifeline

mainsheet

cabin top/
coach roof/
trunk

Sailboat Accommodations

The area between a vessel's cabin sole and its hull is called the *bilge*. Boats with overnight accommodations usually have a *navigator's station*, featuring a *chart table*.

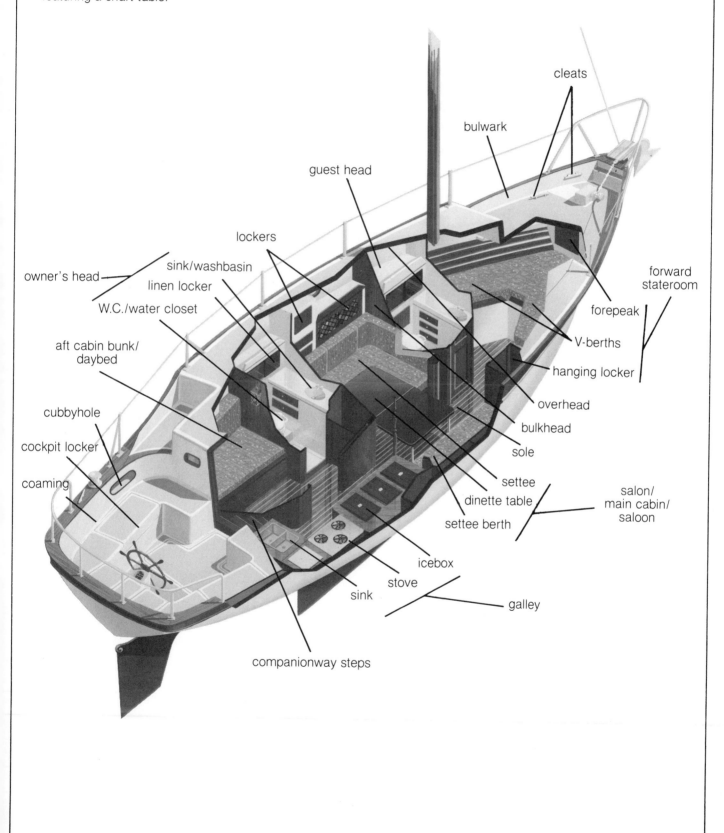

cleats

bulwark

guest head

lockers

sink/washbasin

owner's head

linen locker

W.C./water closet

aft cabin bunk/ daybed

cubbyhole

cockpit locker

coaming

forward stateroom

forepeak

V-berths

hanging locker

overhead

bulkhead

sole

settee

dinette table

settee berth

salon/ main cabin/ saloon

icebox

stove

sink

galley

companionway steps

Boats and Ships

Sail

Sails fall into two broad categories: *standing sails,* or *suits of sails,* and extras. Standing sails, such as those found on a modern *sloop,* would be mainsail and *headsail,* or *jib.* Extras, set to keep the vessel moving at optimum speed, include *spinnakers,* and, in bad weather, *trysails.* There are two types of compass: the *magnetic compass,* shown below, and the electrically-driven *gyro compass.*

head

headboard

panels

tabling

seams

class insignia/logo

sail number

leech

luff

batten pocket

telltale window

luff telltale

reef cringle

luff zipper

reef points

window

tack

clew

foot

foot zipper

Mainsail

Compass

hood/housing

dome

shadow pin

bearing line

pivot

card

lubber's line

binnacle

corrector magnet controls

1224

Outboard Engine

Three basic types of engines are used to power vessels: outboards, *inboard-outboards,* or *sterndrives,* and *inboards.* A marine sextant, a successor to the *octant* and *quadrant,* is used to measure the angle between a celestial body and the earth's horizon to help mariners determine their position at sea.

vent screw

fuel-tank cap

starter rope/ rewind starter

steering and throttle arm

cowling/cowl

clutch lever

carrying handle

swivel bracket

transom clamp

clamp screw

exhaust-relief port

trim-adjustment rack

driveshaft housing

anti-cavitation plate

exhaust port

fairwater

hub

root

propeller

blade

tip

skeg

Sextant

index sunshades

index mirror

handle

telescope

horizon mirror/ horizon glass

frame

index arm

limb

horizon sunshades

index mark

arc

micrometer drum

release lever

Boats and Ships

Powerboat

There are basically two kinds of powerboat *hull forms: displacement* and *planing.* Within these categories there are *V-bottom, cathedral, gull-wing, flat-bottom* and *round-bottom hulls. Houseboats* are boxlike vessels designed to provide maximum living space aboard. Projecting steel fittings used to hoist and carry a dinghy on a yacht are called *davits.*

Control Console

engine hour meter

fuel gauge

compass

tachometers

gear oil-pressure gauge

engine oil-pressure gauge

water temperature gauge

bilge & fuel alarms

voltmeter

port throttle

starboard throttle

port-engine clutch

starboard-engine clutch

wheel

engine stop

trim tabs

flying bridge/flybridge

foredeck

cabin trunk

rub rail

stem

portlight

boot stripe

chine

feature stripes

platform

tuna tower/tower

helmseat

control console

venturi
windshield

ladder

spreaders

companion
benchseat

safety rail

outrigger

after bulkhead

gin pole

cockpit freezer

cockpit

fighting chair

coaming padding

transom
door/gate

transom

handrail

side deck

window

sheer line

ladder

sliding door

live-bait well

rod holders

gunwale

135

Boats and Ships

Tanker

Cargo ships include *roll on-roll off ships; container ships; barge carriers; pallet ships; refrigerator ships,* or *reefers; dry-bulk carriers;* and *liquid-bulk carriers* such as the *super tanker* seen here. A *merchant ship* carrying *cargo* or *freight* is called a *liner* if it travels on scheduled routes at regular intervals, or a *tramp* if it does not have a fixed or scheduled route.

foremast

"crow's nest"/ lookout area

"catwalk"/ fore & aft gangw

pressure & vacuum relief valves

belowdeck storage entrance

anchor windlass & mooring winch

anchor windlass & mooring winch

radar mast & radar antennas

bridge/wheelhouse

bridge wing

wireless, telegraph &
navigation aerials

king post

lifeboat

hose-handling
derrick

stowed derrick
brackets

aft superstructure/
deckhouse

pressure &
vacuum relief valves

deck manifold

tank hatches

rail

foam monitors &
fire-fighting stations

gas-vent lines

137

Boats and Ships

Passenger Ship/ Ocean Liner

Main bulkheads, steel walls running athwartships on a ship, are normally watertight. A *collision bulkhead* is a *watertight bulkhead* near the bow to prevent flooding in the event of collision. Circular windows aboard ship are called *ports* or *portholes.* A ship is boarded at the pier by a portable stairway, or *gangplank,* which fits in an opening in a ship's *rail* or *bulwark.* A metal shield on *berthing hawsers* to prevent rats from coming aboard is a *ratcatcher.*

kennels

theatre bar

stack/funnel

bank

lifeboat

casino

shopping arcade

library

sun deck

nightclub

florist shop

miniature golf course

jogging track

outdoor pools

bar

bar

windscreen

fantail

name

home port

hawsehole

launderette

crew's quarters

car lift

barbershop & beauty salon

garage

staterooms

pool

engine room

card room

stabilizer controls

elevators

signal & lookout tower

restaurant

children's playroom

restaurant

signal deck

deluxe suites

bridge

sports deck

boat deck

weather decks

theatre & lecture hall

upper deck

hawsehole

quarterdeck

passenger decks

CUNARD

anchor

bow thrusters

wine cellar

chapel

gymnasium

stabilizer

pool & sauna

hospital

Surface Fighting Ship

Beginning with *dreadnoughts*, or *battleships*, modern surface *warships*, such as this *destroyer*, or *tin can*, have the capability to protect *shipping lanes*, deter invasions or support military operations on land. Today military vessels carry *surface-to-air missiles* and *surface-to-surface missiles*, as well as a range of *defensive guided weapons*. Many are *nuclear-powered*.

TACAN antenna

VHF (Very High Frequency) antennas

long-wire antennas

full-dress ship guideline

VHF antenna

ladder

helicopter flight deck

telescopic helicopter ranger

stack flue

mack

main dec

fantail

lifelines

ensign

flagstaff

stern light

bits

chock

watertight doors

rudder

strut

shaft

accommodation ladder

propeller

helicopter control tower

secondary con

motor whaleboat

direction finder

surface search radar

electronic
warfare antenna

air search radar

yardarm &
signal blinker

mast

wind indicator

signal halyard

fog whistle

gun director radar

safety observer
station

full-dress
ship guideline

gunmount

gun
director

towing lights

gun barrel

masthead light

forward anchor light

flying bridge

forecastle/fo'c'sle

jack
staff

bridge

ASROC launcher

1092

bull nose/
closed chock

bow number

air intake

02 level

liferafts

signal bridge

running light

waterline/boot top

fin stabilizer

01 level

VHF antenna

bridge wing

launcher
control station

sonar dome

signal shelter

Boats and Ships

Aircraft Carrier

The superstructure on an aircraft carrier, or *flattop,* is called the *island.* On take-off, aircraft are assisted by steam-driven catapults located on the *flight deck* or *angled deck.*

electronic
countermeasures
and radio antennae

air search radar

bridge   light mast

control tower

aircraft control radar

carrier landing system radars

air search radar

missile director

arresting gear pendant

aircraft elevator

boat and
aircraft crane

TACAN
navigation
system

surface
search
radar

missile launcher

aircraft
elevator

bomb elevators

catapults

TV camera

optical
landing
system

catapults

jet blast deflectors

hangar bay

landing signal
officer platform

aircraft elevator

life rafts

boat boom

jet engine
test area

point defense
missile launcher

landing area
line-up lights

missile launcher

personnel
safety nets

Submarine

Submarines, formerly called *U-boats* or *pigboats*, have thick inner *pressure hulls* and lighter *outer hulls*. The space between hulls is divided into several *ballast tanks*, used to control the vessel's buoyancy and trim. The conning tower contains *radio* and *radar antennas* and various *periscopes*, used for observation and navigation. In older submarines the sail also contained a *snorkel tube*. Navigation underwater is accomplished by means of an *inertial guidance system*. In addition to missiles, submarines can carry *torpedoes*.

fairweather planes/sailplanes

bridge/conning tower

sail/fairweather

missile deck

rudder

propeller

Fleet Ballistic Missile Submarine

Nuclear-Powered Attack Submarine

safety-line track

hull number

688

turtleback

Boats and Ships

Tugboat and Fireboat

A *pudding fender* is a large fender made of old rope, formerly fitted to the bow of many *tugs*, or *towboats*. A *pusher tug*, also called a *pushboat*, is specially designed with a high flat bow for *barge cluster* push-towing. A fireboat is usually a tug fitted with such items as *high-pressure pumps*, *hoses* and *nozzles*.

name board
mast
searchlight
aft controls
towing lights
running light
side bits
radar
pilothouse
searchlight
mast bits
line box

hatch
stern line
cleat
scupper
tarp/tarpaulin
towing hawser
capstan
main towing bits
life raft
master's quarters
pilot boarding ladder
side fender
bow fender

Tugboat

Fireboat

masthead light
tower monitor
after steering
tower
radar
flybridge monitors
aft monitors
stack
running light
pilothouse
forward monitor
hose reels
davit
punt
searchlights
nameplate
hose reel

life ring
side bit
scuppers
hawse hole

Hovercraft and Hydrofoil

Air Cushion Vehicles *(ACV)*, or *ground-effect machines,* are *amphibious vehicles* that ride on a cushion of air blown by *lift fans* through *slots* or *jets* around the underside of the hull. There are four classes of hydrofoils: *ladder, depth-effect, surface-piercing* and *submerged foils.*

fin

car deck

propeller gearbox

passenger cabin

radio aerial

engine air intake

passenger cabin

propeller

pylon

radar scanner

lift-fan air intake

flexible skirt/ air cushion

cabin ventilation pack

control deck

forward car ramp

Hovercraft / Air Cushion Vehicle

Hydrofoil

wheelhouse

forward passenger cabin

passenger cabin

steerable front strut

hydrofoil/wing

Boats and Ships

Helicopter

The main body of a helicopter, *chopper*, *whirlybird*, or *eggbeater*, is called the *fuselage*. The rescue helicopter shown here has an *amphibious hull*. Armed military helicopters are called *gunships*.

engine cowl

controllable landing light

rotor head

turbine engine

horizontal stabilizer

tail rotor

rotor blades

glide slope antenna

cockpit

rotary fairing

rescue hoist

sponson support strut

VHF/UHF antenna

tail pylon

sponson

stabilizer supports

main undercarriage wheels

high-frequency antenna

sliding door

cabin

marker beacon

rescue platform

tail wheel

automatic direction finder

A aircraft's central body portion is called the *fuselage*. To land on water, an airplane uses *pontoons*. To become airborne and begin *soaring*, a glider is pulled behind a motor-driven airplane or car by a cable attached to a *tow hook*. A glider lands on either a *landing wheel* or a *skid*.

tail assembly

rotating beacon

vertical fin

registration number

manufacturer's logo

fuselage

antennas

handle

cockpit/cabin

windshield/windscreen

engine cowling

engine air inlet

spinner

rudder

elevator

horizontal stabilizer

wing root

wing

flap

aileron

cabin door

shock absorber

propeller blades

wheel speed fairing

wing gear/main gear

baggage compartment door

nose wheel

running light

wing tip

Single Engine Airplane

Glider / Sailplane

cockpit canopy

vertical fin

rudder

elevator

stabilizer

aileron

nose cone

dive break/spoiler/airbrake paddle

Civil Aircraft

The *trailing edge* of the wings on a *jumbo jet,* such as the one shown here, has small *static discharge wicks* to reduce electrical-charge buildup. Passengers store carry-on belongings in *overhead bins,* or *stowage compartments,* or in front *closets.* Aboard many aircraft, seat cushions double as *flotation devices. Life rafts* are stored in overhead ceiling compartments above the doors, and *emergency escape chutes* are folded inside the doors.

VHF aerial

outboard ailerons

leading edge flap

outboard flaps

outboard spoilers

inboard ailerons

inboard flaps

inboard spoilers

upper lounge

flight deck

radar cone

lavatories

galley modules

business-class section

stairwell

first-class section

tail fin/vertical stabilizer

upper rudder

lower rudder

inboard elevator

outboard elevator

coach/tourist/
economy-class section

exit/door

tail plane/horizontal stabilizer

lavatories

galley modules

baggage compartment/belly

pylon

air inlet door

thrust cone

fan

turbofan engine

engine pod

Aircraft

747 Cockpit

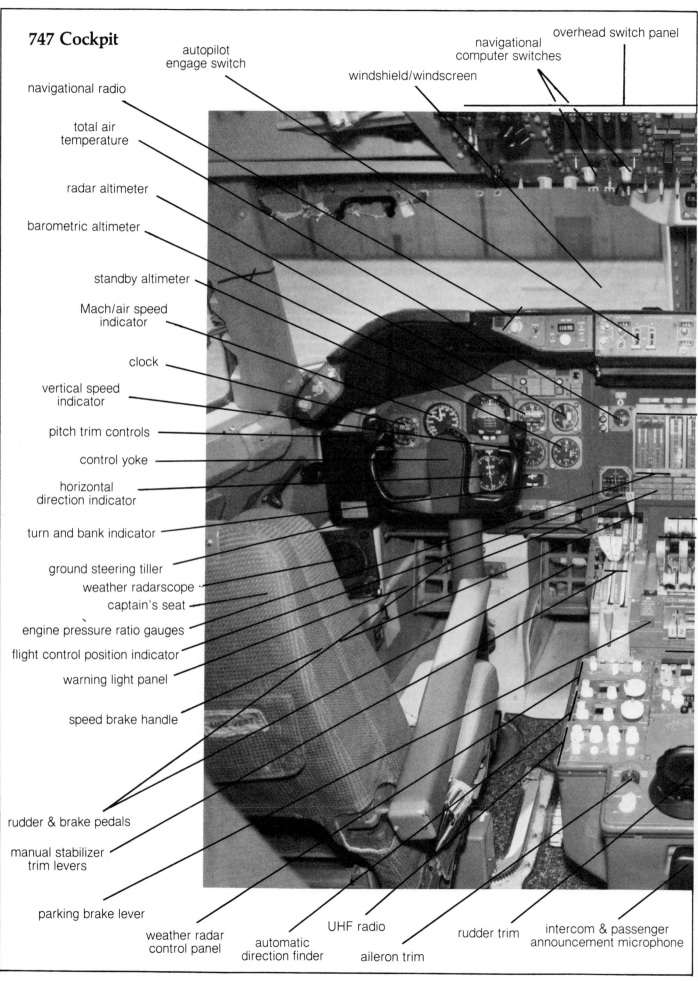

autopilot
engage switch

navigational
computer switches

overhead switch panel

windshield/windscreen

navigational radio

total air
temperature

radar altimeter

barometric altimeter

standby altimeter

Mach/air speed
indicator

clock

vertical speed
indicator

pitch trim controls

control yoke

horizontal
direction indicator

turn and bank indicator

ground steering tiller

weather radarscope

captain's seat

engine pressure ratio gauges

flight control position indicator

warning light panel

speed brake handle

rudder & brake pedals

manual stabilizer
trim levers

parking brake lever

weather radar
control panel

automatic
direction finder

UHF radio

aileron trim

rudder trim

intercom & passenger
announcement microphone

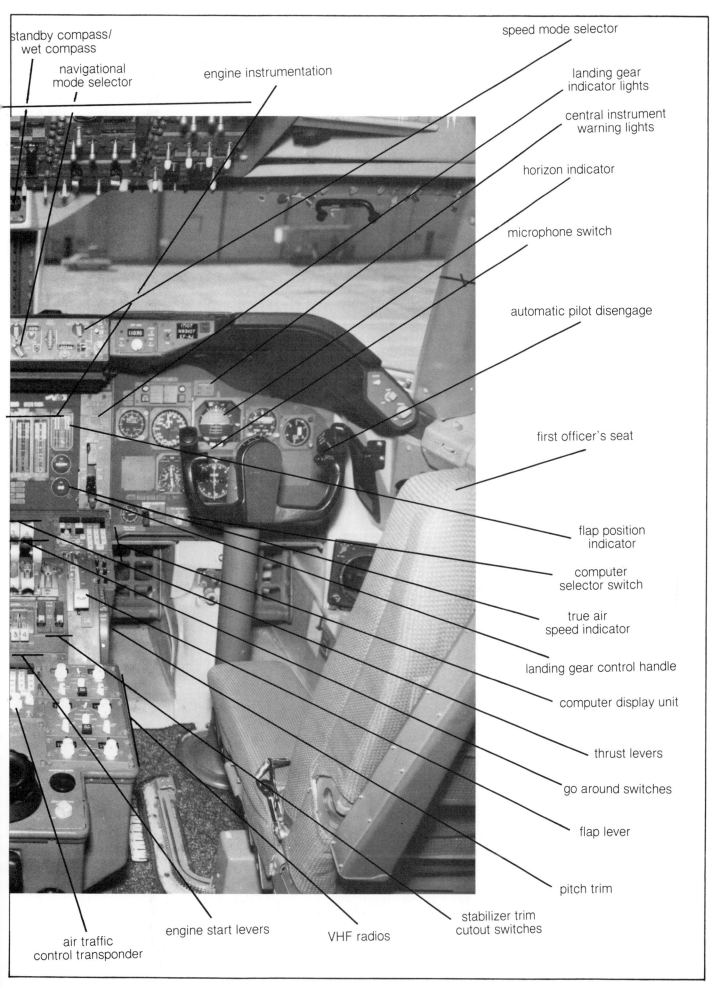

standby compass/
wet compass

navigational
mode selector

engine instrumentation

speed mode selector

landing gear
indicator lights

central instrument
warning lights

horizon indicator

microphone switch

automatic pilot disengage

first officer's seat

flap position
indicator

computer
selector switch

true air
speed indicator

landing gear control handle

computer display unit

thrust levers

go around switches

flap lever

pitch trim

stabilizer trim
cutout switches

air traffic
control transponder

engine start levers

VHF radios

Aircraft

Combat Aircraft

A fighter, such as the one shown here, has an advanced *airframe* with a *variable sweep wing* and a *long-range weapon system*. It is flown at speeds in excess of the speed of sound, or *mach speeds*.

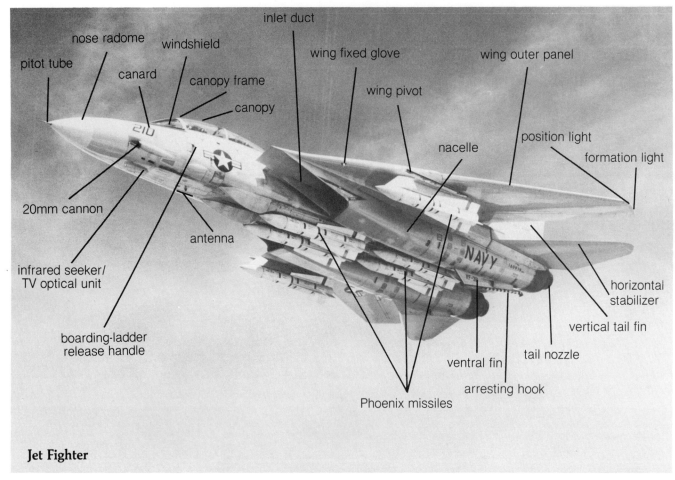

pitot tube
nose radome
canard
windshield
canopy frame
canopy
inlet duct
wing fixed glove
wing pivot
wing outer panel
nacelle
position light
formation light
20mm cannon
antenna
infrared seeker/ TV optical unit
boarding-ladder release handle
Phoenix missiles
ventral fin
arresting hook
tail nozzle
horizontal stabilizer
vertical tail fin

Jet Fighter

Weaponry

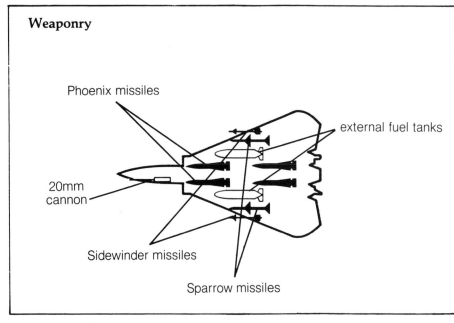

Phoenix missiles
external fuel tanks
20mm cannon
Sidewinder missiles
Sparrow missiles

Pilot's Instrument Panel

Behind the *pilot* is a *flight officer,* or *missile control officer,* who monitors the *tactical information display, armament* and *electronic counter-armament panel* and *electronic countermeasures panel.*

rearview mirrors

approach indexer

angle of attack indicator

left engine fuel shutoff handle

air combat maneuver panel

vertical velocity indicator

radar altimeter

servopneumatic altimeter

tachometer indicator

airspeed mach indicator

wheels-flaps position indicator

rate of flow indicator

landing gear control panel

launch bar abort

wing sweep indicator

target designate switch

fuel management panel

situation display indicators

hydraulic hand pump

brake pressure indicator

integrated control panel

throttle controls

UHF radio controls

oxygen-vent airflow controls

cabin pressure altimeter

liquid oxygen quantity indicator

control stick

master generator controls

air conditioning controls

external environmental control panel

countermeasure warning lights

standby compass

wing sweep indicator

right engine fuel shutoff handle

standby altitude indicator

accelerometer

clock

bearing distance heading indicator

canopy jettison handle

windshield frame

UHF remote indicator

arresting hook panel

displays control panel

elevation lead panel

fuel quantity indicator

caution-advisory indicator

compass control panel

master light control panel

master test panel

defog control lever

153

Aircraft

Space Shuttle and Launch Pad

A shuttle has three main components: an orbiter, external tank and two solid-rocket boosters. Many launch pads have *flame buckets* designed to direct *fireballs* and steam away from the pad itself. A gantry is a movable structure used for erecting and servicing a rocket prior to launch.

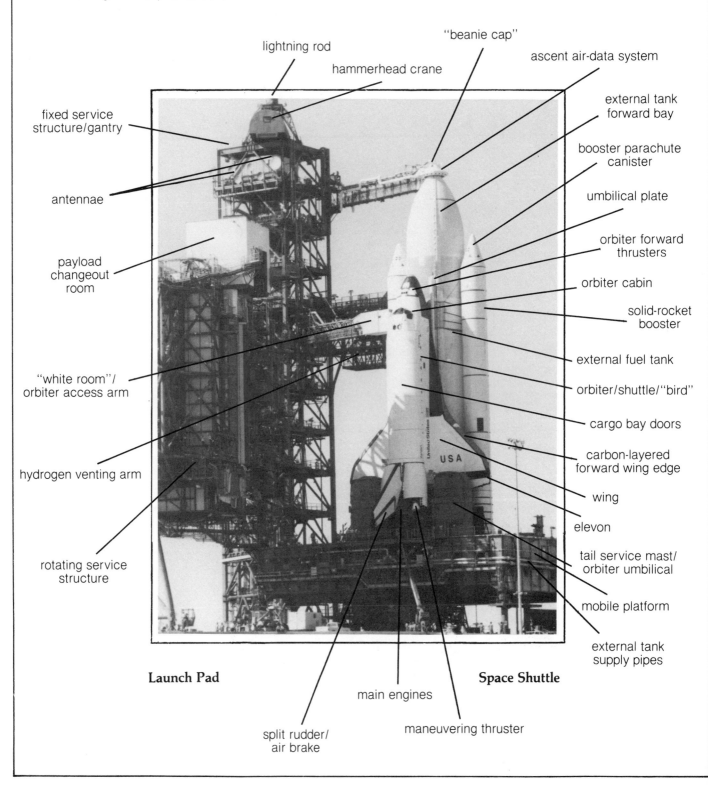

lightning rod

"beanie cap"

hammerhead crane

ascent air-data system

fixed service structure/gantry

external tank forward bay

booster parachute canister

antennae

umbilical plate

orbiter forward thrusters

payload changeout room

orbiter cabin

solid-rocket booster

external fuel tank

orbiter/shuttle/"bird"

"white room"/ orbiter access arm

cargo bay doors

carbon-layered forward wing edge

wing

hydrogen venting arm

elevon

tail service mast/ orbiter umbilical

rotating service structure

mobile platform

external tank supply pipes

Launch Pad

Space Shuttle

main engines

split rudder/ air brake

maneuvering thruster

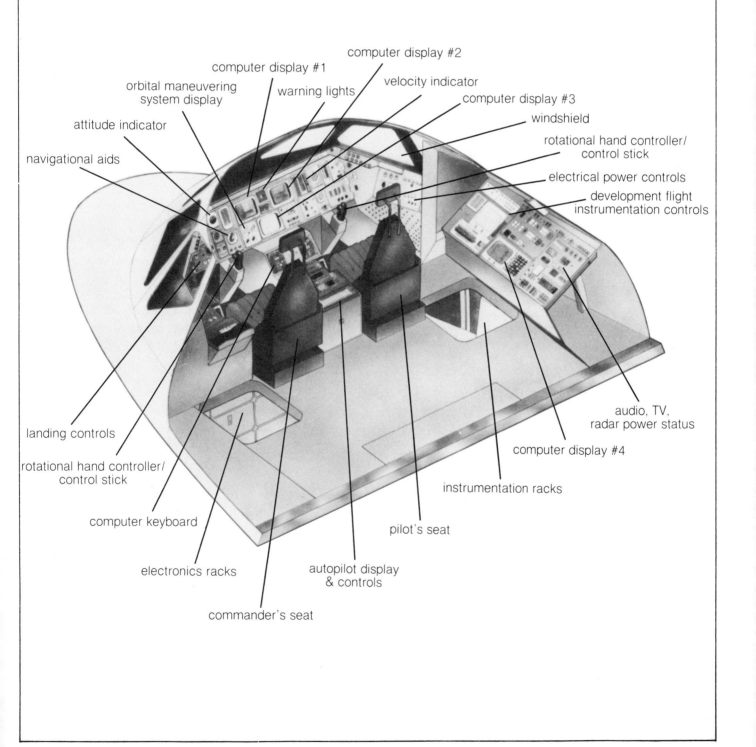

Space Shuttle Flight Deck

Overhead controls include *circuit breakers*, *environmental monitors* and *fuel cell monitors*. The *orbiter* has work and living quarters for as many as seven people, including two pilots, *mission specialists* and *payload specialists*. It also features a *quad-redundant computer system*, including a fifth computer to arbitrate disputes among the first four.

computer display #2

computer display #1

orbital maneuvering system display

velocity indicator

warning lights

computer display #3

attitude indicator

windshield

rotational hand controller/ control stick

navigational aids

electrical power controls

development flight instrumentation controls

audio, TV, radar power status

computer display #4

landing controls

rotational hand controller/ control stick

instrumentation racks

computer keyboard

pilot's seat

electronics racks

autopilot display & controls

commander's seat

Lunar Lander

The *lunar module* consists of a lower *descent stage* which houses the *landing engine, exploration equipment, secondary tanks* and landing gear. The *ascent stage* contains *crew compartment* and *controls, equipment compartment, tanks* and *takeoff engine*, used to rejoin the *command module*.

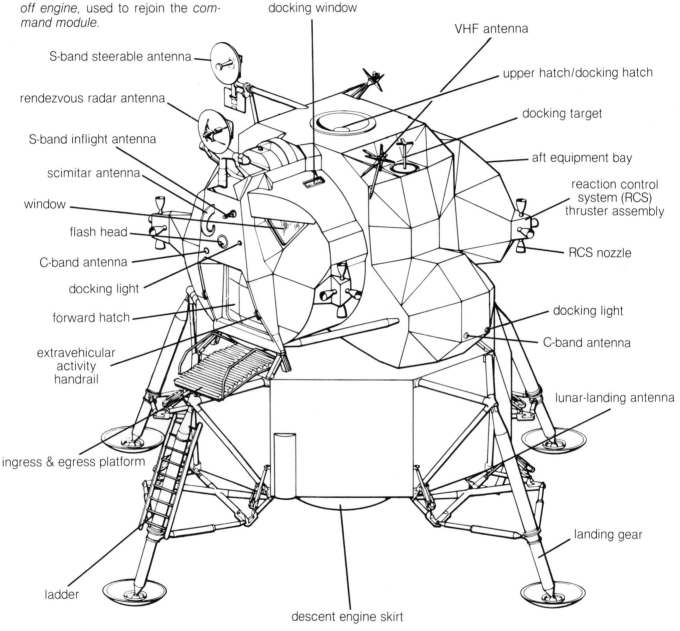

S-band steerable antenna

rendezvous radar antenna

S-band inflight antenna

scimitar antenna

window

flash head

C-band antenna

docking light

forward hatch

extravehicular activity handrail

ingress & egress platform

ladder

docking window

VHF antenna

upper hatch/docking hatch

docking target

aft equipment bay

reaction control system (RCS) thruster assembly

RCS nozzle

docking light

C-band antenna

lunar-landing antenna

landing gear

descent engine skirt

Lunar Rover

Officially called the *Lunar Roving Vehicle*, the *moon buggy* is folded in the Lunar Lander and deployed to transport astronauts and equipment on the lunar surface. The spacesuit, or *integrated thermal meteoroid garment*, is a many-layered structure laced to a *torso limb suit* which consists of an inner cloth *comfort lining*, a *bladder*, and a *restraint layer*.

high-gain antenna

control console & instrument panel

low-gain antenna

16mm camera

handhold

safety belt

buddy umbilical system bag

seat

lunar drill

extension handle

TV camera

stereo camera

payload pallet

tongs

magnetometer stowage bags

lunar communications relay unit

tool carrier

battery box

sample bag dispenser

lunar brush bag

70mm camera position

under-seat bag stowage

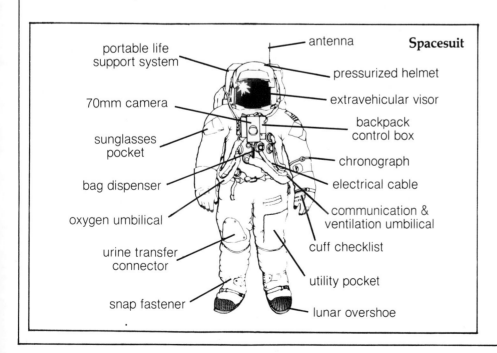

Spacesuit

antenna

portable life support system

pressurized helmet

extravehicular visor

70mm camera

backpack control box

sunglasses pocket

chronograph

bag dispenser

electrical cable

oxygen umbilical

communication & ventilation umbilical

urine transfer connector

cuff checklist

utility pocket

snap fastener

lunar overshoe

Spacecraft

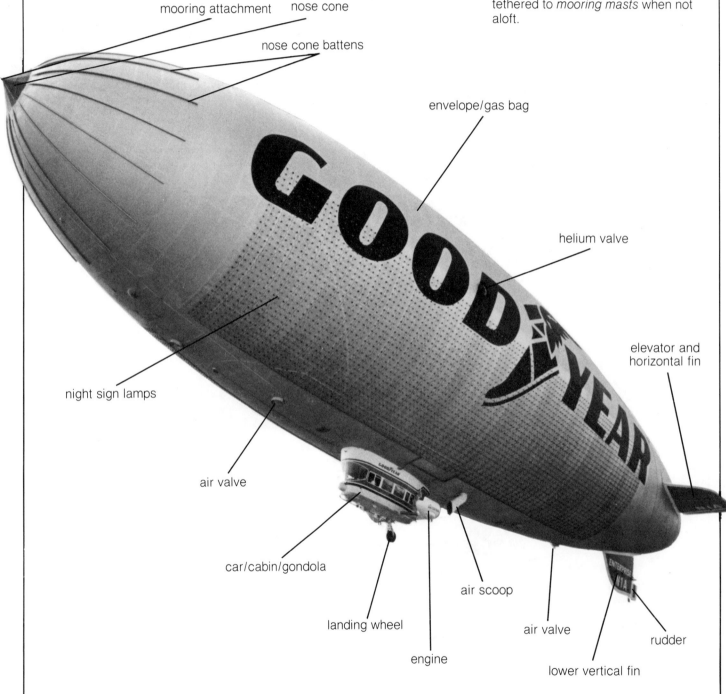

Lighter-than-air Craft

Engine-driven, steerable lighter-than-air craft are called blimps, or dirigibles. They can be *nonrigid* or *semirigid*, dependent on interior *ballonets*, or *air bags*, to maintain their shapes. *Rigid airships*, with metal *frameworks* within their *envelopes*, are referred to as *Zeppelins*. Airships are tethered to *mooring masts* when not aloft.

mooring attachment

nose cone

nose cone battens

envelope/gas bag

helium valve

night sign lamps

elevator and horizontal fin

air valve

car/cabin/gondola

air scoop

landing wheel

air valve

engine

rudder

lower vertical fin

Blimp/Dirigible

Communications

Communications ranks among the fastest-growing areas of modern life. Nevertheless, as this book is meant to demonstrate by providing visual access to language, print communications remains a vital part of the future. Print is therefore examined in some detail, up to and including a close look at the mailing label affixed to periodicals received every day by millions of subscribers.

Space limitations prevent presentation of industrial items such as transmitting stations and microwave towers, sound-recording and television studios and film-processing equipment.

But the devices used in all forms of communications—visual, aural and audiovisual—are represented by objects commonly used in most households. The single exception to this is the satellite which appears at the end of the section. It is included because of the vital role it plays in modern communications of all kinds.

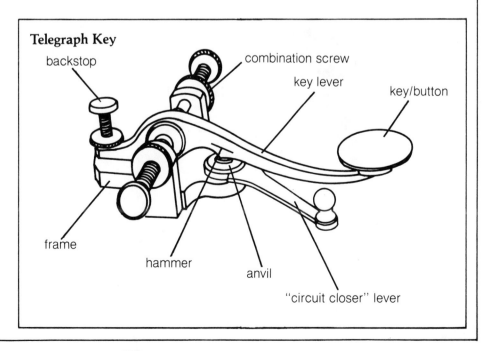

Telegraph Key

backstop

combination screw

key lever

key/button

frame

hammer

anvil

"circuit closer" lever

Pen and Pencil

In refillable *lead pencils* a *barrel cap* is turned in order to push new lead out the tip. Some fountain pens are *cartridge-loaded* but older models have a barrel, *ink reservoir* and *self-filling mechanism. Quills,* or *feather pens,* made from the horny, hollow barrel of bird feathers, were dipped in *ink wells.*

eraser

shoulder

ferrule

grade/lead hardness

push button/ cap mounting

brand name & product number

extending & retracting ball

thrust tube

plug

clip

barrel/casing

case

ink cartridge/ reservoir tube

spring

Fountain Pen

barrel

air hole

feed tube

nib

Ballpoint Pen

point

ballbearing/writing tip

point/"lead"

Pencil

Correspondence

A note appended to a completed letter is called a *postscript,* abbreviated as *P.S.* When items are enclosed with a letter they are indicated by the word *enclosure(s)* or *encl.* The back portion of an envelope which is glued down after a letter has been inserted is the *flap.* Postage stamps can be purchased in *books, strips, blocks, coils* and *sheets,* or *panes.*

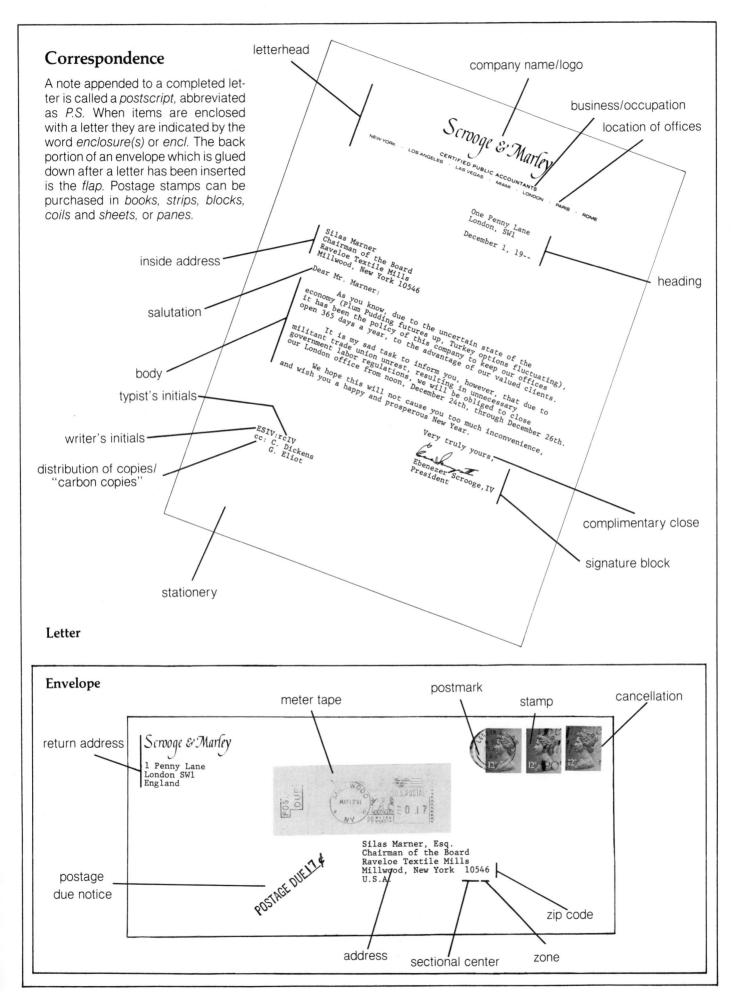

letterhead

company name/logo

business/occupation

location of offices

NEW YORK

Scrooge & Marley

CERTIFIED PUBLIC ACCOUNTANTS

LOS ANGELES · LAS VEGAS · MIAMI · LONDON · PARIS · ROME

One Penny Lane
London, SW1
December 1, 19--

heading

inside address

Silas Marner
Chairman of the Board
Raveloe Textile Mills
Millwood, New York 10546

Dear Mr. Marner:

salutation

As you know, due to the uncertain state of the economy (Plum Pudding futures up, Turkey options fluctuating), it has been the policy of this company to keep our offices open 365 days a year, to the advantage of our valued clients.

It is my sad task to inform you, however, that due to militant trade union unrest, resulting in unnecessary government labor regulations, we will be obliged to close our London office from noon, December 24th, through December 26th.

We hope this will not cause you too much inconvenience, and wish you a happy and prosperous New Year.

Very truly yours,

body

typist's initials

writer's initials

ESIV:rcIV
cc: C. Dickens
G. Eliot

distribution of copies/ "carbon copies"

Ebenezer Scrooge, IV
President

complimentary close

signature block

stationery

Letter

Envelope

meter tape

postmark

stamp

cancellation

return address

Scrooge & Marley

1 Penny Lane
London SW1
England

POS DUE

MILLWOOD
MAY 13'91
NY

U.S. POSTAG
≡ 0.17
PR····
····

POSTAGE DUE 17¢

postage due notice

Silas Marner, Esq.
Chairman of the Board
Raveloe Textile Mills
Millwood, New York 10546
U.S.A.

zip code

address

sectional center

zone

161

Print Communications

Typewriter

On standard manual or *office type-writers*, lightweight *portables* and older *electrics*, when a key labeled with a *character* is struck, it sends the appropriate type bar toward an inked *ribbon*. On modern electric typewriters type bars in the *type basket* have been replaced with a ball.

automatic line finder

carriage release

paper guide

erasure table

line space regulator

retractable paper support

variable spacer

platen

margin stop

bail roller

paper bail/positioning scale

carriage return & line space lever

paper release

platen knob

type guide

ROYAL

carriage

margin release

card holder

ribbon color control

card loop

shift & lock key

top plate

shift key

type bars

tabulator control

space bar

backspace key

keys

keyboard

Manual Typewriter

Ribbon Cartridge / Electric Typewriter

ball/core

separator wire

correctable ribbon

element release lever

correction tape

impression control

guide post

roller

take-up spool

typestyle

character

spindle/knob

ribbon end indicator

tape load lever

ribbon load lever

Type with serifs is called *book type.*
Type without serifs is *sans serif.*

Typeface Composition

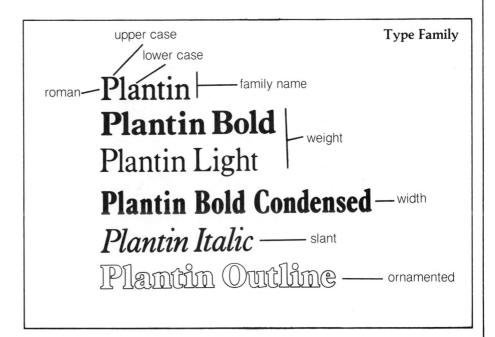

Type Family

All *metal type* is known collectively as *hot metal,* in contrast to *cold type,* which is produced photographically. The letterpress method of printing uses a raised surface, or *relief,* while gravure uses a depressed surface, or *intaglio,* and lithography uses a *plane,* or *flat surface.* Printing is done on sheets of paper on *sheet-fed presses* or on rolls of paper on *web-fed presses.*

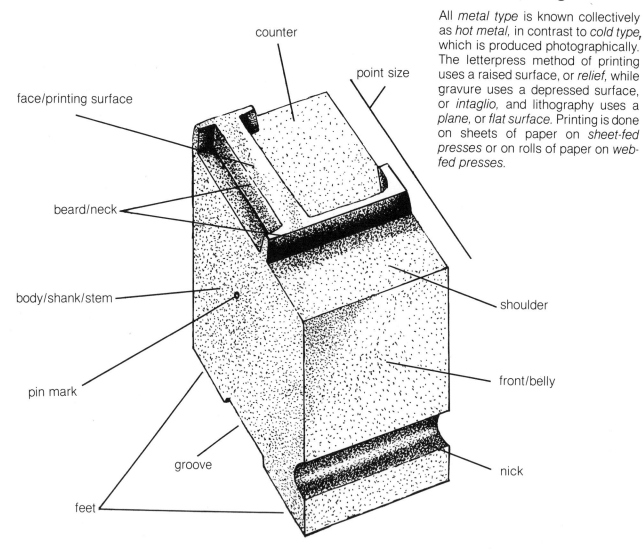

counter

point size

face/printing surface

beard/neck

body/shank/stem

pin mark

groove

feet

shoulder

front/belly

nick

Type

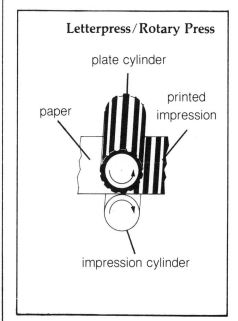

Letterpress/Rotary Press

plate cylinder

paper

printed impression

impression cylinder

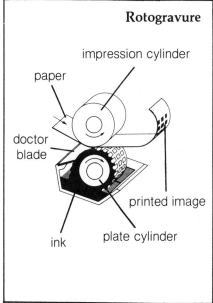

Rotogravure

impression cylinder

paper

doctor blade

ink

plate cylinder

printed image

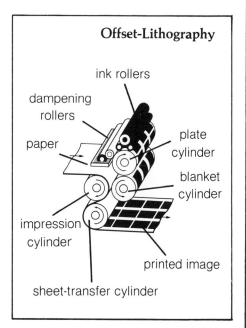

Offset-Lithography

ink rollers

dampening rollers

paper

plate cylinder

blanket cylinder

impression cylinder

printed image

sheet-transfer cylinder

The *body* of a book is made up of *leaves*, each side of which is a *page*. Two facing pages form a spread. Pages leading up to the actual *text* are called *preliminaries* or *front matter*. Those pages following the text are *back matter, end matter* or *reference matter*. A box for a book, open at one end, is called a *slipcase* or *forel*.

endpapers/endleaves/end sheets/linings

back flap

fore-edge

gatherings

joint/hinge

author's photograph

headband

spine/
backbone/
backstrip/
shelfback

cover/case

front flap

title

illustration/artwork

author

specific edition

GONE WITH THE WIND

Margaret Mitchell

DELUXE EDITION

GONE WITH THE WIND

publisher

front cover/front face

spine

back cover/back face

dust jacket/jacket/dust cover

**Hardback/Hardcover/
Casebound Book**

**Paperback/Softback/
Softcover/Softbound Book**

covers/wrappers

publisher

colophon/
trademark

price

spine

blurb

International
Standard
Book Number/
ISBN

order number/
inventory control
number

MARGARET MITCHELL'S
GONE WITH THE WIND
THE EPIC NOVEL OF OUR TIME

Spread

head of page

gutter margin/
back margin/
inside margin

head margin/top margin

chapter number

vignette/
illustration/
headpiece/
cut

chapter title/
chapter heading

copyright
notice

copyright
symbol

recto/
right-hand page

text

verso/
left-hand page

foot of page

gutter

folio

lower margin/bottom margin

outside margin

Print Communications

Newspaper

Terms vary from newspaper to newspaper. Those shown here are used at *The New York Times*. Small-size newspapers are called *tabloids*.

Labels around the newspaper page:

- nameplate/flag/logo
- skyline
- out-of-town prices
- copyright
- issue date
- weather ear
- left ear
- volume number
- price
- folio line
- banner headline
- dingbat
- head
- readout dash
- deck/bank
- agate line
- bar line
- byline
- dateline
- lead/lede
- twinned stories
- italic refer
- body of story
- subhead
- credit line
- jump line
- caption/cut line
- art
- hairline rule
- index

TODAY: SIX PAGES OF BICENTENNIAL ARTICLES AND PICTURES

"All the News That's Fit to Print"

The New York Times

LATE CITY EDITION

Weather: Partly cloudy and less humid today through tomorrow. Temperature range: today 64-80; Sunday 61-82. Details on page 20.

VOL. CXXV ... No. 43,262

© 1976 The New York Times Company

NEW YORK, MONDAY, JULY 5, 1976

20 CENTS

Nation and Millions in City Joyously Hail Bicentennial

ISRAELIS RETURN WITH 103 RESCUED IN UGANDA RAID

Toll Is Put at 3 Hostages, 7 Hijackers, Army Officer and 20 of Amin's Men

FORD LAUDS OPERATION

Freed Captives Are Received Joyously at Airport After Their 7-Day Ordeal

By TERENCE SMITH
Special to The New York Times

JERUSALEM, July 4—An Israeli commando unit that last night conducted a daring raid on the Entebbe airport in Uganda flew home today with the hostages it released.

Military officials said that 103 hostages had been flown to Israel. They said that four Is-

Text of the Rabin address will be found on page 2.

raelis, seven of the 10 hijackers and about 20 Uganda soldiers had been killed.

Some of the hostages arrived exhausted, some exuberant, to a noisy, joyous reunion here with family and friends. A majority of those freed last night were Israelis.

[President Ford sent a message of congratulation to Prime Minister Yitzhak Rabin, voicing "great satisfaction" that the passengers of the hijacked plane had been saved and "a senseless act of terrorism thwarted." Page 3. President Ford, Amin of Uganda condemned the Israeli action.]

Back at Same Airport

A week to the day after they set off on an Air France airbus, the Israeli passengers and French crew members were back at the same airport where they had originally started their trip. They were weeping, laughing and literally falling into each other's arms with relief.

Their return here brought to an end seven days of terror that culminated in the spectacular rescue operation, in which Israeli airborne troops traveled 2,500 miles to pluck the hostages from the gunpoints of their captors at the Entebbe airport.

Rabin Address Parliament

The success of the operation, which surprised most Israelis, electrified the country. Flags were brought out, people rejoiced openly in the streets, and in the sky over Jerusalem a skywriter wrote in Hebrew, "Kol hakavod zahal," or "All honor to the army."

Addressing a specially convened session of the Israeli Parliament, Prime Minister Yitzhak Rabin declared: "This operation will become a legend. It is Israel's contribution to...

Continued on Page 2, Column 4

French Officials See Signs Amin, Hijackers Colluded

PARIS, July 4 — Officials and released hostages said here today that they had substantial evidence that President Idi Amin had been in collusion with the hijackers of an Air France airbus in the seizure of the plane as well as after it landed in Uganda.

Although the officials refused to be quoted publicly, one said that negotiations got "much tougher" last night after President Amin returned to Uganda from a meeting of the Organization of African Unity in Mauritius.

A highly placed French source said that President Amin had refused to allow Pierre Renard, the French Ambassador to Uganda, or a special French envoy to deal with the hijackers directly.

While President Amin was out of the country, messages sent from Israel had to be passed by French Government representatives through the Somali Ambassador. Hashi Abdullah Farah in the hijacking. Messages back to the Israelis followed the same route.

Uganda Guards

When Gen. Amin returned from Mauritius yesterday, he resumed the role of mediator. He told the French Ambassador that demands for the release of 53 pro-Palestinian prisoners in Israel, Kenya and Europe must be met by early today or all the hostages would be killed.

Officials here pointed out that on the list of prisoners were five Ugandans held in

Continued on Page 4, Column 2

Kenyatta orders to assassinate President Jomo Kenyatta.

They also noted that during the first 24 hours after the aircraft reached Entebbe, the hijackers withdrew to rest and Ugandans guarded the hostages.

Other evidence pointing to the Uganda President's involvement with the terrorists was included in comments by French diplomats and the reports of hostages freed earlier by the terrorists. At the time of the Israeli rescue operation nearly all of the hijackers' captives were Israelis or dual nationals.

Among the passengers released last week were Michel Cojot and his 12-year-old son, Olivier. Mr. Cojot, a French management consultant, served as interpreter for the hostages and negotiated on their behalf for small conveniences during the ordeal.

'No Shadow of Doubt'

Mr. Cojot said that he had not a shadow of a doubt" that the Uganda President knew of the hijack plan in advance and had prepared for the action.

He said that the airbus, a new European-built plane with a normal four-hour flying capacity, flew non-stop to Entebbe after a refueling stop in Benghazi, Libya — a six-hour flight. "We couldn't possibly have made any other airport by then," he said. "The hijackers were obviously certain they...

Continued on Page 4, Column 4

CARTER TO BEGIN TALKS ON TICKET

Will See Muskie Today and Other Possible Running Mates Soon After

By CHARLES MOHR
Special to The New York Times

PLAINS, Ga., July 4—Jimmy Carter has asked Senator Edmund S. Muskie to visit him here tomorrow and discuss the Maine Senator's qualification to serve as Mr. Carter's running mate on the 1976 Democratic ticket.

Mr. Carter told reporters at his home in this small Georgia town this morning that he expected to talk to at least four other persons about the Vice-Presidential nomination between now and the Democratic National Convention, which convenes July 12.

The former Georgia Governor, who is assured of the Presidential nomination, said that it would be wrong to assume that there was any special significance in the fact that Senator Muskie was the first to be invited to meet with him. And, indeed, few political observers seem to feel that Mr. Muskie is a front-runner for the job. He was the Vice-Presidential nominee in 1968 and an unsuccessful candidate for the Democratic Presidential nomination in 1972.

A highly knowledgeable source said that the three men

Continued on Page 10, Column 4

PRESIDENT TALKS

Philadelphia Throngs Told U.S. Is Leader— Liberty Bell Rings

By JAMES T. WOOTEN
Special to The New York Times

PHILADELPHIA, July 4 — With its famous bells ringing and prayer, bands blaring, choirs singing and fireworks exploding, this city today staged a joyous, cacophonous commemoration that day two centuries ago when the representatives of the 13 English colonies met here to renounce their allegiance to the British Crown.

At least one million people were in Philadelphia for the centerpiece of the Bicentennial observance.

President Ford came here from Valley Forge to recall that first Fourth of July as "the beginning of a continuing adventure," unfinished, unfulfilled, but still unchallenged as a model of social and political achievement.

"The world is ever conscious of what Americans are doing, for better or for worse," he said at Independence Hall, "because the United States remains today the most successful realization of humanity's universal hope.

Says Nation Leads

"The world may or may not follow, but we lead because our whole history says we must."

Then, after he left for New York City, the Liberty Bell, that faulted but venerated symbol, was softly sounded with a rubber mallet as millions across the nation watched on television. In clamorous response, hundreds of other bells rang out in Philadelphia's steeples and towers.

Meanwhile, several miles from the official observances, more than 30,000 other Americans, most of them members of a loose coalition, staged their own peaceful Bicentennial celebration. Mayor Frank L. Rizzo had warned of potential disorders, but there were none.

At the main celebration, blue-shirted policemen cordially gave

Continued on Page 10, Column 1

PANOPLY OF SAILS

Harbor Armada Led by Tall Ships in Salute to Fourth

By RICHARD F. SHEPARD

Buoyed by panoramic spectacles that included a unique armada of tall masted ships, a massive fireworks display and a series of festivals that took over downtown Manhattan, millions of New Yorkers and visitors in a happy mood observed the nation's Bicentennial yesterday.

It was a day of mammoth presentations.

Uncounted crowds lining the waterfront of the magnificent but underused harbor saw a virtually unbroken bridge of small craft that reached from the shores of Brooklyn to the coast of New Jersey.

More than 225 sailing ships, under 31 flags paraded up the Hudson, a river that foretold their doom in 1807 when Robert Fulton's smoky little Clermont started steamboat service on it.

International Review

A 22-nation fleet of 53 naval units gray and grim—even ships festooned with pennants—lined the upper Bay and the Hudson for the International Naval Review, which had Vice President Rockefeller as the chief United States official present.

President Ford flew onto the hulking 78,000-ton aircraft carrier Forrestal, the host ship of the review, and later went by helicopter to the U.S.S. Nashville, anchored in mid-Hudson. He watched the sailing ships and was stranded for 40 minutes by a sudden squall before taking off again, headed for Washington, without having set foot alone in the city.

As night fell, hundreds of thousands jammed onto the shore of lower Manhattan—some dangling from trees like so many Christmas decorations —to watch the dazzling fireworks display over the harbor and the Statue of Liberty. When it was over, the tide of the departing throng sometimes swept people out of control.

Continued on Page 20, Column 3

A Day of Picnics, Pomp, Pageantry and Protest

By JOHN L. HESS

The nation celebrated its 200th birthday yesterday with pageantry and prayer, with games and parades, with picnics and fireworks, with the peal of bells and the chant of protests.

It began with a flag-raising atop Mars Hill Mountain in Maine, where dawn reached the continent, and moved on to pounding, at Baltimore, the last brick in Baltimore's fireworks display, in Washington, D.C., the largest gathering of sailing ships, in New York Harbor.

Yet many sponsors of celebrations were disappointed at the turnout. The Philadelphia parade, planned for 70,000 marchers drew about half that

Continued on Page 18, Column 5

Philadelphia, and bells rang in the 50 states and in American communities overseas. At Independence Hall, President Ford read the day's keynote address.

This being an American festival, many new records were claimed: the largest cherry pie (60 square feet), at George Washington's birthplace, and the rockets' red glare of the national anthem. The activities were to end nearly a day later with an indigenous festival in brannon were disappointed at the turnout. The Philadelphia parade, planned for 70,000 marchers drew about half that number.

Preceded by a fireboat, the Coast Guard training ship Eagle leads the armada of ships past the Battery up the Hudson for the naval review.

The New York Times/Edward Hausner

Ethnic Diversity Adds Spice to the Holiday

By FRED FERRETTI

New Yorkers and their friends poured into lower Manhattan yesterday and compressed 200 years of their history and varied ethnic heritages into a day-long birthday party crammed with prayer, martial music, high spirits and good fellowship.

It was the tall ships and the warships that drew them there, but it was Dr. Quackenbush's Traveling Medicine Show, Delsin's Loyalist Red Coat Brigade, Pfautsch's Tavern, Oscar Brand, falafel and pecan and egg rolls, and John Philip Sousa that kept them there.

Not even a succession of perilous downpours late in the afternoon could drive them away. They watched George III beheaded at Federal Hall National Memorial, listened to Terence Cardinal Cooke pray at Castle Clinton, watched the Turks take over Wall Street for

Continued on Page 22, Column 4

President Ford waves to the crowd at Valley Forge, Pa., where he signed a bill making it a national historical site. He stands on a covered wagon that represented Michigan, his home state, in the Bicentennial wagon train.

The New York Times/Teresa Zabala

O, Say, It Was a Glorious Patchwork-Quilt of a Fourth

By McCANDLISH PHILLIPS

The Fourth of July celebration in New York City yesterday was as American as a patchwork quilt—full of a joyous order-in-disarray and a series of brilliantly improbable juxtapositions.

It was an exercise in patriotic progression, demonstration, declamation, delineation, commemoration, celebration, titulation, subornation and for some indignation.

The free and independent citizens of New York City girt themselves into a grand, many unusual positions as they scrambled for perspective on events, sometimes at the price of mild peril.

In parks and on piers on fences, bakeshops, ramps, rooftops, chimneys, ledges, elevations and the ladders of water storage tanks they sat stooped stood and clung chiefly to watch great ships come sailing out of the distant past and go up the hazy Hudson like a vision.

It was a great day for family portraits to be taken with the most senior member of the American family. The process began early in the day in front of the Federal Hall National Memorial on Wall Street, on the site where George Washington took the oath as President on April 30, 1789.

Washington's statue dominates the steps leading up to the eight columns of the hall and the bare sit of the pedestal is a stage large enough for at least half a dozen persons.

As soon as one group posed and left, the next moved up to be photographed with the unblinkingly obliging founding father.

Seven small children in bright summer colors nearly ringed the great figure, standing under his outstretched right hand, their heads reaching to half the height of the pedestal. They looked very serious for the moment or so they stood there.

Though few noticed it, Christopher Columbus was in town. But the idol boy from

Continued on Page 28, Column 3

City Hall is the scene of street dancing and music in July 4th in Old New York Festival.

The New York Times/Jim Wilson

NEWS INDEX

(index listing — partially illegible)

Magazine Cover and Contents Page

Periodicals may be consumer magazines, intended for the general public; *trade* or *technical magazines,* intended for particular industries and businesses; or *journals,* published for people engaged in professions. *House organs* are distributed within a specific company. Covers may have *cover blurbs* with *selling copy,* describing inside stories, and *cover captions.*

cover flap/cover inset

masthead

issue date

logo

border/border logo

cover lines

subhead

cover billing/main cover title

subhead

foreign prices

cover photo/cover art

logo

feature well

title & blurbs

articles

bylines/author credit

folio/page number

departments/regular sections

preview

indicia

copyright notice

Cover

Contents Page

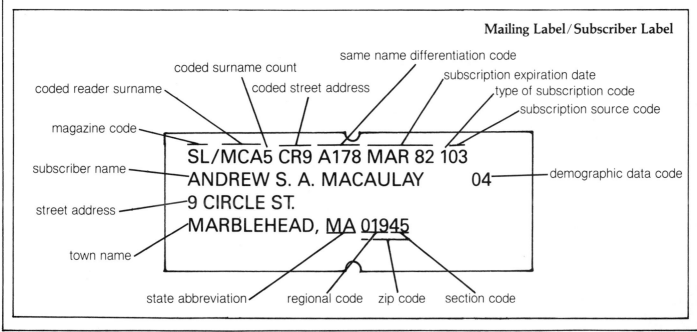

Mailing Label/Subscriber Label

coded surname count

same name differentiation code

coded reader surname

coded street address

subscription expiration date

type of subscription code

subscription source code

magazine code

SL/MCA5 CR9 A178 MAR 82 103

subscriber name

ANDREW S. A. MACAULAY   04

demographic data code

street address

9 CIRCLE ST.

town name

MARBLEHEAD, MA 01945

state abbreviation

regional code

zip code

section code

Magazine Feature

The design of a magazine page is called the *layout*. In the feature shown here *dummy type* has been substituted for *text* or *copy*. Two facing pages are called a spread, *double spread,* or *double-truck.* A *sidebar* is a self-contained, boxed *article* bearing on the main feature.

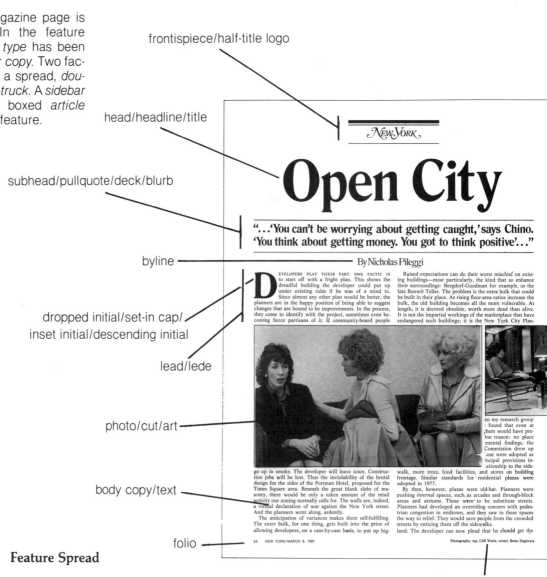

frontispiece/half-title logo

head/headline/title

subhead/pullquote/deck/blurb

byline

dropped initial/set-in cap/
inset initial/descending initial

lead/lede

photo/cut/art

body copy/text

folio

Feature Spread

New York

Open City

"…'You can't be worrying about getting caught,' says Chino. 'You think about getting money. You got to think positive'…"

By Nicholas Pileggi

photo credit

Service Articles

scotch rule

art/illustration

oxford rule

head

column rule

special-feature
photo treatment

sign-off

"nuts and bolts"

flush-left type

ragged-right type

Reviews

running title

subhead

decorated initial

introduction

breaker

boldface/highlight

column

A page that folds out to twice the size of a regular page is called a *gatefold*. A *jump line*, or *continued line*, at the end of a page refers the reader to the remaining text of a story appearing elsewhere in the magazine. A brief descriptive headline above the main head, designed to attract the reader's attention, is a *kicker, teaser, eyebrow,* or *highline*. Subscription cards bound into a magazine are called *inserts*. Those not physically connected are called *blow-ins*.

gutter/gutter margin

italics

margin

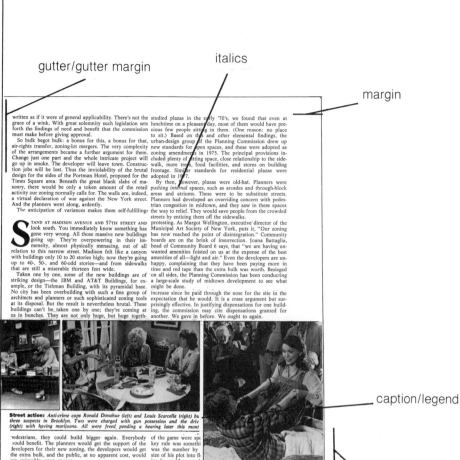

caption/legend

bleed

cutoff rule

footnote

date & running foot

Column

slug

two-deck head

bold face lead-in

art

end slug/closed quad

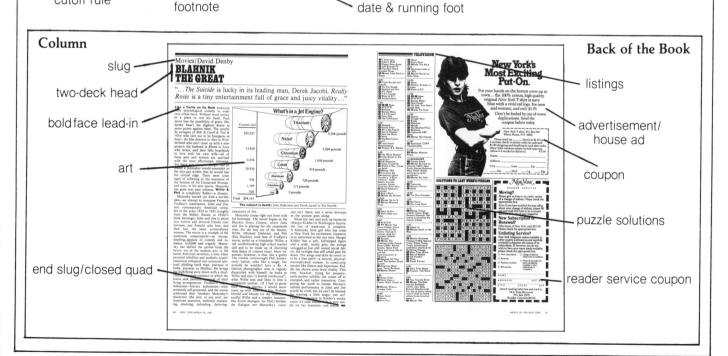

Back of the Book

listings

advertisement/ house ad

coupon

puzzle solutions

reader service coupon

Still Camera

Modern instant cameras have *battery-powered film packs* that produce *prints* moments after the picture is taken. Pocket cameras use snap-in *110 film cartridges.* Some instant and pocket cameras use *flash cubes, FlashBars* or *Q-lights* to provide artificial light.

viewfinder cap

viewfinder eyepiece

manual focus switch

manual focus wheel

shutter button

shutter-button remote control

bellows

film-door button

film door

FlashBar socket

sonar focus transducer

flash, tripod sensor

light & dark control

electric eye/ photocell

lens

distance scale

POLAROID SX-70 LAND CAMERA
SONAR **OneStep**

picture exit slot

Instant Camera

Pocket Camera

shutter release/ automatic film advance

film compartment cover latch

extended-range flash switch

battery compartment

electronic flash power switch

film wind & shutter release lock

viewfinder

830 AW

Vivitar

Vivitar
·24 mm 1:5.6
LENS

lens

built-in flash

strap/lanyard

Still Camera and Film

To focus on an *image,* a *photographer* looks through the *viewfinder* on the back of the camera. In addition to the motor drive, or *power winder,* shown on this model, camera accessories include *interchangeable lenses— telephoto, wide-angle, zoom* and *special-purpose—lens caps* and *hoods, shutter-release cables, filters, focusing screens, eyecups, chest pods* and *action straps.*

hot shoe/flash attachment

scale illumination window

selector release

back-cover release knob

rewind crank

exposure adjustment

film-speed selector

neckstrap eyelet

aperture scale/aperture ring

depth-of-field scale

distance scale

focusing ring

lens

film advance lever

mode selector

shutter release

shutter-speed selector

frame-counter window

motor drive coupler lug

strap lug

camera body

self-timer

motor drive

Single Lens Reflex Camera

Film Roll

canister/cartridge/cassette/magazine

sprocket holes

felt

tongue

leader

spool

Slide

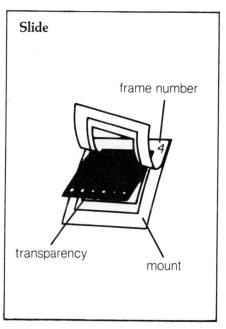

frame number

transparency

mount

Movie Camera

Home-movie cameras, such as the one shown here, use film contained in *drop-in cartridges*. In large commercial models, *unexposed film* moves through the body from the *supply reel* to the *take-up reel*. The reels in these cameras are often housed in a *blimp*, a soundproof device that fits on top of the body. *Single-system sound cameras* record both *image* and *sound* on the same film. Sound tracks on film may be either *optical* or *magnetic*.

directional-microphone contacts

accessory socket

run light

eyepiece guard

power-zoom control

FM/auxiliary contacts

FM/auxiliary attaching socket

sound-test button

earphone jack

battery-check button

microphone and remote filming jacks

auxiliary selector

frame-speed selector

back light button

manual zoom lever

run & lock switch

filming trigger

handgrip

battery chamber

head

cord

"mike" stand

manual zoom ring

zoom-focus range indicator

focal-length scale

distance scale

zoom-macro lens

focusing grip/lens hood

zoom-speed selector

Microphone

Movie Film

sound track

frame line

image

frame

sprocket holes/ perforations

The film projector shown here is a *self-threading, reel-to-reel model* with a built-in *speaker*. Slide projectors may have circular, or *carousel*, trays, *slide cubes* or *straight trays*.

carrying handle

framing knob

supply spindle

supply reel

take-up spindle

take-up reel

supply-reel arm

loop-former bar

film-loading port

operating control

zooming ring

volume control

lens

projection-speed selector

audio-input

focusing knob

microphone input plug

tilting knob

monitor

dubbing control

DIN socket

recording lever

recording-lever lock

Movie Projector

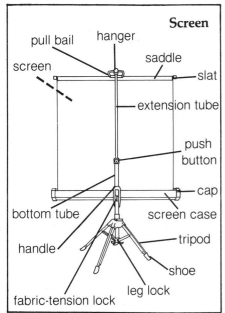

Screen

pull bail

hanger

saddle

screen

slat

extension tube

push button

reverse

forward

cap

bottom tube

screen case

handle

tripod

shoe

fabric-tension lock

leg lock

Slide Projector

slides/transparencies

lock ring

slide tray

gate index

slide-changing controls

handle

elevating wheel

leveling foot

focusing knob

lens

remote control

Photographic Accessories

In addition to the accessories shown here, *carrying straps, gadget bags,* and *cleaning supplies* such as *brushes, lens tissue* and *cleaning fluid* are used.

incident-light measuring diffuser

reflected-light window

high-low scales

high-low selector

indicator needle

light-reading scale/ indicator scale

exposure-time scale

aperture scale/f-stop scale

cine scale

computer ring

film-speed setting/ ASA-DIN exposure index

film-speed setting disk

incident light-reading index

exposure-value shutter scale

transfer scale

spot-meter reading index

Exposure Meter / Light Meter

Electronic Flash / Strobe

bounce-angle scale

flash head

calculator dial

flashtube

battery compartment

sensor

mounting foot

Tripod

camera platform

table lock

head lock

elevator lock

leg hinge/leg swivel

pan lock

leg

leg clamp collar

center post

spiked foot

Tape Recorders

Sound is recorded on *magnetic tape* by passing the tape over a *recording head*. Most cassette recorders have *built-in microphones* but are designed to work with *external mikes* as well. They are *battery-powered,* have *rechargeable battery packs* or *AC power cords.*

monitor switch

speed switch

equalizing switch

bias switch

power button

recording-mode buttons

right-channel volume unit meter

supply reel

front panel

reel lock/keeper

take-up reel

record indicator

direction indicators

left-channel volume unit meter

pause button

pause indicator

record button

headphone jack

play button

microphone jacks

stop button

microphone-recording level control

fast-forward button

tape counter

capstan

fast-rewind button

pinch roller

reset button

line-recording level control

repeat button

pinch roller

pitch-control dial

Reel-to-Reel Recorder and Playback Unit

Cassette Tape

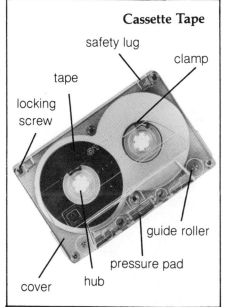

safety lug

clamp

tape

locking screw

guide roller

pressure pad

cover

hub

Cassette Tape Recorder

speaker

cassette holder

telephone input jack

tape counter

line-in jack

tone control

speech & music selector

volume control

record & battery button

telephone indicator

microphone

telephone monitor

eject button

pause button

cue button

telephone-record button

review button

stop button

record button

Aural Communications

Phonographic Equipment

A *long-playing record,* or *LP,* contains several *recordings* on both the front and *flip sides.* A *stereo record* has *twin soundtracks* in a single groove, whereas a *monaural record* has one and a *quadraphonic record* has four. Records are protected by a *sleeve* which is slipped into an *album cover,* or *jacket.* A *jukebox* is a coin-operated phonograph that plays selected music.

dust cover

counterweight dial/ tracking-force dial

hinge

gimbal suspension

spindle

tone-arm lock

rubber mat

anti-skate dial

tone-arm lifter/automatic cue

base

tone arm

headshell

arm grip

speed selector

cartridge/needle/stylus

cabinet

start/cut control

platter

record size selector

power on & platter speed indicator

repeat control

Turntable

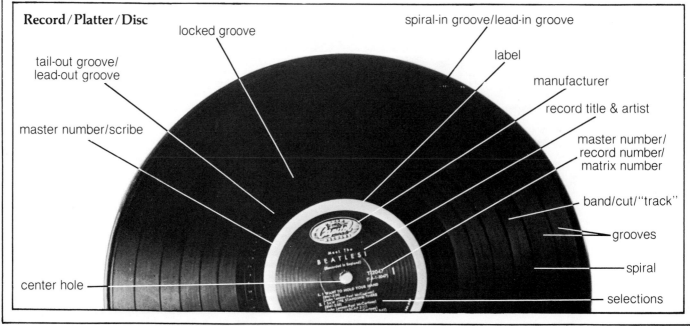

Record/Platter/Disc

locked groove

spiral-in groove/lead-in groove

tail-out groove/ lead-out groove

label

manufacturer

record title & artist

master number/scribe

master number/ record number/ matrix number

band/cut/"track"

grooves

spiral

center hole

selections

Phonographic Equipment

A phonographic system produces minimally distorted sound, or *high fidelity*. It is usually comprised of a *tuner*, a *pre-amp*, an amplifier and speakers. Its power output is measured in *watts*.

FM tuning/AM signal meter

power output meter

stereo indicator light

speaker indicator lights

tuning dial

AM/FM radio tuning dial

cabinet

volume dial

power/on & off knob

function indicator lights

headphone jack

bass dial

treble dial

speaker balance dial

mode & FM mute

loudness control

speaker selectors

function selector

tape-monitor switches

Receiver / Amplifier

Headphones

headband

ear cushion

pad

grille

retainer

plug body

housing

Speakers

cabinet

supertweeter

equalizer

level controls

grille

tweeter

midrange

woofer

cone

diaphragm

corrugations

manufacturer's identification & model number

177

Aural Communications

Telephone

The colored shell of a telephone is the *casing*. The *handset* rests in the *cradle* on *plungers*. The recessed area in the back of the casing, by which the phone is lifted, is the *grasper*.

notch

clip

cradle

handset

speaker/transmitter

receiver/earpiece

mounting cord

dial plate

rotary dial

AREA CODE 202
456-1414

directory number/
listed number

finger stop

number plate

finger hole

phone base

pad

handset cord

Standard Desk Phone

Pay Phone

coin slot

coin-release lever

switch hook

number strip

pushbutton digits

instruction cards

coin-box vault door

coin-return assembly

armored cord

Candlestick Phone

cradle

mouthpiece

handle

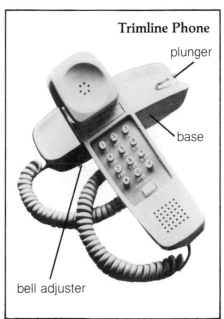

Trimline Phone

plunger

base

bell adjuster

Transceiver

A *walkie-talkie* is a hand-held transceiver used to transmit and receive over short distances. *CBs,* or Citizens Band radios, like the one shown here, have greater but still limited range. *Amateur radio operators,* or *"hams,"* use transceivers capable of communicating over vast distances.

transmit light/ broadcast indicator

S/RF meter/ power & wattage indicator

modulation indicator

emergency channel selector

emergency channel indicator

channel display

speaker

channel selector

microphone jack

headphone jack & indicator

power & wattage selector

Citizens Band & public address switch

squelch control

on-off switch/ volume control

automatic noise limiter

Base Station

Microphone

talk switch

housing

element

driven element

boom-to-mast clip

Antenna/Aerial

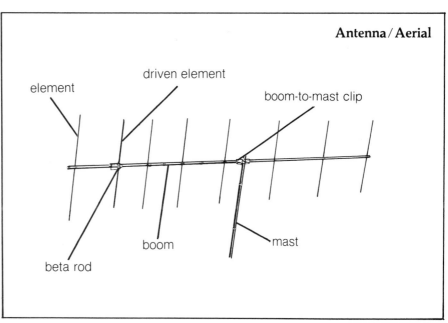

grille

cord strain relief

beta rod

boom

mast

cord

Aural Communications

Video Recorder

Video recorders are used in conjunction with *television sets*, or *monitors*. They can be operated by hand-size *remote control units*. Some recorders use a grooveless *disc*, others use a *video cassette tape.*

tape speed control buttons

still-frame button

recording mode
select switch

recording indicator

tape cassette holder

tape counter

search switch

pre-tuning controls

channel set indicator

channel
selection
controls

function indicator

function switch

select button

set button

video-TV switch

video-TV indicator

microphone jack

headphone jack

remote terminal

sub-control panel

tape control keys

program button

cancel button

display function
select switch

day & time recording pre-set

camera connector

Playback Unit

Video Camera

aperture scale

zoom ring

focus ring

zoom lens

zoom control

pistol trigger switch

eye cup

sensitivity controls

head/shell/body

handgrip

Television

The picture tube, or *"gun,"* is the largest single component in a television set's *chassis.* Today's sets are capable of receiving 105 channels, including *ultra-high frequency, very-high frequency, midband* and *super-band signals.* A low-power *laser beam* located in the player's *cabinet* translates 54,000 circular *tracks,* or *"frames,"* into pictures.

infrared remote-control command

cabinet

screen/picture tube

mask

speaker

base/pedestal

power key

remote-control detector

response lamp

channel indicator

volume & contrast indicator

volume keys

channel number keys

channel keys

picture keys

cable television indicator

cable television controls

speaker

Television Set / Monitor

LaserDisc ™ Player

viewer

spindle cover

spindle

disc/record/software

turntable

program setting, search & display buttons

freeze function

slow forward & reverse

scan button

fast forward and reverse

play button

pause button

reject button

power button

sound-track controls

Satellite

Active repeater satellites are communications satellites that amplify signals beamed to them for retransmission. *Passive* or *reflector satellites* mirror signals without amplifying them. Satellites used for space exploration, such as the one shown here, make scientific measurements and transmit the information back to earth.

magnetometers

plasma science

infrared radiometer

sunshade

rocket motor nozzle

steerable high-gain antenna

occulation ultraviolet spectrometer

charged particle telescope

airglow ultraviolet spectrometer

TV cameras

low-gain antenna

solar panel

Personal Items

This section includes items people are likely to wear, carry or use in the course of their everyday lives. Thus, coverage includes clothing, hats, shoes, jewelry and money.

Wherever men's and women's apparel differ appreciably, items have been separated. But in the case of items such as sweaters and overcoats, articles worn by both sexes, only one version has been presented. Liberal use has been made to show the variations possible on single objects. However trendy clothing fashions or hairstyles may be, they share the same basic parts and details shown in the illustrations on the pages that follow.

Because cosmetics, grooming, hairstyles and jewelry are an important part of everyday life, they have been included in this section, as have such items as eyeglasses, handbags and wallets, timepieces and smoking materials. And because on rainy days an umbrella is essential to carry, it, too, appears here.

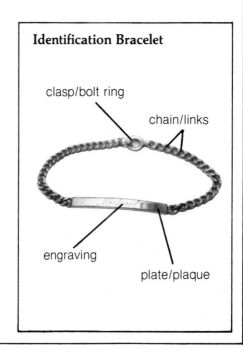

Identification Bracelet

clasp/bolt ring

chain/links

engraving

plate/plaque

Jacket and Vest

A jacket, or *coat,* can be *single-* or *double-breasted.* A *handkerchief pocket* or *chest pocket* is usually found on the upper left front panel. The pouchlike attachment inside a side pocket is called a *change pocket.* Most jackets have a *vent* or *double vent* cut into the hem in the *back panel.* Vests have an adjustable *backstrap* in the back.

lapel seam/gorge

collar

shoulder seam

lapel buttonhole/boutonniere buttonhole

armhole/sleeve seam

lapel

back sleeve seam/outseam

sleeve

front panel

inseam/inside sleeve seam

ticket pocket flap

piping

welt pocket flap

sleeve buttons

sleeve vent

dart

vest button

watch pocket/fob

buttonhole

vest bottom

jacket hem

Shirt

This illustration combines all the elements found in shirts suitable for casual or formal occasions.

label
yoke
tailor's loop

spread collar
collar stay
bib
pleats
front placket

neckband
button-down collar
button hole/stud hole

flap
breast pocket
sleeve

cuff-link hole

body of shirt

sleeve placket
French cuff/double cuff

button
single cuff/ barrel cuff

shirttail

Men's Apparel

Belt and Suspenders

Large, often elaborately engraved buckles are called *plaque buckles.* *Military buckles,* or *ratchet buckles,* are adjusted by pushing a *tension rod* inside the *frame.* Some belts come with reinforcing *eyelets* in the punch holes. The composite pair of suspenders shown here are *fireman's, policeman's,* or *working man's suspenders.* They all have a single elastic band at the back, whereas *dress suspenders* have crossed bands.

piping

filler

lining

punch holes

frame

buckle

tongue/prong

keeper

tip

panel

top stitching

Belt

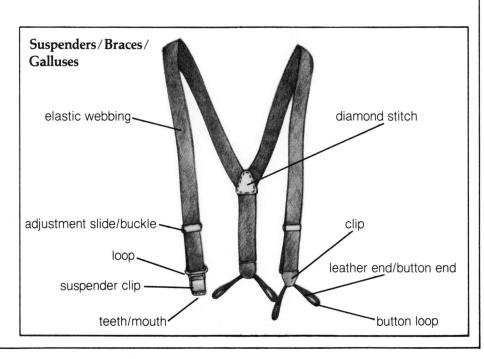

Suspenders/Braces/ Galluses

elastic webbing

diamond stitch

adjustment slide/buckle

clip

loop

leather end/button end

suspender clip

teeth/mouth

button loop

Pants

The back of a *pair of pants* is called the *seat*. Mid-thigh or knee length pants are *shorts*. *Jeans* often have pockets and seams reinforced with *rivets*. *Waistband closures* on pants are secured with *button tab closings* or metal *hook and eye closings*.

waistband

belt loop/belt carrier

self-belt

watch pocket/fob

slash pocket

jean pocket/western pocket

zipper shield/fly front

front crotch seam

side seam

crease

straight leg

flare/bell-bottom

cuff

inseam/inside leg seam

Trousers / Slacks

Men's Apparel

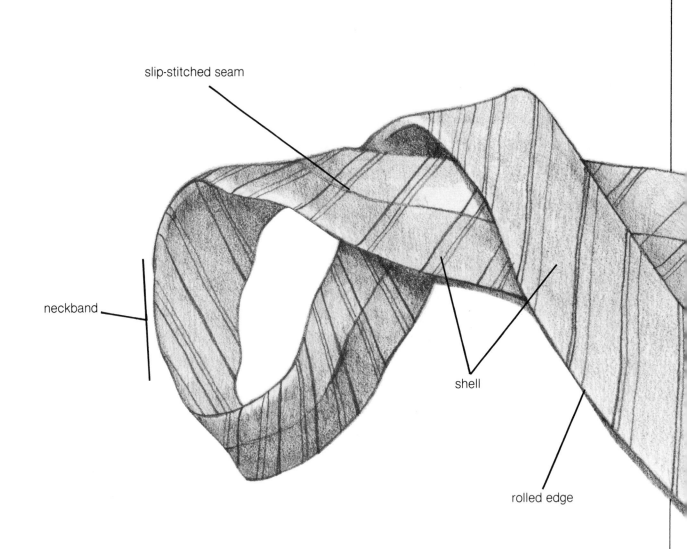

slip-stitched seam

neckband

shell

rolled edge

Necktie/Four-in-Hand

Bow Tie/Butterfly Tie

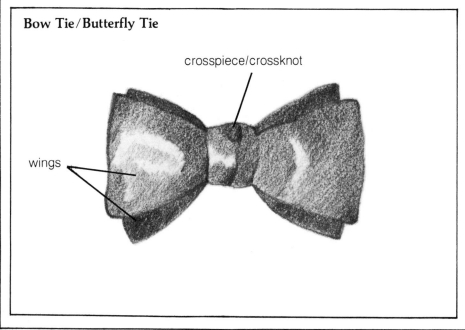

crosspiece/crossknot

wings

String Tie/Bolo Tie

slide

string/cord

aglets

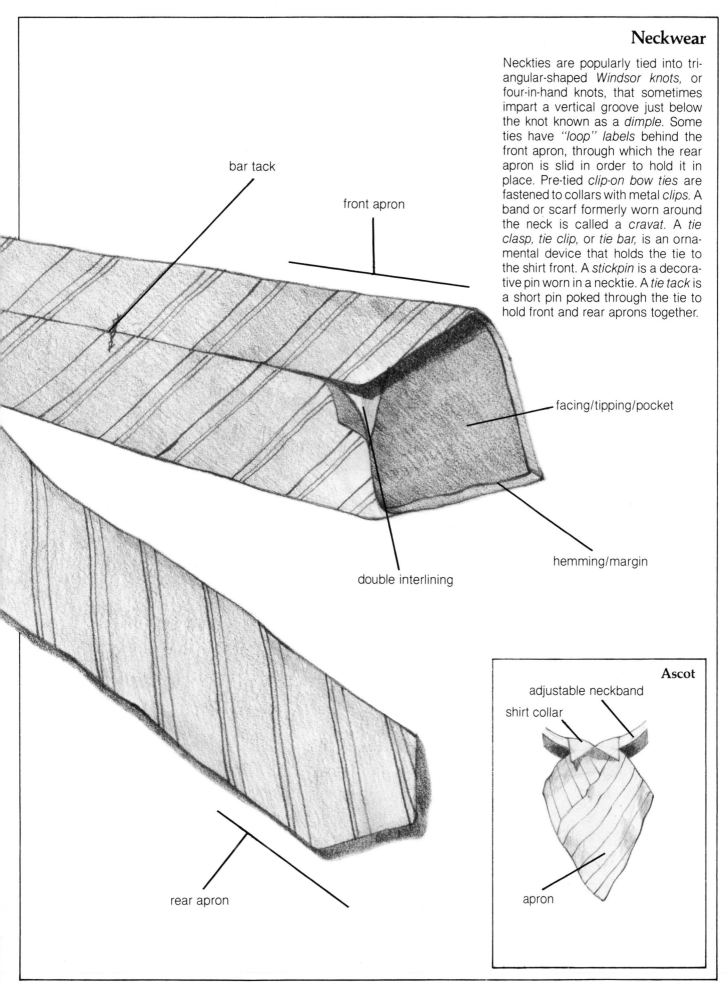

Neckwear

Neckties are popularly tied into tri-angular-shaped *Windsor knots,* or four-in-hand knots, that sometimes impart a vertical groove just below the knot known as a *dimple.* Some ties have *"loop" labels* behind the front apron, through which the rear apron is slid in order to hold it in place. Pre-tied *clip-on bow ties* are fastened to collars with metal *clips.* A band or scarf formerly worn around the neck is called a *cravat.* A *tie clasp, tie clip,* or *tie bar,* is an orna-mental device that holds the tie to the shirt front. A *stickpin* is a decora-tive pin worn in a necktie. A *tie tack* is a short pin poked through the tie to hold front and rear aprons together.

bar tack

front apron

facing/tipping/pocket

hemming/margin

double interlining

rear apron

Ascot

adjustable neckband

shirt collar

apron

Men's Apparel

Underwear

A *T-shirt* has short sleeves rather than shoulder straps. Loose-fitting *boxer shorts* have short, trouserlike legs rather than leg openings. Some athletic supporters, or *jockstraps,* have pockets in the pouch to accommodate rubber-lined *protective cups.*

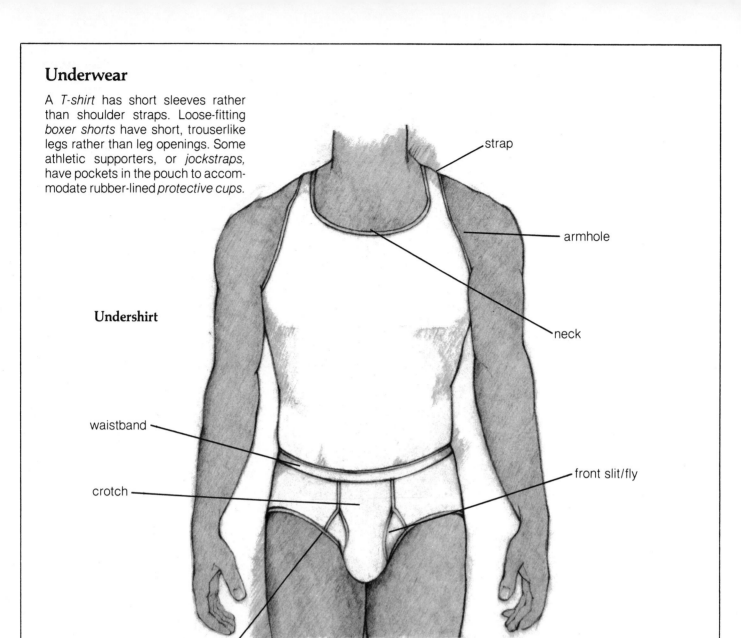

Undershirt

strap

armhole

neck

waistband

crotch

front slit/fly

leg hole

Underpants / Jockey Shorts

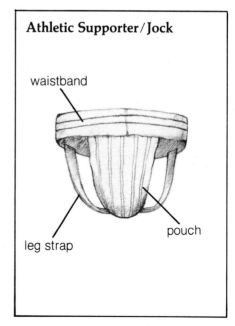

Athletic Supporter / Jock

waistband

leg strap

pouch

Foundation Garments

Most *bras* are secured with *hook-and-eye closures* either on a *back-strap* or in the front of the garment. Many have *underwiring* and/or *side-bones* for added support. *Cup padding* is another optional element. Girdles are sometimes stiffened with *spiral bones* or *stays*. Corsets are similar to girdles.

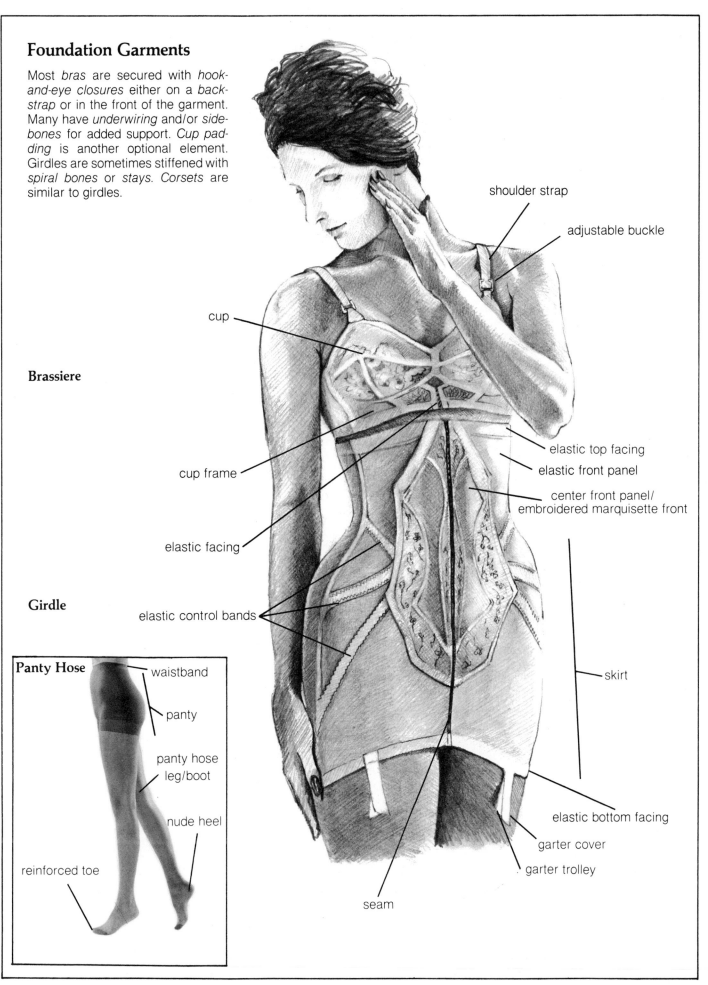

Brassiere

shoulder strap

adjustable buckle

cup

elastic top facing

elastic front panel

center front panel/
embroidered marquisette front

cup frame

elastic facing

Girdle

elastic control bands

skirt

Panty Hose

waistband

panty

panty hose
leg/boot

nude heel

reinforced toe

elastic bottom facing

garter cover

garter trolley

seam

Women's Apparel

Jacket and Pants

Facing material is used on the underside of a lapel. *Lining* is used on the inside of a garment to cover up seamwork and provide body. A pair of lined pants has inside material from cuff to waist. In half-lined pants, the material stretches from waist to knee. In unlined garments, *seams* are clean finished with *bias tape,* or bias binding, sewn on a diagonal to provide stretch and support and to protect fabric from raveling.

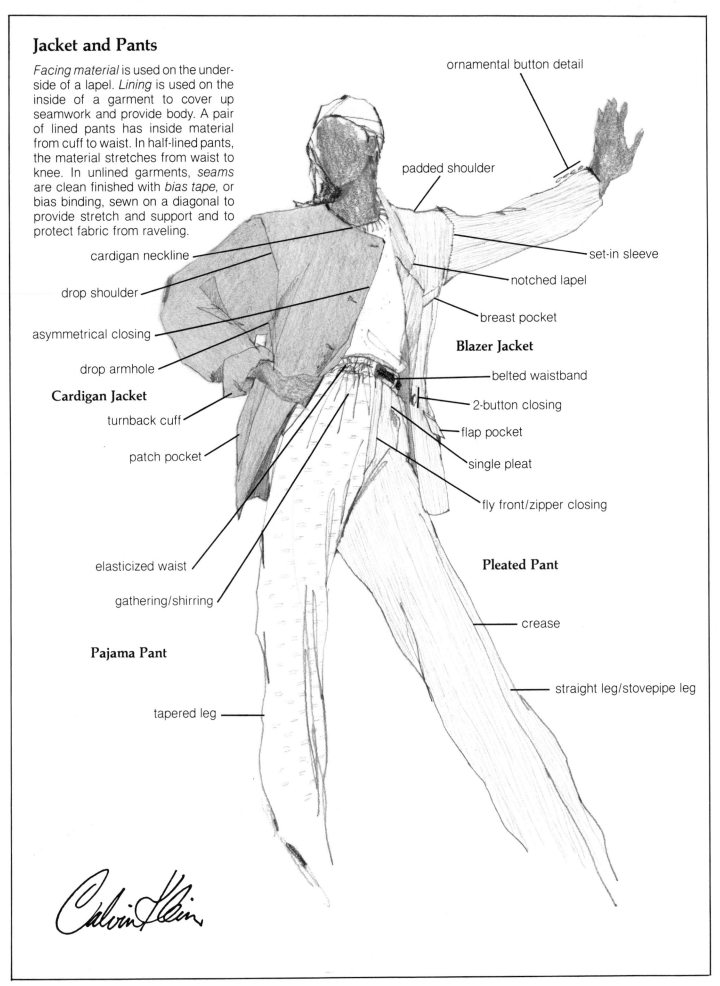

ornamental button detail

padded shoulder

set-in sleeve

notched lapel

breast pocket

Blazer Jacket

cardigan neckline

drop shoulder

asymmetrical closing

drop armhole

Cardigan Jacket

turnback cuff

patch pocket

belted waistband

2-button closing

flap pocket

single pleat

fly front/zipper closing

elasticized waist

gathering/shirring

Pajama Pant

tapered leg

Pleated Pant

crease

straight leg/stovepipe leg

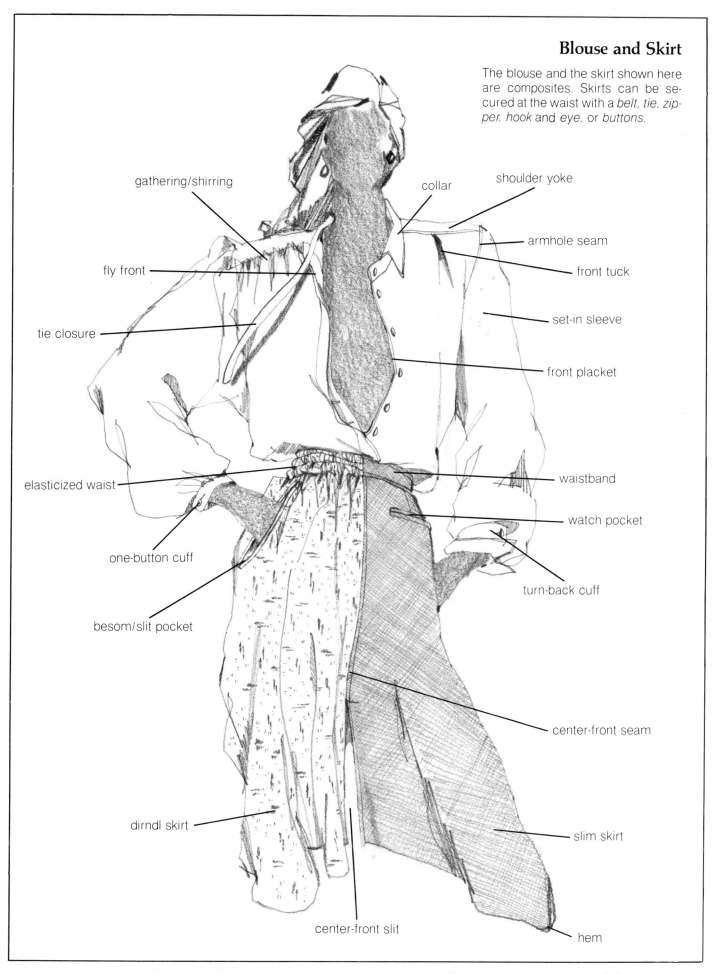

Blouse and Skirt

The blouse and the skirt shown here are composites. Skirts can be secured at the waist with a *belt, tie, zipper, hook* and *eye,* or *buttons.*

gathering/shirring

collar

shoulder yoke

armhole seam

front tuck

fly front

set-in sleeve

tie closure

front placket

elasticized waist

waistband

watch pocket

one-button cuff

turn-back cuff

besom/slit pocket

center-front seam

dirndl skirt

slim skirt

center-front slit

hem

Women's Apparel

Dress

This composite dress, or *gown,* has a *camisole top.* A dress hanging straight from the shoulders is a *chemise.* Some dresses have a fitted or shaped piece at the shoulder called a *yoke. Bratelles* are ornamental suspenderlike straps. Dresses are stored on hangers by means of *keepers, carriers, riders, loops* or *hangers.*

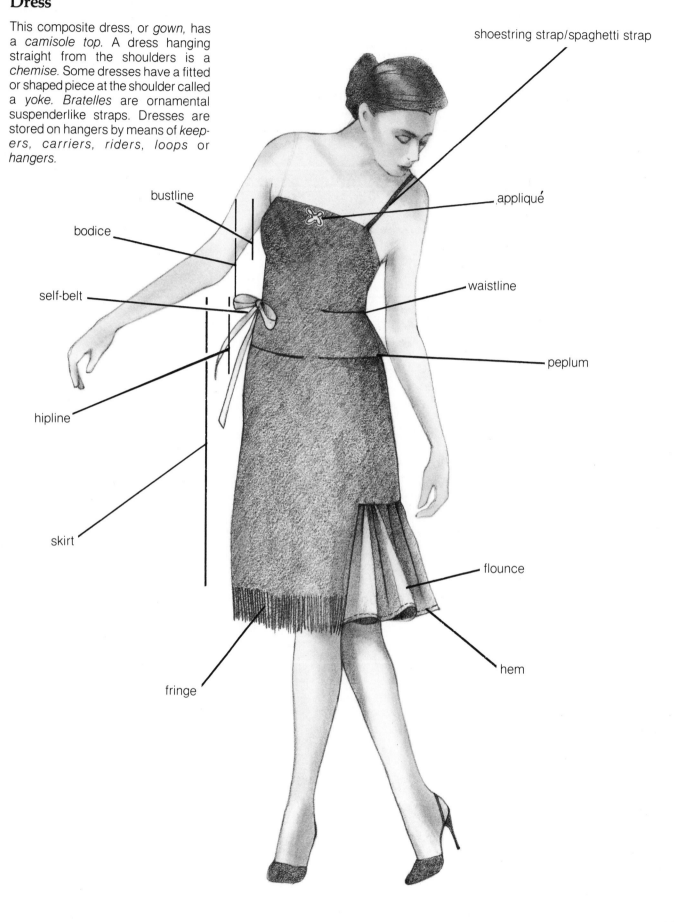

shoestring strap/spaghetti strap

bustline

bodice

self-belt

hipline

skirt

fringe

appliqué

waistline

peplum

flounce

hem

Sweater

A *crew neck sweater* is a pullover with a high, round neck. A *turtleneck* has a high neck that turns back over itself. A sweater with a neck opening that stretches from shoulder to shoulder is a *boat neck,* or *bateau neck.* A sweater without arms is a *vest,* or *knit vest.*

shawl collar

ribs/ribbing

covered button

inset sleeve

wrap belt

patch pocket

Cardigan/Jacket Sweater

Pullover/V-Neck

V-neck

body

ribbed cuff

ribbed bottom

Unisex Clothing

Outerwear

The type of combination *overcoat* and *raincoat* shown here usually has a *button-out* or *zip-out robe lining* which provides warmth in cold weather. It also has a *storm shield* on the back, ornamental *'D' rings* hanging from the back of the belt and sometimes a *throat latch* strap around the collar.

button-off wool collar

collar

epaulet/strap

raglan sleeve

button

belt loop

sleeve strap

strap buckle

button-through flap pocket

storm patch

belt buckle

belt

sleeve strap loop

Trench Coat

elastic

lining

Mitten

liner

hook & ring

glove strap

Glove

fourchette

Outerwear

Fur pelts used in apparel by *furriers* are first *dressed,* or cleaned, then fleshed, stretched and tanned. The furry parts of a pelt's facial hair are called *gills.*

hood

outer shell

raglan sleeve

map pocket

zipper pull

hand warming slot

bellows cargo pocket

hem

drawstring closure/leather tab

double slide zipper

bellows breast pocket

snap closure

placket

Velcro cuff closure

cloth lining

Parka / Anorak

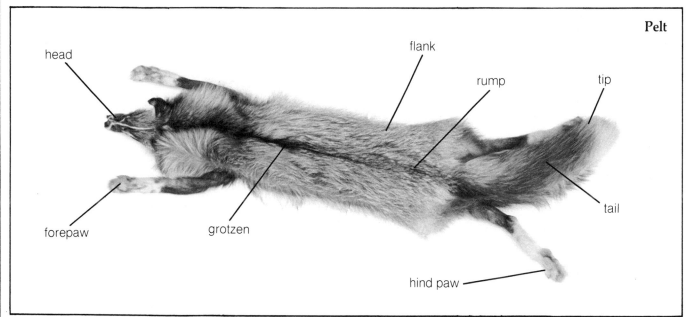

Pelt

head

flank

rump

tip

forepaw

grotzen

tail

hind paw

Unisex Clothing

Men's Hats

Hats are *styled,* or *blocked,* by a *hat-maker* or *hatter.* Hats that have not been creased have an *open crown.* Some hats have *plastic linings.*

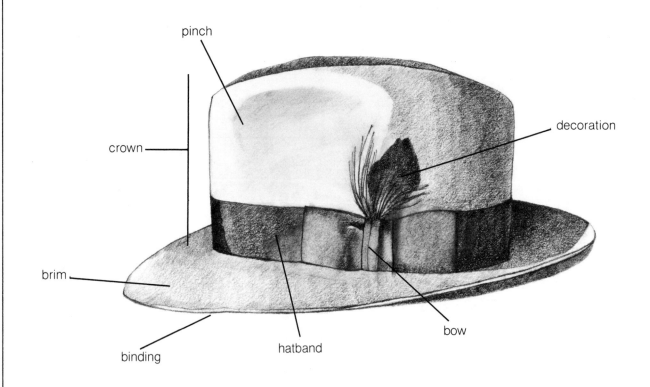

pinch

crown

decoration

brim

binding

hatband

bow

Cowboy Hat / Ten-Gallon Hat

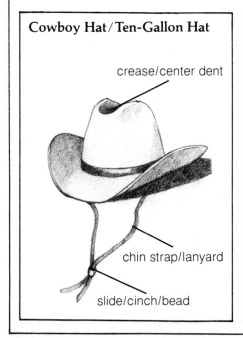

crease/center dent

chin strap/lanyard

slide/cinch/bead

Beret

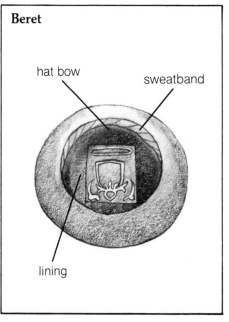

hat bow

sweatband

lining

Cap

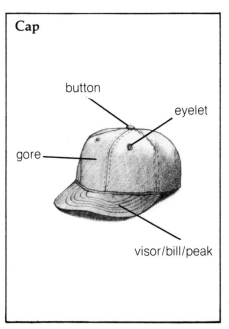

button

eyelet

gore

visor/bill/peak

Women's Hats

Women's hats are designed, made and sold by *milliners. Malines*, or stiff, fine *netting,* is often used as a veil. *Buckles, sequins, plastic fruit, fabric flowers, buttons, tassels* and *braids* are among the many items used as decorative *trimming.* Brimless, close-fitting hats include a *toque*, a *cloche*, and a *turban*. A *picture hat* has a broad flexible brim and is often decorated with trimming. A shallow, round hat with vertical sides is a *pillbox.* A netlike hat or part of a hat or the fabric that holds or covers the back of a woman's hair is a *snood*.

crown

trim/feather

hat pin

hatband

brim

veil

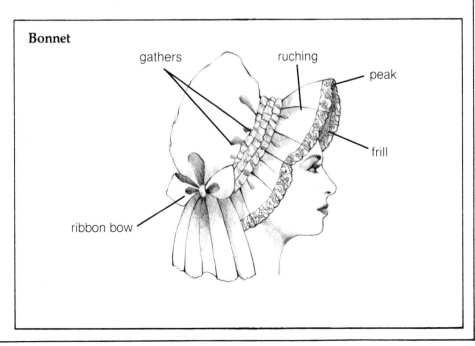

Bonnet

gathers

ruching

peak

frill

ribbon bow

Headwear

Man's Shoe

A shoe consists of a *bottom,* or heel and sole, an *inner sole,* or *insole,* and an *upper.* Shoes like the one shown here, in which the flaps fold over the tongue or vamp, are *bluchers.* Shoes without this construction are *barrels.* A step-in shoe without laces is a *loafer,* whereas a *moccasin* has neither laces nor a heel. The fringed leather decoration on some shoes that covers the laces is the *kiltie.*

binding

lining

tongue

counter

shoelace

aglet

flap

eyelet

instep

throat

vamp

broguings/ decorative perforations

quarter

heel

shank

welt

sole/outsole

wing tip/toe box

Woman's Shoe

A shoe with an open front is an *open-toed shoe,* whereas a shoe with an open back, held on by a strap, is a *slingback,* or *sling shoe.* The *high-heel shoe* seen here is similar to a *pump* in that it grips both the toe and the heel. A high, thin heel is a *spiked,* or *stiletto, heel.* A shoe with a thick layer between the *inner sole* and the outsole is a *platform.*

piping/trim

instep strap

ankle strap

counter

throat

collar

vamp

tip

heel seat

heel

shank

heel breast

heel lift

outsole

Andy Warhol

Boot and Sandal

The upper section of a boot, called the *shaft,* may extend from ankle to knee. The lower section is called the *foot.* Many boots have a contoured steel *shank,* located between outsole and *insole,* to provide support for the arch area. A *thong* is a type of sandal in which the strap comes up between the big toe and the toe next to it.

pull strap

piping

side seam/side welt

front quarter

fancy stitching

back quarter

vamping stitching

foxing stitching

vamp

foxing/counter

toe medallion

rand

box toe

outsole welt

heel base

Boot

outsole

heel lift

Sandal

strap/thong

buckle

upper/insole

vamp

rivet

strap slot

stitching

midsole

crepe sole

arch cookie/scaphoid pad

Shoe Accessories

Shoes can be protected in wet weather by *rubbers, rain boots* or *galoshes*. Socks, or *hose*, which extend to the ankle are *ankle socks*, whereas *knee socks* reach to the knee. *Support* hose have a higher *denier*, or mesh count, than regular hose, which provides additional support for the foot and leg. *Peds* are liners that cover the toes, sole and heel. *Boot hooks*, which fit into *boot loops*, help pull boots on, while V-shaped *bootjacks* hold the boot heel for easier removal. *Athletic socks*, or *sweat socks*, absorb perspiration. Shapeless *tube socks* mold to any foot shape.

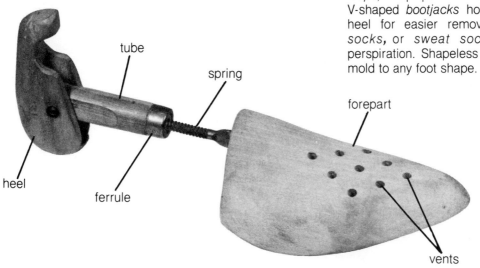

tube

spring

forepart

heel

ferrule

vents

Shoe Tree

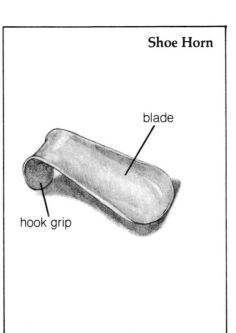

Shoe Horn

blade

hook grip

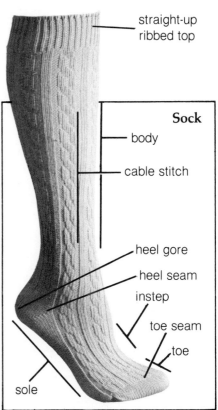

straight-up ribbed top

Sock

body

cable stitch

heel gore

heel seam

instep

toe seam

toe

sole

Footwear

Fasteners

Heavy-duty hook-and-eye closures are called *hook and bars.* In a *cinch fastener,* a *strap* is pulled through two *rings* then back through the second ring to fasten. A *frog* consists of an intricately knotted *cord loop* through which a button is hooked.

point

shafts

coil

head/cap/guard/sheath/clasp

Safety Pin

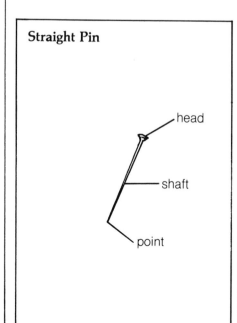

Straight Pin

head

shaft

point

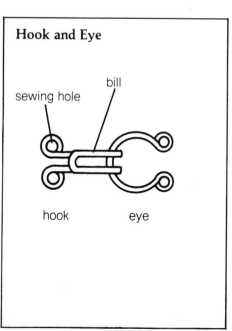

Hook and Eye

bill

sewing hole

hook   eye

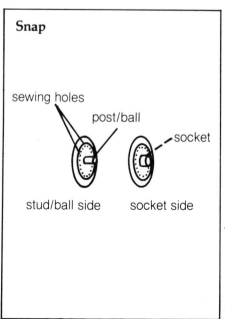

Snap

sewing holes

post/ball

socket

stud/ball side   socket side

Closures

A *divider* within the zipper slide separates teeth when it is moved downward. Some zippers have a *synthetic coil* rather than teeth. A *pull ring* is occasionally attached to the slide for decorative purposes. A *two-way zipper* can be opened from either end, while an *invisible zipper* is concealed when closed and appears to be a *seam*.

protruding upper face

pull tab

top stop/ top-end piece

hollow lower face

zipper tape

teeth

slide

chain/closed teeth

bottom stop/ bottom-end piece

Zipper/Slide Fastener

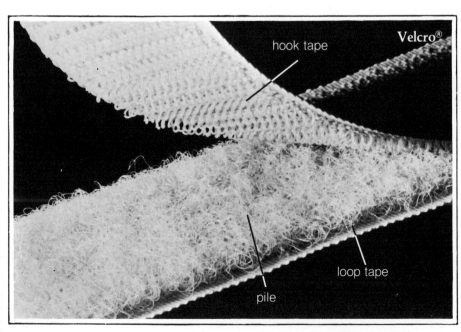

hook tape

Velcro®

pile

loop tape

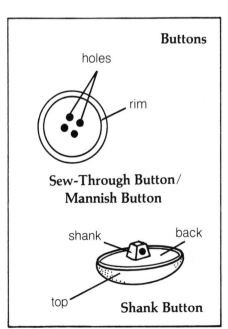

Buttons

holes

rim

Sew-Through Button/ Mannish Button

shank

back

top

Shank Button

Shavers

A *straight razor* has a single, long blade which folds into a *handle*. It is sharpened on a long strip of leather called a *strop*. Other, older barbering equipment includes *shaving brushes* and *shaving mugs*. A *safety razor* has two *wings* on the *head* which are opened by a screw at the base of the handle. Bleeding from shaving cuts or nicks can be stopped with a *styptic pencil*.

combs

tension bar

long-hair slots

cutters

shaving head

trimmer

top housing

logo

on & off switch

rear housing

front housing

Electric Razor

Razor Blade / Double-Edged Blade

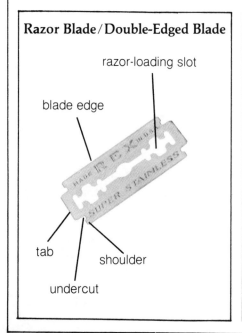

razor-loading slot

blade edge

tab

shoulder

undercut

Blade Injector

blade loader

rail

front tab

stem

used-blade box

gash

bump

Disposable Razor

blade cartridge

blade

overcap/
protective cap

handle

Men's Hair

Chevelure is a head of hair. A man without any hair on his *scalp* is said to be *bald*. *Wigs, hairpieces, toupees* or "rugs" can be used to conceal *bald spots*. *Pogonotrophy* is beard-growing and *pogonotomy* is beard-cutting. A partial growth is known as *stubble*. A small, tufted chin beard is a *goatee*. A trim, pointed one is a *Vandyke*. A mustache having long, curled ends is a *handlebar mustache*.

distribution point

crown

cowlick/tuft

hairline

part

spit curl

widow's peak

sidewall

sideburn

mustache

muttonchop/
side whiskers

beard/whiskers

Hairstyles and Facial Hair

Hair Grooming Implements

Among other attachments available for use with a *pro-style dryer* are combs, brush and an *air-flow nozzle,* to limit the amount of hot air.

air vents

barrel grille

CONAIR®
Pro Style 1250 Watts

barrel

motor housing

handle

high heat switch

low heat switch

on-off switch

hang ring

cord strain relief

Hair Dryer

spine

comb strip

bristles

comb holder

Electric Brush

Comb

fine teeth

coarse teeth

heat indicator

on-off switch

Women's Hair

A small portion of hair in a woman's *hairdo*, or *coiffure*, is a *lock*. *Bouffant* is a puffed-out hairdo. *Teased*, or *back-combed*, hair is achieved by taking hold of a strand and pushing the short hairs toward the scalp with a comb. A braid on the back of the head is a *pigtail*. Hair that turns inward at the end, rather than outward, is a *pageboy*. A long piece of store-bought hair clipped to real hair is a *fall*.

knot/bun/beehive/chignon

kiss curl

bangs

eyebrow

eyelashes

flip

ponytail

curl

braid/plait/tress

tendril/ringlet

strand/wisp

Hairstyles and Facial Hair

Hairstyling Implements

A curling iron is used to curl a *strand* of hair or to straighten it. Hair clips and bobby pins, which may be long or short, can be used to secure a roller while hair is being set. The roller shown here, however, is *self-clasping*. *Barrettes*, *combs*, *hair ribbons*, *headbands* and *hair bands* hold hair in place or serve as decorative *hair ornaments*. Professional *hairdressers* use *permanent rods* and *papers*, *applicator bottles* filled with *permanent lotion*, *setting lotion*, *rinse* or *dye*, plastic *caps*, *dryers* and *infrared lamps* to treat and style *hairdos*.

on-off switch

thumb press

power cord

strain relief

main housing

stand

thermal dot

tongue

safety cool tip

barrel

Curling Iron

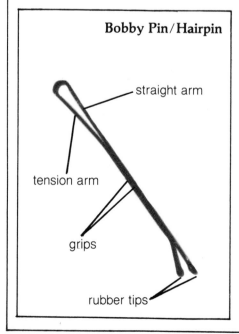

Bobby Pin/Hairpin

straight arm

tension arm

grips

rubber tips

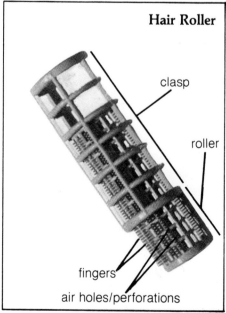

Hair Roller

clasp

roller

fingers

air holes/perforations

Hair Clip

finger grip

spring

leaf

Toothbrush

The stimulator tip on a toothbrush fits in what is called a *hang-up hole.* Teeth can also be cleaned with *dental floss,* a waxed string, and *high-pressure water-spray units.* Nails can be smoothed with an *emery board,* a cardboard strip covered with *powdered emery,* or a *nail file.*

bristles

tuft hole

block head

stimulator tip

block handle

Toothbrush

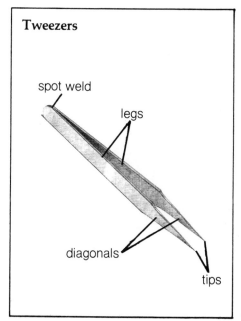

Tweezers

spot weld

legs

diagonals

tips

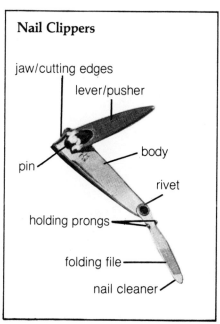

Nail Clippers

jaw/cutting edges

lever/pusher

pin

body

rivet

holding prongs

folding file

nail cleaner

Makeup

A skin-colored *concealer,* or *coverup,* can be used to cover blemishes or undesirable shadows under the eyes. *Pancake makeup* is a thick face powder used by actors and actresses as a foundation. Makeup can be removed with a *cleansing cream* or *cold cream.*

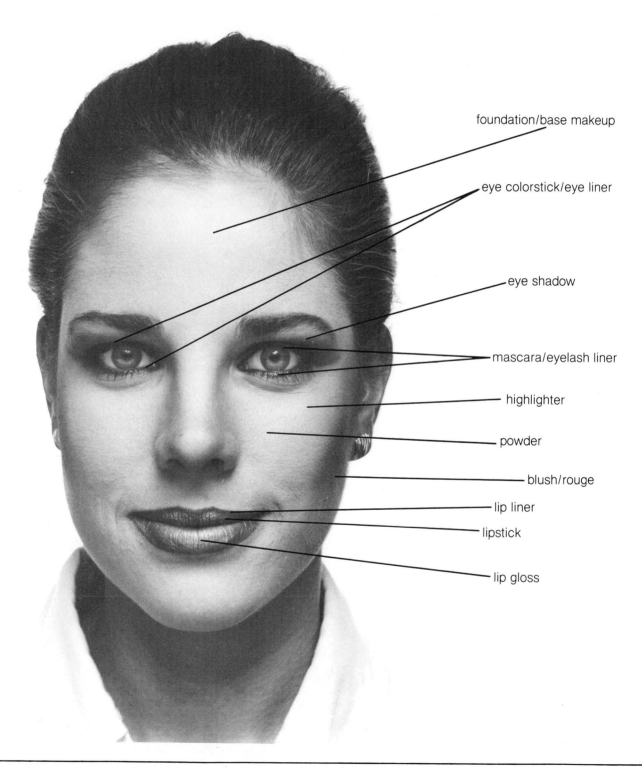

foundation/base makeup

eye colorstick/eye liner

eye shadow

mascara/eyelash liner

highlighter

powder

blush/rouge

lip liner

lipstick

lip gloss

Beauty Products

Colored *nail polish* is often used to "paint" fingernails and toenails. In addition to those beauty products shown here, there are *scents,* such as *perfume,* applied by women to *pulse points; bath oils; body oils; moisturizers* and *lotions.* Men use *colognes* or *after-shave lotions.*

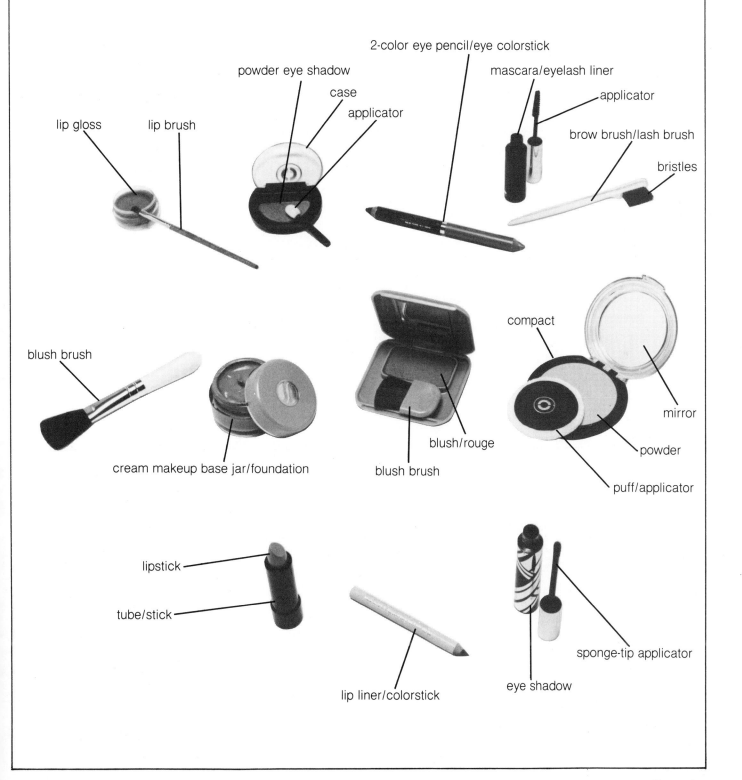

lip gloss

lip brush

powder eye shadow

case

applicator

2-color eye pencil/eye colorstick

mascara/eyelash liner

applicator

brow brush/lash brush

bristles

blush brush

cream makeup base jar/foundation

blush/rouge

blush brush

compact

mirror

powder

puff/applicator

lipstick

tube/stick

lip liner/colorstick

eye shadow

sponge-tip applicator

Gemstone

The shades of color a gemstone gives off are called *fire.* A matched set of jewelry, or *parure,* often includes a necklace, earrings and a *brooch.* A *cameo* is a gem on which a relief carving has been made. Nonprecious *costume jewelry* is made to simulate its precious counterparts. The end of a *cuff link* that is passed through the buttonhole and fastened is called a *wing-back,* or *airplane-back.*

Cut Gemstone

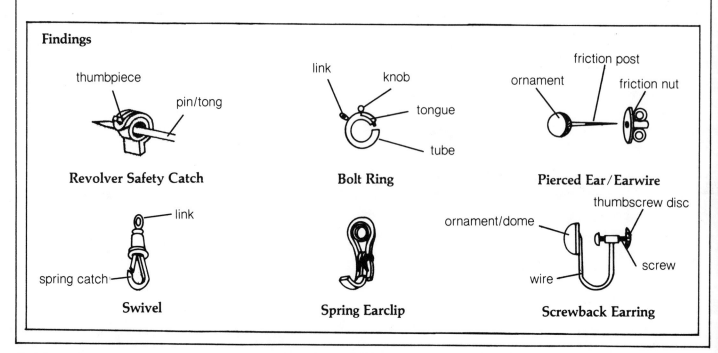

Ring

A *lavaliere* is a pendant worn on a chain as a necklace. A *charm* is a trinket worn on a bracelet or necklace, often having personal or symbolic meaning. An *ouch* is a brooch or a setting for a precious stone. *Spangles* are glittering pieces of metal used on clothing for decoration. A *riviere* is a multi-stringed necklace containing many precious stones.

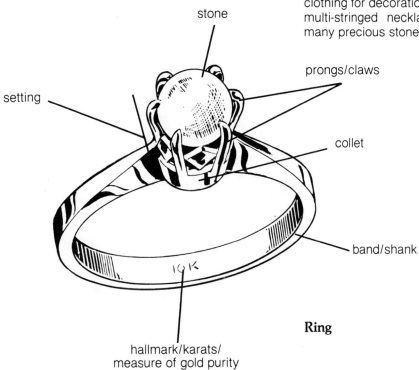

stone

prongs/claws

setting

collet

band/shank

hallmark/karats/
measure of gold purity

Ring

Pendant

chain

hook

link

stone

bezel

trim

stone

Pieces

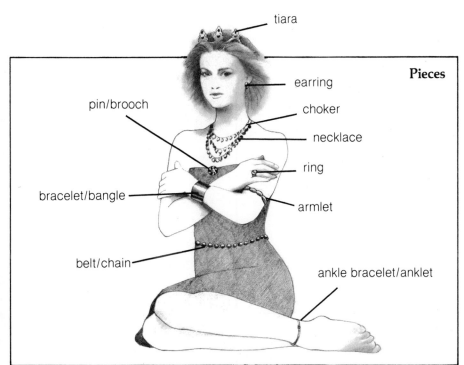

tiara

earring

pin/brooch

choker

necklace

ring

bracelet/bangle

armlet

belt/chain

ankle bracelet/anklet

Jewelry

Watches

The digital display on this watch can indicate date, seconds, time in a different time zone, and it can perform *stopwatch* functions. An extremely accurate timepiece is called a *chronometer.* A watchband, or *strap,* is attached to the case by *push-pins,* or *spring-bars.*

link

watchband/bracelet

zero mark

case

dial/face

minute hand

hour hand

protective shoulder

crown

Liquid Crystal Display (LCD)

LCD second time zone display control

LCD second and date display control

elapsed time bezel

luminous indices/markers

Wristwatch

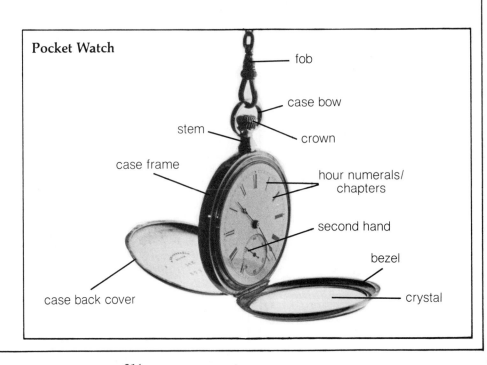

Pocket Watch

fob

case bow

stem

crown

case frame

hour numerals/chapters

second hand

bezel

case back cover

crystal

Eyeglasses

This is a composite pair of eyeglasses, or *spectacles*. The *frame* consists of a *front* and two temples. The front is formed by two *eyewires* which hold the lenses and are connected by a bridge.

skull temple

end piece

bifocal

rivets

double bar

bridge

comfort-cable temple

screw

hinge

rectangular lens

tabs/nose pads

distance

intermediate

trifocal

aviator lens

reading

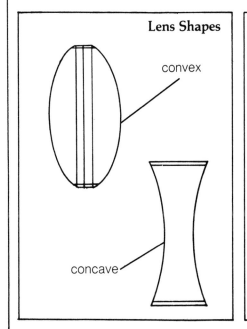

Lens Shapes

convex

concave

Monocle

gallery

rim

Lorgnette

eyewires

handle

Eyeglasses

Handbag

A handbag can also be referred to as a *pocketbook* or *purse*. A bag with no handles is a *clutch*. *East-west* describes a handbag which is wider than it is long. A *north-south* bag has a long, narrow shape. The metal ornaments and closures on bags are collectively called *hardware* or *fittings*.

adjustable shoulder strap

loop

flap

top stitching

side belt/side loop

tab

top eyelet

turn-lock

piping/welting

back plate

double-front pocket

accordion gusset

Shoulder Bag

Swagger Bag

knob closure

double top handles

frame

outside flap pocket/ open outside pocket

foot

handle attachment tabs/handle holders

gusset

Wallet / Billfold

A wallet's exterior covering is called the *cover*. Women's wallets often have a *coin purse* within and a *tab closing* on the outside. *Photo holders* that unfold and become a long strip are called *accordion windows*.

photo & card windows/photo & card wings/pass case windows

bill compartment/currency pocket

credit card slots/credit card pockets

pocket

flap

Texas Oil

clip

stay facing/stay

pass case/photo & card case

Checkbook Clutch

flap

top stitching

open ID window

credit card slots

stay facing/stay

pen holder/pen loop

checkbook cover

Wallet and Currency

Money

There are three types of U.S. paper currency in circulation: green *Federal Reserve Notes*, or *"greenbacks,"* red *United States notes*, and blue *Silver Certificates*. *Bills* are printed from *engraved plates* on paper containing colored *fibers*. Notes damaged during printing are replaced with *star notes*. Money printed illegally and passed off as *legal tender* is called *counterfeit money*.

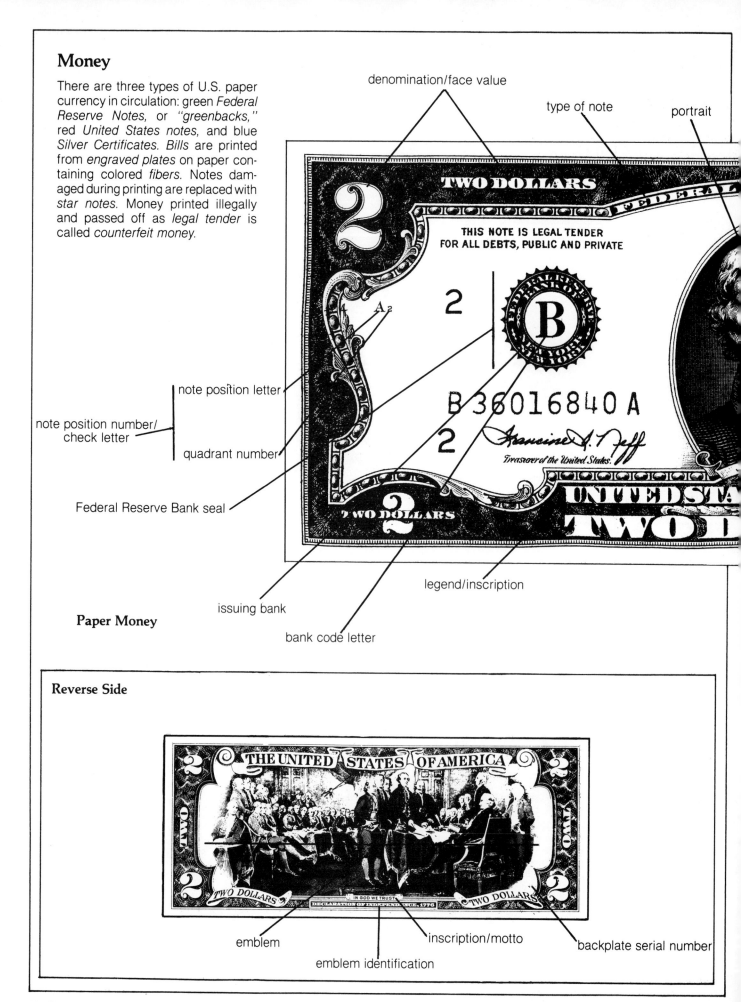

denomination/face value

type of note

portrait

note position letter

note position number/ check letter

quadrant number

Federal Reserve Bank seal

legend/inscription

Paper Money

issuing bank

bank code letter

Reverse Side

emblem

emblem identification

inscription/motto

backplate serial number

prefix letter/issuing Federal Reserve Bank's code number

serial number

suffix letter/run number

Money

One- and five-cent coins are *minor coins.* Ten-, twenty-five- and fifty-cent *pieces* are *subsidiary coins.* A steel *stamp,* or *die,* is used to impress, or strike, a coin design on a metal *blank* called a *flan,* or *planchet.* *Commemoratives* are coins issued to mark a special event or to honor an outstanding person. *Bullion* is un-coined gold or silver. A person who studies and collects money is a *numismatist.* An *exonomist* collects *tokens, medals, scrip,* etc., as well as money.

Federal Reserve Bank number

faceplate numbers & letters

plate serial number/ faceplate number

note position letter/ check letter

Treasury seal

statesman's name

series identification

border

Coin

inscription

portrait

main device

field

motto

mint mark

motto

designer's initials

denomination/ face value

symbolic date

reeding/milled edge/serrations

Obverse Side/"Heads"/"Face"

Reverse Side/"Tails"/Back

Wallet and Currency

Check and Credit Card

A check must be signed by the payee, or *endorsed,* on the back to be valid. The back of a credit card contains a *signature panel* and a *magnetic strip* which contains account number, expiration date, name, address, personal identification number and *service code.* Some credit cards have a *card security number* hidden within the plastic to help prevent fraud.

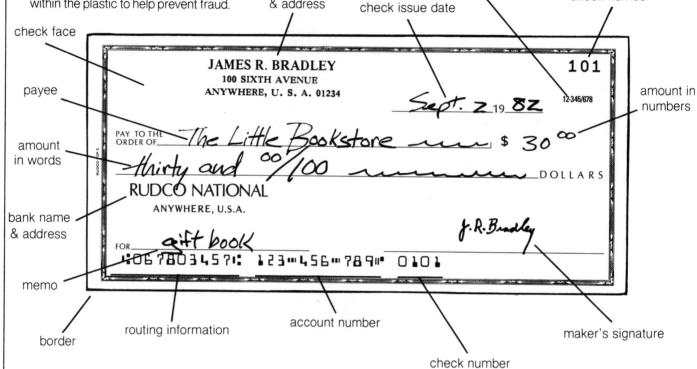

check face

maker's name & address

check issue date

American Bankers Association routing number/ABA number

check number

payee

amount in words

bank name & address

memo

border

routing information

account number

check number

maker's signature

amount in numbers

Check

Credit Card

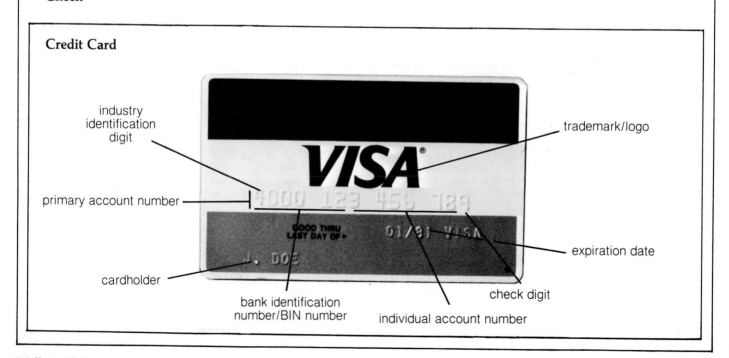

industry identification digit

primary account number

cardholder

bank identification number/BIN number

individual account number

check digit

trademark/logo

expiration date

Money Order and Traveler's Check

A money order has a tear-off *customer's receipt* and *department voucher*. On the reverse side of the money order is an *endorsement block*, a *validation statement* and a *warning* to the cashing agency. Telegraph company money orders permit an individual to authorize payment to a specified individual at a distant location without the recipient having the original document.

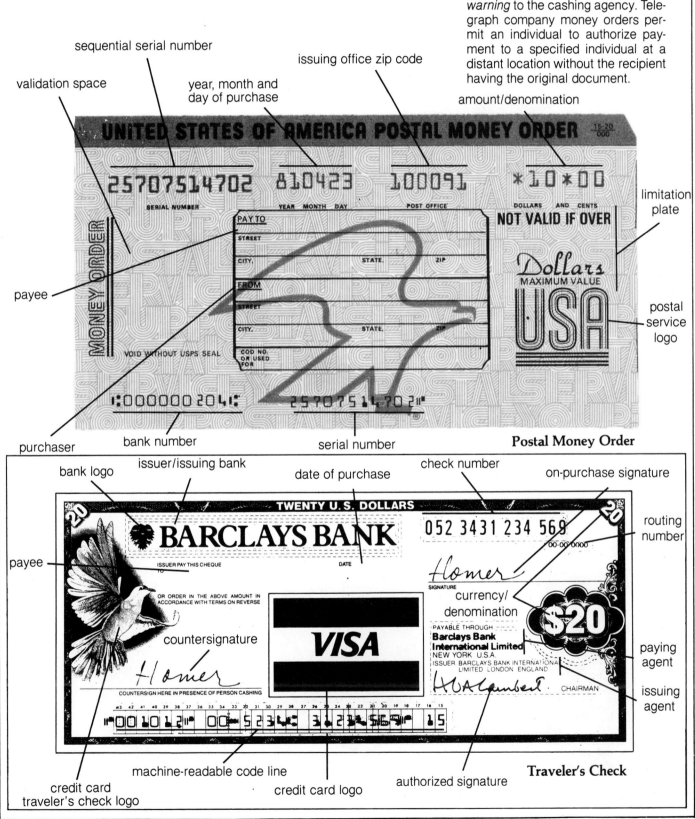

sequential serial number

validation space

year, month and day of purchase

issuing office zip code

amount/denomination

UNITED STATES OF AMERICA POSTAL MONEY ORDER 15-20 000

25707514702   810423   100091   *10*00

SERIAL NUMBER   YEAR MONTH DAY   POST OFFICE   DOLLARS AND CENTS

limitation plate

MONEY ORDER

PAY TO
STREET
CITY.   STATE.   ZIP
FROM
STREET
CITY.   STATE.   ZIP
COD NO. OR USED FOR

VOID WITHOUT USPS SEAL

NOT VALID IF OVER

Dollars
MAXIMUM VALUE
USA

postal service logo

payee

⑆000000204⑆   25707514702⑈

purchaser   bank number   serial number   **Postal Money Order**

bank logo   issuer/issuing bank   date of purchase   check number   on-purchase signature

payee

TWENTY U.S. DOLLARS
20   20

❧ **BARCLAYS BANK**

052 3431 234 569
00-00-0000

ISSUER PAY THIS CHEQUE   TO   DATE

OR ORDER IN THE ABOVE AMOUNT IN ACCORDANCE WITH TERMS ON REVERSE

Homer
SIGNATURE

routing number

currency/ denomination

countersignature

Homer

VISA

COUNTERSIGN HERE IN PRESENCE OF PERSON CASHING

PAYABLE THROUGH
Barclays Bank International Limited
NEW YORK U.S.A.
ISSUER. BARCLAYS BANK INTERNATIONAL
LIMITED LONDON ENGLAND

H.V.A.Lambert CHAIRMAN

$20

paying agent

issuing agent

⑈3 42 41 40 39 38 37 36 35 34 33 32 31 30 29 28 27 26 25 24 23 22 21 20 19 18 17 16 15

⑈00 10 12⑈ 00⑆523⑉ 3⑉234 569⑈ 15

credit card traveler's check logo

machine-readable code line

credit card logo

authorized signature

Traveler's Check

Cigar and Cigarette

The cigar wrapper, as well as the interior *binder*, is a spirally-rolled *leaf*. Cigars, or *"stogies,"* are stored in *humidors* to insure freshness. The residue of smoked tobacco is *ash*. The remains of a smoked cigar or cigarette is the *butt*. The abrasive striking surface or *friction strip* on which matches are struck is on the *back cover* of a matchbook.

foot

cigar band

wrapper

filter

head

foot

tuck

band

tobacco/filler

paper

tobacco

Cigar

Cigarette

Cigar Cutter

slide

slide box

blade

blade hole

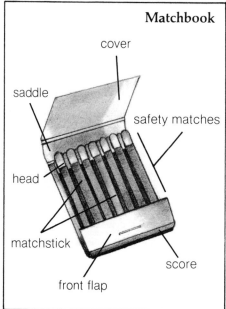

Matchbook

cover

saddle

safety matches

head

matchstick

score

front flap

Gas Lighter

flame adjustment wheel

striker wheel

gas lever

butane well

Pipe

Pipe smoke is also called *lunt,* and un-smoked tobacco in the bottom of the bowl after smoking is called *dottle.* The pliable, tufted rod used to clean the inside of a pipe's stem is a *pipe cleaner.* Pipe tobacco is kept in a *pouch.* Some bowls are covered with a *pipe umbrella* or *bowl lid.* An Eastern pipe with a long, flexible tube by which the smoke is drawn through a jar of water and thus cooled is a *water pipe, hookah,* or *hubble-bubble.*

stem

bit/mouthpiece

saddle

bowl

shape

shank

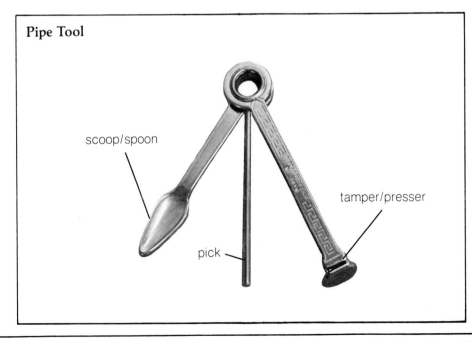

Pipe Tool

scoop/spoon

pick

tamper/presser

Smoking Materials

Umbrella

An umbrella's water-repellent *fabric* is attached to a *frame,* or *skeleton.* The specific points where the fabric is sewn to the skeleton are called *tacks.*

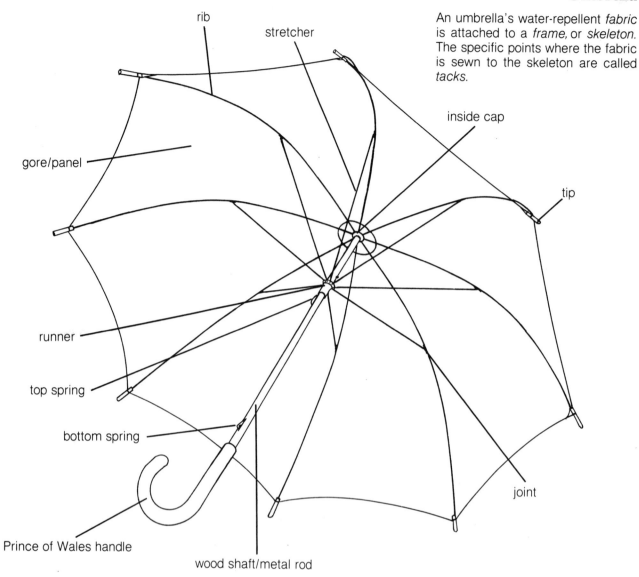

rib

stretcher

inside cap

gore/panel

tip

runner

top spring

bottom spring

joint

Prince of Wales handle

wood shaft/metal rod

Runner

stop wire

finishing wire

stretcher

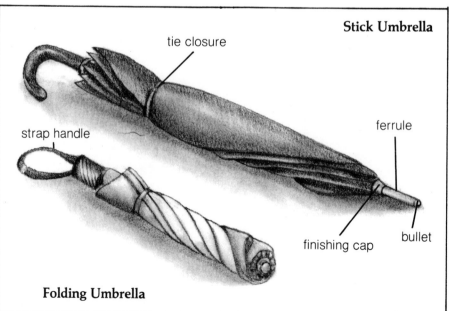

Stick Umbrella

tie closure

strap handle

ferrule

finishing cap

bullet

Folding Umbrella

The Home

To facilitate locating items found in the home, the objects in this section have been grouped according to where they are most likely to be encountered: living room, dining room, kitchen, bedroom, bathroom, playroom, utility room or yard.

The kitchen subsection, for example, includes implements for preparing food as well as appliances that make food preparation easier. In addition to identifying the parts of containers used to bring groceries into the kitchen, coverage includes all the terms used in the designing and packaging of food and kitchenware. Knowing the names for these components will surely change how the reader views his or her cereal box at the breakfast table in the future.

The terms for details of desk equipment, found in the playroom/utility room subsection, apply as well to office furnishings. The seven parts of a paper clip, for example, are valid wherever this unique little device is used.

Although a nursery is not included as a subsection, objects used for or by children—stroller, car seat, playpen, and swings—have been incorporated in the subcategory of yard equipment.

Mailbox/Rural Mailbox

latch/handle/lock

flag

residence number

440

door

box

mounting post/support

Fireplace

Many fireplaces have glass and metal *fire screens* to prevent heat loss and to keep sparks from flying into the room. Others have a low metal *fender* between the inner and outer hearth. A metal cover, used to shield a banked or dying fire, is called a *curfew*. Fireplace accessories include air-blowing *bellows, coal hods* and *wood carriers,* and *grates* or *heat exchangers* which can be used instead of andirons. A *firebrand* is a piece of burning wood.

mantle/mantlepiece

firebrick/fireback

poker
shovel
log forks
fire irons

outer hearth

inner hearth

andiron

spark arrester/hood

chimney cap

flue liner

chimney

flue

mantle

smoke chamber

smoke shelf

throat

lintel

damper

firebox

hearth

ash dump

ashpit

ashpit door

Fireplace Cross Section

Clock

A *pendulum clock* tall enough to stand on the floor, either a grandfather or the shorter *grandmother clock*, is called a *tall-case clock*. The machinery or *movement* within is called the *clockworks*. A *rating*, the length of a pendulum swing, can be adjusted by a *rating nut*, usually found beneath the bob.

finial

moon dial

crest

break-arch

dial plate

spandrel ornament

hood door

hour hand

chapter ring

dial/face

seconds dial

minute hand

hour numeral/chapter

calendar

hood

concave molding

trunk door

rope/chain

pendulum rod

weight

pendulum

bob/lead weight

trunk

base/plinth

Grandfather Clock

Clock Radio

clock & alarm settings

AM/FM radio controls

snooze alarm

digital display

radio dial

Hourglass/Sandglass

bulb

waist

frame

sand

foot

Chair

A single broad center upright used in place of spindles in a seat back is called a *splat*. Horizontal•members across the seat back are called *slats*, or *crosspieces*. *Braces* are two spindles that form a "V" at the back of a chair seat. The crest of a chair may have a shape called a *handgrip, roll top* or *pillow*. A *slip seat* is a seat that is fitted into a molding and can be removed and covered with fabric, then replaced. An extended arm with a flat surface is called a *writing arm*.

headpiece/back rail

crest

ear

spindles

stile

seat back

arm/armrest

arm post/
arm stump/
arm support

spindle

seat

rear stretcher

rung/side stretcher

leg

rocker/curved slat

front stretcher

Rocking Chair/Rocker

Lounger

When the backrest of this *recliner*, or *Barcalounger*, is pushed back, the *footrest* rises to seat level. The term *ottoman*, or *pouf*, is often used to refer to an overstuffed *footstool*. An *arm pad* on an *easy chair* is also called a *manchette*.

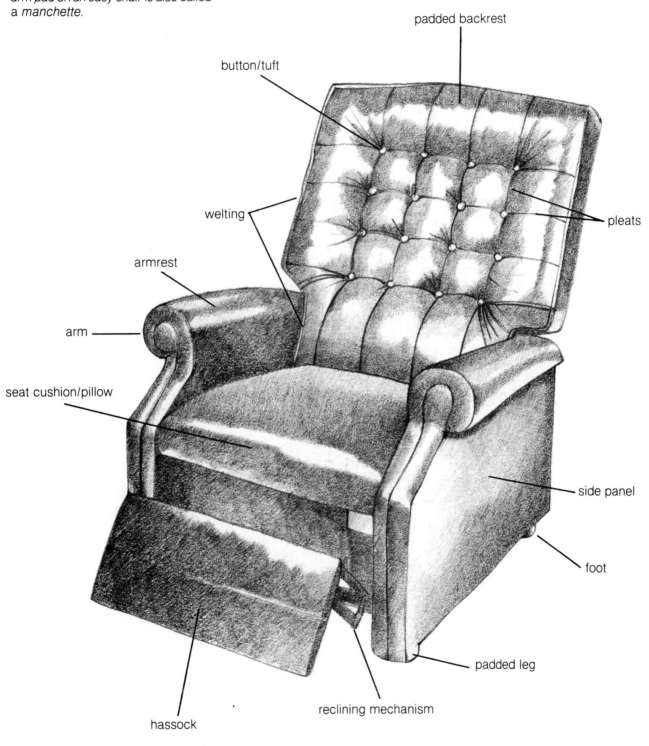

padded backrest

button/tuft

welting

pleats

armrest

arm

seat cushion/pillow

side panel

foot

hassock

reclining mechanism

padded leg

Sofa

A sofa is an upholstered *couch* with a back and two arms or raised ends. If it is composed of several independent sections that can be arranged individually or in various combinations, it is a *sectional*. A *davenport* or *convertible* can be converted into a bed for nighttime use, whereas a *divan* is a large couch without back or arms that is often used as a bed. A sofa for two is a *loveseat,* or *courting seat.* Cylindrical pillows, or *bolsters,* and *fitted* or *tailored pillows* or *cushions* are often used on sofas.

armrest

scrolled arm

upholstered back

crest rail

rosette

buttons/tufts

inlay

side cushion

ornament

foot

caster

seat-rail

upholstered seat

Candle and Candelabrum

Candles, or *tapers*, are made of *tallow*, *wax* or *paraffin*. Most are *dripless*. A collar placed at the top of a candle is a *burner*. The charred or partly consumed portion of a candlewick, or *snaste*, is the *snuff*, formerly referred to as the *snot*. The remains of a used candle is the *stub*. Many candlesticks have a pointed *pricket* on which a candle is impaled, rather than a socket. Small candles used for religious purposes are called *devotionals*.

flame

wick

candle

bobèche/drip pan

socket

candlestick

post/stem

branch/arm

base

Candle Snuffer / Extinguisher

bell/snuffer

handle

Lamps and Lighting

Light output, measured in *lumens*, depends on the amount of electricity used by a bulb. *Long-life bulbs* have heavier filaments. *Three-way bulbs* have two filaments, used separately for two of the light levels and together for the third. Two general types of bulb glass are soft, or *lime glass*, and hard, or *heat-resistant glass*. Lamp shades come in *drum, empire* and *bell* shapes. Lighting fixtures suspended from the ceiling are called *chandeliers*. The ceiling cap that covers the *junction box* for hanging lighting fixtures is the *canopy*.

ring
spider
shade
ribs

Lampshade

finial

harp

switch
socket shell
socket cap
harp sleeve
nipple
harp wing
neck
lamp cord
lock nut
lamp pipe/tube
lock washer
washer
channel
hex nut
power cord

Table Lamp

Incandescent Bulb

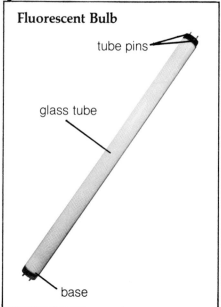

filament
lead-in wire
bulb
button
support wire
mica disc
button rod
exhaust tube
stem press
base
ring contact
tip contact

Fluorescent Bulb

tube pins

glass tube

base

Lamps and Lighting

Adjustable lamps, such as the one seen here, have an *inner reflector* around the bulb to help ventilate the shade. *Gooseneck lamps* have flexible shafts which permit the shade to be turned in any direction. *High-intensity* lamps produce a strong beam of light that illuminates only a small area.

neck assembly

on & off switch/turn

neck angles

wiring tube/arm

shade

mid-angle

support tube/arm

adjustment knob

springs

spring hangers

mounting-shaft sleeve

mounting assembly

tension clamp

mounting shaft

Adjustable Lamp

Track Lighting

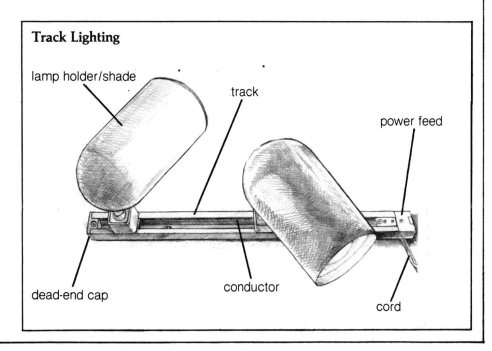

lamp holder/shade

track

power feed

dead-end cap

conductor

cord

Window Coverings

The gathering of material at the top of draperies, hidden by the valance in this illustration, is called the *heading*. A *curtain rod* is a simple metal or wooden rod on which curtains are hung and moved by hand, without aid of pulley mechanisms. A curtain *panel* is a vertical section of fabric. *Cafe curtains* are suspended from rings and cover only part of a window.

valance/cornice

trim

shade body

pull

scallop

hem

tassel

skirt

pleats/folds

curtain/drape/ side panel

window shade

tieback

Curtains/Draperies and Shade

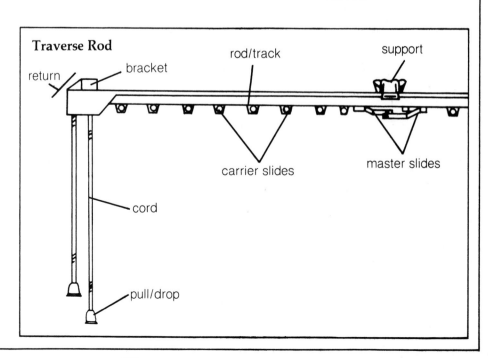

Traverse Rod

return

bracket

rod/track

support

cord

carrier slides

master slides

pull/drop

Window Coverings

Braided ladders are used in place of ladder tapes on some venetian blinds, and tubular wands are sometimes used instead of tilt cords. In roll-up blinds, slat tilt cannot be adjusted. A shutter consists of panels, each one of which contains louvers within a frame.

worm gear

tilter

tilt rod

drum

cradle

head

headbox/headrail/
head channel

end brace

lift lock

slats

tilt cord pulley

tilt cord

blind

equalizer clip/
equalizer buckle

tassel/knob

lift cord

end cap

lift cord

bottom rail/
bottom bar

tape/ladder tape

Venetian Blinds

Shutters

outside stile

hanging strip

hinge

top block

louvers

tilt rod/control rod

bottom block

frame

Shade Roller

roller

shade body

flat pin/spear

slat

round pin/
gudgeon

hem/pocket

ring pull

Living Room

Table

A drop-leaf table is any table with a leaf that drops down to the side, such as a *gateleg* or a *butterfly table*. In a butterfly table, which has *splayed legs,* wooden wing-shaped *brackets* support the leaves. *Pedestal tables* rest on a single *base* rather than on legs. Some tables have an *apron,* wooden slats that run along the sides just beneath the top, to provide additional support. *Card tables,* or *bridge tables,* are lightweight, portable tables with folding *frames.*

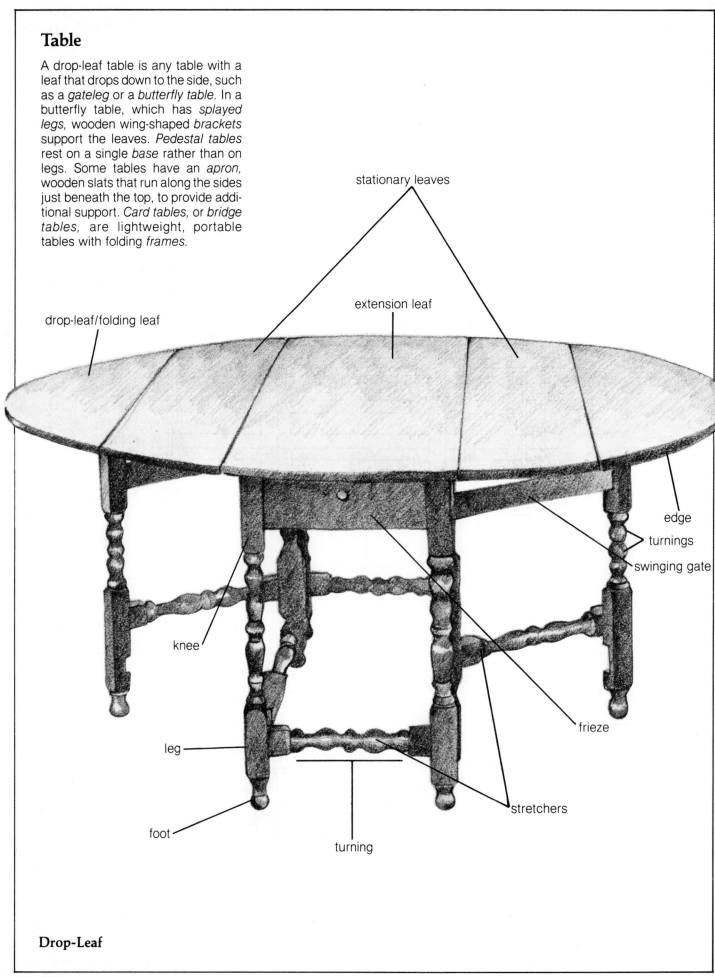

stationary leaves

extension leaf

drop-leaf/folding leaf

edge

turnings

swinging gate

knee

frieze

leg

stretchers

foot

turning

Drop-Leaf

cornice

keystone

rosette

molding

domed shell

shell hub

arched-top glass door

latch

pilaster/column

shelf/cupboard

hinge

front pilaster

paneled door

cupboard doors

return end

Side Pieces

Storage cabinets and receptacles are known as *casework furniture.* Some sideboards have *candle slides,* which are boards that slide out to support candlesticks. *Knife boxes,* or *knife cases,* sit atop the sideboard at either end. Other side pieces include *breakfronts, hutches* and *dry sinks.*

Corner Cupboard/China Cabinet

Sideboard/Buffet

top

silverware drawer

wine drawer/wine bin

china cupboard

hardware/ pulls/brasses

side panel

stile

inlay

leg

foot

serving silverware drawer

Dining Room

Place Setting

There is no universally accepted way of setting a table. The elements and their proper position vary. The arrangement shown here is based on that used by the White House on formal occasions.

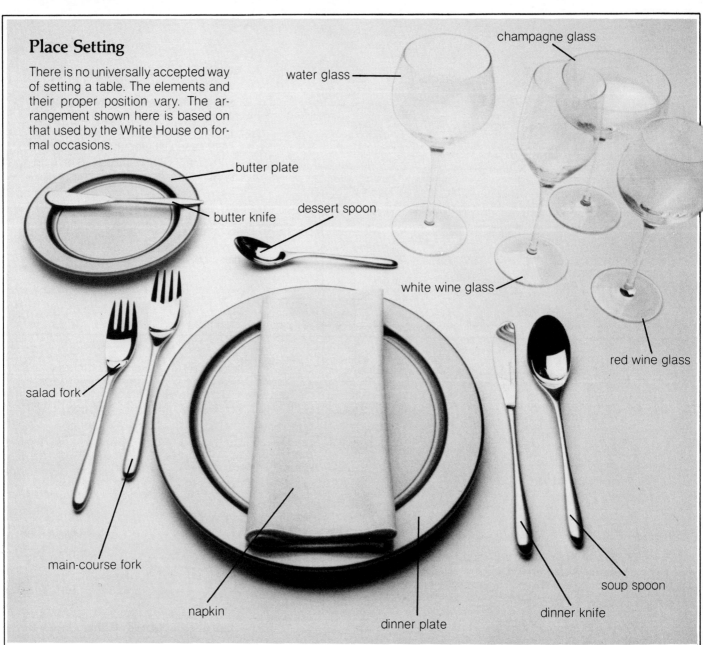

water glass

champagne glass

butter plate

dessert spoon

butter knife

white wine glass

red wine glass

salad fork

main-course fork

napkin

dinner plate

dinner knife

soup spoon

Flatware/Silverware

blade

handle

tang

prongs/tines

bowl

Stemware

rim/lip

head

bowl

stem

foot

Dessert Setting

Among other plates used for serving dessert and sweets are multi-tiered *terrace servers*, *serving trays*, *cake plates*, *fruit bowls* called *center-pieces*, and *compotes*. After-dinner drinks are often poured from ornamental glass bottles called *decanters*.

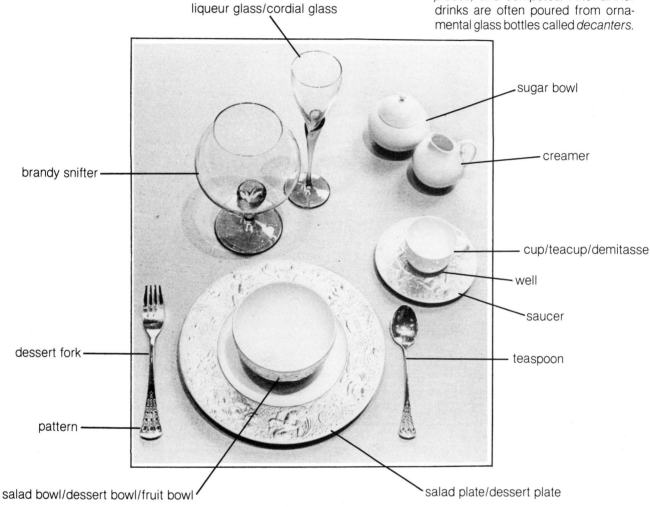

liqueur glass/cordial glass

sugar bowl

creamer

brandy snifter

cup/teacup/demitasse

well

saucer

dessert fork

teaspoon

pattern

salad bowl/dessert bowl/fruit bowl

salad plate/dessert plate

Chafing Dish

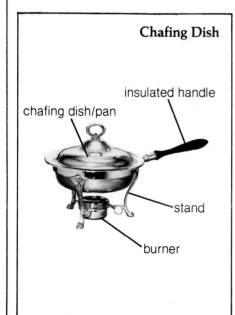

chafing dish/pan

insulated handle

stand

burner

Tea Set / Tea Service and Kettle

spout

handle

lid/cover

coffeepot

water kettle

burner

teapot

serving tray

creamer

sugar bowl

Dining Room

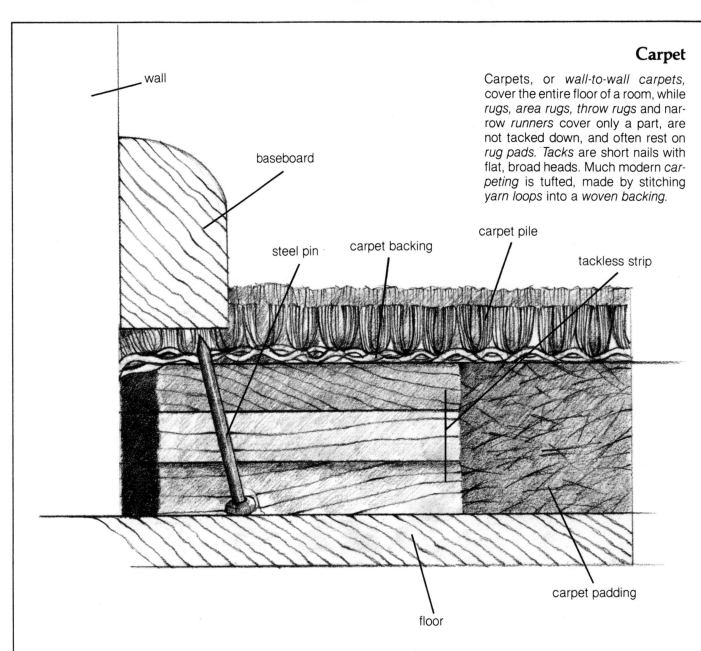

Carpet

Carpets, or *wall-to-wall carpets,* cover the entire floor of a room, while *rugs, area rugs, throw rugs* and narrow *runners* cover only a part, are not tacked down, and often rest on *rug pads. Tacks* are short nails with flat, broad heads. Much modern *carpeting* is tufted, made by stitching *yarn loops* into a *woven backing.*

wall

baseboard

steel pin

carpet backing

carpet pile

tackless strip

floor

carpet padding

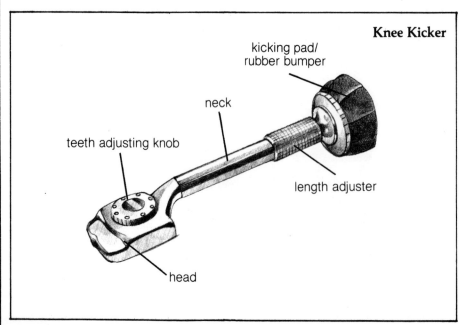

Knee Kicker

kicking pad/ rubber bumper

neck

teeth adjusting knob

length adjuster

head

Sink and Compactor

The hardware in a sink, the faucet handles and spout, are known as *fixtures*. Sink drains usually have perforated *drain baskets* which trap debris but allow water to pass through. Many baskets are two-piece units that form a watertight seal when the *inner basket* is twisted. *Instant hot-water devices* mounted on the spout of some sinks have a constantly heated coil that produces small amounts of hot water on demand.

faucet handle/
hot-water handle/
spigot

spray hose

escutcheon plate

spout/mixer

faucet handle/
cold-water handle/
spigot

soap dispenser

splashboard

aerator

lotion dispenser

counter/worktop

deck

rim

garbage-disposal
compartment

bowl/basin compartment

Kitchen Sink

Garbage Disposal/Trash Compactor

control panel

litter bin

lock

cabinet

trash drawer

trash basket

storage
compartment
cover

latch rod &
slide hook

bag-holding button

basket-release handle

leveling foot

Stove/Range

On an *electric range, heating elements* connected to *terminal blocks* are used in place of burner grates on a gas model. The permanent flame, used to ignite individual burners on a gas stove, is called a *pilot light.* Some models have an *electric pilot.* The walls of a *self-cleaning oven* are covered with a heat-sensitive porcelain enamel finish.

clocks/timers

vent/flue

oven light switch

griddle

accessory panel/ back guard/ backsplash

cook top

burner base

burner cap/head

burner control knobs

oven & broiler control knob

burner trim/ drip plate

burner grate

control panel·

griddle control knob

oven wall

rack guide

oven

oven rack/ oven shelves

door gasket

oven window

oven door

handle

hinge

Gas Range

Broiler Compartment

broiler pan

broiler door

grid

handle

Refrigerator

Some refrigerators, or *iceboxes*, have an *ice dispenser* in the freezer section. Others have *ice trays*. A *frostfree*, or *no-frost*, model does not require defrosting.

freezer compartment

thermostat and air control

hinge cover

egg rack

door gasket

juice rack

butter compartment

storage basket

handle

icemaker

door shelf/bin

slide-out shelf

ice dispenser

sealed vegetable compartment

freezer basket

storage

vegetable crisper/ fruit compartment

bulk storage basket

meat keeper

light switch

base grille/toeplate

Dishwasher

The *cycle-selector control panel* and *timer* are located on the outside of the door of this built-in dishwasher. The machine will operate only when the *external door switch,* or latch, is engaged.

cabinet

door gasket

china guard

tub

lower spray arm

heating element

fill unit float

strainer

door

latch

upper rack track

upper rack

rack partition

upper spray arm

air inlet cap

lower rack track

pump

detergent dispenser

Openers

With manual openers, the can rim is held between a *cutting blade* and a *turning gear,* with pressure applied by squeezing two *handles* and the can rotated with a winged *key.* The blade and handle device used by military personnel to open food ration cans is called a *"John Wayne."* The corkscrew shown below is used by *sommeliers,* or *wine stewards.*

cutting lever

blade shaft

cutting blade/plow

pivot pin

magnetic lid lifter

drive wheel

nameplate

shaft

front housing

rear housing

release knob

motor housing

can ledge

Electric Can Opener

Corkscrew

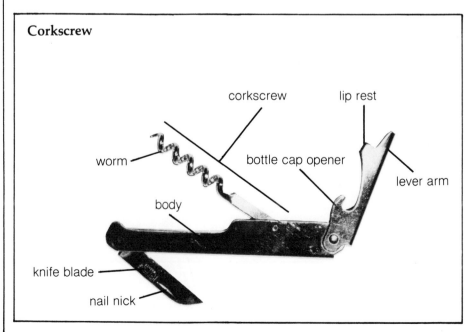

corkscrew

lip rest

worm

bottle cap opener

lever arm

body

knife blade

nail nick

"Church Key"/Can Piercer

can piercer/
can punch

lance-form

handle

lid lifter/
crown cap opener/
bottle cap opener

hanging ring

Coffee Makers

Coffee is *brewed* by passing boiling water through *ground coffee* beans. *Espresso* is brewed by forcing steam through roasted beans. *Cappuccino* consists of espresso and steamed milk.

brew control

fill opening

filter basket

lid

water reservoir

handle

brew starter/automatic timer

carafe/decanter

on-off switch

warming unit/hot plate

indicator light/signal light

cup level scale

Drip Coffee Maker

Percolator

dome

spout

lid

pot/body

brewing & warming element

plug outlet

brew selector

Brewing Basket

cool-tip

cover/perforated spreader

basket

stem/pump

base

Infusion Maker

knob/plunger

lip/spout

rod

frame

beaker/carafe/jug

filter assembly

Many toasters have removable *crumb trays*. The heating elements in toasters are flat *nichrome wires*. Toasters have either a spring-and-cylinder *dash-pot* or a simple spring device to pop toast up once it is browned. Toaster ovens have removable *baking trays*.

toast wells/bread slots

carriage/bread rack

bread guides

lift knob

front panel

keeper/lift lock

selection plate

housing/shell

toasting control knob

foot

Toaster

Toaster Oven

shell

rack/tray

door

temperature dial

toast color selector

temperature knob

indicator light

on-off switch

cord strain reliever

foot

crumb tray

Food Processor

Food processors have interchange-able accessories such as *mixing blades, slicing discs* and *shredding discs.*

pusher

feed tube

cover

work bowl

handle

steel blade

Cuisinart
FOOD PROCESSOR
Caution

ON   PULSE/OFF

motor housing base

control switch

rubber foot

Blender

pouring lip

feeder cap

cover

handle

container

container bottom

motor base ring

motor base

speed control buttons

Juicers

The soft mass of *tissue* remaining after the *juice*, or *liquid*, has been extracted from a piece of fruit or vegetable is called the *pulp*.

spring clip

hex nut

bowl

base top

sidearm

motor base housing

spout

cord

cover/lid

foot

plunger

cutter blade

spring clutch nut

strainer basket

Fruit and Vegetable Juice Extractor

push knob

Automatic Citrus Juicer

Manual Citrus Juicer

reamer

bowl

handle

gear bracket

strainer

pressure cup

reamer

column

spout

strainer cone

funnel bracket

base

drip cup/ juice collector cup

base

bumper

cup support

Kitchen

Knife

The part of a knife blade that extends into the handle is called the *tang,* and the blade's formation is known as the *grind.* In a *flat grind,* the sides of the blade are smooth. In a *hollow grind* there is a marked curve or bevel along the length of the blade.

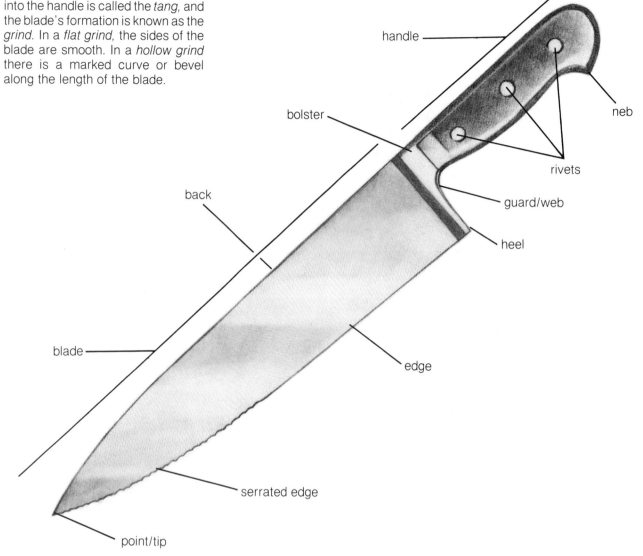

handle

neb

bolster

rivets

back

guard/web

heel

blade

edge

serrated edge

point/tip

Peeler

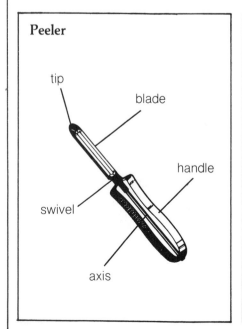

tip

blade

handle

swivel

axis

Sharpening Steel

tip/point

sharpening surface/ honing surface

handle

guard

rivets

Cheese Plane/Cheese Slicer

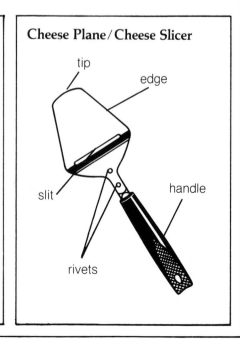

tip

edge

slit

handle

rivets

Pots and Pans

Pots and pans are often described by their function—for example, a *boiler* or *steamer*. *Crockpots* are pots made of earthenware. *Casseroles* are earthenware, glass or cast-iron pots in which food can be both baked and served. A *pipkin* is a small saucepan with a long handle used to melt butter.

knob

cover/lid

handle

Stock Pot/Stew Pot

lift-out stem

perforated panel

Steamer Basket

rim

leg/foot

side

Saucepan

tang

bottom

hanging ring

handle

Skillet/Frying Pan

Electric Wok

knob

dome cover/lid

tempura rack

handle

bowl/wok

feet

heat-control dial

plug

cooking chopsticks

Pressure Cooker

pressure regulator

air vent/cover lock

vent pipe

overpressure plug

body handle

cover handle

Mixing and Measuring Tools

In addition to the *meat*, or *rapid-response thermometer*, seen here, well-equipped kitchens have *oven* and *freezer thermometers, deep-frying thermometers, scales* and *funnels*.

egg beater/rotary beater

mixing bowls

scoops

whisk

kitchen timer

liquid measuring cup

meat thermometer

measuring spoons

dry measuring cups

Preparation Utensils

Additional preparation implements include *molding scoops*, for soft foods, wooden *spaghetti spoons* with long *prongs* to wrap pasta and lift it from boiling water, *basting ladles* with an egg-shaped *bowl* for easy pouring, and cylindrical one-piece *pastry pins*.

skimmer

slotted lifter/ drainer

draining spoon

lifter

spatula/ pancake turner

kitchen spoon

ladle

pot fork/ two-pronged fork

wooden spoon/ tasting spoon

spaghetti tongs

tongs

potato masher

ice cream scoop

grease skimming brush/ basting brush

skewers

rolling pin

pastry brush

icing syringe

icing nozzles/tubes/tips

Strainers and Drainers

Clean dishes, vegetables and fruits may be left on a *draining rack,* or *dish rack,* to dry. *Cooling racks* are used in conjunction with baked foods. A *sieve* has a mesh bottom for straining. A *food mill,* or *food foley,* is a heavy colander through which food is pressed by means of a flat *plate* attached to a *rotating handle.*

colander

strainer

sifter

tea ball/ tea infuser

tea and coffee strainer

deep frying basket

lettuce dryer/salad shaker

dredger/sugar and flour shaker

Cutters, Grinders and Graters

A *potato peeler* has a swivel blade for following contours and a sharp tip for gouging. Hand-cranked *meat grinders* chop meats and other foods. A *zester* is a tool that shaves the thin surface off fruits.

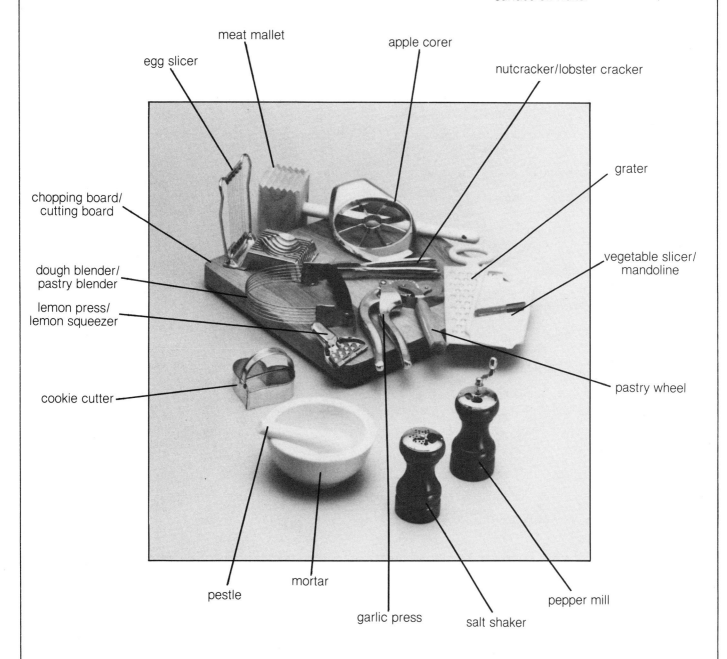

egg slicer

meat mallet

apple corer

nutcracker/lobster cracker

grater

chopping board/ cutting board

dough blender/ pastry blender

lemon press/ lemon squeezer

vegetable slicer/ mandoline

cookie cutter

pastry wheel

pestle

mortar

garlic press

salt shaker

pepper mill

Raw Ingredients

On *lettuce*, the entire mass of leaves is called the *head*, while the center leaves are the *heart*. A small slice of meat is a *collop*. A *peppercorn* is a dried berry of black pepper.

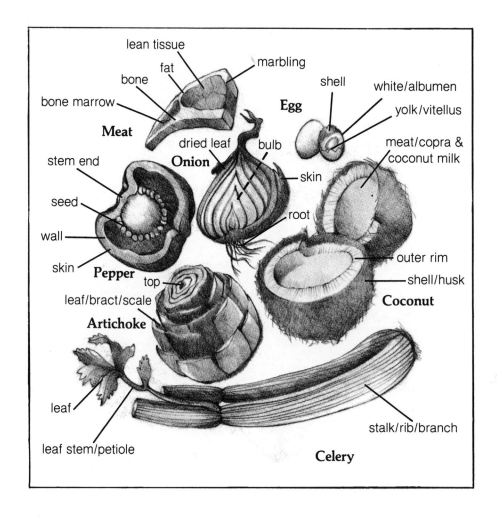

Prepared Foods

Appetizers, or *hors d'oeuvres,* are served before the main *course,* or *entree.* An ingredient, such as a *condiment, spice* or *herb,* added to food for the savor it imparts, is *seasoning.* Cheese is made by separating the *curd,* milk solids, from the *whey,* milk liquids. *Crumb* refers to both the soft inner portion of bread and any tiny piece that flakes off the loaf or a slice.

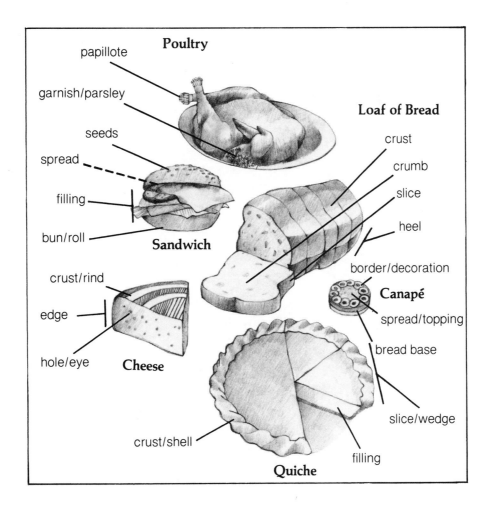

Poultry

papillote

garnish/parsley

seeds

spread

filling

bun/roll

Sandwich

crust/rind

edge

hole/eye

Cheese

Loaf of Bread

crust

crumb

slice

heel

border/decoration

Canapé

spread/topping

bread base

slice/wedge

filling

crust/shell

Quiche

Kitchen

Desserts

Baked desserts, or *sweet goods,* made of dough or having a crust made of enriched dough, such as *pies,* tarts and *turnovers,* are *pastries.* A *parfait* is similar to a sundae but may have layers of fruit and be frozen.

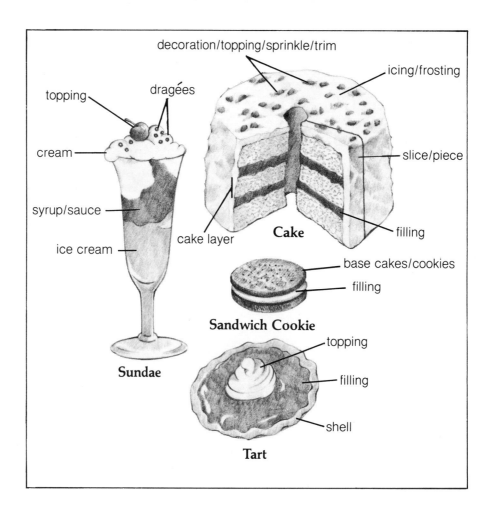

Snack Foods

Ice cream scoops are also put in flat-bottomed *wafer cones* and topped with other *fixings,* including *nuts* and *cherries.* When ice cream melts and drips down the cone, it forms *lickings.* The part of a hot dog roll that remains attached after the roll is sliced is the *hinge. Smoked sausages* are larger than franks and often include additional *seasonings.* Among other pizza toppings are *anchovies, extra cheese, pepperoni* and *onions.*

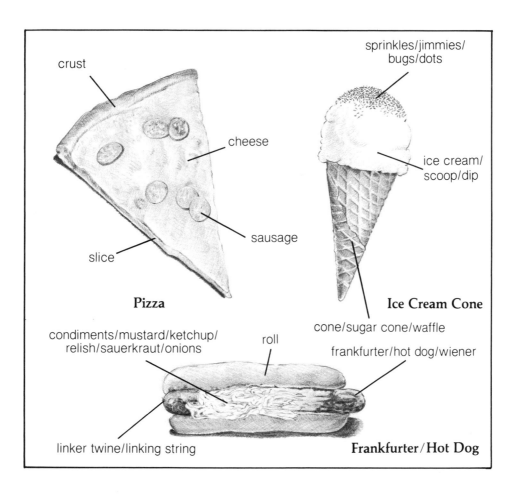

crust

cheese

sausage

slice

Pizza

sprinkles/jimmies/ bugs/dots

ice cream/ scoop/dip

Ice Cream Cone

cone/sugar cone/waffle

condiments/mustard/ketchup/ relish/sauerkraut/onions

roll

frankfurter/hot dog/wiener

linker twine/linking string

Frankfurter/Hot Dog

Kitchen

Containers

Most baskets are made by weaving individual *strands* or *rods* in front of one *stake* of the *frame* and behind the next. Some baskets have a border, or *foot,* on the bottom, just above the *base,* as well as a *cover,* or *lid,* which often rests on an inside *ledge.* A small, oblong veneer basket with rounded ends, the kind used for mushrooms, is a *climax basket,* and a little wooden paillike container with one stave extending up for a handle is a *piggin.*

serrated edge

twisted handle

patch

face

body

bellows

Paper Bag

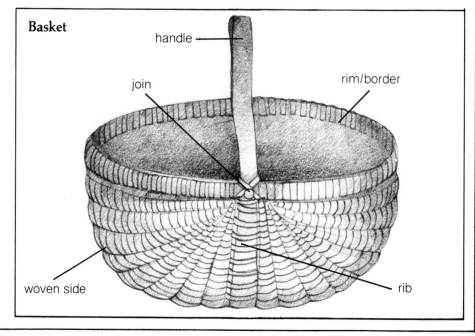

Basket

handle

join

rim/border

woven side

rib

Containers

The empty space inside a bottle, between the liquid and the top, is *ullage*. The wire arrangement covering the cork of a champagne bottle is called a *coiffe* if the bottle is from the Champagne region, a *wire hood* if it is domestic. Some barrels and *kegs* have a *taphole* in the top and a *bunghole* in the side. Large barrels are called *hogsheads* or *puncheons*.

mouth

cork

muzzle

lip

neck

capsule

shoulder

kick/punt

Bottle

saddle head

piston

container cap

accumulator

inductor/dip tube

Dispenser

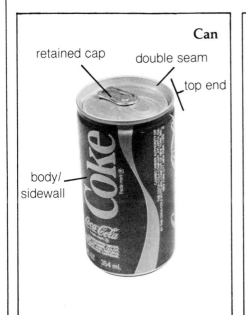

Can

retained cap

double seam

top end

body/ sidewall

Barrel/Cask

staves

chime

head

bottom

chime hoop

quarter hoop

Kitchen

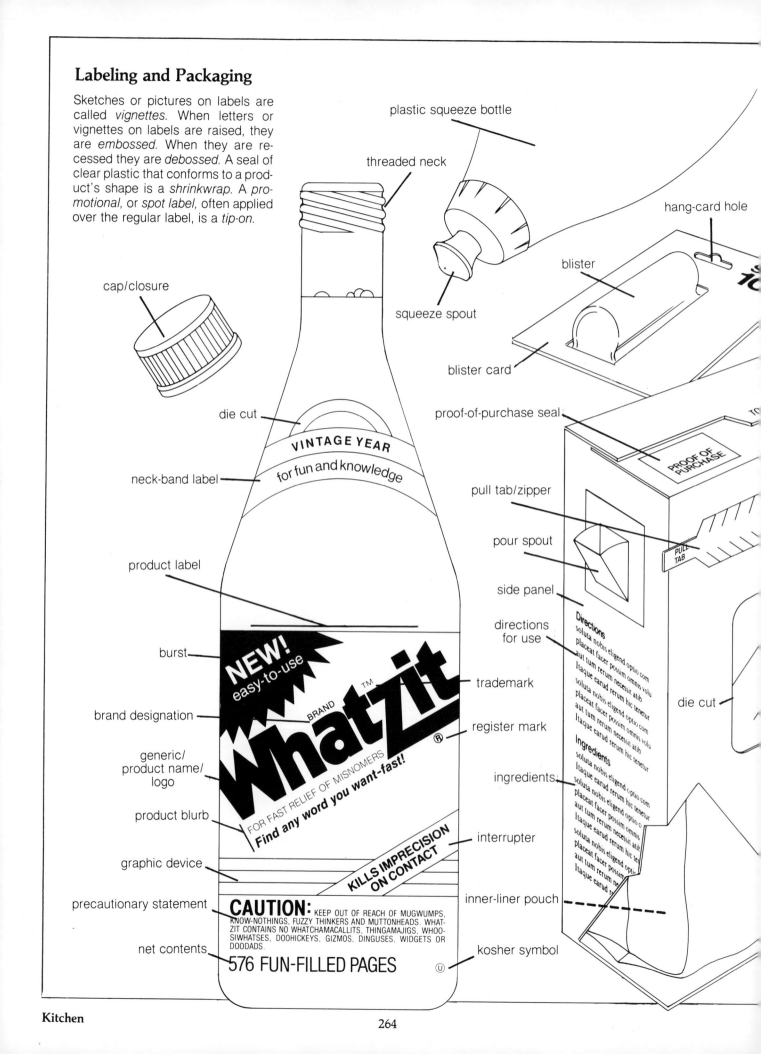

Labeling and Packaging

Sketches or pictures on labels are called *vignettes*. When letters or vignettes on labels are raised, they are *embossed*. When they are recessed they are *debossed*. A seal of clear plastic that conforms to a product's shape is a *shrinkwrap*. A *promotional*, or *spot label*, often applied over the regular label, is a *tip-on*.

plastic squeeze bottle

threaded neck

hang-card hole

blister

squeeze spout

cap/closure

blister card

proof-of-purchase seal

die cut

VINTAGE YEAR
for fun and knowledge

neck-band label

pull tab/zipper

pour spout

product label

side panel

directions for use

NEW! easy-to-use

BRAND

Whatzit ™

trademark

burst

register mark ®

brand designation

FOR FAST RELIEF OF MISNOMERS

generic/ product name/ logo

Find any word you want–fast!

ingredients

product blurb

KILLS IMPRECISION ON CONTACT

interrupter

graphic device

precautionary statement

inner-liner pouch

CAUTION: KEEP OUT OF REACH OF MUGWUMPS, KNOW-NOTHINGS, FUZZY THINKERS AND MUTTONHEADS. WHATZIT CONTAINS NO WHATCHAMACALLITS, THINGAMAJIGS, WHOOSIWHATSES, DOOHICKEYS, GIZMOS, DINGUSES, WIDGETS OR DOODADS.

net contents

576 FUN-FILLED PAGES

kosher symbol

Ⓤ

Directions

Ingredients

die cut

PROOF OF PURCHASE

PULL TAB

twist-off cap

credit line —————— **SCHECHTER**GROUP
descriptor ————— **Design for Marketing**

plasti-shield

corporate logo

tuck flap

ents-off corner mark

tuck flap

price spot | perforation

heat seal

foil pouch

dust flap

folding box

closure

foil bundling

tear tape

cautionary statement

Warning The Surgeon General Has Determined That Cigarette Smoking Is Dangerous to Your Health

see-through window

cello wrap

poly bag

Free Offer

0 12300 11113

deal patch

fin-seal wrap

mortise

Universal Product
Code symbol

twist tie

Bed and Bedding

A bedstead or *bed frame* consists of *side rails,* or *bedrails,* which connect the headboard to the *footboard.* A *twin bed* is a single bed, or one of a matching pair or beds, while a *double bed* is large enough to sleep two adults. A *comforter* is a small, thick quilt, while a *throw* is a bedspread with a short *side drop* rather than long *skirts.*

finial

flame

urn

canopy

head post

headboard

foot post

draperies/side curtains

pillows

quilt

foot

dust ruffle

Four-Poster / Canopy Bed

quilt

bedcover/bedspread

blanket

mattress cover/
bed pad

top sheet

anchor/
elastic band

bottom sheet/
fitted sheet

mattress

frame/
bedstead

welting/
cording

caster

binding

box spring/inner spring

Bedroom

Dressers

A dresser without the drawers in it is called the *main body,* or *carcass.* The thin plywood sheets between drawers, to keep *drawer cases* rigid, are *dust panels.* An *armoire,* or *wardrobe,* is a tall, movable closet in which to hang clothes. A *chiffonier* is a high, narrow chest of drawers.

finial

mirror frame

pivot

ornament

swing mirror/ dressing glass/ toilet mirror

jewel drawers

drawer

knobs/pulls

pedestal

tabletop

center drawer

kneehole

base

Dressing Table / Vanity

Bureau / Chest of Drawers

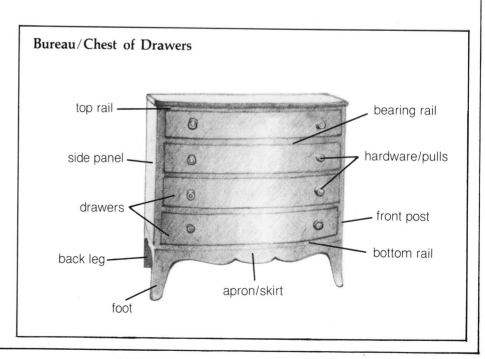

top rail

bearing rail

side panel

hardware/pulls

drawers

front post

back leg

bottom rail

apron/skirt

foot

Faucet and Sink

Some basins have *rubber plug* and *chain stoppers* to hold water, and *splash rims* or *lips* to prevent water from overflowing.

handle

spindle/stem

packing nut/bonnet

packing

washer

valve stem

stem washer

faucet body

set screw

valve seat

spout/nozzle

Faucet/Spigot/Tap/Bibcock

Sink Drain

tailpiece

slip nuts

wall flange

trap

cleanout plug/trap plug

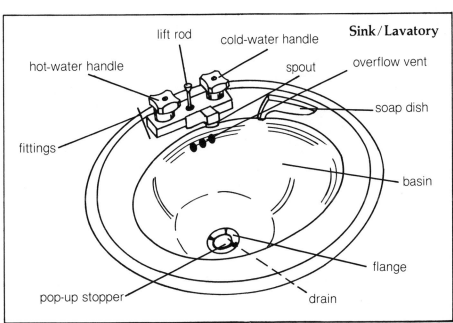

Sink/Lavatory

lift rod

cold-water handle

hot-water handle

spout

overflow vent

soap dish

fittings

basin

pop-up stopper

flange

drain

Bathroom

Bath and Shower

Waterproof *shower curtains* or sliding glass *doors* enclose baths and showers and smaller *shower stalls.* Hand-held shower heads, *massagers,* or *spray heads* are popular shower accessories. Some *tubs* have *whirlpool jets* to circulate water. Floors of tubs and showers may have *non-skid,* or *non-slip,strips.*

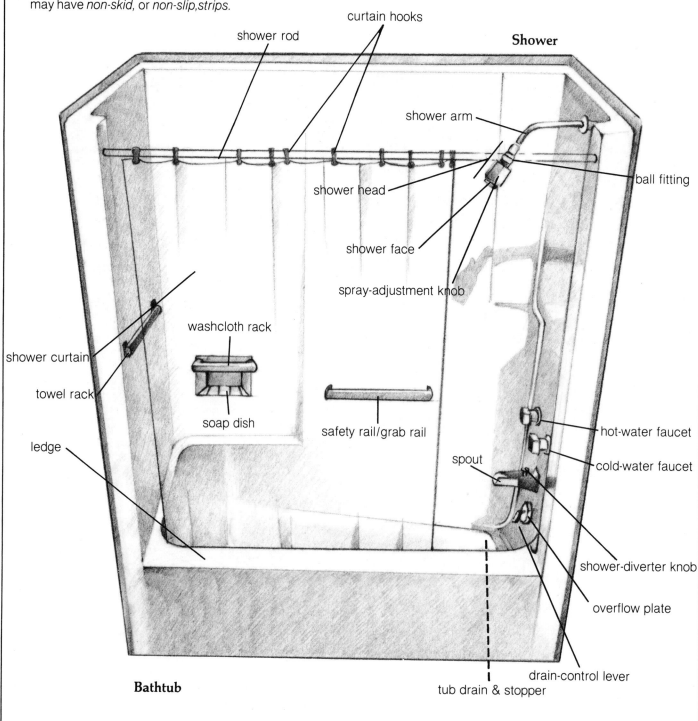

curtain hooks

shower rod

Shower

shower arm

ball fitting

shower head

shower face

spray-adjustment knob

shower curtain

washcloth rack

towel rack

soap dish

safety rail/grab rail

ledge

spout

hot-water faucet

cold-water faucet

shower-diverter knob

overflow plate

drain-control lever

Bathtub

tub drain & stopper

Toilet

This is a standard ball-float toilet. The seat is held in place by *posts* and rests on *bumpers*.

flush/trip handle

filler tube

float arm

ball-cock assembly

tank lid

tank

float ball

lift wires

guide arm

tank ball

valve seat

cover

inlet tube

overflow tube

shutoff valve

seat

rim

bowl

bolt cap

Bathroom

Desk

A *rolltop* or *cylinder desk* has a *sliding cover* that covers the desk's *writing area* when not in use. In *slant-front, falling-front* or *drop-lid desks,* the *front* flips down to offer a writing area which is supported by two *slide-out supports.* Some modern office desks have *elevator platforms* that can be raised and locked in place to hold a business machine, or lowered and closed behind a *cabinet door.*

work surface/top

center drawer

box drawer

lock

writing slide/
reference slide

return top

return section

left pedestal

leg

floor glide

file drawer/
letter drawer

modesty panel

kneeholes

stationery rack

secretarial pedestal

Desktop Equipment

Strips of staples are loaded into a stapler's *channel*. Pencils are sharpened in a *carrier* which holds two grooved cylinders called *cutters*. A paper clip is a piece of bessemer stock wire given three *twists*.

plastic cap

metal cap

hinge pin

case assembly

follow spring

staples

front foot

anvil

magazine & tie plate assembly

base

rail

follow block

rear foot

Stapler

Paper Clip/Gem Clip

#2 bend

#1 leg

#2 leg

#3 leg

#4 leg

#1 bend

#3 bend

Pencil Sharpener

guide spring

aperture

guide

crank/handle

knob

receptacle

stand

base/vacuum mount

actuating lever knob

actuating lever

Sewing Machine

The standard presser foot can be replaced by a variety of special attachments, including a *zipper foot, hemmer foot* and *roller foot.* Some machines have a *slide plate* as well as a needle plate that opens to provide access to the bobbin case.

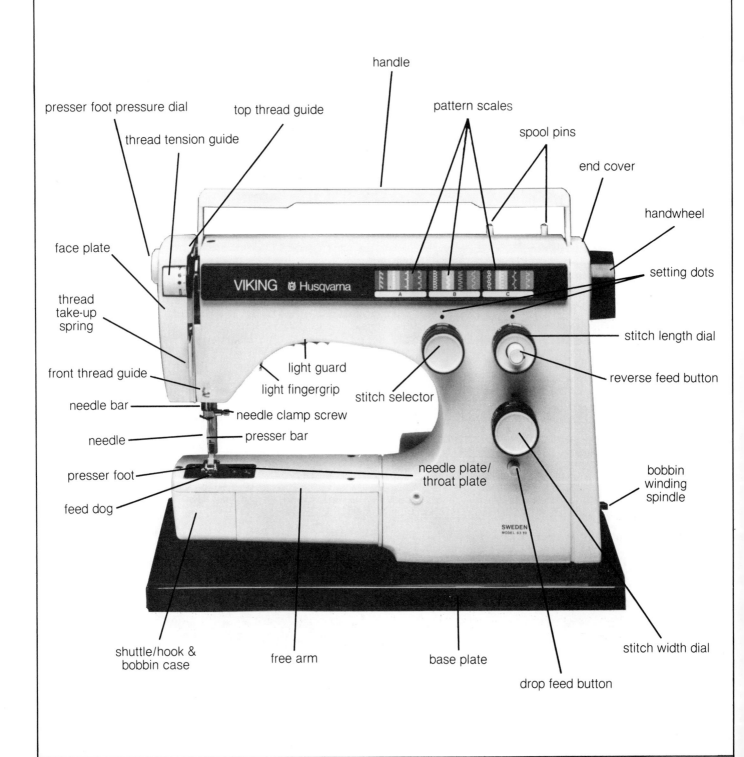

handle

pattern scales

spool pins

end cover

handwheel

presser foot pressure dial

top thread guide

thread tension guide

setting dots

face plate

stitch length dial

thread take-up spring

reverse feed button

light guard

front thread guide

light fingergrip

stitch selector

needle bar

needle clamp screw

needle

presser bar

presser foot

needle plate/ throat plate

bobbin winding spindle

feed dog

shuttle/hook & bobbin case

free arm

base plate

stitch width dial

drop feed button

VIKING Husqvarna

SWEDEN MODEL 63 10

Iron

The *steam-and-dry iron,* or *flatiron,* shown here has *steam vents,* or *steam ports,* in the soleplate. Some irons have *front spray nozzles* as well.

handle

on-off steam button

thumb rest

cord

filling port/
water fill opening

reversible
cord
assembly

temperature guide plate

temperature control lever

heel rest

shell

water tank/reservoir

button nook

soleplate

saddle plate/
fabric temperature guide

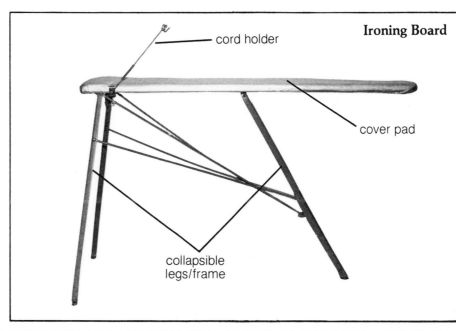

Ironing Board

cord holder

cover pad

collapsible
legs/frame

Playroom/Utility Room

Washing and Drying

Formerly, clothes were washed in a *washtub* with a *scrubboard* and *wringer* before being hung out to dry on *clotheslines,* or *washlines,* with clothespins. Wash-and-wear shirts are still air-dried on hangers. In automatic *top-loading washing machines* and *front-loading washers,* the basket, which has *drain holes* inside it, is contained within a metal *tub.* Some washers and dryers have a *window* in the *door* and a *tub light.*

gripping hole

spring slot

claw end

pinwood

spring

handle

Clothespin

Washing Machine

temperature selector

cycle selector

load-size selector

lid

tub ring and filter/ splash guard

liquid-bleach dispenser

cabinet

basket

lint filter

agitator cap

agitator

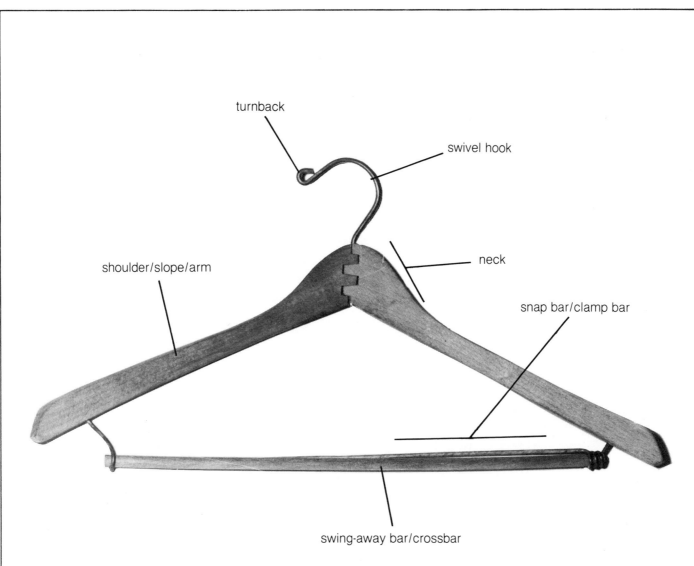

turnback

swivel hook

shoulder/slope/arm

neck

snap bar/clamp bar

swing-away bar/crossbar

Suit Hanger

temperature selector

starting switch

exhaust duct

door latch

drum

lint trap/filter

Dryer

control panel

cycle selector/
timer

door

277   **Playroom/Utility Room**

Household Cleaning Equipment

A conventional mop has absorbent *strands* rather than a sponge. An *electric broom* is a lightweight vacuum cleaner on a handle. A *carpet sweeper* contains two revolving brushes in a box at the end of a pushing handle.

sleeve

brace

rail

toggle link

handle

spring

bridge & socket assembly

presser plate

sponge/mophead

Sponge Mop

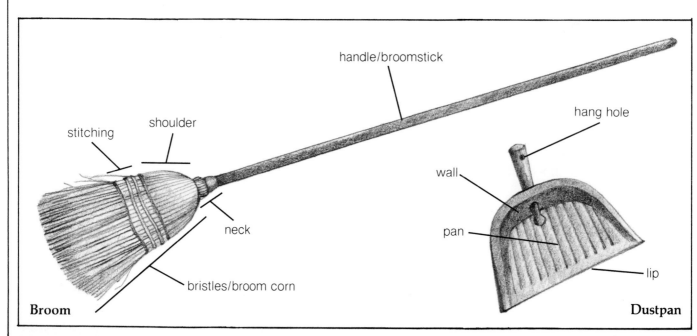

handle/broomstick

shoulder

hang hole

stitching

wall

neck

pan

bristles/broom corn

lip

Broom

Dustpan

Vacuum Cleaner

In an *upright vacuum cleaner,* shown here, *spiral brushes* under the hood and *beater bars* stir up dust and dirt. A *fan* blows these into a *disposable bag.* In a *cylinder model,* all the cleaning components are mounted horizontally. Dirt is sucked directly from the *intake tube* into a *vacuum bag,* or *dust bag.*

handle grip

manual operation button

handle

dust bag jacket

motor housing

handle release pedal/ height adjustment pedal

nozzle adjustment lever

wheel

bumper/furniture guard

hood

Vacuum Cleaner

Attachments

multipurpose brush

extension wands

hose grip

hose

dusting brush

converter

furniture nozzle

crevice tool

hose connector/ collar

Firefighting Devices

Dry chemical extinguishers, containing chemicals and gas under pressure, are activated by squeezing or twisting the handle. *Soda-acid extinguishers,* inverted to mix the contents, produce a smothering *foam.*

pull-pin/locking pin

operating lever

handle

band

pressure gauge

discharge tube/hose

collar

instruction panel

shell/cylinder

horn

Fire Extinguisher

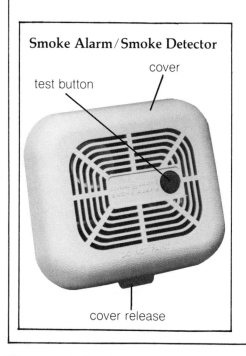

Smoke Alarm/Smoke Detector

cover

test button

cover release

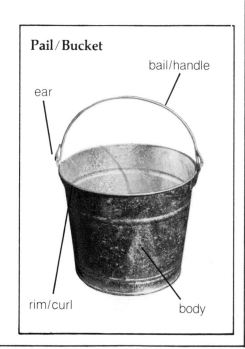

Pail/Bucket

bail/handle

ear

rim/curl

body

Luggage

The exterior parts of a *suitcase* or *bag* are identical to those of an *attaché* case. A suitcase that unfolds to be hung up is called a *garment bag*. Briefcases sometimes have zippered *file folders* or *portfolios* as well as paper storage *pockets*.

handle

identification tag

lock

shell

frame

rivet

foot

beading

Attaché Case/Briefcase

Overnight Bag

curtain fasteners

curtain

cross straps

Cosmetic Case

adjustable mirror

cosmetic tray

Two-Suiter

tie holder

Children's Gear

Modern strollers have largely replaced more elaborate *baby carriages,* or *perambulators.* A portable, basketlike infant bed, often with a *hood* at one end, is called a *bassinet.* An indoor *baby chair,* or *high chair,* has long legs, a *footrest* and a *serving tray.*

handle grip

canopy

handle

canopy support

backrest

backrest adjustment lever

wing

seat

frame

rear axle

footrest

swivel fork

wheel pin

swivel wheel holder

brake

wheel

Stroller

Car Seat

shoulder strap

top pad

safety shield

crotch strap

adjustment lever

recliner stand

Playpen

padded top rail

handle

hinge cover

drop rail lock

mesh net

padded side leg

mattress pad

floor support

closure

floorboard

Backyard Equipment

Other popular backyard and *playground* equipment includes *seesaws,* or *teeter-totters; jungle gyms,* or *monkey bars; climbing nets; overhead ladders* and *sandboxes.*

platform tower

safety guardrail

welded channel

top rail/tubing

swing hanger

end assembly

platform

safety guardrail

ladder

swing chain

chinning bar/
leg support

slide bed

side rail

tubing

exit angle

glider seat

foot rest

protective
chain cover

swing seat

leg

slide support

Slide/Sliding Pond

Glider

Swing

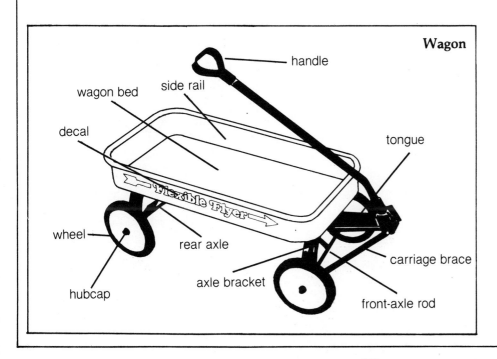

Wagon

handle

side rail

wagon bed

decal

tongue

wheel

rear axle

carriage brace

hubcap

axle bracket

front-axle rod

Patio Accessories

On regular grills and *braziers,* food is cooked over *charcoal briquettes* resting in a *fire bowl,* whereas on gas and electric models food is grilled over *volcanic rock.* Other grills include *hibachis* and *kettle grills* featuring *damper controls, adjustable grills,* and *ash catchers.* On some outdoor lounges and *settees,* small springs, or *helicals,* connect the frame to metal supporting straps.

handle

lid

warming grid

cooking grid

cutting board

burners

towel bar

heat control

fuel gauge

electric starter

gas tank

Barbecue Grill / Gas Barbecue

Chaise Lounge

arm

back

pad/cushion

positioning ratchet

leg

strapping

frame

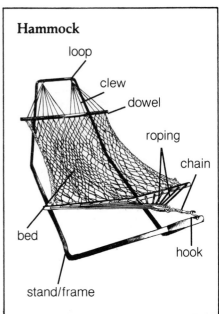

Hammock

loop

clew

dowel

roping

chain

bed

hook

stand/frame

Sports and Recreation

Emphasis in this section is given to major sports and forms of recreational activity which involve gear and equipment. Word and picture games, for example, have been omitted, since the nomenclature involved is so limited.

In order to enable the reader to find particular items quickly, recreational activities have been grouped in the following way: team sports, competitive sports, individual sports, equestrian sports, automobile racing, outdoor sports, bodybuilding, board games, and casino games.

Because playing areas involved in team and competitive sports are an integral part of the activity, fields, courts and rinks have been diagramed with all the vital areas, lines and demarcations identified.

And to show the parts of clothing and equipment used by players, real athletes rather than models have been photographed: batter Rod Carew, football running back Bruce Harper, basketball guard Mike Glenn, hockey defenseman Ken Morrow and goalie Billy Smith.

Trophy

ornament

ornament pedestal

panel

riser

base attachment

base

plate

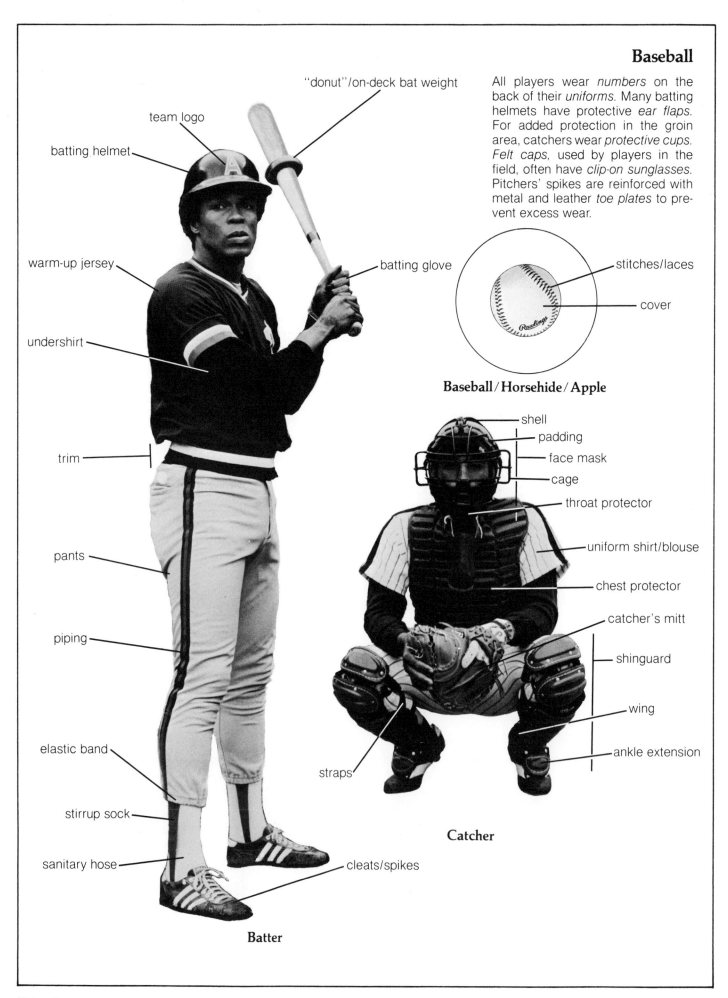

Baseball

"donut"/on-deck bat weight

team logo

batting helmet

All players wear *numbers* on the back of their *uniforms*. Many batting helmets have protective *ear flaps*. For added protection in the groin area, catchers wear *protective cups*. *Felt caps*, used by players in the field, often have *clip-on sunglasses*. Pitchers' spikes are reinforced with metal and leather *toe plates* to prevent excess wear.

warm-up jersey

batting glove

undershirt

stitches/laces

cover

Baseball/Horsehide/Apple

trim

shell

padding

face mask

cage

throat protector

pants

uniform shirt/blouse

chest protector

piping

catcher's mitt

shinguard

wing

elastic band

ankle extension

stirrup sock

straps

sanitary hose

cleats/spikes

Catcher

Batter

Baseball

Artificial turf has replaced natural *grass* in the outfield and certain portions of the infield in many *stadiums*, or *ballparks*.

fence/wall

foul pole

warning track

center field

right field

left field

outfield

infield

right-field foul line

fair territory

left-field foul line

shortstop area

second base/"keystone sack"

foul territory

third base/"hot corner"

first base

baseline/basepath

coaches' box

pitcher's mound

pitcher's rubber

batter's box

dugout/bench

home plate/"dish"

umpire's area

catcher's box

on-deck batter's circle

Baseball Field/Diamond

Bat

"meat"

label/trademark

signature

barrel

tape

handle

knob

Glove/Mitt

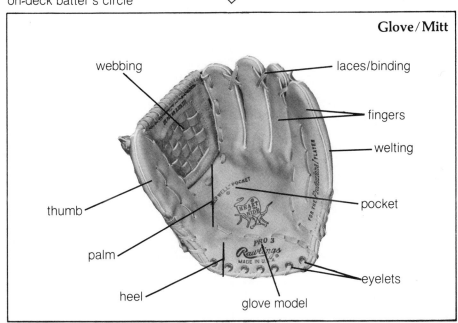

webbing

laces/binding

fingers

welting

thumb

pocket

palm

eyelets

heel

glove model

Team Sports

Football

Protective equipment worn on the upper body is covered with a *numbered jersey*. A *tear-away jersey* is loosely sewn and meant to rip apart when grabbed by an opponent. Helmets are manufactured with different *suspension systems*, some of which are air-inflated. Football covers have a rough *pebble finish* and an air-retaining *bladder* which is filled by inserting an *inflation needle* in the valve.

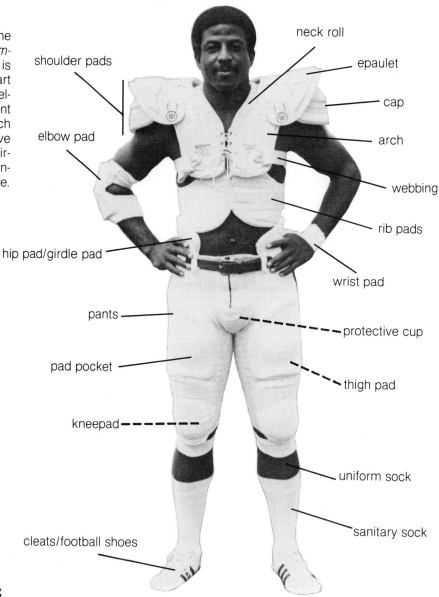

shoulder pads

neck roll

epaulet

cap

arch

webbing

rib pads

wrist pad

elbow pad

hip pad/girdle pad

pants

protective cup

pad pocket

thigh pad

kneepad

uniform sock

sanitary sock

cleats/football shoes

Uniform and Protective Padding

Football

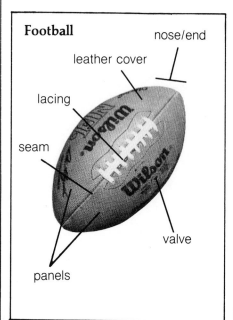

nose/end

leather cover

lacing

seam

valve

panels

Helmet

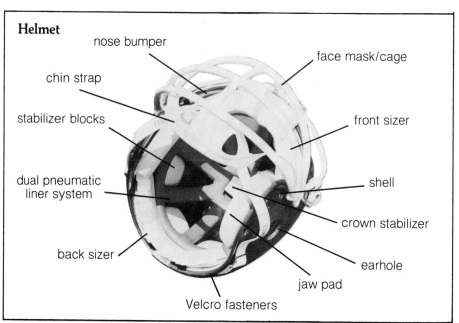

nose bumper

face mask/cage

chin strap

stabilizer blocks

front sizer

dual pneumatic liner system

shell

crown stabilizer

back sizer

earhole

jaw pad

Velcro fasteners

Football

A *down marker* is used to mark the exact location of the ball on the field between downs. The *flip chart* at the top of the down marker has *flip panels* to indicate what down is about to be played. The goalpost in college football has two support *standards* instead of a gooseneck, used in professional games. *Flags* are located at the junction of the goal line and sideline to mark in bounds. Small, rubber inverted V-shaped *yard markers* are placed at five-yard intervals along the sidelines.

3-yard line (college)

2-yard line (pro)

10-yard lines

inbound lines/ hash marks

50-yard line/midfield

yard lines

bench

sideline/out-of-bounds line

goal line

coffin corner

end zone

goalpost/uprights

end line

Football Field / Gridiron

Field Equipment

Goalpost / Uprights

fluorescent banner

panel assembly

upright

crossbar

Yards Marker / Sideline Chains

pole

10-yard chain

main standard/gooseneck

foot peg

safety padding

spike

Ice Hockey

Hockey players' pants are held up by *suspenders*. Socks are attached to a *garter belt*. The angle between the shaft of a hockey stick and the blade is called the *lie*. The game is played with a black vulcanized rubber *puck*. A blinking *red light* atop the goal judge's box indicates a goal.

helmet

crossbar

stick glove

body pad/ chest protector

face mask

catch glove

shoulder & arm protector

cuff

back pad

goalpost

net/cage

goal pad

goalkeeper's stick

goal line

heel

skate

Goal and Goalie/Goalkeeper/Goaler

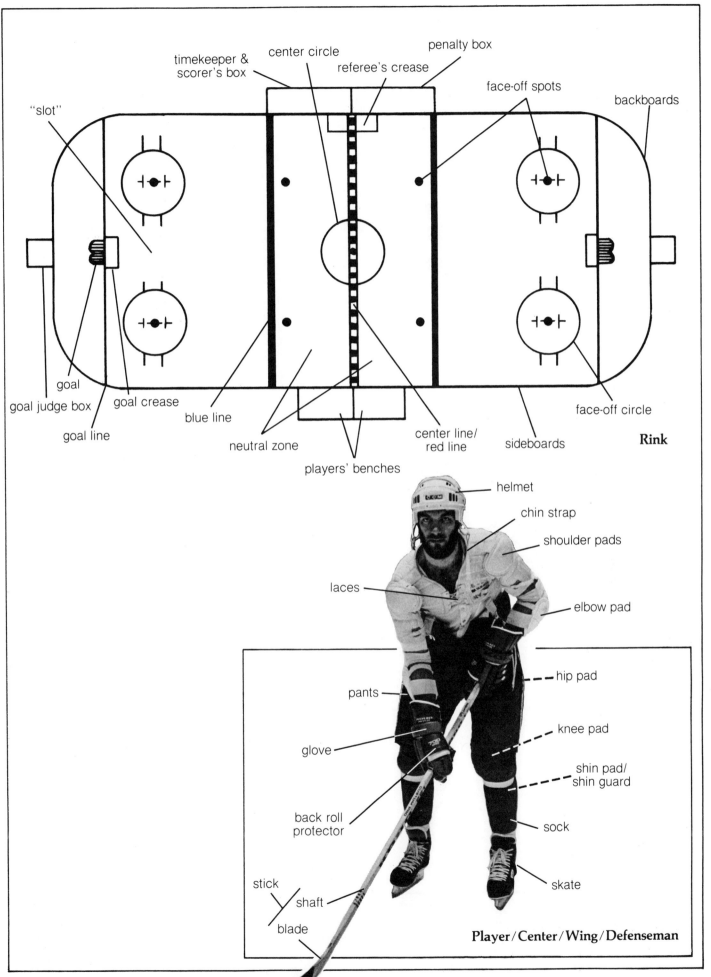

timekeeper & scorer's box

center circle

referee's crease

penalty box

face-off spots

backboards

"slot"

goal

goal judge box

goal crease

goal line

blue line

neutral zone

players' benches

center line/ red line

sideboards

face-off circle

Rink

helmet

chin strap

shoulder pads

laces

elbow pad

hip pad

pants

knee pad

glove

shin pad/ shin guard

sock

back roll protector

skate

stick

shaft

blade

Player/Center/Wing/Defenseman

Team Sports

Basketball

The offensive team advances from its own *backcourt* into the *forecourt*. The area at the top of the free-throw lane, usually patrolled by the *center* (as opposed to one of two *guards* or two *forwards*), is called the *pivot*. Many players wear *kneepads* and *elbow pads* for protection, and *warm-up suits* prior to games.

shot timer/
24-second clock

backboard

glass

rectangle

rim/hoop/ring

attachment loops

basket/hoop/goal

net

backplate

basketball

brace member

support unit

column/
upright/
stanchion

padded base

player's surname

number

jersey

GLEN
34

shorts

socks

sneakers

Backstop and Player

Court

sideline

bench

scorer's table

3-point line

center circle

lane space marks

end line

free-throw circle

basket

free-throw lane/key/
3-second lane

floor

midcourt line/
division line

restraining circle

foul line/
free-throw line

Soccer and Lacrosse

In soccer, or *association football*, players protect their legs with *shin-guards*. In lacrosse, players wear *helmets* and *face masks* for protection.

goal net

goal

flag

center circle

midfield line/halfway line

touch-line

penalty kick mark

penalty arc

penalty area

corner kick arc

goal line

goal area/crease

Soccer Field

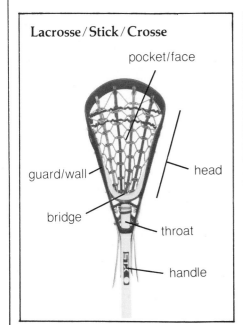

Lacrosse/Stick/Crosse

pocket/face

guard/wall

head

bridge

throat

handle

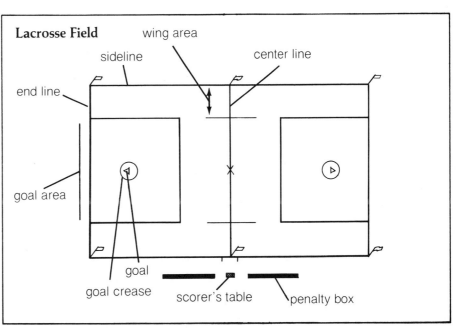

Lacrosse Field

wing area

sideline

center line

end line

goal area

goal

goal crease

scorer's table

penalty box

Team Sports

Track and Field

Track-and-field events take place on a *running track* and the enclosed *field* within. Besides *jumping events* and *throwing events*, there are *footraces*, including *walking races, hurdle races, steeplechase, relay races, medley relays, runs* and the *marathon*. The *decathlon* is a ten-event contest, while the *pentathlon* consists of five events.

long jump/
broad jump

triple jump/
hop, skip & jump

takeoff far

pole vault

landing pits

jumping pit

high
jump

throwing sector

scratch lines/
takeoff boards/
stamp boards

lanes

chute

staggered starting line
for distance events

safety cage

sector flag

hammer throw/discus

shot put

stopboard/toeboard

throwing circle

javelin

scratch line/foul line

runway/approach

finish line

Competitive Sports

Running Shoe

These *training shoes*, or *trainers*, are more durable than lighter-weight *racing flats*. Lightweight running shoes are worn by *joggers* or *distance runners* in long races such as *marathons*. *Track shoes*, shoes with *spikes*, are used for most track-and-field events.

tongue

eyelets

binding

heel patch/
Achilles' tendon pad

padding

eye stay

laces

vamp

toe box

trim

uppers

outsole

sole

manufacturer's ornament

midsole wedge

foxing

heel counter

point/tip

head

Tread

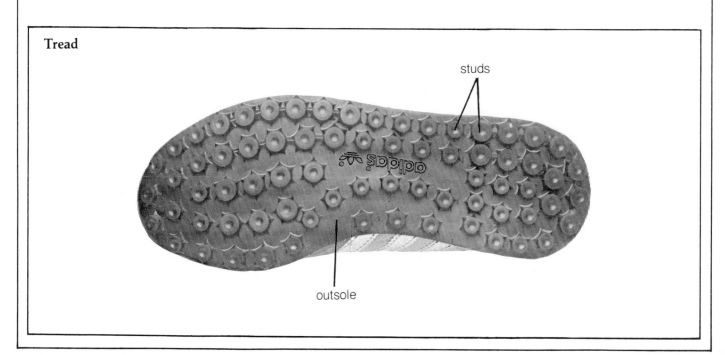

studs

outsole

Field Events Equipment

In addition to the equipment shown here, a round metal ball called a *shot put,* or *shot,* is also used in field events. Hammer throwers often wear *gloves* with padded palms.

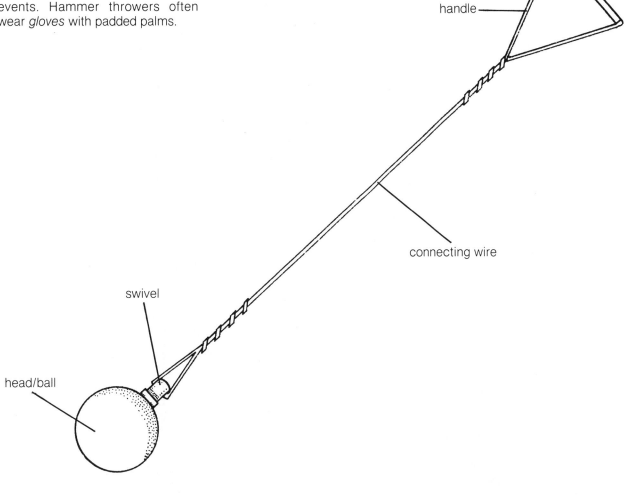

grip

handle

connecting wire

swivel

head/ball

Hammer

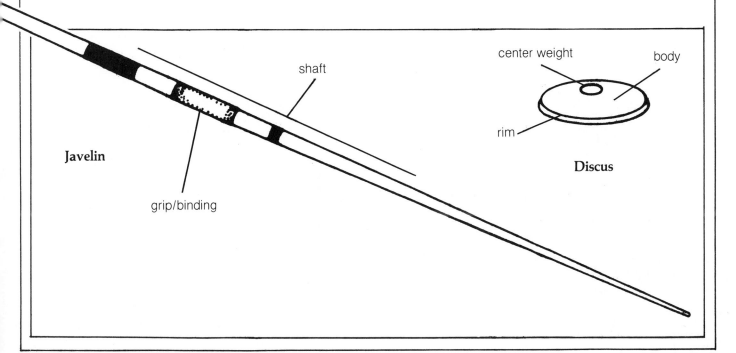

shaft

center weight

body

rim

Javelin

grip/binding

Discus

Hurdle

The height of hurdles can be adjusted for use in *high, intermediate* and *low hurdle* events. Base weights can also be adjusted to provide the proper *pull-over,* or *flipover,* the force required to knock them over. *Fixed hurdles* are used in a *steeplechase race,* an event that includes *water hazards.* Roller, or notched *lever locks* permit runners to adjust the slant on starting blocks, and a *plunger snap lock* allows them to position the blocks individually on the rail.

gatebar/top bar

gate upright

gate tube

plunger snap lock

wing nut & bolt

base upright

base weight

foot

Hurdle

Stopwatch

lanyard

bow

crown/start & stop button

reset button

minute hand

second bits

bezel

second hand

Starting Block/Blocks

pedal/block

face

rails

pin & cap/anchor

end piece

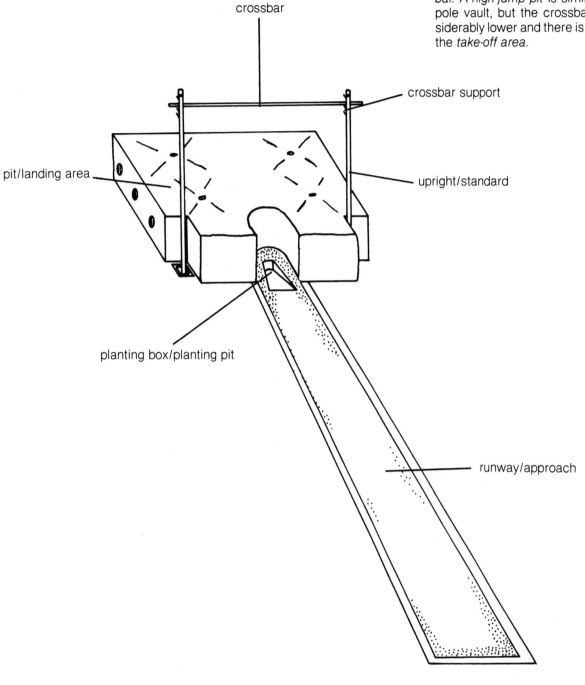

Pole Vault

The *fiberglass pole,* which replaced traditional *bamboo* and *metal poles,* enables a *vaulter* to catapult over the *bar.* A *high-jump pit* is similar to the pole vault, but the crossbar is considerably lower and there is no *box* in the *take-off area.*

crossbar

crossbar support

pit/landing area

upright/standard

planting box/planting pit

runway/approach

base

handgrip/binding

Pole

Competitive Sports

Gymnastics

Protective *landing mats* are placed around each piece of gymnastic equipment when it is in use. In addition, during practice sessions, assistants called *spotters* stand by to aid the *gymnast*. Gymnastic competition called *floor exercises* takes place on lined *floor exercise mats*.

bars

uprights

piston

lock

protection pad

leg leveler/base pad

base

leg

Parallel Bars

Horizontal Bar/High Bar

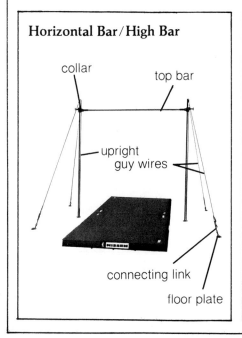

collar

top bar

upright
guy wires

connecting link

floor plate

Uneven Parallel Bars

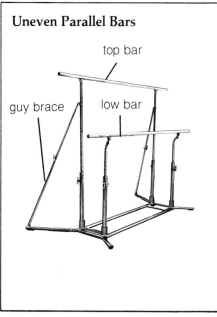

top bar

guy brace

low bar

Balance Beam

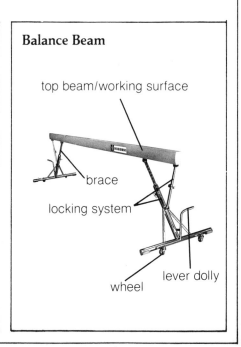

top beam/working surface

brace

locking system

wheel

lever dolly

Some pommel horses, or *side horses*, can be converted into *vaulting*, or *long*, *horses* by removing the pommels and plugging the holes they fit in. *Vaulting boards*, or *springboards*, are used by *vaulters* to gain height when mounting the apparatus.

pommel/handle

saddle

croup

neck

horse

NISSEN

piston

T-handle/lock

upright

base

pad

Pommel Horse

Stationary Rings

frame

swivel housing

suspension cable

guy wires

strap

ring

floor plate

Trampoline

Trampolining, trampoline tumbling, or *rebound tumbling* is performed on the canvas or elastic-webbing bed. Smaller *trampolets* are often used as *springboards* for mounting gymnastic apparatus.

bed/jumping bed

frame pad/safety pad

frame

leg

springs

Boxing

In addition to the *sparring,* or practice, equipment shown here, *boxers* use a *mouthpiece* or *mouthguard* for protection of teeth. A *bell* at *ringside* is used to indicate the beginning and end of each *round.* Boxers rest on *stools* placed in their corners by assistants, or *handlers,* between rounds. Corners not used by fighters during these periods are called *neutral corners.*

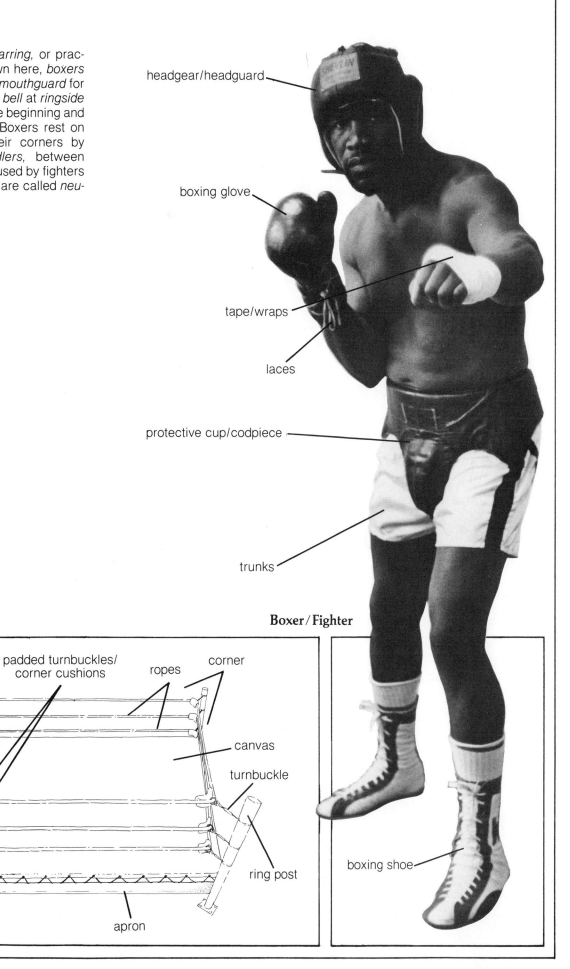

headgear/headguard

boxing glove

tape/wraps

laces

protective cup/codpiece

trunks

Boxer/Fighter

boxing shoe

Boxing Ring

padded turnbuckles/
corner cushions

ropes

corner

canvas

turnbuckle

ring post

apron

Competitive Sports

Golf

Clubs are numbered in order of increasing *loft,* the angle of the club-face from the vertical, with woods numbered from one to five and the irons numbered two through nine. A *golfer* may also carry a *pitching wedge,* a *sand wedge* and a putter. The spot where the ball lands after being hit is called the *lie.*

shaft

hosel

neck

head

screw

scoring lines

heel

sole

toe

face

Clubs

ball identification

dimples

tee

Ball

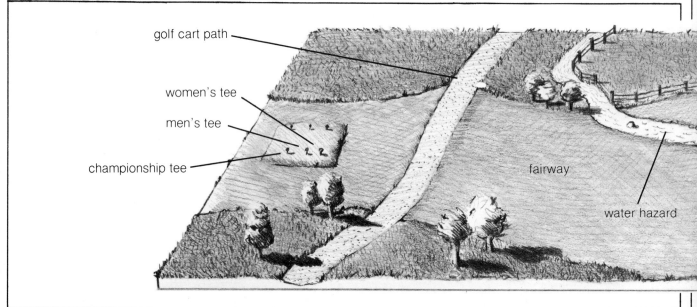

golf cart path

women's tee

men's tee

championship tee

fairway

water hazard

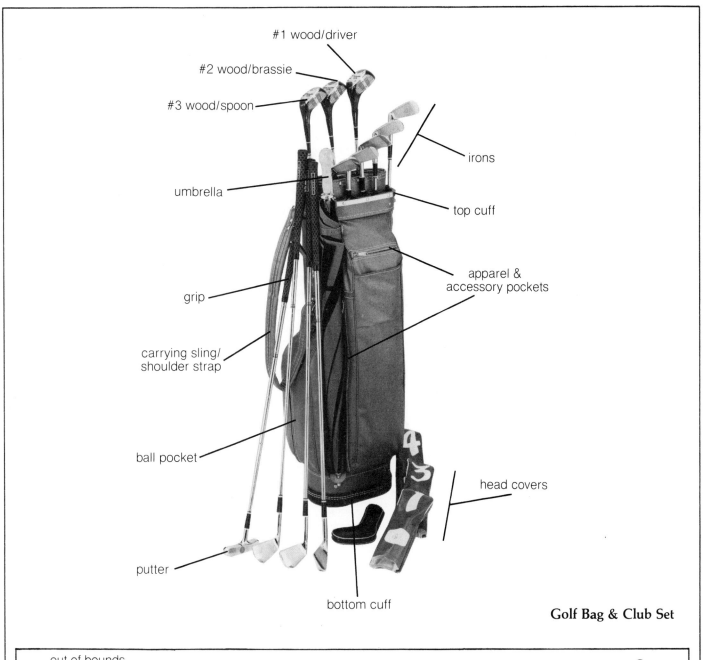

#1 wood/driver

#2 wood/brassie

#3 wood/spoon

irons

umbrella

top cuff

grip

apparel &
accessory pockets

carrying sling/
shoulder strap

ball pocket

head covers

putter

bottom cuff

Golf Bag & Club Set

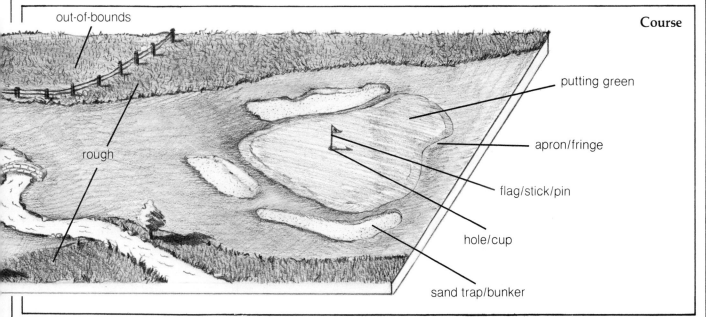

Course

out-of-bounds

putting green

apron/fringe

rough

flag/stick/pin

hole/cup

sand trap/bunker

305

Competitive Sports

Tennis

Some rackets have an interchange-able *handle,* or *pallet,* and a replace-able *throatpiece,* or *yoke.* The *"sweet spot"* is the prime hitting area of a racket *face.*

trim cord

crown

main strings

head

string holes

"sweet spot"

cross strings

throat

binding/trim tape

shoulder

handle

shaft

flake

grip

butt cap

heel

Racket

Court

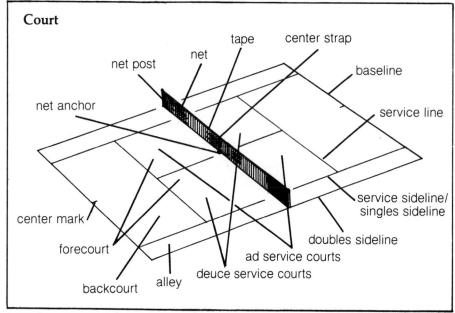

net post

net

tape

center strap

baseline

net anchor

service line

center mark

service sideline/
singles sideline

forecourt

doubles sideline

backcourt

alley

deuce service courts

ad service courts

Ball

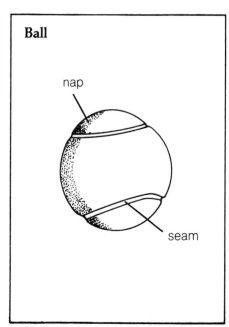

nap

seam

Handball and Squash Courts

The composite court shown here includes both handball and squash rackets terms. In each case, the court is entered through a small *door* in the *back wall.* In handball, players alternately hit a hard black *ball* with their hands, whereas in squash a soft rubber ball is hit with a *racket.*

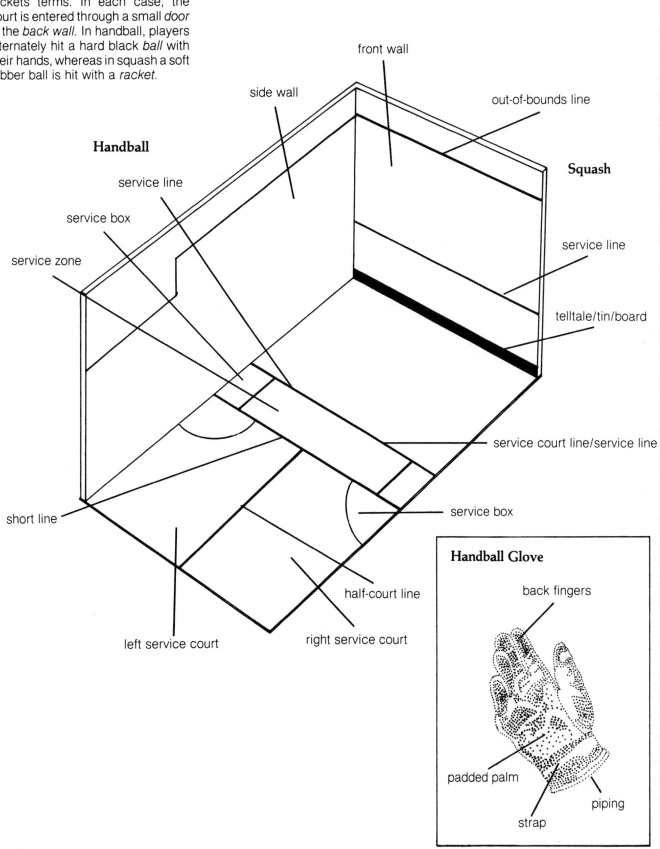

front wall

side wall

out-of-bounds line

Handball

Squash

service line

service box

service line

service zone

telltale/tin/board

short line

service court line/service line

service box

half-court line

left service court

right service court

Handball Glove

back fingers

padded palm

strap

piping

Competitive Sports

Jai Alai/Pelota

Jai alai is played in a *fronton,* an auditorium that includes the court, a tiered spectator seating area, and *parimutuel betting* facilities. A clearvision mesh *screen* separates the spectators from the playing area.

helmet

rabillo/string

fondo

team number/post position

faja/sash

pelota/ball

trousers

costilla/ribs

punta/point

guante/glove

rubber-soled shoes

aro/frame

taco

Cesta/Basket

Cancha/Court

rebote/back wall

odds board/scoreboard

underserve line/ fault line

frontis/front wall

serving player's line

overserve line/ pass line

service line

service area

out-of-bounds area

cushion/fault line

players' lounge

players' cage

the "wood"

position lines

judges' entrance

Fencing

Foils, *sabres* or *épées,* which differ slightly in weight and design, are used in fencing *matches* or *bouts.* Each *fencer* must wear a chest-protecting *plastron* under his jacket, and women must also wear *breast protectors.* Four *judges* and a *director,* or *president,* referee *dry* or *non-electric* matches.

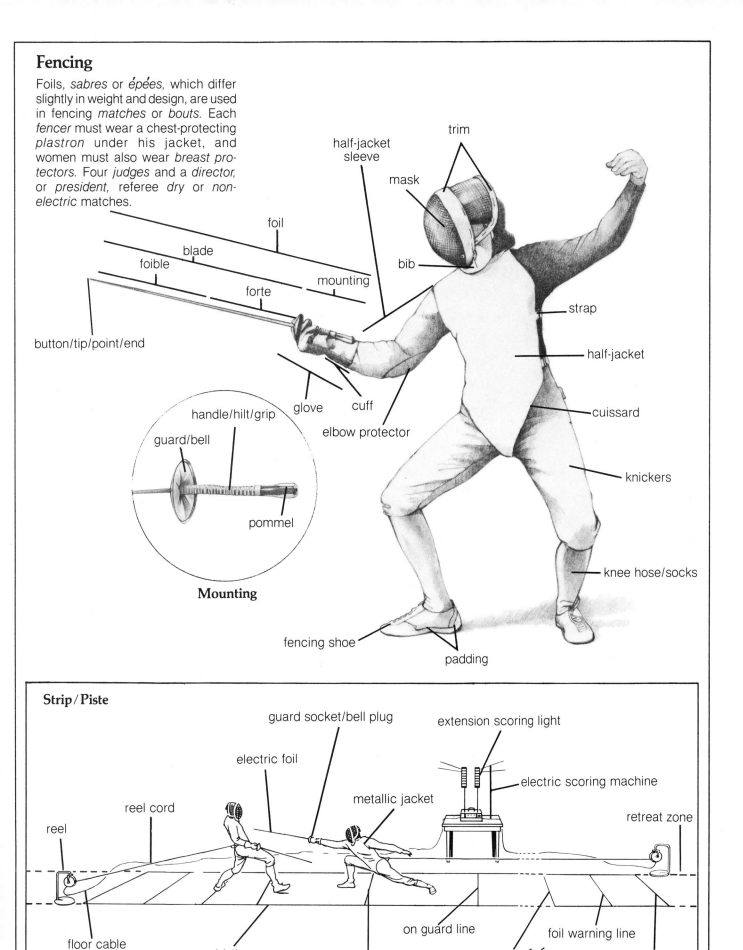

trim

half-jacket sleeve

mask

foil

blade

foible

bib

forte

mounting

button/tip/point/end

strap

half-jacket

glove

cuff

cuissard

handle/hilt/grip

elbow protector

guard/bell

knickers

pommel

Mounting

knee hose/socks

fencing shoe

padding

Strip/Piste

guard socket/bell plug

extension scoring light

electric foil

electric scoring machine

reel cord

metallic jacket

reel

retreat zone

floor cable

sideline

on guard line

foil warning line

center line

sabre and épée warning line

rear limit line

Swimming and Diving

During a swim *meet,* swimmers compete in *individual* or *team races* in the *freestyle, backstroke, breaststroke* and *butterfly,* as well as the *medley,* a combination of all strokes. To begin the backstroke, swimmers grasp the *handgrip* on the starting block. The flexible springboards and the rigid *diving platforms* used in competition are covered with *non-skid surfaces.*

lane numbers

end wall/ turning wall

8 7 6 5 4 3 2 1

gutter

lanes

sidewall

lane markers

back stroke flags

starting block/ platform

Pool

Diving Board / Springboard

rear anchor

board

front end/diving end

adjustable fulcrum

pedestal

Bowling

The strike pocket opposite to the hand delivering the ball is called the *Brooklyn pocket* or *Jersey pocket*. Pins are reset by a mechanical *pinsetter* or *pinspotter*. *Duckpins* and *candlepins* are forms of bowling in which differently shaped pins and lighter, smaller balls are used.

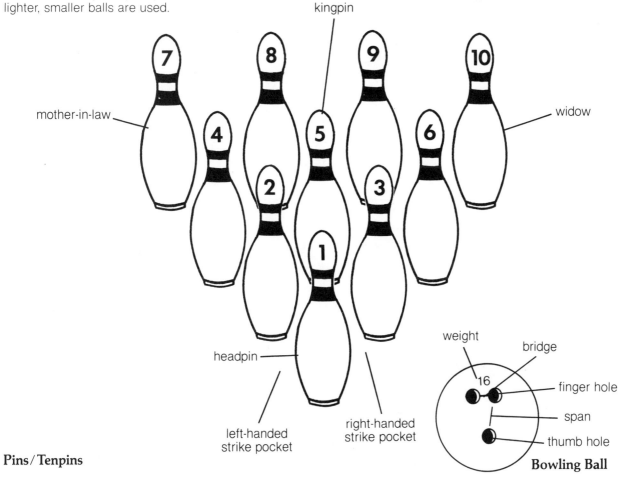

kingpin

mother-in-law

widow

headpin

left-handed strike pocket

right-handed strike pocket

Pins/Tenpins

weight

bridge

finger hole

16

span

thumb hole

Bowling Ball

Lane/Alley

pit

gutter/channel

spots/target arrows

foul line

approach/runway

cushion

setup/rack

ball return

12' markers

15' markers

Competitive Sports

Shuffleboard and Croquet

A shuffleboard game may begin at either end of a *court*. That end is designated the *head*. The opposite end is the *foot*. In croquet, *strikers* start at the *home stake* and return to it after going through wickets and hitting the *turning stake*.

neutral zone

dead lines

scoring diagram/
scoring triangle

clear

10-off square/minus square

disc

cue

separation triangle

Shuffleboard

base line

Croquet

mallet

shaft/handle

wicket/hoop/arch

crown

stake/peg

face

head

ball

upright

Volleyball and Badminton

In volleyball, an inflated ball hit sharply is called a *spike* or *kill.* Badminton is played with a *racket* or *bat* whose parts are similar to those of a tennis racket. Some badminton shuttles have nylon *skirts* rather than feathers.

tape

vertical aerial

net

net post

center line/net line

rear spikers' line/attack line

sideline

service area

back line/end line/boundary line

Volleyball Court

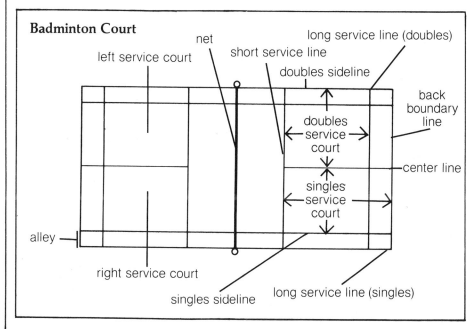

Badminton Court

net

left service court

long service line (doubles)

short service line

doubles sideline

back boundary line

doubles service court

center line

singles service court

alley

right service court

singles sideline

long service line (singles)

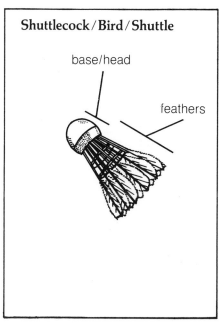

Shuttlecock/Bird/Shuttle

base/head

feathers

Billiards and Pool

Billiard and pool tables are usually covered with a dark green cloth called *felt,* or *bed cloth.* A triangular *rack* is used to position object balls at the beginning of a pool or *snooker* game. *Chalk* is used on cue tips. A point scored in billiards is called a *carom.*

head spot

playing surface

pockets

object balls

foot spot

cue ball

sights

cushion

rail

rail trim

score counters

leg

cross support

ball return/ball storage box

apron

leveler

Pocket Billiard Table/Pool Table

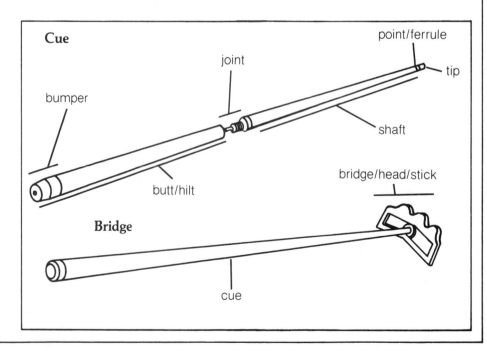

Cue

point/ferrule

joint

tip

bumper

shaft

butt/hilt

bridge/head/stick

Bridge

cue

Ping-Pong/Table Tennis

Paddles have two types of grips, *shake-hands grips* and *penhold grips,* and two types of faces, *rubber* and *sponge.* The game is played with a ping-pong *ball.*

Ping-Pong Table

Racket/Paddle/Bat

Net

Table Games

Darts

Darts, or *darting,* is played by two *dartists* or teams of from two to eight. Darts are scored on *point of entry* on the board *face.* Of the *clock-face games,* tournament darts is the most popular. Other games include *round-the-clock, all-fives, baseball, high score, cricket, 51-in-5's, 14-stop, killer, Mulligan, 301, sudden death,* and *Shanghai.*

triple ring/triple-score ring

double bull's-eye/ 50-point ring

bull's-eye/25-point ring

double ring/ double-score ring

single ring/ single-score ring

no-score ring

Dart Board/English Clock

Dart

flight

shaft

barrel

point

Kites

Bridle lines are attached to the spine through holes in the front cover. They are shown here on the rear of the kite only for illustrative purposes. Among the limitless varieties of kites, there are six major categories: flat, *plane*, or *two-stick kites; bowed kites*, sometimes known by their classic example, the *Eddy;* box, or *cellular,* kites; *compound kites*, represented by the *Conyne kite; semiflexible kites*, such as *delta-keels;* and *Rogallos,* or *flexible,* kites. *Fighting kites* have two flying lines.

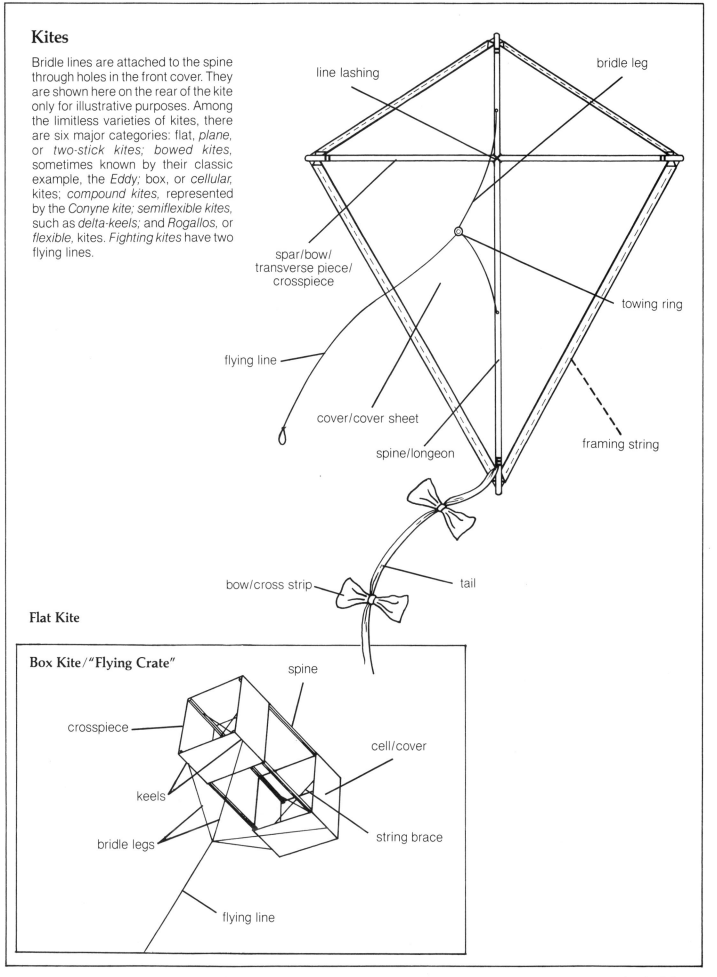

line lashing

bridle leg

spar/bow/ transverse piece/ crosspiece

towing ring

flying line

cover/cover sheet

framing string

spine/longeon

bow/cross strip

tail

Flat Kite

Box Kite/"Flying Crate"

spine

crosspiece

cell/cover

keels

string brace

bridle legs

flying line

Individual Sports

tongue

boot

Roller Skating and Skateboarding

On the skateboard seen here, the raised tail is called a *kicktail*. The degree to which a board bends is its *flex*. Auxiliary roller sports equipment includes *helmet*, *kneepads* and *elbow pads*.

toe cup/toe box

heel

toe stop

CHICAGO CUSTOM
PAT. 2 510 722

CHICAGO VANATHANE 11k

CHICAGO VANATHANE 11k

sole plate/plate

ball bearings

pivot

wheel

action nut/lock nut

axle

cushions

axle nut

king pin/action bolt/truck bolt

truck

Roller Skate

Skateboard

tail

deck

nose

riser pad

grip tape

truck

wheel

bearings

Ice Skates

Uppers refer to the area of a skate above the sole. *Inserts* can be used to reinforce the uppers and tighten the heel, and *lunge pads* provide extra protection in the toe area. Hockey skates often have L-shaped *ankle guards* built into the boot. *Skate guards* or *blade booties* protect skate blades when not in use.

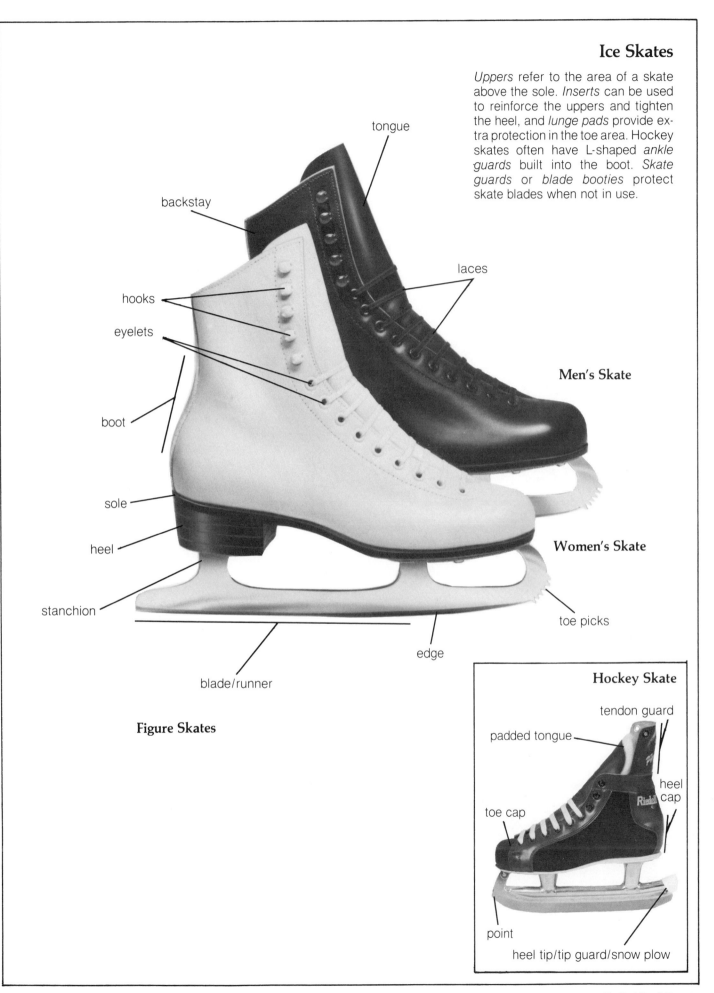

tongue

backstay

laces

hooks

eyelets

boot

Men's Skate

sole

heel

Women's Skate

stanchion

toe picks

blade/runner

edge

Figure Skates

Hockey Skate

tendon guard

padded tongue

heel cap

toe cap

point

heel tip/tip guard/snow plow

helmet

goggles

faceplate

bandana

protective padding

Alpine Skiing/ Downhill Skiing

A shallow *groove* along the bottom of a ski helps the *skier* track in a straight line. *Ski retention devices* include ski brakes, or *ski stops,* and *leashes.* There are four main events in skiing: *jumping,* downhill, *slalom* and cross country. Older bindings include *bear-trap* and *safety bindings.*

ski sweater

wrist strap

ski glove

pole grip

ski pole

shaft

knee padding

stretch pants

cuff

ski boot

basket/snow ring

tail

heel binding

buckles

toe binding

edge

Alpine ski/downhill ski

shovel

tip

Binding

release adjustment screw

height adjustment screw

brake plate

heel

release adjustment screw

mounting screw

indicator

anti-friction pad

ski

ski brake

brake-plate interface

heel cup pivot

pompom
ski hat
skiing rucksack
cross-country glasses
turtleneck/T-neck

headband
pullover sweater

mitten
lining

vest

bota/wineskin

knickers

knee sock

snow cuff

touring boot

gaiter

heelplate

toe binding/pin binding

ski pole

cross-country ski

Cross-Country Skiing/ Ski Touring

Since cross-country skiing includes climbing slopes as well as sliding down them, *ski tourers* apply *climbing waxes* to their skis. Snowshoes are made in two basic styles: the long *trail shoe,* seen here, and the broader *bearpaw shoe,* which usually has a rounded back.

Snowshoe

body lacing
master cord
crossbar
crossbar
toe lacing

heel lacing

tail

frame

toe hole

Sledding and Tobogganing

Bobsleds, driven by two- or four-man crews, have a racing *cowl* and toothed metal *brake.* Small racing sleds called *luges* are controlled by reclining drivers using their feet and *hand ropes.*

steering bar

tongue

side rail/handrail

center slat

side slats

deck

bumper

rope hole

front rail

runner

standard/strut

bench

Sled

Toboggan

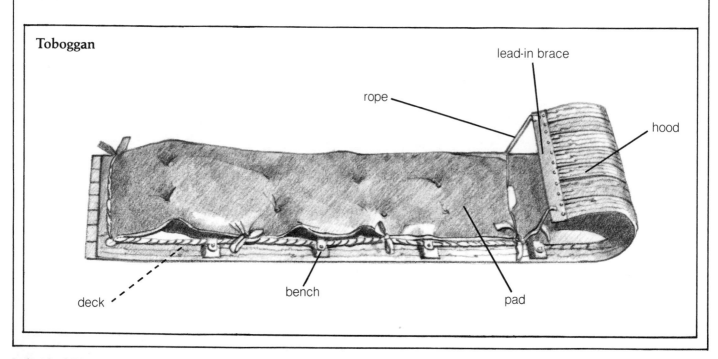

rope

lead-in brace

hood

deck

bench

pad

Waterskiing

Many skis have concave or *tunnel bottoms* for better control and stability. *Rocker,* or *camber,* is the continuous bend from a ski's tip to its heel. *Combination skis,* as well as slalom skis, have rear *keels, fins,* or *skegs.* Rear *binding heel pieces* are optional on slalom skis. Other ski types include *jumpers* and freestyle *trick skis.*

tip

front rocker

sidewall

foot binding/ "wet boot"

toe bar

toepiece

heel piece/ heel flap

rear toe binder

heel glide

tail rocker

trigger

heel plate

drop-through fin cover

tail

Slalom Ski

Ski Vest/Safety Jacket

reinforced shoulder

strap/belt

buckle

snap

Ski Rope/Towline

rope

bridle

hand protector

handle

end cap

323

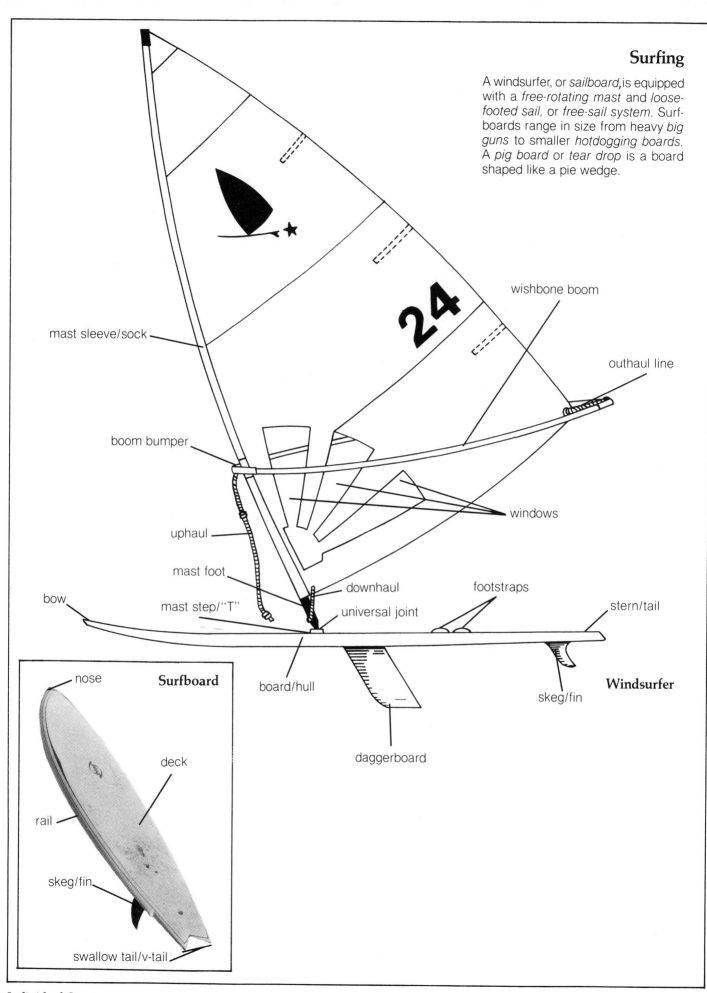

Surfing

A windsurfer, or *sailboard,* is equipped with a *free-rotating mast* and *loose-footed sail,* or *free-sail system.* Surfboards range in size from heavy *big guns* to smaller *hotdogging boards.* A *pig board* or *tear drop* is a board shaped like a pie wedge.

mast sleeve/sock

wishbone boom

outhaul line

boom bumper

windows

uphaul

mast foot

downhaul

footstraps

bow

mast step/"T"

universal joint

stern/tail

board/hull

skeg/fin

Windsurfer

daggerboard

nose

Surfboard

deck

rail

skeg/fin

swallow tail/v-tail

Skin Diving

Skin diving, as opposed to *helmet* or *hard-hat diving*, is a catch-all term that includes *snorkeling, breath-hold diving* from the surface, and *scuba diving*, breathing *compressed air* from tanks underwater. A face mask may have a *purge valve* in it to facilitate removal of water from within.

mask/face mask
lens
skirt
strap
snorkel
regulator mouthpiece
air hose/regulator hose
inflation hose
buoyancy compensator/ flotation device
auto inflation hose
automatic inflator
wet suit jacket
pressure gauge hose
BC inflator mouthpiece
pocket
pressure gauge
weight belt
depth gauge
diver's watch/submersible watch/dive timer
compass
glove
wet suit pants
lead weight
knife
sheath
boot/bootie
heel strap
foot pocket
side rail
vent
rib
blade
fin/swim fin/flipper

Tank and Regulator

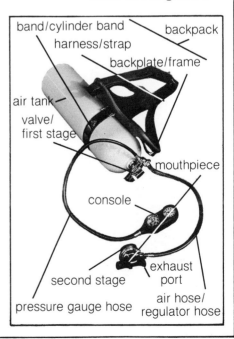

band/cylinder band
backpack
harness/strap
backplate/frame
air tank
valve/ first stage
mouthpiece
console
second stage
exhaust port
pressure gauge hose
air hose/ regulator hose

Hot Air Balloon

A balloon, or *montgolfier*, rises when *ballast*, usually water or *sandbags*, is jettisoned. A *drag*, or *trail rope*, hangs from the balloon to give it stability in flight and slow it down upon landing. To deflate the balloon a *ripping panel*, or *rip panel*, near the top is opened.

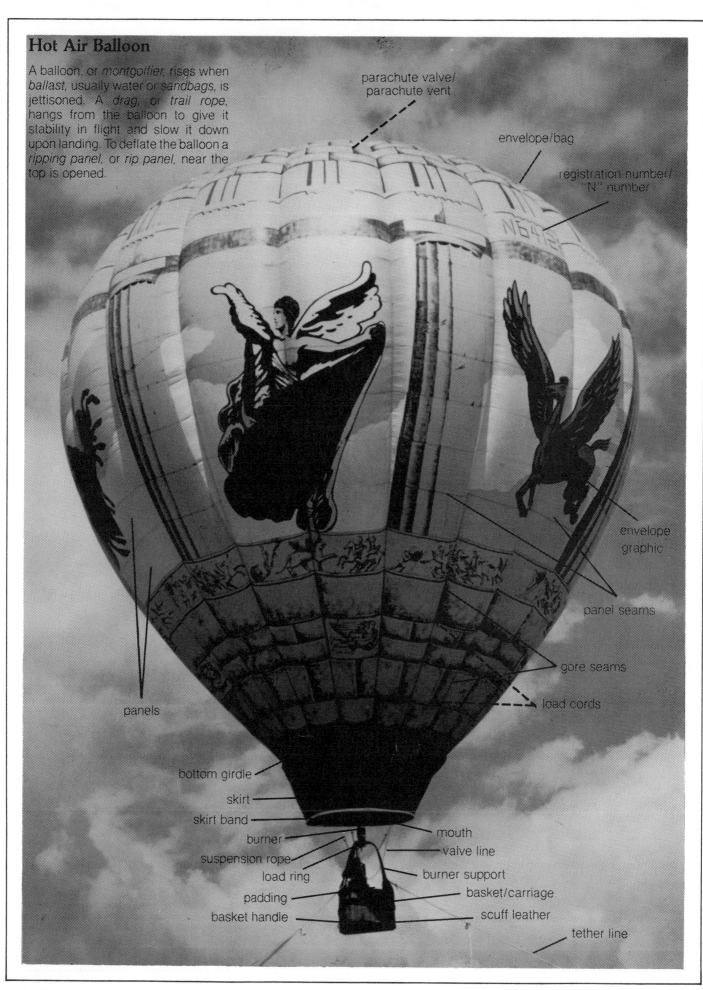

parachute valve/parachute vent

envelope/bag

registration number/"N" number

envelope graphic

panel seams

gore seams

load cords

panels

bottom girdle

skirt

skirt band

burner

suspension rope

load ring

padding

basket handle

mouth

valve line

burner support

basket/carriage

scuff leather

tether line

Parachuting and Hang Gliding

Unless attached to a *static line*, which automatically opens a *chute* once a *jumper* has cleared the *jump plane*, a *sky diver* can *free-fall* before pulling his *rip cord*.

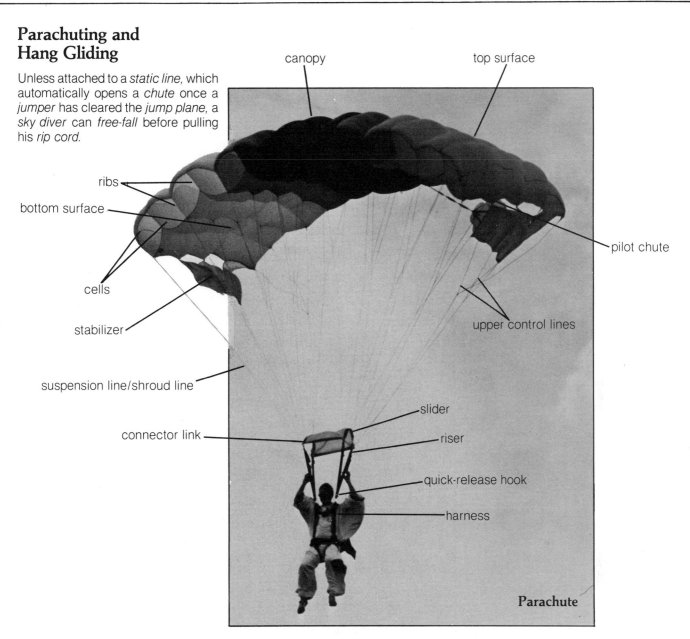

canopy

top surface

ribs

bottom surface

pilot chute

cells

upper control lines

stabilizer

suspension line/shroud line

slider

connector link

riser

quick-release hook

harness

Parachute

Hang Glider

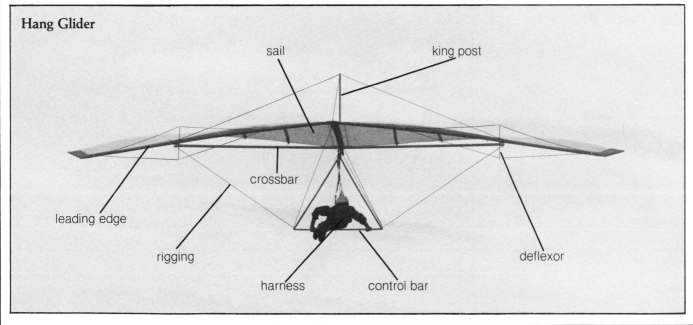

sail

king post

crossbar

leading edge

rigging

deflexor

harness

control bar

Individual Sports

Mountain Climbing

Mountaineers use nylon webbing for *shoulder slings* and *swami belts.* Carabiners, either oval- or D-shaped, have spring-loaded *gates* for connecting various pieces of climbing equipment. Unlike *pitons,* which are hammered into cracks, nuts are wedged into cracks and easily removed. *Icescrews,* ring-topped threaded tubes, are actually screwed into the ice for protection.

hardware sling

carabiners

climbing harness

tape

chocks & nuts

climbing rope

rand

smooth-soled climbing shoe/
klettershoe/PA

Ice Climbing Boot

crampon straps

lace lock

front points

points/spikes

crampon

corrugated sole

Ice Tools

adz

carabiner hole

shaft

spike

pick

Ice Axe

hammer

handle

wrist sling

teeth

pick

Ice Hammer

Riding Equipment

A saddle is built on a frame called a *saddle tree*. A *saddle blanket* or *saddle pad* is placed between horse and saddle. Metal stirrups, or *stirrup irons*, are attached to the saddle by *stirrup leathers*. *Saddlebags* fit over the back of the saddle.

horn cap

horn

fork/swell

pommel

seat

horn neck

gullet

lining

front jockey

rope strap

stirrup strap

hobble strap

cantle/hind bow

rear jockey/
back housing

skirt

rear rigging ring/dee ring

saddle string/tie

fender

rear cinch/
flank billet/
flank cinch

stirrup

Western Saddle/Stock Saddle

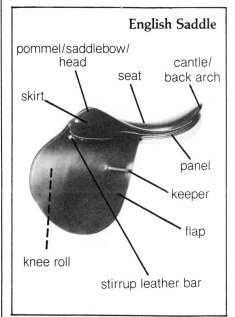

English Saddle

pommel/saddlebow/
head

cantle/
back arch

seat

skirt

panel

keeper

flap

knee roll

stirrup leather bar

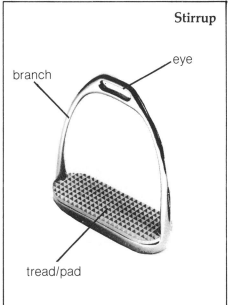

Stirrup

branch

eye

tread/pad

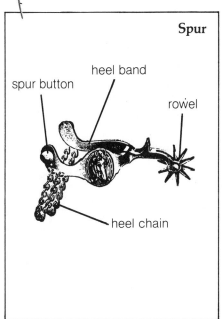

Spur

heel band

spur button

rowel

heel chain

Flat Racing

The equipment used on a racehorse is called the *tack*. *Thoroughbreds* start from a fixed *starting gate,* while harness racers start from a car-pulled *moving gate*. The most desirable *post position* in a race is gate number one, the *pole position* closest to the *rail*. Bettors pick horses to finish first, second and third, or *win, place* and *show*. Picking all three finishers in the right order is called a *trifecta*.

number cloth · jockey · silks · goggles · crash helmet/"skull cap" · whip/bat/crop · blinkers/blinders · rein · bridle · saddle · "tote board"/totalizer board · boot · bandages · lead weight/handicap weight · turf/track · spur · stirrup iron · girth & surcingle · leathers · bit

Racing Program Entry

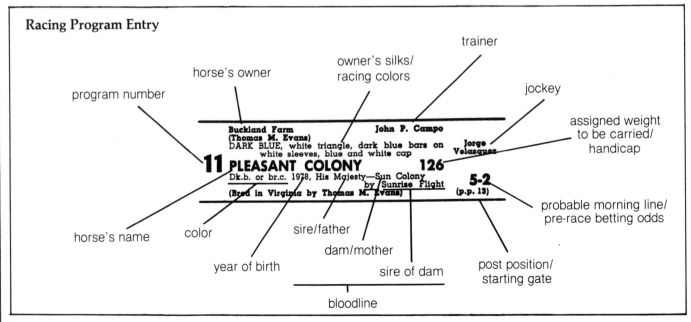

program number · horse's owner · owner's silks/racing colors · trainer · jockey · assigned weight to be carried/handicap · horse's name · color · year of birth · sire/father · dam/mother · sire of dam · post position/starting gate · probable morning line/pre-race betting odds · bloodline

Buckland Farm
(Thomas M. Evans)   John P. Campo
DARK BLUE, white triangle, dark blue bars on
    white sleeves, blue and white cap   Jorge
                                               Velasquez
11 PLEASANT COLONY   126
Dk.b. or br.c. 1978, His Majesty—Sun Colony
                by Sunrise Flight   **5-2**
(Bred in Virginia by Thomas M. Evans)   (p.p. 13)

Harness Racing

Trotters and pacers race in *harness*. Trotters move front and opposing rear legs in unison, *laterally gaited,* while pacers move front and rear legs on the same side in unison, *diagonally gaited.* Horses are assembled, saddled and paraded in the *paddock area.*

Driver

helmet

racing colors

whip

handholds

crupper

hobble hangers

saddlecloth

shaft carrier

saddle

water hook

check rein

bridle

driving bit

check bit

reins

thimble

breast collar

knee-boot suspender

suspender

buckle

knee boot

shin & ankle boot

bell boot

shaft

stirrup

hobbles

girth

Pacer

hind scalpers

seat

tire

plastic disc

spokes

Sulky/"Bike"

Racetrack/Mile Track

backstretch

7 furlong chute/ 7/8 mile chute

3/8 pole

1/2 pole

5/8 pole

3/4 pole

turf course/ steeplechase course

far turn

inside rail

outside rail

clubhouse turn

infield

tote board

1/4 pole

1/8 pole

nursery course

1¼ mile chute

3/16 pole

homestretch

1/16 pole

finish line

7/8 pole

grandstand & clubhouse

Grand Prix Racing

International *road racing* takes place on *closed-circuit tracks* laid out through the countryside, as opposed to *speedway racing,* which takes place on banked, oval-shaped *race tracks. Formulas* primarily limit engine size and car weight, and range from *Super-Vee* to *Formula One,* used in Grand Prix racing.

adjustable rear wing/spoiler

engine air intake

life support system

crash helmet

monocoque chassis

velocity stacks

roll bar

shield

cantilevered suspension

engine

cockpit

mirror

nose

radiator air exit

brake duct

racing slick

side pod

cowling

rim

trim tab

skirt

hub

spring

front wing/spoiler

wing strut

side plate/end plate

radiator air intake

Formula One Racing Car

Drag Racing

Each drag racing *event*, or *acceleration contest*, involves two-car *heats*, the winner of which is deemed the *eliminator*. Vehicles include *slingshot dragsters* and *funny cars* whose mismatched bodies, or *"hulls,"* and *chassis* give them an unusual appearance. The Christmas Tree is situated in the middle of a divided, two-lane *straight-line course*, *drag strip* or *dragway*. *Elapsed time*, or *"ET,"* is computed from the moment a car breaks a *light beam* at the *starting line* until it breaks a similar beam at the *finish*. A car leaving the starting line prematurely, in either *handicap* or *heads-up racing*, is said to be *"red-lighting."*

wing/air foil

intake valves

roll cage

support bar

cockpit

racing slick/ tire

aluminum rim

body

front wheel

fuel tank

fire extinguisher

air blower

exhaust header

engine compartment

Dragster / Rail

amber pre-starting lights

amber sequenced starting lights

green GO light

base

red foul light

Starting Lights / Christmas Tree

eyeport shield

neck sock

vent port

helmet skirt

nose shroud & breathing filter

shoulder harness

driving glove

driving suit

lap belt

anti-submarine belt/ crotch strap

racing shoe

Driver's Fire Suit

handle

foot/pole mount

leg/reel stem

bail/pick-up arm

trip/dog

crank handle

spool skirt

spool

anti-reverse lever

PENN
750 SS

3 BALL BEARINGS
SKIRTED SPOOL

rear bearing

gear housing

bearing cover

silent
anti-reverse
housing

drag-adjustment knob/
drag knob

line roller/line guide

Reel/Spinning Reel

Rod/Spinning Rod

hood

rear hood/
reel seat ring

foregrip

butt cap

lock ring

chuck

butt guide

male ferrule

handle/butt grip

reel seat

winding/wind

female ferrule

butt section

Fishing

Fishermen, or anglers, use a variety of tackle, from simple cane rods, or bank rods, to sophisticated fly rods and trolling gear. Sinkers hold bait underwater, while floats, or bobbers, keep it suspended from the surface. A gaff or landing net is used to land fish.

leader

snap

swivel

eye

shank

body

eye

point

gap

lip/bill

hook hanger

barb

treble hook

Plug

Fishhook

eye

skirt

bend

Lures

head

hook

Jig

graduated guide

tip top

top ring/end ring

blade/tip

Camping

Wall tents and pup tents are held up by tent poles. Many modern tents have *exterior frame* construction. Features in all the above-mentioned tents include *lap-felled* or *French seams*, which provide four layers for keeping out water, *webbed–tape backing* and pressed-on *grommets* or sewn-in *rings* for *ropes* secured to the ground with *pegs* or *stakes*, and sewn-in *flooring*. A lantern is primed by pumping the *pump valve* and lit by a match placed in the *lighting hole*.

grommet

ridgepole

eave pole

awning/canopy/flap

mosquito netting screen

zippered door

upright pole

awning pole/ canopy pole

stake loop

pole tip

brace pole

window flap

Tent

Camp Stove

stove lid

wind baffle

wire support

grate

burner ring

fuel tank cap

fuel tank

main control valve

finger pump/ pump plunger handle

Lantern

ventilator

bail

mantle

globe

heat shield

fuel valve

base rest

tank/fount

fuel cap

Loft is the trade term for fluffiness in sleeping bags. *Bonded insulation filling* eliminates the need for *quilting* and reduces "cold spots." The various pockets of backpacks, *knapsacks* or *rucksacks,* are called *local organizers.* Small camping items are packed in *stuffsacks,* which are then put inside a hiker's *pack.*

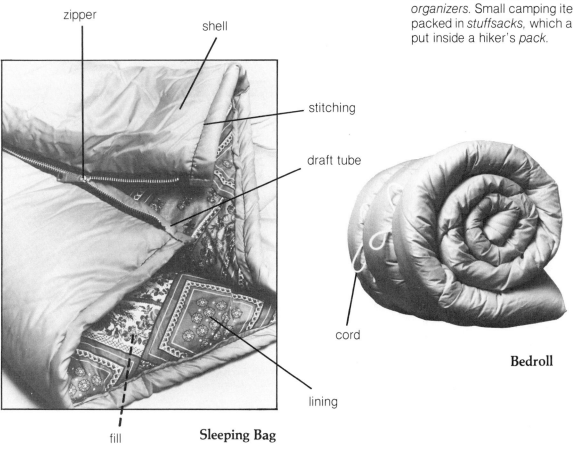

zipper

shell

stitching

draft tube

cord

Bedroll

lining

fill

Sleeping Bag

Backpack

main compartment

top pocket flap

storm flap

side pocket

zipper

cordlocks/togglelocks

bag compression strap/ cinch strap

compartment partition

hip belt

lower compartment

shoulder pad strap

external frame

cap/stopper

release buckle

Body Building

Among other *stations* in the universal gym, designed to improve muscle development through *isotonic exercises*, are *dead lift* and *low pulley*. Muscle-building and toning equipment includes *dumbbells, hand grips,* or *hand flexors, scissor grips, tone-up wheels, power twisters, exercise bikes, neck developers, ankle* and *wrist weights, triceps exercisers* and *waist trimmers.*

high pulley/
lateral pulley

chinning station

leg press

hip flexor

dipping station

shoulder press

thigh &
knee machine

abdominal board

weights

chest press

Universal Gym

Jump Rope/Skip Rope

swivel

handle/grip

ferrule

rope

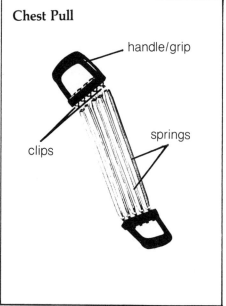

Chest Pull

handle/grip

clips

springs

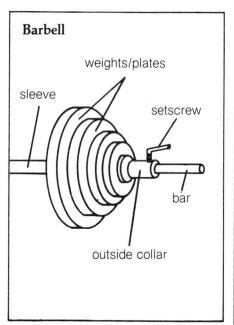

Barbell

weights/plates

sleeve

setscrew

bar

outside collar

Chess, Checkers, Backgammon and Tile Games

When chessmen and checkers are arranged at the start of a game, they are positioned in a *setup*. A chessboard's horizontal rows are called *ranks*. Vertical rows are *files*. In backgammon, a player increases the stakes by turning a dicelike *doubling cube*. A single backgammon piece on a point is called a *blot*. Two or more on a point make a *block*. In dominos, pieces with identical numbers on both ends are called *doubles* or *spinners*. Dominos that have been played form a *layout*. In mah-jongg, tiles are arranged in a *wall* to begin a game.

white square

double corner

checkers/checker men

king

single corner

king row

chessmen/ chess pieces

black square

queen rook/ queen castle

queen rook pawn/ queen castle pawn

queen knight

queen bishop

queen knight pawn

queen bishop pawn

queen pawn

queen

king pawn

king

king bishop pawn

king bishop

king knight

king knight pawn

king rook/ king castle

king rook pawn/ king castle pawn

Chessboard / Checkerboard

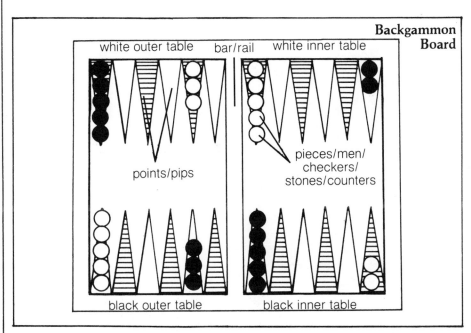

Backgammon Board

white outer table   bar/rail   white inner table

points/pips

pieces/men/ checkers/ stones/counters

black outer table   black inner table

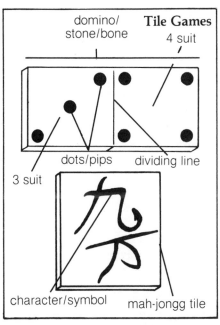

Tile Games

domino/ stone/bone

4 suit

3 suit

dots/pips

dividing line

character/symbol

mah-jongg tile

Gambling Equipment

A roulette wheel is operated by a *croupier*. Bets are placed on a *layout*. Slots are divided into *red* and *black* for betting purposes. Dice players bet either with the person rolling the dice, the *shooter*, or with the casino, or *house*. The blackjack dealer pushes money won by the house into a double-locked *drop box* below the betting table. Other casino games include *baccarat, chemin de fer, wheel of fortune*, and *chuck-a-luck*, a game played with three dice.

coin slot

face

coin viewer/window

arm

wheels

bars, bells & fruit

payoff chart

EXTRA AWARD

casing/frame

payoff return/ coin return

stand

Slot Machine / One-Arm Bandit

Roulette Wheel

bowl

ball

ball rest

pan/wheel

spindle

canoe/diamond

slot/groove

pip/spot/dot

die

Dice

dice-dealer position

on & off puck

rail

chip rail

chips

boxman's position

for shooter

against shooter

hard-way bets

proposition area

stick

stickman's position

place bets

don't-come box

come box

dice boat

pass line/front line

don't-pass bar

field

big 6/big 8

Craps Table/Dice Table

Blackjack/21 Layout

discard holder

money slot

dealer's hand

chip rack

dealer's station

shoe/sabot

home plate/anchor spot

spots

hand

first base

Casino Games

Playing Cards

There are 52 cards in a *deck* or,*pack.* The *aces,* shown below, and cards numbered two through ten,are called *spot cards* or *pip cards.* An additional card, the *joker,* or *mistigris,* is used in *card games* requiring a *wild card.* A *marked deck* is one in which the card *backs* have been altered slightly to allow a player to read their *values* illegally.

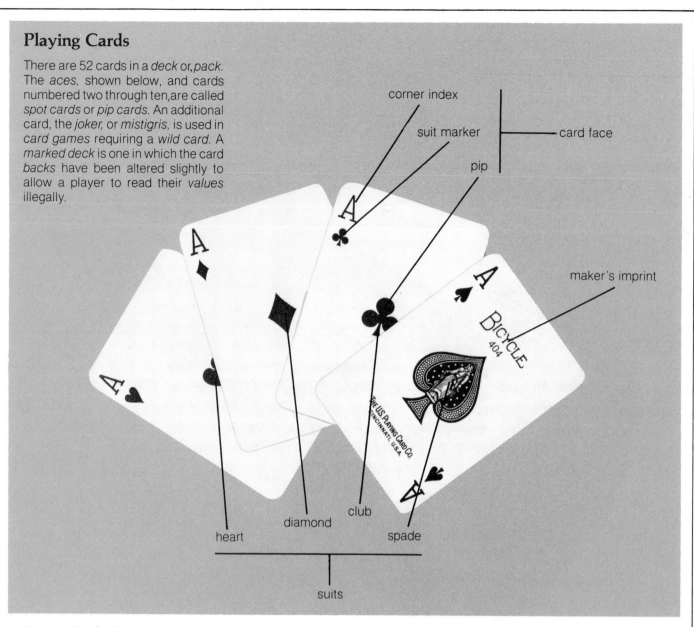

corner index

suit marker

card face

pip

maker's imprint

heart

diamond

club

spade

suits

Picture Cards/Court Cards/Face Cards

Jack/Knave

La Hire/One-eyed Jack

Hector

Lancelot

Ogier/One-eyed Jack

Queen

Judith

Rachel

Argine

Palas

King

Charlemagne/Suicide King

Caesar

Alexander

David

Arts and Crafts

The main subsections here include the platforms on which the performing arts take place; coverage of the music field, ranging from the symbols that appear on sheet music to the parts of various musical instruments; the fine arts and crafts.

In the fine arts subsection an effort has been made to identify the terms for elements of style, rather than to cover styles themselves. The equipment used in everything from painting and sculpting to relief arts and stained glass are also illustrated and their parts labeled. The crafts subsection covers decorative stitching, knitting and weaving, and also includes the terms used to identify a sewing pattern.

Cartooning has a subsection all to itself. Here, for the first time, the reader will be able to identify everything from the beads of fear on a comic character (plewds) to the meaning of double XX's on a cartoon bottle (boozex). In addition the reader will henceforth be able to recognize the difference between a thought balloon, a speech balloon and an idea balloon in a cartoon panel.

Ticket/"Ducat"

stub/rain check

price

event information

seat type & location

Stage

Also found on many stages are *tormentors,* or *legs,* which frame the stage to narrow the acting area, a *trapdoor,* or *scruto,* an *elevator,* and a fabric backdrop, or *scrim.* Everything used on stages, or *boards,* are *props,* or *properties.* The arrangement of *scenery,* properties and lighting is called a *set.*

counterweight pulleys

fly lines

gridiron/grid

stage left wall

flies/loft

loading platform/weight floor

drop/border

fire curtain/iron curtain

pipe batten

grand drape/valance

spotlight batten

spotlights

cyclorama floodlights/"cyc floods"

teaser/act drop

proscenium arch/portal

border lights

act curtain

teaser

traveler

cyc"/sky drop

drop/border

fly deck/gallery

brace

pin rail

leg

footlights

batten

floor plate

flat/scenery

Cross Section

Theater

In a *performance hall*, the orchestra sits in a sunken *orchestra pit* between the audience and the stage. For some shows a *runway*, or *ramp*, extends from the stage into the *center aisle*. The seating area above the orchestra is the *balcony*. In theaters with more than one balcony, the lowest one is the *mezzanine*, the front section of which is the *loge*.

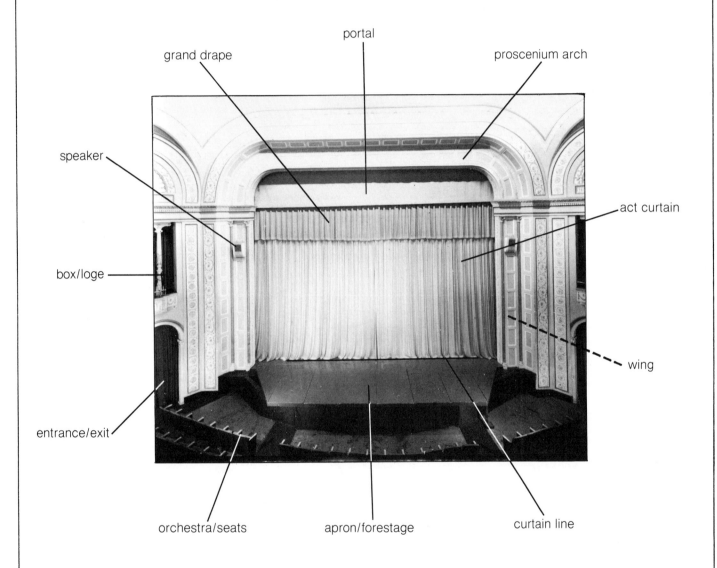

portal

grand drape

proscenium arch

speaker

act curtain

box/loge

wing

entrance/exit

orchestra/seats

apron/forestage

curtain line

Performing Arts

Sheet Music Notations

Words to be sung, or *lyrics,* appear below the staff on sheet music. The notation ' is a *breath mark* indicating that the singer or musician should briefly pause. A combination of tones that blend harmoniously is a *chord.* Sharps, flats and naturals appearing directly in front of specific notes are called *accidentals.* A *quasihemidemisemiquaver* is a 128th note.

Orchestra

In symphony orchestras, string, woodwind and brass parts are performed by many *musicians.* In *chamber music ensembles,* each part is usually played by a single *player. Bands* do not normally include stringed instruments. *Marching bands* generally use no oboes or bassoons, and flutes are replaced with piccolos or *fifes. Dance bands* and *jazz bands* are loosely structured.

Brasses

French horn

trombone

tuba

trumpet

timpano

Percussion

snare drum

bass drum

cymbals

tambourine

triangle

harp

clarinet

bass clarinet

bassoon

contra-bassoon

piccolo

flute

oboe

second violin

viola

string bass/double bass

first violin

Woodwinds

cello

English horn/cor anglais

Strings

Strings

Symphony Orchestra

choir riser

conductor

conductor's podium

riser

concertmaster

Music   348

Violin

Stringed instruments produce tones when a bow is drawn across the strings (arco) or they are finger-plucked (pizzicato). The sympathetic vibration produced between the instrument's belly and back adds resonance and volume to the sound.

scroll

peg/screw

pegbox

nut

fingerboard

strings

neck

purfling

belly/table/top/soundboard

f-hole/soundhole

bridge

point/tip

hair

nut

stick

frog

screw/adjusting screw

Bow

side/rib

chin rest

tail piece

button

Viola da Gamba

upper bout

waist

lower bout

Cello / Violoncello

retractable spike

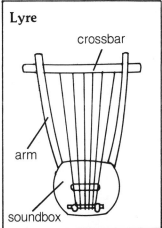

Lyre

crossbar

arm

soundbox

Bass Fiddle / Double Bass / Bass

G string

D string

A string

E string

Woodwinds

Woodwinds produce *tones* by the vibration of one or two reeds of pliant cane in the mouthpiece or by the passing of air across a blow hole.

middle section/middle joint/main body

tail section/foot joint

rod

key

ring keys

plates

fingerplate

pad

cover

Flute

bell

double reed

Clarinet

head section

body section

Piccolo

Oboe

head section/head joint

embouchure hole/blow hole

embouchure plate

mouthpiece

reed

cork

barrel

ligature

thumb screws

upper joint

lower joint

double reed

bell

crook

neck

mouthpipe key

body

long joint/
bass joint

wing/tenor joint

buttons

boot/butt

Saxophone

English Horn/Cor Anglais

Bassoon

Brasses

Brasses are *wind instruments* that produce *tones* when lips are buzzed against the mouthpiece. The range of brass instruments is increased by added lengths of tubing called *crooks* or *shanks*.

brace flange

bell brace

outer slide brace

inner slide brace

balancer

bell lock

cup

rim

shank

slide lock

mouthpiece

tuning-slide crook

tuning slide/ tuning bow

Trombone

Sousaphone

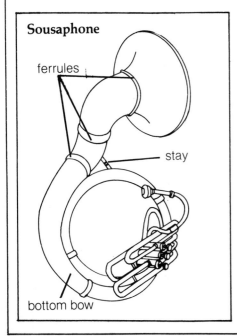

ferrules

stay

bottom bow

Tuba

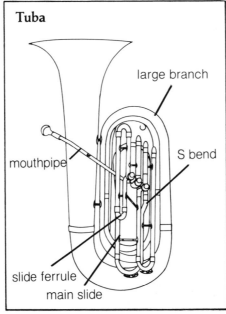

large branch

mouthpipe

S bend

slide ferrule

main slide

French Horn

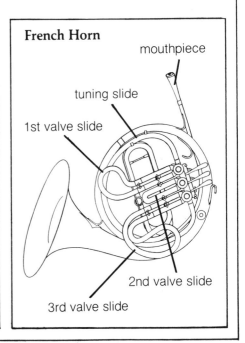

mouthpiece

tuning slide

1st valve slide

2nd valve slide

3rd valve slide

bell flare

hand slide

water key/spit key

bumper

bell wire

valve buttons

1st valve

2nd valve

3rd valve

pinky ring/
finger hook

mouthpipe/lead pipe

mouthpiece

1st valve slide

2nd valve slide

3rd valve slide

valve casings

lyre holder

tuning slide

water key/spit key

Trumpet

Cornet

throat

valve caps

tuning slide

Bugle

cup

edge/"bite"

rim

bell rim

Music

Organ

The keyboards, or *manuals,* pedal board and *pipes* of a pipe organ, such as the one shown here, are contained in the body, or *console.* Music is produced when air, sent into a *wind chest* from an internal *bellows,* is directed into one of the organ's pipes. An *electric organ* produces tones mechanically. An *electronic organ* uses *transistors* and *tubes* to make sounds.

coupler-tilt tablets

music arch

indicators

manufacturer

on & off switch

clock

sharp keys

stops/voices/ draw-knobs

natural keys

arm

swell keyboard

sforzando/ full-organ button

great keyboard

choir keyboard

memory locks

pistons/presets

lock

keybed

cancel button

toe studs

swell shoes/ expression pedals

side

pedal board

crescendo shoe

sharps

Piano

A piano is made up of a *structural unit,* a *tone unit* and a *mechanical unit.* The keys activate a mechanism that throws felt-covered *hammers* against the strings in the piano *case.* A *digitorium* is a silent machine for piano practice.

front half/front lid

prop stick/
long lid prop

back lid/
back half

heel

music desk

straight side

fall/
fallboard

keyboard

keyslip

cheek/arm

lyre

una corda pedal

Sostenuto pedal

damper pedal

lyre brace/
lyre stay

short stick/
short lid prop

bent side

leg

caster/castor

Grand Piano

Upright Piano

top door/
upper frame/
upper panel

keybed

leg/column

pedal rail/
front rail

bottom frame/
bottom door

toe

C#/Db
D#/Eb
F#/Gb
G#/Ab
A#/Bb

C
D
E
F
G
A
B
C

keys

Keyboard Octave

Guitar

These *chordophones,* or *stringed instruments,* are members of the lute family. They are played by plucking or strumming the strings with the fingers or with a stiff *plectrum* or *pick.* A movable device attached to a guitar neck, used to raise the pitch of the strings, is a *capo.* There are *sympathetic strings* inside the hollow neck of a sitar that vibrate in response to the drone or melody strings.

tuning pegs/tuning keys

head

tuning machine

nut

neck

frets

position marks

fingerboard

shoe brace/heel

body

sounding board

sound hole

rosette

strings

waist

bridge base

pick guard

bridge bone/saddle

Acoustic Guitar

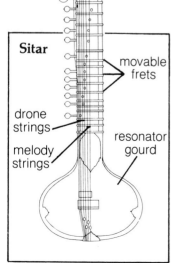

tuning pegs

gourd

Sitar

movable frets

drone strings

melody strings

resonator gourd

Banjo

nut

thumb-string peg

resonator

belly

tension hoop

sleeve protector

tailpiece

tension screw

Mandolin

paired strings

shell plate

belly

Appalachian Dulcimer

tuning pegs

sound box

Electric Guitar

The electric guitar has a *solid body* rather than the *hollow* or *semi-hollow body* of an acoustic guitar. *Special-effects pedals*, among them *fuzz*, *fuzz-phaser*, *wah-wah* and *distortion*, can be linked to the amplifier. *Pre-amplifiers*, which serve to magnify weak signals, can also be hooked up to the amplifier.

key/peg

head

nut

strings

fingerboard

frets

neck

instrument input

volume control

tone control

on & off switch

rate control

pilot light

depth control

foot-switch input

pickguard

bass pick-up/ rhythm pick-up

middle pick-up

tremolo arm

cabinet

trebel pick-up/ lead pick-up

speakers

tone and volume control

grille

Amplifier / Amp

bridge

jack-plug socket

Electric Guitar

Double-Neck Bass and Guitar

position markers

guitar neck

bass neck

controls

Synthesizer

output/amplifiers

oscillators & controllers

mixer

modifiers

keyboard

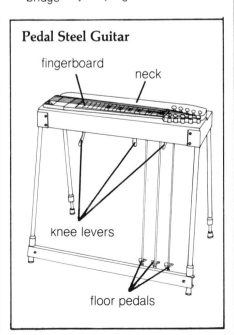

Pedal Steel Guitar

fingerboard

neck

knee levers

floor pedals

Music

Drums

Drums, or *membranophones,* in a *drum set* such as the one shown here, are played with *drumsticks, mallets* or *brushes.* A *gong* is struck with a *beater.* Adjustable metal, nylon or gut strings, called *snares,* are stretched across the bottom head, or *snare head,* of a snare drum. Timpani can be adjusted by screws or pedals to produce sounds of different pitches.

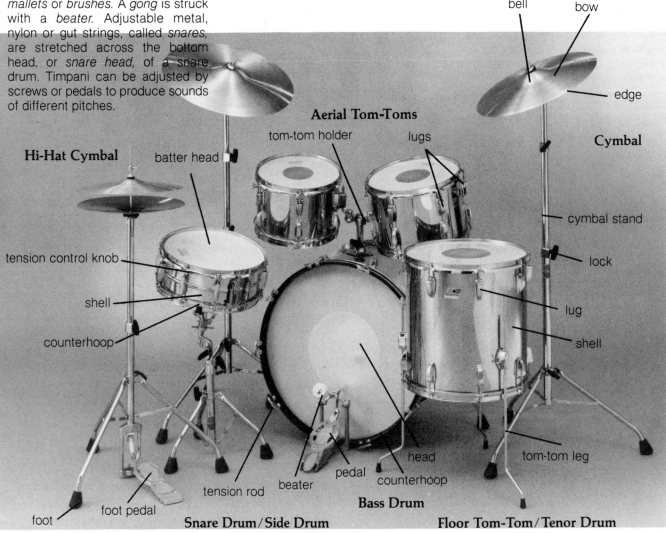

bell

bow

edge

Aerial Tom-Toms

tom-tom holder

lugs

Cymbal

Hi-Hat Cymbal

batter head

cymbal stand

lock

tension control knob

lug

shell

shell

counterhoop

head

tom-tom leg

foot

foot pedal

tension rod

beater

pedal

counterhoop

Bass Drum

Snare Drum/Side Drum

Floor Tom-Tom/Tenor Drum

Bongos

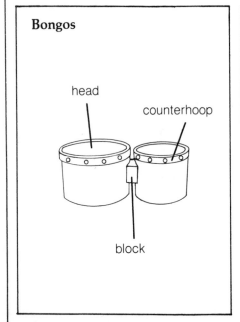

head

counterhoop

block

Tambourine

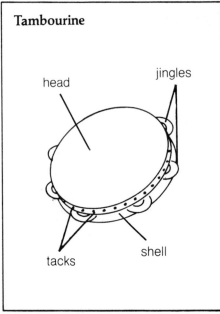

head

jingles

tacks

shell

Kettledrum/Timpano

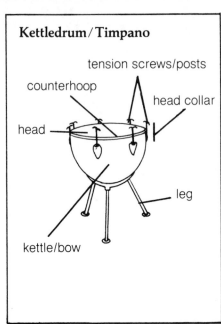

tension screws/posts

counterhoop

head collar

head

leg

kettle/bow

Bagpipe

A *drone reed*, or *double-reed*, held inside the chanter by a *tenon*, creates music when air is blown into the *pipes* by a *bagpiper* or by pumping *bellows* strapped to the *piper's* body. The melody is played on the eight *open holes* in the chanter. The *leather bag* is usually covered with a decorative *bag cover*.

cord

tassel

mounts

tenor drones

bass drone/drone pipe

blowpipe

bag/windbag

stock

chanter/melody pipe

Folk Instruments

Like the harmonica, the accordion, or *piano-accordion,* is a *free-reed instrument.* Many accordions have *treble* and *bass register buttons* which allow the *accordionist* to change the tone of the instrument.

fingerboard

chord buttons & bass buttons

bass part

bellows strap

bellows

grille

treble part/ melody part

shoulder strap

piano keys

reed selector switch

keyboard

Accordion

Tub Fiddle

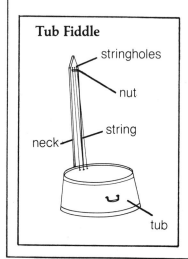

stringholes

nut

neck

string

tub

Kazoo/Mirliton

diaphragm

outlet

mouthpiece

Harmonica/ Mouth Organ

housing/ case

openings/ air holes

mouthpiece

Jew's Harp

tongue

frame

lamella

Musical Accessories

A metronome, used to find the correct speed for music in beats per minute, can be spring wound or electric. A tuning fork is constructed and tempered so as to give a pure *tone* when caused to vibrate. It can be used in conjunction with a *resonance box* to amplify its sound.

graduated scale

shaft

box/case

pendulum

weight

pivot

key

on-off button

Metronome

Tuning Fork

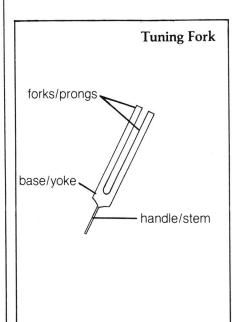

forks/prongs

base/yoke

handle/stem

Pitch Pipe

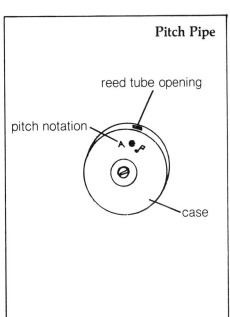

reed tube opening

pitch notation

case

Music Stand

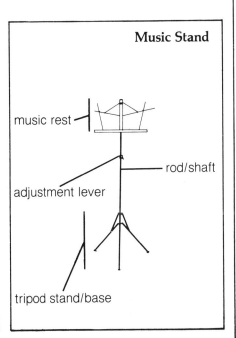

music rest

rod/shaft

adjustment lever

tripod stand/base

Elements of Composition

The forms of *linear perspective* illustrated here allow an artist or illustrator to show *dimension – height, width* and *depth –* on a *flat surface.* The central focus of a work of art is the *subject.* The way an artist renders a subject, which ranges from *literal rendition* to forms of *abstraction,* is called *style.*

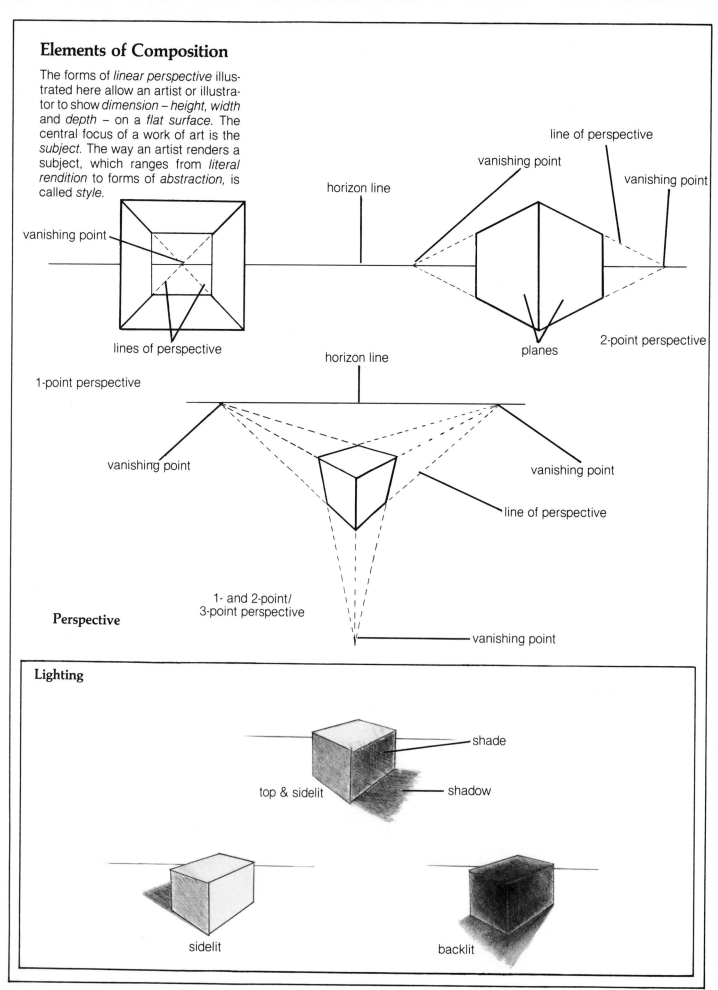

vanishing point

horizon line

line of perspective

vanishing point

vanishing point

lines of perspective

planes

2-point perspective

1-point perspective

horizon line

vanishing point

vanishing point

line of perspective

1- and 2-point/
3-point perspective

Perspective

vanishing point

Lighting

top & sidelit

shade

shadow

sidelit

backlit

Composition

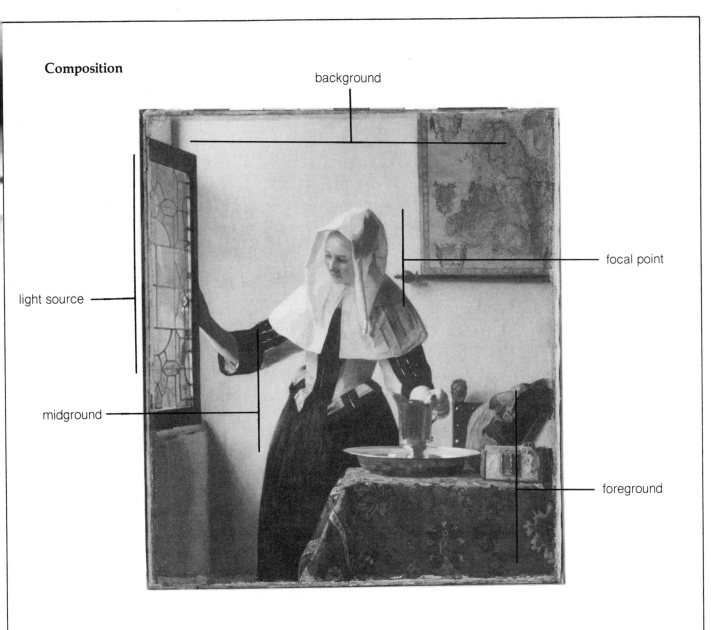

background

focal point

light source

midground

foreground

Texture

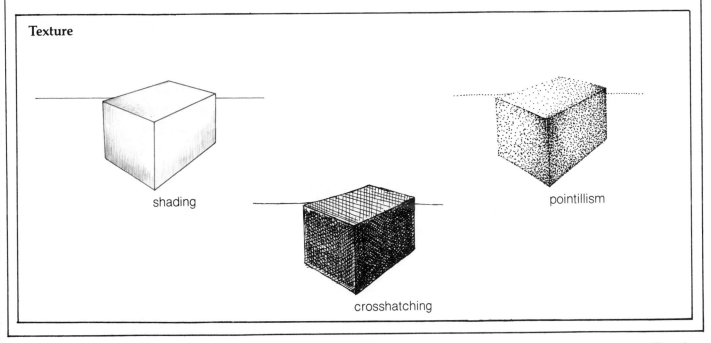

shading

crosshatching

pointillism

Painting

Before paint is applied to a *canvas* it must be drawn taut on a *stretcher* and the surface coated with *primer,* usually a substance called *gesso.* The *artist,* or *painter,* chooses a type of paint, or *medium,* in which to work, the most common of which are *tempera, acrylic* and *oil.* A thin blade set in a handle, used for mixing colors or applying them to a canvas, is a palette knife.

upright

left wing

right wing

short bar

upper back-stick

canvas holder

hand crank

box tray

lower back-stick

short bar

base

brake caster

long bars

Easel

Brushes

bristles/hair

ferrule

crimp

handle

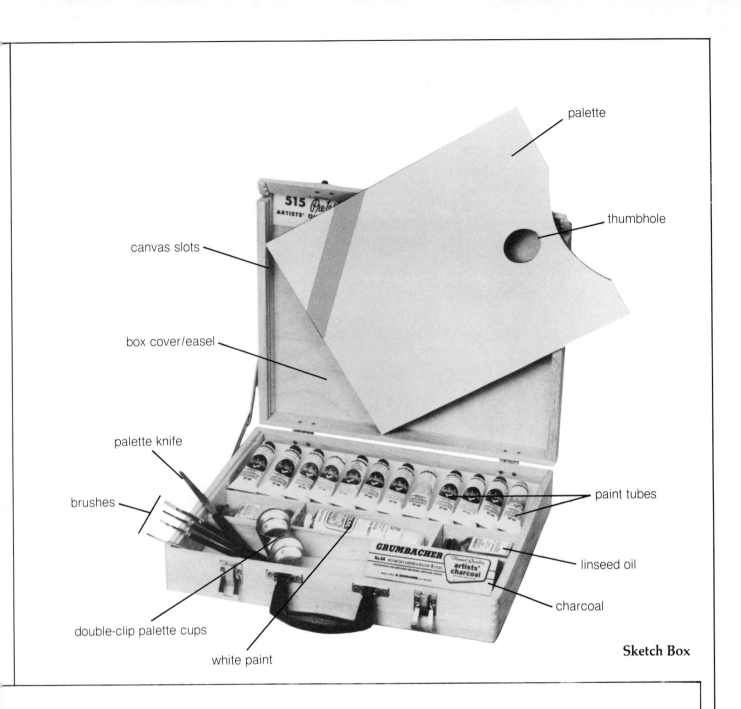

palette

thumbhole

canvas slots

box cover/easel

palette knife

brushes

paint tubes

linseed oil

double-clip palette cups

charcoal

white paint

Sketch Box

brush size

manufacturer

series number

Sculpting Tools

In stone sculpture, a *subtractive process,* forms or objects are created in *three dimensions* or in *relief.* Works may be carved or built up from some flexible material. Whenever a pliant material is used, it may be laid upon an inner skeleton, or *armature.* To make the finished product more durable, it may be fired or cast.

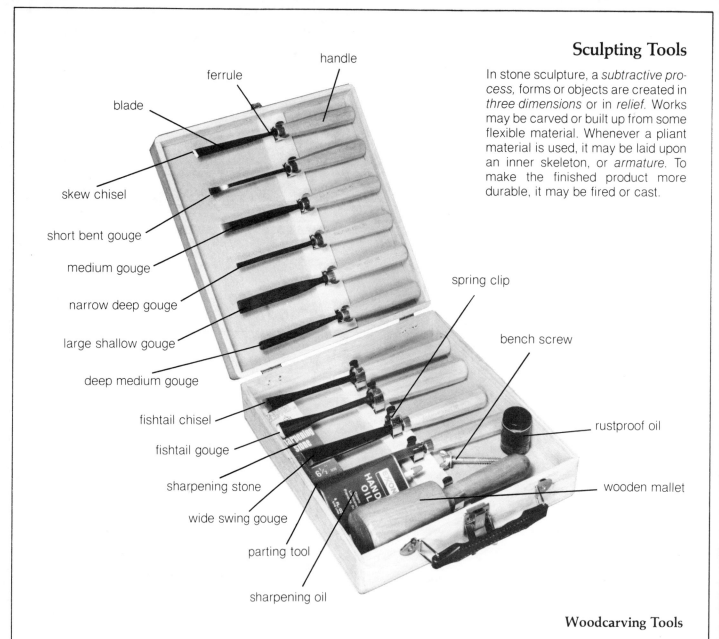

ferrule

handle

blade

skew chisel

short bent gouge

medium gouge

narrow deep gouge

large shallow gouge

deep medium gouge

fishtail chisel

fishtail gouge

sharpening stone

wide swing gouge

parting tool

sharpening oil

spring clip

bench screw

rustproof oil

wooden mallet

Woodcarving Tools

Clay Modeling Tools

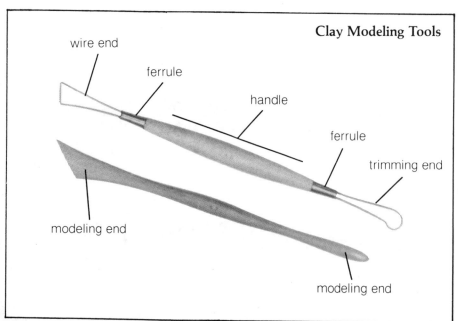

wire end

ferrule

handle

ferrule

trimming end

modeling end

modeling end

Stonecutting Tools

flat chisel

point chisel

round-end chisel

cape/splitting tool

toothed chisel

stone carving hammer

Potting

An object made on a potter's wheel is *thrown*. The object is then put in a kiln where it is *fired*, or hardened. Its surface is usually covered with a glasslike coating, or *glaze*. A knifelike *fettling tool* is used to cut and shape soft clay, as is a wooden strip called a *paddle*. A manually operated potter's wheel is called a *kick-wheel*.

bat pins

wheel head

splash pan

worshelf

motor housing

on-off button

forward-reverse button

electric cord

hand lever

foot pedal

adjustable foot

Electric Potter's Wheel

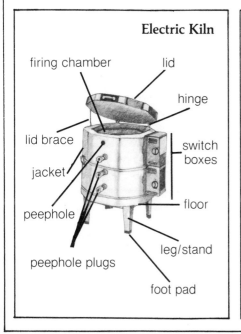

Electric Kiln

firing chamber

lid

hinge

lid brace

switch boxes

jacket

floor

peephole

peephole plugs

leg/stand

foot pad

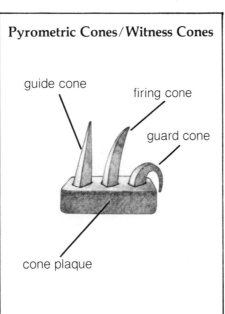

Pyrometric Cones/Witness Cones

guide cone

firing cone

guard cone

cone plaque

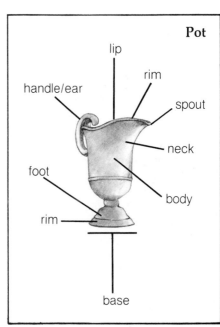

Pot

lip

rim

handle/ear

spout

neck

foot

body

rim

base

Woodcut Printing

The art of making *engravings* with wooden blocks is *xylography,* and the tools used to create the designs are called *gravers.*

U-gouge

liner/slant

straight gouge/chisel

U-gouge

V-gouge

handle

ferrule

shank

sharpening stone

blade

Gouges

Wood Block

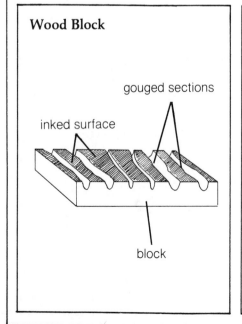

gouged sections

inked surface

block

Brayer/Roller

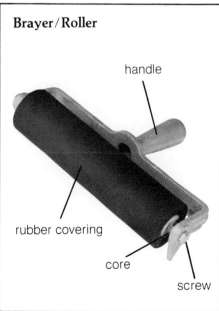

handle

rubber covering

core

screw

Baren

handle

SPEEDBALL

band

body

teflon pad

Silk Screen and Scrimshaw

The *silk-screen printmaking process* is called *serigraphy*. A *stopping medium*, called a *resist*, blocks out or *masks* an area of the screen. Ink or paint passes through the unprotected areas of the screen to become the print. A person who does *decorative engravings* or *carvings* in *ivory* or *whalebone* is called a *scrimshander*.

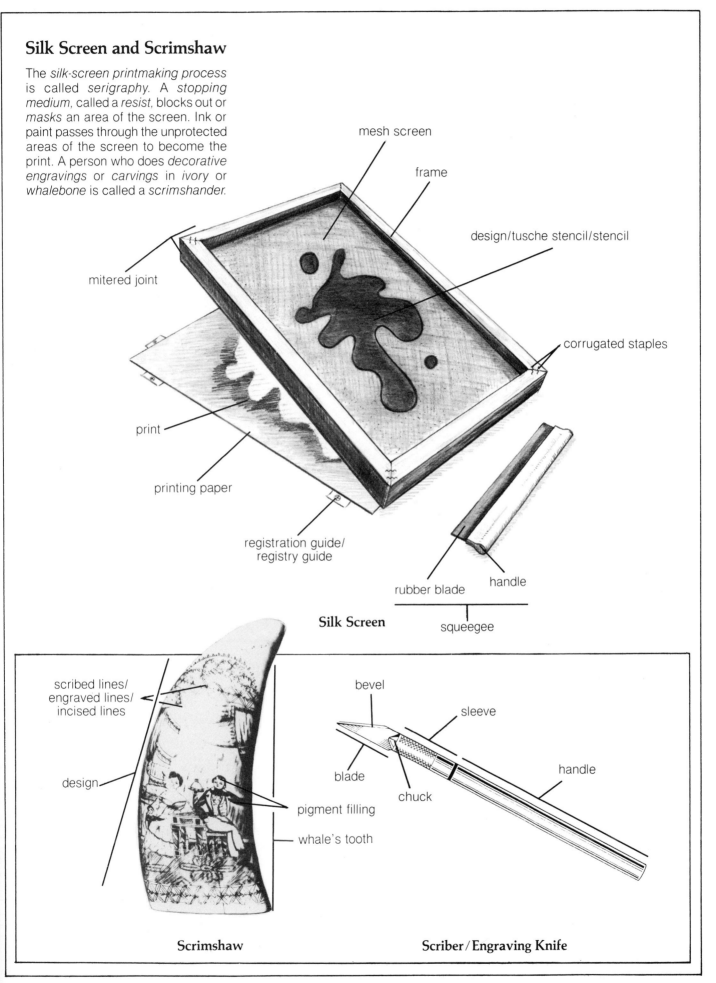

mesh screen

frame

design/tusche stencil/stencil

corrugated staples

mitered joint

print

printing paper

registration guide/
registry guide

rubber blade

handle

squeegee

Silk Screen

scribed lines/
engraved lines/
incised lines

design

pigment filling

whale's tooth

bevel

sleeve

blade

chuck

handle

Scrimshaw

Scriber/Engraving Knife

Fine Arts

Lithography

Lithography is a form of *planographic printing.* The design is made on a stone, prepared, or "grained," by spinning the levigator over its surface, or on a metal *plate* with a *lithographic crayon, lithographic pencil, rubbing ink* or *asphaltum.*

adjustment screw

manufacturer's identification

locknut

pressure bar

screws

cambox

uprights

cambox shaft

crank handle

scraper bar holder

gear box

lock screw

scraper

clutch

stone

printing surface

chain guard

stand

press body

press bed

bed handle

Lithographic Press

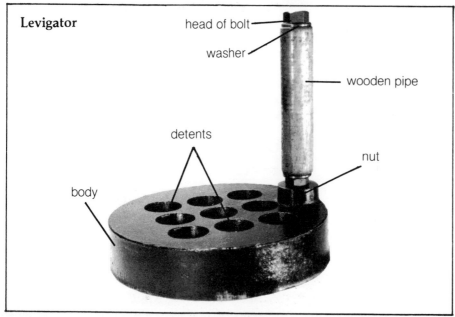

Levigator

head of bolt

washer

wooden pipe

detents

nut

body

Intaglio and Etching

Intaglio, or *incised printing*, is a type of *printmaking* in which a design is cut into a *plate* by techniques such as etching, *engraving, soft ground* or *aquatint*. A person who engraves metal is called a *chaser*.

top roller

pressure screw

pressure screw

micro-dial indicator gauge

blanket bar

screw

upright

gearbox

gearbox shaft

spring

wood form

crank handle

press bed

springs

press bed stops

machine stop

stand

carrier roller

press body

Etching Press

Dabber

handle

muslin wrapping

leather pad

Burnisher

blade

ferrule

handle

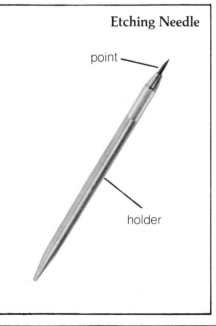

Etching Needle

point

holder

Fine Arts

Stained Glass

Cut sections of *colored glass* are separated by *breakers.Grozing pliers* are used to grind or bite away irregular glass edges.

finished edge

cartoon/pattern

stained glass

tip

heating element/
heating head

handle

Soldering Iron

Lead Came

heart of came

face

channels

Copper Foil

tapper

foil

handle

paper backing

cutter head

wheel

Glass Cutter

Frame

The frame shown here is a long-lasting *archival frame*. The area cut out of the mat to reveal the artwork is the *mat window*. A wire hanger can be attached to L-shaped *shoulder hooks*, *picture hooks* or *nails* as well as to screw eyes. The process of permanently affixing artwork to a backing is called *mounting*. A *free-standing easel-back* or *piano frame* consists of an easel, backing and an angled support *stand*. In *passe-partout*, the framing elements are held together by strips of cloth or paper pasted over the edges.

molding

glass

mat

artwork

acid-free backing

non-porous backing

stiff backing

hanger

screw eye   wire

seal

Cartooning

Many one-panel cartoons use *captions* or *labels* below the *illustration* for dialogue or explanation. Those appearing on the editorial pages of newspapers are called *editorial* or *political cartoons* and usually feature an exaggerated likeness, or *caricature*, of some well-known figure, as the main *character*. *Comics*, or *comic books*, use cartooning throughout. A complete *sphericasia*, or *swalloop*, is used by a *cartoonist* to depict a complete swing at an object, be it a golf ball or another person.

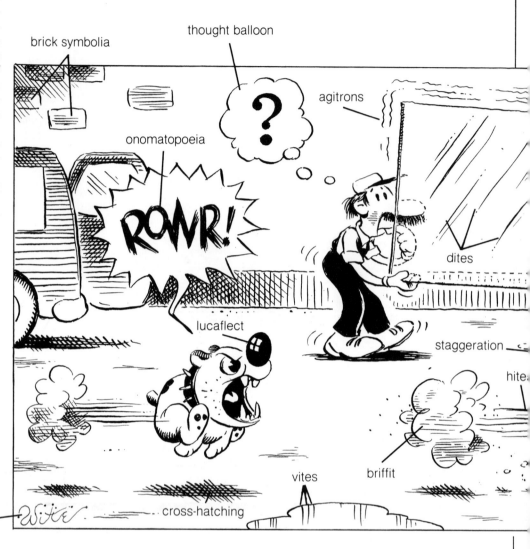

brick symbolia

thought balloon

agitrons

onomatopoeia

dites

lucaflect

staggeration

hite

briffit

vites

cross-hatching

artist's signature

Comic Strip

strip title

cartoonist

cartoon panel/frame

border

speech balloon

spurl
idea balloon
symbolia
squean
oculama
boozex
plewds
ZZZAT!!!
jarns
quimp
grawlix
maladicta balloon
nittles
solrads
digiton
waftarom
blurgits

balloon pointer

WELL?!

dialogue

I THINK I SAW IT ON YOUR WHATCHAMACALLIT

punch line

SURE IS TOUGH TO GET AN ANSWER AROUND HERE

Cartooning

Sewing

Each in-and-out movement of a threaded needle produces à *stitch*. A scissor's *bite* is the distance it cuts into a fabric on a single stroke. A small cushion into which pins or most-used needles are stuck until needed is called a *pincushion*.

crown

edge

eye/hole

shank

knot

point

strands/cords

Needle and Thread

Scissors/Shears

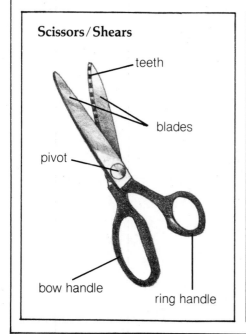

teeth

blades

pivot

bow handle

ring handle

Thimble

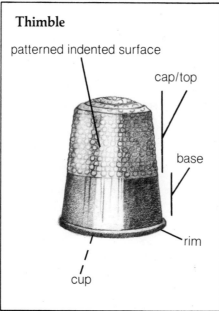

patterned indented surface

cap/top

base

rim

cup

Spool/Reel

flange/end

nick/notch

bore/hole

barrel

thread

rim

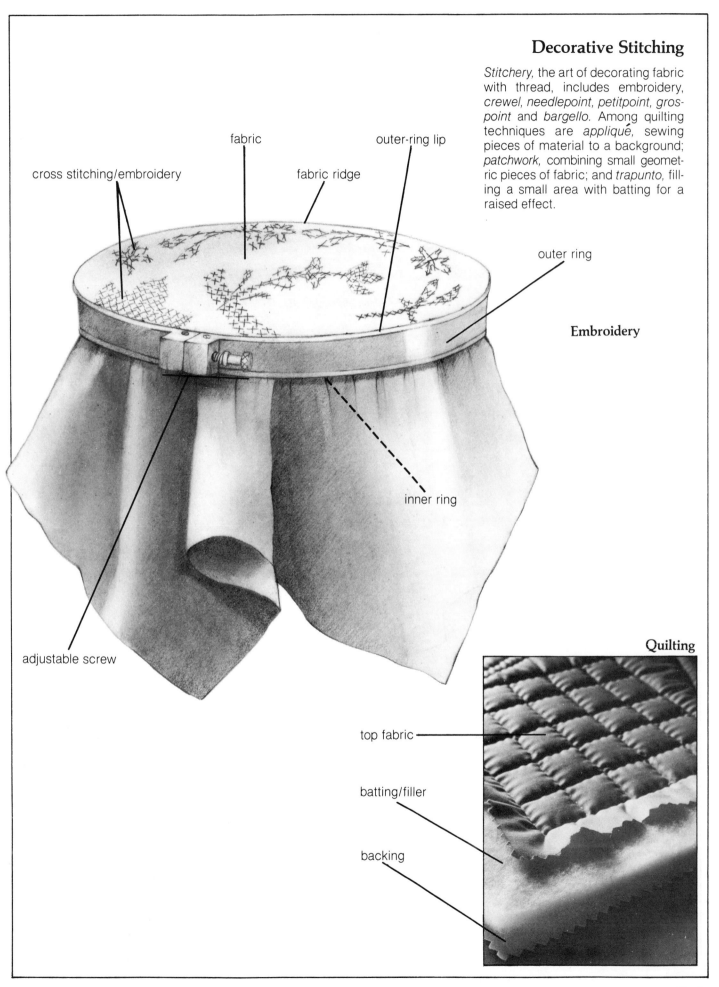

Decorative Stitching

Stitchery, the art of decorating fabric with thread, includes embroidery, *crewel, needlepoint, petitpoint, grospoint* and *bargello.* Among quilting techniques are *appliqué,* sewing pieces of material to a background; *patchwork,* combining small geometric pieces of fabric; and *trapunto,* filling a small area with batting for a raised effect.

cross stitching/embroidery

fabric

fabric ridge

outer-ring lip

outer ring

Embroidery

inner ring

adjustable screw

Quilting

top fabric

batting/filler

backing

Crafts

Knitting

Knitting is the interlacing of *loops*. The main stitches are the *knit stitch,* or *stitch,* and the *purl stitch,* or *purl*. *Crocheting* is a form of *needlework* done by looping thread with a *crochet needle. Macrame* is knotting, and *tatting* is done by looping and knotting with a single cotton thread and a small shuttle.

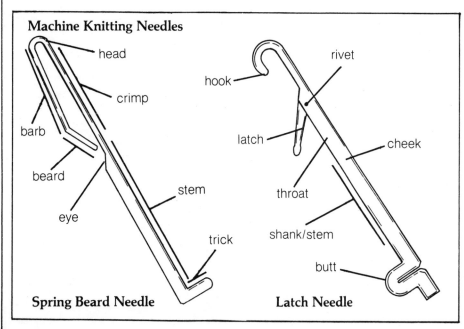

head

needle/knitting needle

stitches

skein of yarn/ hank of yarn

fabric

rows

point

Hand Knitting

Machine Knitting Needles

head

crimp

hook

rivet

barb

latch

cheek

beard

throat

eye

stem

shank/stem

trick

butt

Spring Beard Needle

Latch Needle

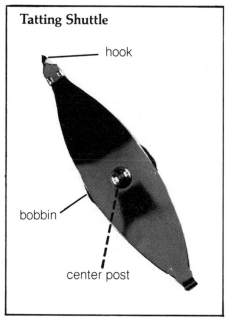

Tatting Shuttle

hook

bobbin

center post

Weaving

The lengthwise (front to back) *yarn* or *threads* on a loom are called the warp. Threads taken together which run from side to side, or from *selvage* to selvage, are called the *weft*. The weft is also often called the *woof,* although more correctly, the woof is the same as the *web,* or finished *fabric.*

harness frame
harness box cover board
harness slides
beater/batten
reed
warp
back beam/ whip roll
ratchet wheel
cloth beam/ fore beam
heddles
shuttle race
warp beam
breastbeam
treadle cords
lams
crossbeam
take-up motion handle
rear post
upright
release treadle
front post
crossbeam
crosspiece
treadles

Hand Loom

Spinning Wheel

driving band/ cord band
bobbin, spindle & flyer
wheel
distaff
standard
the mother-of-all
treadle

Sewing Pattern

A roll of fabric of a specified length is called a *bolt*. A sample of a fabric is a *swatch*. Fabrics sold at lengths specified by the customer are called *piece goods* or *yard goods*.

cutting line

seam allowance

straight of goods/lengthwise grain line

seam line/stitching line

notch

fold line

dart

button marks

alteration lines/adjustment lines

zipper line

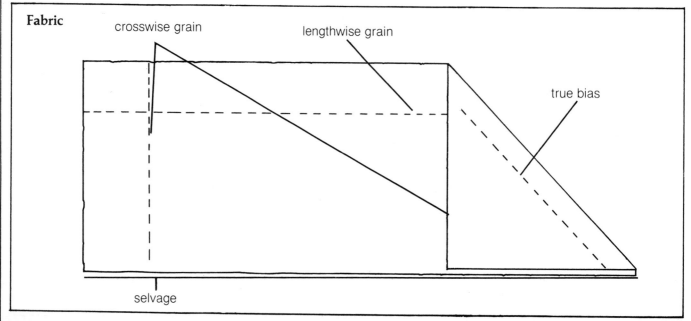

Fabric

crosswise grain

lengthwise grain

true bias

selvage

Machinery, Tools and Weapons

Except for office and industrial equipment, which is outside the scope of this book, this section covers all the man-made equipment one is likely to encounter in everyday life, daily reading or classroom learning. It includes basic power systems and offshoots, everything from a nuclear power plant to an electrical plug, equipment used to control temperature in a house, and components of various engines.

Considerable space has been devoted to illustrating the parts of tools used around the home and in the yard while not ignoring the basic gear used by ranchers, trappers, farmers, scientists and doctors. Even penal equipment used for capital punishment has been included.

The weaponry subsection traces the names and parts of articles used in warfare from medieval times to objects used today. Thus, a student reading about King Arthur for the first time will be able to identify the parts of a sword as easily as a newspaper reader is able to identify the parts of a modern missile.

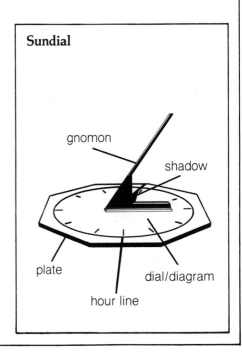

Sundial

gnomon

shadow

plate

dial/diagram

hour line

Wind Systems

The cloth sail on this *smock mill* is in a *first reef,* or *curled,* position, as opposed to *sword point, dagger point* or *full sail.* Sails or *shutters* on a fantail are called *vanes.* Some mills have *petticoats,* or vertical boards, below the cap, to provide protection where cap and tower meet, and *beards,* or decorated boards, behind the cannister.

sail/sweep/rotor/blade

cord/line

cloth sail

heel

leader board

sail bars

stock

helmath

whip/sail back

windshaft/axle

cannister/poll end

cap

fantail/fly tackle

tower

Windmill

machine cabin

knob

Wind Turbine

rotor

post

Solar Power System

Solar energy can be collected by systems such as the one shown here, which operate like *radiators* working in reverse to produce hot water. The sun's energy can also be converted directly into *electricity* by *solar cells*. *Concentrating solar collectors* use *lenses* or *reflecting sufaces* to direct sunlight on a trough-type collector to produce large amounts of heat which can be converted into electricity.

flat-plate solar-collector unit

solar-collector differential thermostat

sensor

domestic hot-water tank

hot-water pipe

cold-water pipe

hot-water differential thermostat

thermal-storage tank

pump

main circulating pump

hand valve

heating-unit return pipe

heating-unit pipe

heating unit

Solar Heating System

Collector Panel

glass cover plate

heat-transfer fluid

return pipe

upper header

frame

collector tube

heat-absorber plate/
blackened copper surface

insulation

supply plate

Nuclear Power Reactor

In order to generate *electricity* by using the heat produced by *fission*, the *chain reaction* must be slowed down and controlled. To control the reaction rate in a reactor, or *pile, rods* of neutron-absorbing material are moved in and out as required. The smallest amount of *fissionable material* in which fission is self-sustaining is called the *critical mass*. If more fissionable material is produced than consumed, the reactor is called a *breeder reactor*.

concrete shield & steel inner shell

relief valve

remote-operated block valve

steam generator

steam line

generator

condensate pump

turbine

pressurizer

control rods

reactor

reactor core

condenser

emergency core-cooling system pump

borated-water storage tank

demineralizer

sump pump

block valve

auxiliary feedwater pump

radioactive-waste storage tank

drain tank

sump

reactor coolant pump

main feedwater pump

Auxiliary Building

Turbine Building

Containment Building

transformer

circulating water pump

condensate storage tank

Cooling Tower

Reactor Cross Section

plenum assembly

control-rod guide tube

inlet nozzle

outlet nozzle

upper grid

core support assembly

core basket

fuel assembly

lower grid assembly

guide lugs

flow distributor head

incore-instrument guide tubes

Power Systems

Power Line, Vacuum Tube and Transistor

An *overhead line support, lattice-work tower* or *double-circuit tower* transmits high-voltage electrical power from *generating plants* to various parts of a *power network*. A transistor consists of a small block of a *semiconductor* with at least three *electrodes*.

strain insulator/protective sleeve

drip loop

pole

primary cable

secondary cable

crossarm/traverse arm

tower

Overhead Power Line

Transistor Chip

region of interaction

emitter

collector

base/chip

Vacuum Tube/Electron Tube

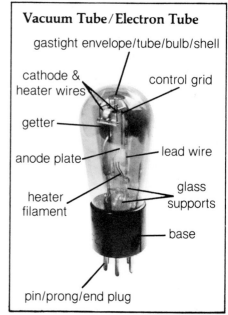

gastight envelope/tube/bulb/shell

cathode & heater wires

getter

anode plate

heater filament

control grid

lead wire

glass supports

base

pin/prong/end plug

Battery

Batteries are marked with *polarity symbols,* + identifying the positive terminal, − the negative. *Secondary cells* can be recharged, while *primary cells* cannot.

positive terminal/post

vent cap

cell compartments

negative terminal/post

cover

case

Lead Acid Battery

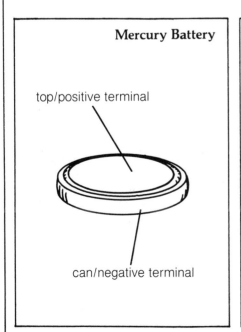

Mercury Battery

top/positive terminal

can/negative terminal

Zinc Carbon Cell/Battery

jacket

positive terminal

cover

bottom/negative terminal

Switch, Receptacle and Plug

A wall switch conducts *electrical current* only when it is in the up, or *on position,* as opposed to the down, or *off position. Ground wires* are located inside the junction box. *Attachment plugs,* or *"dead front" plugs,* such as the one shown here, have no exposed current-carrying parts except prongs, blades or *pins.* A *male plug* is fitted into a *female receptacle.*

Cover Plate/Switch Plate

Wall Switch

Receptacle/Outlet/Wall Socket

Plug

Meter and Fuse Box

Fuses "blow" and circuit breakers "trip" when there is too much heat in the wires of a particular *circuit*. The fuse or circuit breaker acts as a safety device to keep fire from starting by heat caused by an *overload* or by a *short circuit*.

usage registers

shaft

KILOWATT HOURS

glass casing

primary cell

SINGLE-PHASE WATTHOUR METER TYPE I-30-A
15 AMPERES   115-120 VOLTS
Kh=1.5   60 CYCLES   3-WIRE
MODEL AC103

18 690 382

specifications

electrical connection

LINE   LOAD

Electric Meter

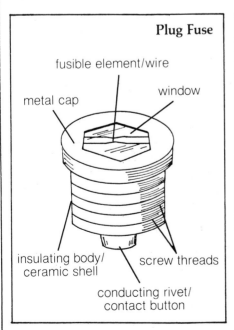

Plug Fuse

fusible element/wire

metal cap

window

insulating body/
ceramic shell

screw threads

conducting rivet/
contact button

Cartridge Fuse

casing

link/metal strip

insulation

end cap

conducting blade

Circuit Breaker Box

entrance cable

main breaker

ground
wire

circuit breaker

Power Systems

Furnace

The furnace shown in this schematic illustration provides *steam heat* to radiators located in various parts of a building.

tubes

air vent

handle

packing nut

shutoff valve

Radiator

chimney

exhaust duct/stack

steam main

air vent

steam pressure gauge

safety valve

instruction plate

water return pipe

overflow pipe

water level
sight glass

boiler

water make up feed line

burner

drain cock

Furnace

Hot Water Heater

The unit shown here is *gas-fired*. Other models include *electric water heaters* and *oil water heaters*.

relief valve/pressure relief valve

flue

cold-water supply pipe

hot-water supply line

overflow drain

cold-water shutoff valve

gas supply line

water tank

gas supply shutoff valve

instruction plate

reset button

gas cock

union

pressure regulator

thermostat

vent

sediment bleed valve/drain valve

access plate

heater/burner unit

Climate Control Units

Air Conditioning

An air conditioner's *front grille* has *louvers* which allow cooled air to be directed to any part of a room. *Condenser coils* in the rear of the unit discharge heat outdoors. Hand-held *folding fans, overhead fans* and *rotary fans* circulate air without actually cooling it. A *dehumidifier* removes moisture from the air, whereas a humidifier adds moisture to it.

cabinet

inner enclosure

filter retainer

control panel

function selector

temperature control

power cord

air filter

moisture-collector pan

evaporator coils

evaporator fins

Air Conditioner

Humidifier

grille

trough

control panel

drum/blower wheel

cabinet

Heat Exchanger

This schematic shows the basic elements used to extract cold from outside air in summer and heat from outside air in winter. A *heat pump* consists of two exchangers and a compressor, or *condenser. Cooling/heating fluid* is compressed in one exchanger or the other, depending on the season.

supply duct

cooling/ heating coils

filter

blower

return duct

hot- gas pipe/warm -liquid pipe

exhaust

fan

air intake

heating/cooling coils

warm- liquid pipe/hot- gas pipe

compressor

Woodburning Stove

When the *stove damper* is closed, interior *baffles* direct air into the *secondary combustion chamber*, then through the *smoke path* until it exits through the flue collar. A stovepipe led through a wall is attached to a *thimble*. The original *Franklin stove* was built into the wall, but three sides extended into the room to radiate heat.

stovepipe

flue collar

griddle

stove top

thermostat control

finials

front-door handle

stove-damper handle

side loading door

front door

loading-door handle

bottom

loading-door ash lip

pin hinge

ash lip

primary combustion chamber

leg

Steam Engine

The steam engine was used to generate *mechanical power* from *thermal energy*. A *piston* inside the steam cylinder, or *engine cylinder*, was driven by *high-pressure steam*. It moved the crankshaft to provide *rotational motion*.

lubricating valve

connecting rod/ pitmans

crank wrist

crank

crankshaft

sliding block/ crosshead

flywheel

pressure gauge

exhaust

piston rod

steam cylinder

stuffing box

pressure release & bleed valve

steam pipe

boiler/generator

frame/base

bedplate

Internal Combustion Engine

The internal combustion engine is one in which combustion of fuel takes place within the *cylinder*, the product of which is measured in *horsepower*. Engines are *two-cycle*, *four-cycle*, or *Otto cycle*; *gas-* or *diesel-fueled*; *air-cooled* or *liquid-cooled*.

gas cap

gas tank

fuel cock

throttle shaft

spark plug lead

model, specification & serial number plate

air filter

shroud

muffler

control lever

screen

stop plate

governor lever

oil filler dipstick

governor spring

oil-drain plug

exhaust

starter handle

recoil starter plate

crankcase/ cylinder body

WISCONSIN ROBIN

Jet Engines

A *turboprop engine* is like a combustion jet engine or *turbofan jet*, except that its turbine wheel is attached to a *crankshaft* that turns a *propeller*. Unlike a rocket, a *ramjet*, or *flying stovepipe*, combines compressed incoming air with fuel injection and ignition for propulsion.

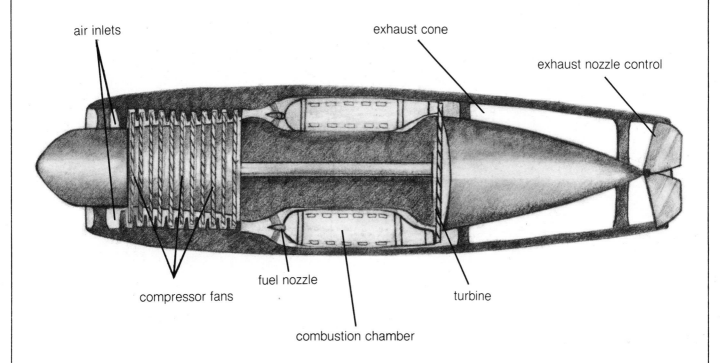

air inlets

exhaust cone

exhaust nozzle control

compressor fans

fuel nozzle

turbine

combustion chamber

Combustion Jet Engine

Rocket

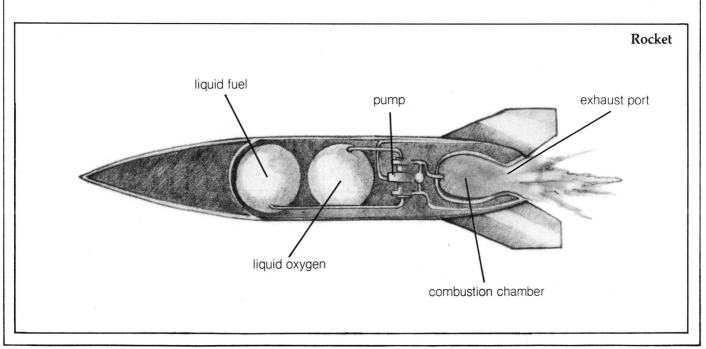

liquid fuel

pump

exhaust port

liquid oxygen

combustion chamber

Engines

Workbench

A *machinist's vise* has two parallel iron *jaws* with a wide *throat opening* to allow as much working room as possible. A *vise dog* is a steel pin in a vise which can be raised to hold materials between the vise and the bench dogs. A *backstop* is a raised portion at the rear of a workbench.

dog blocks/dogs

bench top

tool well

dogholes

end vise/tail vise

vise block

shoulder vise

spindle locking plate

tool drawer

handle

stretcher

guide rod

leg brace

leg

Sawhorse/Sawbuck

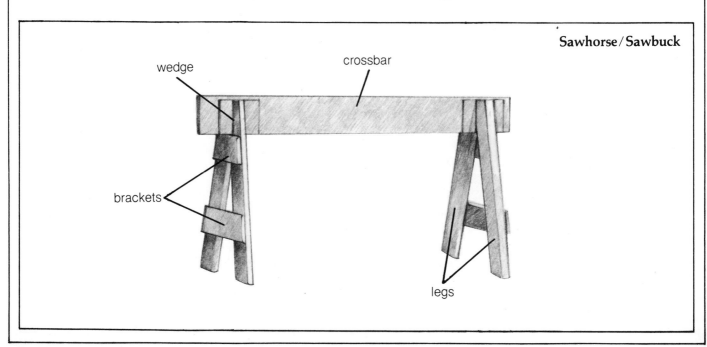

wedge

crossbar

brackets

legs

Clamps

In addition to the *holding tools* shown here, there are *hand screws, bar clamps, miter clamps, band clamps* and *spring clamps.* A *woodworking vise* is similar to a *metalworking vise* except that its jaws are padded in order to hold lumber without marring it. In wood clamps, the steel screws operate through *pivots* so that the jaws can be set at any required angle. *Adjustable C-clamps,* also known as *short bar clamps,* have an adjustable jaw that slides along a flat metal bar to the desired position.

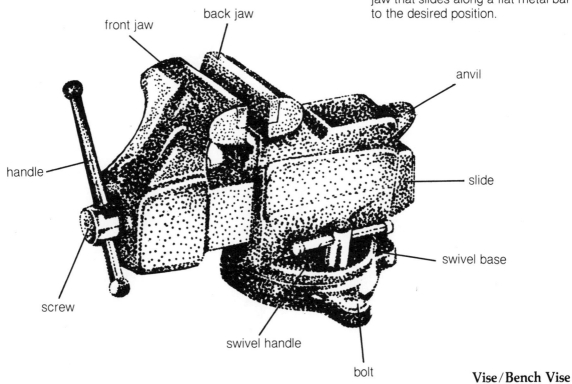

front jaw

back jaw

anvil

handle

slide

screw

swivel base

swivel handle

bolt

Vise / Bench Vise

Hand-Screw Clamp / Wood Clamp

end operating-screw handle

jaws

screw

insert

middle operating-screw handle

C-Clamp

frame

throat

handle

ADJUSTABLE

fixed jaw

movable jaw

swivel head / ball joint head

operating screw

Household Tools

Nails and Screws

A nail is measured in *penny sizes.* A *brad* is a thin *finishing nail* with a tiny *nailhead* used mainly in cabinetwork. *Spikes* are large, heavy nails. The small hole drilled prior to driving a screw is called a *pilot hole.*

head
gripper marks
shank
point

Nail

head
shank
threads
thread crest
root
pitch
point

Screw

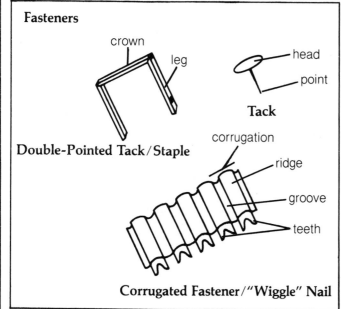

Fasteners

crown
leg

head
point

Tack

Double-Pointed Tack/Staple

corrugation
ridge
groove
teeth

Corrugated Fastener/"Wiggle" Nail

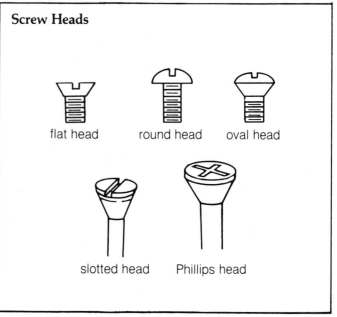

Screw Heads

flat head
round head
oval head

slotted head
Phillips head

Nuts and Bolts

Some bolts have small *collars* below the head to prevent them from turning in a piece of wood. *Washers,* flat discs with a hole in the center, are used to prevent nutheads or bolts from digging into wooden surfaces. *Eyebolts* have rounded tops that enable them to anchor string or rope.

head

bolt

shank

threads

nut

Nuts

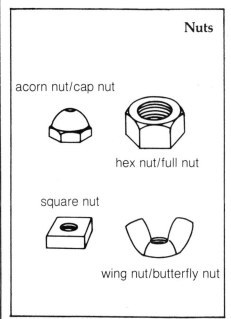

acorn nut/cap nut

hex nut/full nut

square nut

wing nut/butterfly nut

Bolts

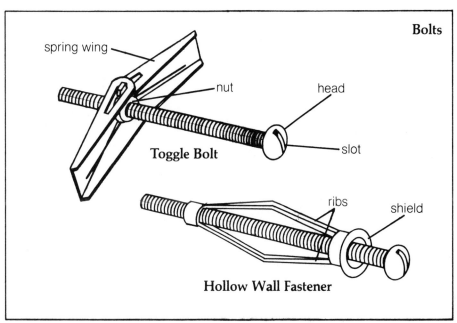

spring wing

nut

head

slot

Toggle Bolt

ribs

shield

Hollow Wall Fastener

Household Tools

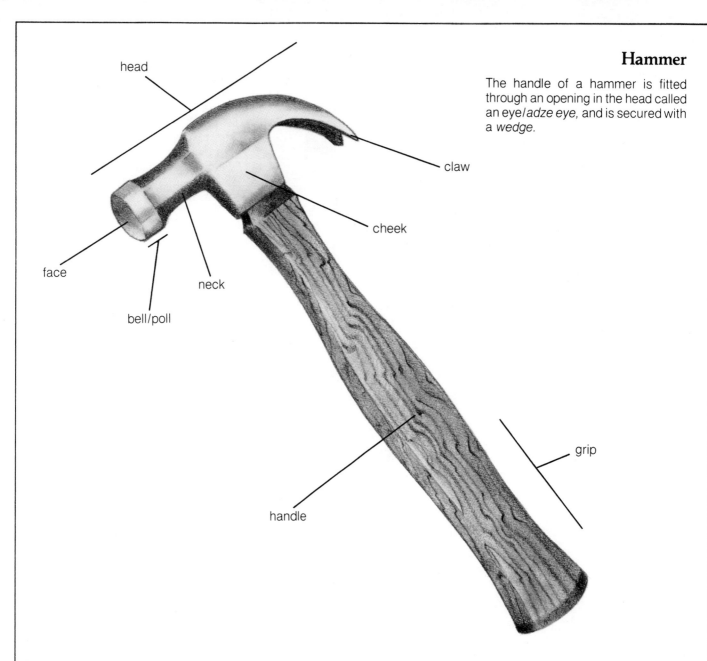

Hammer

The handle of a hammer is fitted through an opening in the head called an eye/*adze eye,* and is secured with a *wedge.*

head

claw

cheek

face

neck

bell/poll

grip

handle

Hatchet

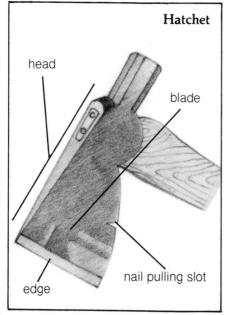

head

blade

edge

nail pulling slot

Ball-Peen Hammer

peen

Mallet/Gavel

eye

Screwdriver

Screwdrivers are specified by the length of the blade and the width of the tip. Some have a *ferrule* where the blade meets the handle. *Offset screwdrivers* are used when working in tight areas where a regular screwdriver will not fit. The *standard ratchet screwdriver* is the predecessor to the spiral ratchet screwdriver. It has a *ratcheting mechanism* in the handle.

head

handle

flute

round shank

blade

square shank

tip

Spiral Ratchet Screwdriver

handle

ratchet shifter

chuck sleeve

cabinet tip

bits

keystone tip

locking ring

chuck

spiral groove spindle

Phillips head tip

Household Tools

Pliers

In addition to the pliers seen here, there are heavy-duty *bolt cutters;* *midget pliers* and *needle-nose pliers,* often used for jewelry work or electrical jobs; *music wire pliers,* used for cutting piano wire; and *duckbill pliers,* used primarily by telephone workers and weavers.

nose

curved jaw

straight jaw

teeth

nest

wire cutter

slip joint/pivot

handle

Combination Pliers/Slip-Joint Pliers

Tongue-and-Groove Pliers

jaw

adjustable channels

bolt slot

nut & bolt

cam

Lineman's Pliers/ Electrician's Pliers

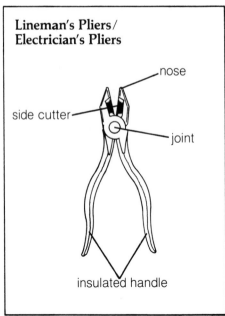

nose

side cutter

joint

insulated handle

Locking Pliers/ Lever-Wrench Pliers

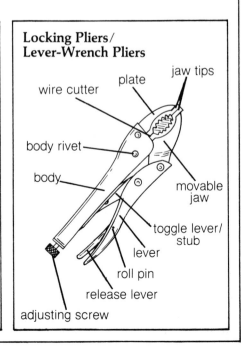

plate

jaw tips

wire cutter

body rivet

body

movable jaw

toggle lever/ stub

lever

roll pin

release lever

adjusting screw

Wrench

Adjustable wrenches come in two styles, *locking* and *non-locking*. A *"cheater"* is a handle extension used to increase leverage. Some wrenches have *offset handles* to provide clearance over obstructions. *Socket wrenches* combine an offset handle with a male *drive piece* which has a spring-loaded *bearing* to lock on various sized *sockets*. Many socket wrenches also have a *ratchet handle* so that reversing is possible.

jaws

web area

open end

handle

box end

web area

points

box

Combination Wrench

Monkey Wrench

handle

stationary jaw/ fixed jaw

adjusting nut

adjustment screw

sliding jaw/ movable jaw

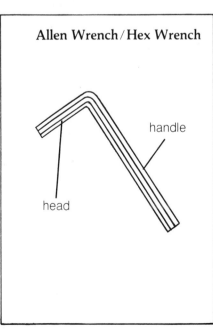

Allen Wrench/Hex Wrench

handle

head

Household Tools

Handsaws

The cut or incision made by a saw blade is the *kerf.* The carpenter's saw, seen here, is similar to a *ripsaw* or *crosscut saw.* A *skewback hand-saw* has an inwardly curved back. On a coping saw, the distance from the blade to the frame is the *throat,* or *throat clearance.* A coping saw with a particularly long throat is called a *deep throat.*

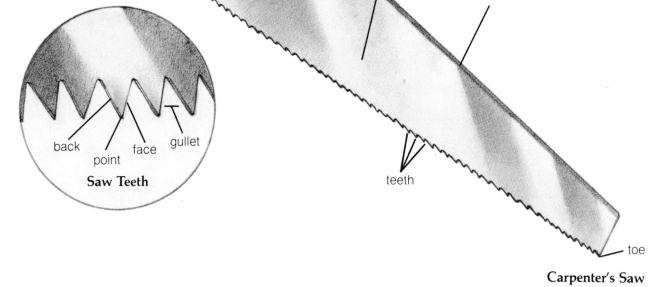

handle

fittings

heel

blade

back

teeth

toe

Carpenter's Saw

back

point

face

gullet

Saw Teeth

Coping Saw

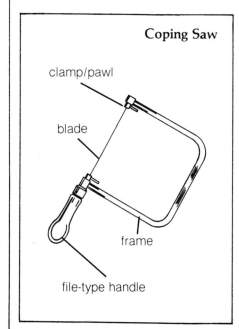

clamp/pawl

blade

frame

file-type handle

Hacksaw

adjustable frame

pistol-grip handle

pin

blade

wing nut

Power Saw

The round blades used in table and circular saws have either *crosscut teeth* or *rip teeth*. Circular saws can be equipped with a *rip guide* and an *ejector chute,* which routes sawdust to the rear or side. Saber units include *variable-speed controls* and a *roller support* behind the blade. The *band saw* derives its name from the fact that its blade is a continuous band revolving on two wheels.

splitter/spreader

slot

anti-kickback pawl

blade guard

table/
cutting surface

miter-gauge slot

grid table extension

rip fence

fence guide bar

adjustable
table extension

miter gauge

fence lock handle

locking switch key

on & off switch

rip fence head

overload reset button

fence adjusting knob

tilting arbor handwheel/
blade-bevel handwheel

saw base

bevel scale

arbor lock/tilt lock

stand leg

blade-elevating
handwheel

stand brace

Table Saw/Bench Saw/Contractor's Saw

Circular Saw

Saber Saw/Jigsaw/Bayonet Saw/Scroll Saw

retaining bolt

handle

handle

upper blade guard

on & off switch

cord-strain
reliever

cord

knob

housing

angle scale

brush retainer
screw

blade

tilt lock knob

baseplate/base

tilting base/shoe

guide knob

retractable blade guard

lubricant port

blade screw

blade

Household Tools

Manual Drill

Drilling accessories include a *bit gage, reamer, auger bits, dowel bits, expanding bits, screwdriver bits, countersink bits, twist drill bits, spade bits* and *power bore bits*. The circle described by turning the handle of a brace is called the *sweep*.

crank handle

file handle

idler pinion

frame

bevel gears

pinion

chuck

auxiliary handle/ side handle

bit/drill point

Hand Drill

Brace/Hand Brace

handle/floating crank

bow

box ratchet

chuck

quill

cam ring

shell

jaws

pawl

head

Gimlet

handle

auger bit

shank

Power Drills

A regular bit, or *drill*, consists of a *point, body* and shank. Some bits have specially configured *tangs* at the end of the shank. If a drill has a *geared key chuck,* the bit is locked in place with a key. Holes can be drilled to predetermined depths by clamping an *adjustable bit gauge* to the bit shank. A drill is classified by the largest bit its chuck will accept. Some drills have *reversible motors.*

belt & pulley safety guard

head

depth stop

push-button switch

mounting collar

keyless chuck

motor housing

belt-tension knob

pilot-wheel feed

rigid table/main table

table-locking clamp

handle

chuck

shank

column

Key/Chuck Key

lower table/base

Drill Press

Hand Drill and Bits

spur/nib

cutting edge

feed screw

shank

motor housing

Auger Bit   twist/throat/flute

jaw

collar

chuck/shell

adjustable arm

Expansive Bit   cutter adjusting screw

trigger

handle

Countersink Bit

cord-strain reliever

Household Tools

Planing and Shaping Tools

The body of a plane is the *frame.* The angle of the blade is the *pitch.* The flat side of a chisel is its *back. Cold chisels* are designed to cut metal and have no handles. *Gouges* are either *in-cannel,* with the bevel ground on the inside of the curved blade, or *out-cannel,* with the bevel ground on the outside. The rough side of a rasp or file is the *face.* The smooth side is called the *"safe" side.*

lateral adjusting lever

handle

heel

plane iron/blade

cam

handle screw

lever cap screw

lever cap

"y" adjusting lever

knob/auxiliary handle

adjustment nut/ adjustment screw

knob nut and bolt

plane iron cap/cap iron

cutting edge

mouth

sole/bottom

toe

Plane

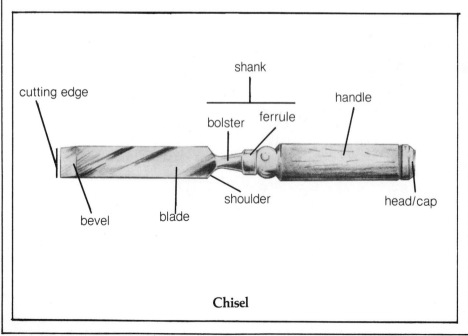

cutting edge

shank

handle

bolster

ferrule

bevel

blade

shoulder

head/cap

Chisel

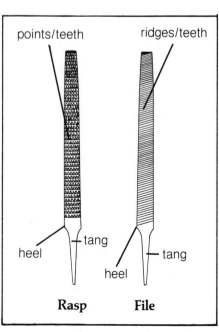

points/teeth

ridges/teeth

heel

tang

heel

tang

heel

Rasp   **File**

Sander

In a finishing, or *straight-line*, sander, the pad moves back and forth, whereas in the similar-looking *orbital sander,* the pad moves in a small orbital pattern. *Belt sanders* use a continuous *belt* of either *natural* or *artificial abrasive material,* and are available with or without *dust bags.* Sandpaper has either an *open* or *closed coat,* depending on spacing between *grains.*

handle

cord strain reliever

trigger switch

front handle

paper clamp

upper housing

lower housing

shoe

pad

paper clamp

Finishing Sander

Sandpaper

grit/abrasive coating

grit number

backing

Household Tools

Plumbing Tools

In addition to the basic plumbing tools shown here, there are *tubing*, or *pipe cutters*, some of which have built-in *polishers; reamers* for removing *burrs* inside cut *pipe;* and *flaring tools*, used to spread the ends of copper *tubing* for *flare fittings*. In *sweat soldering, flux* and *solder* are used. When working with *threaded pipe*, a *pipe threader* (which consists of a *die, diestock* and *handles*) and *joint-sealing tape* or *compound* are used. Other basic plumbing tools are *hacksaws* and *pipe wrenches*.

bulb head/bit/spiral tip

thumbscrew

canister

snake

handle

knob

Drain Cleaner/Snake/Auger

nozzle

Propane Torch

gas-control knob

valve

gas cylinder

Plunger/"Plumber's Friend"

handle

cup/suction cup/force cup

Electrician's Tools

A volt-ohm meter, also known as a *multimeter* or *volt-ohm-milliammeter,* is used with test *leads* and *jacks* attached to needle-type *probes* or *alligator clips.* The markings on the sheath of a wire describe *wire size,* number of *conductors,* the existence of a ground wire and cable type.

pointer

instrument sensitivity

VAC, VDC, MADC scales

ohms scale

DCmv scale

temperature scale

meter movement

zero adjust screw

"negative" test lead jack

ohmmeter zero adjust knob

temperature probe jack

"positive" test lead jack

selector knob

MODEL AM-1A
9000 Ω/V AC
20 000 Ω/V DC

MADE IN JAPAN FOR
AMPROBE INSTRUMENT®
LYNBROOK, N.Y.

METER MOVEMENT
PROTECTION

OHMS
R x 1   R x 10   R x 100   R x 1K
TEMP
DC.mV   60
1200   ΩADJ
DCmA 30 150
3
DCV 15   TEMP PROBE
30   ACV 30 150
300   OFF   300

Volt-Ohm Meter

Wire Stripper and Crimper/Multipurpose Tool

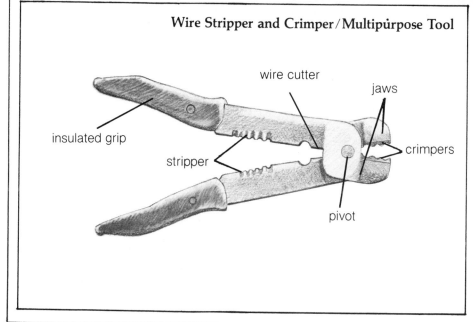

wire cutter

jaws

crimpers

insulated grip

stripper

pivot

Wire/Cable/Cord

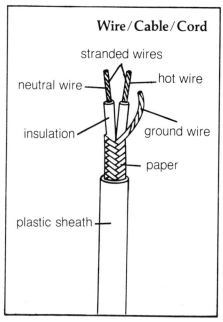

stranded wires

neutral wire

hot wire

insulation

ground wire

paper

plastic sheath

Measuring Tools

The basic measuring tool is the one-piece *bench rule*, or *ruler*. Tape measures also come in *reels* which can be manually rewound. An *L-shaped square* has two *arms* set at right angles. The longer arm is the *blade*, the shorter one is the *tongue*. They meet at the *heel*. A *combination square* substitutes for *try squares*, *depth gauges* and *marking gauges*. When the *air bubble* in a monovial stops between *marks*, the level is on the desired *plane*.

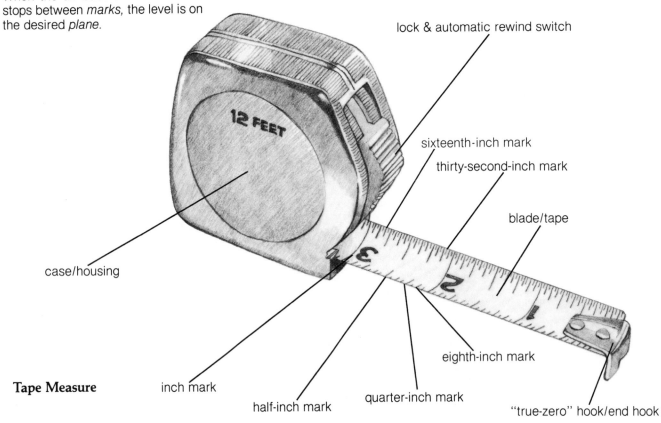

lock & automatic rewind switch

sixteenth-inch mark

thirty-second-inch mark

blade/tape

case/housing

eighth-inch mark

Tape Measure

inch mark

half-inch mark

quarter-inch mark

"true-zero" hook/end hook

Combination Square

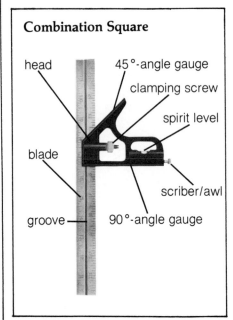

head

45°-angle gauge

clamping screw

spirit level

blade

scriber/awl

groove

90°-angle gauge

Folding Rule / Zigzag Rule

extension slide

hinge

stick/arm

joints

Carpenter's Level

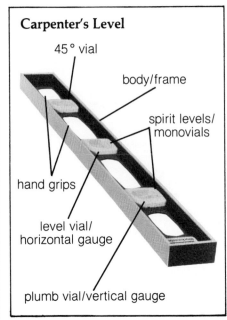

45° vial

body/frame

spirit levels/ monovials

hand grips

level vial/ horizontal gauge

plumb vial/vertical gauge

Painting Tools

A regular *paint brush* has *bristles* with *split*, or *flagged*, *ends*. The *heel* section of a brush is where the *butt ends* of bristles fit into a *ferrule* attached to the handle. Other paint-application tools include *pressure brushes*, *foam brushes* and *pad applicators*. Accessories include *pot* and *brush holders* and *brush spinners*. Paint rollers may have *threaded handles* to accommodate *extenders*. *Tack cloth* is used to clean surfaces to be painted, and a *drop cloth* protects objects and areas against paint spills.

housing

high-pressure pump

control knob

venthole

trigger

handle.

nozzle

safety guard

container cover

container

plug

Paint Spray Gun

Tray and Roller

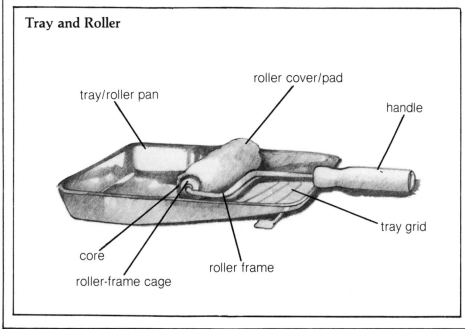

roller cover/pad

tray/roller pan

handle

tray grid

core

roller frame

roller-frame cage

Ladder/Stepladder

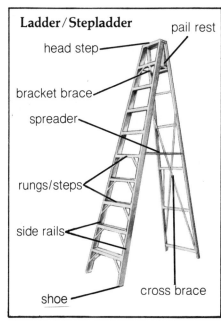

pail rest

head step

bracket brace

spreader

rungs/steps

side rails

shoe

cross brace

Swiss Army Knife

The *dividers* in the *handle* of a *jack-knife,* pocketknife or *camping knife* keep each blade or *tool* separate.

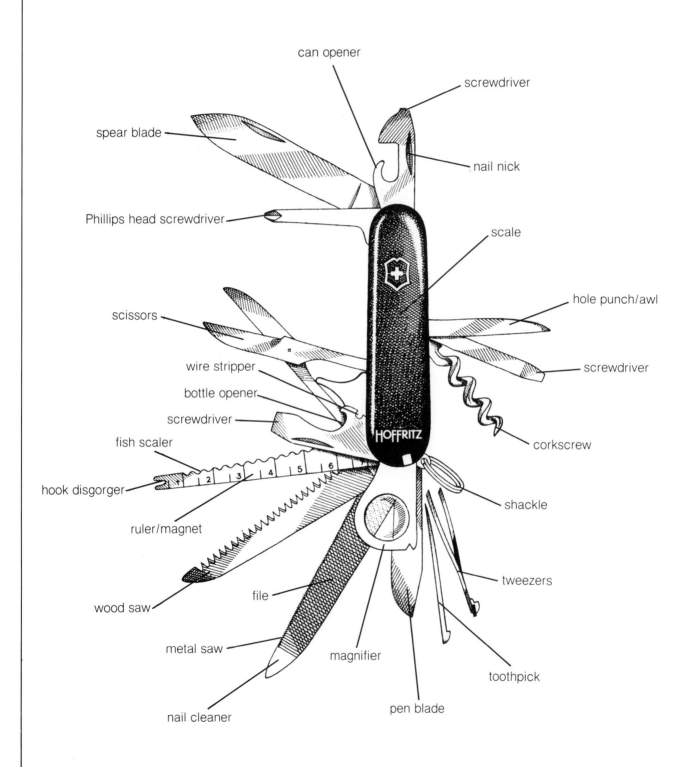

can opener

screwdriver

spear blade

nail nick

Phillips head screwdriver

scale

hole punch/awl

scissors

wire stripper

screwdriver

bottle opener

corkscrew

screwdriver

fish scaler

hook disgorger

shackle

ruler/magnet

tweezers

wood saw

file

metal saw

magnifier

toothpick

nail cleaner

pen blade

HOFFRITZ

Gardening Implements

A hand tool with a small scooped blade used for potting and planting is a *trowel*. A *spading fork* is used for turning soil. Shears are generally of two types: *anvil*, in which a blade cuts through a branch and stops against an anvil, and *by-pass*, which uses a shearing action to cut.

teeth/tines

blade

shank

blade

bow

tang

ferrule

frog

ferrule

socket

rolled shoulder/
turned step

handle

handle

handle

Hoe   **Rake**   **Shovel/Spade**

Shears/Clippers

blade

tension adjustment pin

grip

spring

linkage   stop

Sprinkler and Nozzles

Revolving sprinklers have rotating *arms* that spray water through nozzles at each end. An inverted Y-shaped *coupling*, or *siamese*, makes it possible to connect two *hoses* to a single *faucet*. In making a *hose connection*, the larger *female coupling* is fitted over the *male coupling* and turned until the connection is made fast. *Washers* inside couplings make seals watertight.

plug · spray tube · jet nozzles · oscillating crank · cam · hose connector · motor housing · spray-pattern dial · base/frame

Oscillating Lawn Sprinkler

Hose Nozzle

threaded fitting/socket

adjustable barrel/stem

standard/ screw nozzle

Pistol Nozzle

spray nozzle

barrel

adjustment knob

lever lock clip

control lever

body

threaded fitting/socket

Lawn Mower

Rotary mowers, such as the one shown here, use a single *blade* to slice off grass, as does a *scythe*. *Reel mowers,* such as the *sickle-bar mower,* use multiple blades, called a *reel,* to push grass against a stationary *bed knife* at the base of the mower. Cut grass is contained in a bag called a *grass-catcher.* With a *mulching mower,* bagging is unnecessary. A *lawn sweeper* uses a rotating sweeping action to pick up cuttings and leaves. *Lawn edgers* and *trimmers* are used to cut grass in areas where mowers cannot.

upper handle

lower handle

handle knob

starter handle

primer control

engine

stop control

screen plug

wheel adjuster

rear deflector/
drag shield

gas-tank cap

fuel tank

muffler

governor

toe guard

hinge rod

housing/deck

discharge chute

trim panel

air cleaner

hubcap

DANGER
KEEP HANDS and FEET AWAY

Power Mower

Gardening Tools

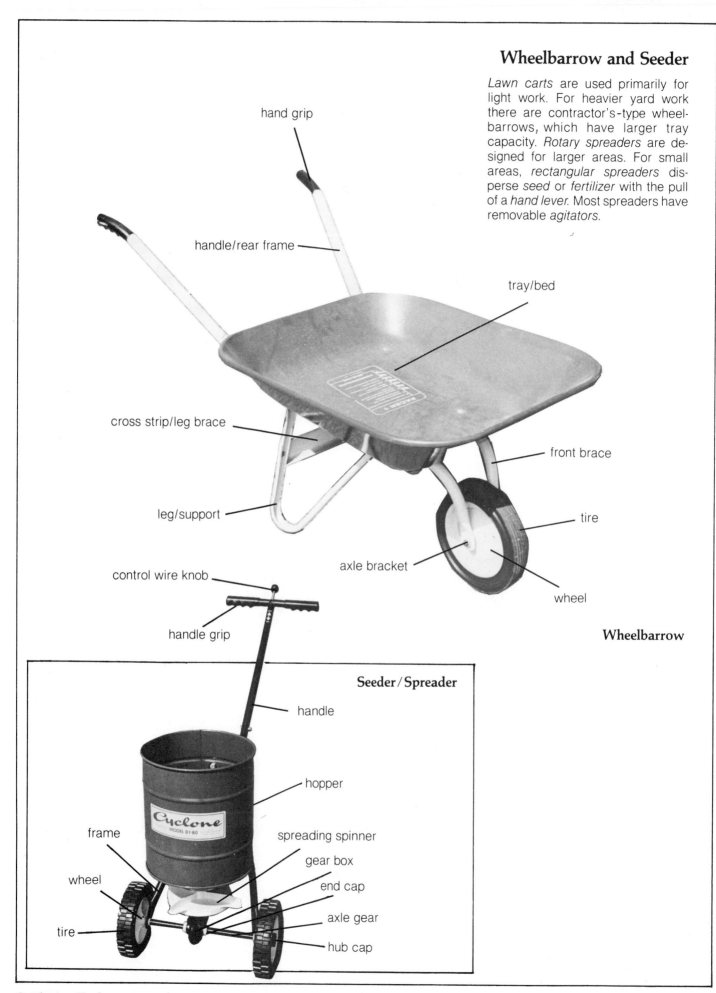

Wheelbarrow and Seeder

Lawn carts are used primarily for light work. For heavier yard work there are contractor's-type wheelbarrows, which have larger tray capacity. *Rotary spreaders* are designed for larger areas. For small areas, *rectangular spreaders* disperse *seed* or *fertilizer* with the pull of a *hand lever*. Most spreaders have removable *agitators*.

hand grip

handle/rear frame

tray/bed

cross strip/leg brace

front brace

tire

leg/support

axle bracket

wheel

Wheelbarrow

control wire knob

handle grip

Seeder / Spreader

handle

hopper

frame

spreading spinner

gear box

wheel

end cap

tire

axle gear

hub cap

Chain Saw

Chain saws are either gasoline- or electric-powered. Power output is measured in cubic inches of *piston displacement* in the *power head* rather than in horsepower. The *cutting head* may be *direct drive* or *gear drive*. A *sprocket-tip cutting bar* increases cutting speed because it eliminates most of the friction around the *bar tip*. Safety devices include a *chain brake* intended to stop the moving chain when the saw begins to kick back, *throttle latches* for safer starting, *safety triggers* to prevent accidental acceleration, *muffler shields*, and *chain catchers* designed to protect the operator from a broken or slipped chain.

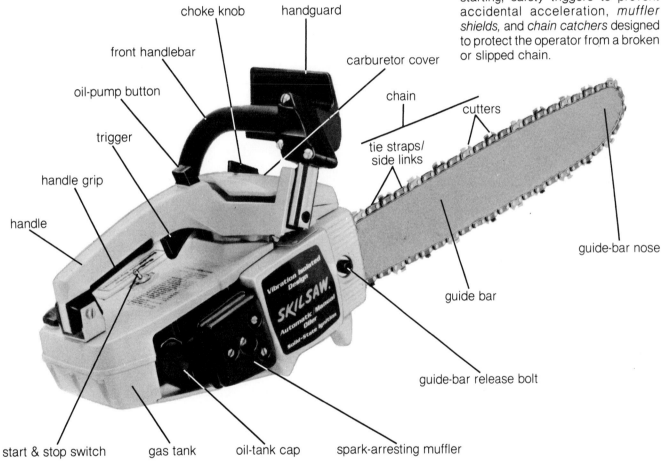

choke knob · handguard · front handlebar · carburetor cover · oil-pump button · chain · cutters · trigger · tie straps/ side links · handle grip · handle · guide-bar nose · start & stop switch · gas tank · oil-tank cap · spark-arresting muffler · guide-bar release bolt · guide bar

SKILSAW.
Vibration Isolated Design
Automatic Manual Oiler
Solid-State Ignition

Gardening Tools

Ranching Gear

In the days of cattle ranching, *ketch hands* would rope *calves,* or "critters," an *iron man* would brand them, and, in some instances, a *knife man* would cut an additional identifying notch, or *earmark,* in their ears. A *tally man* would record the operation.

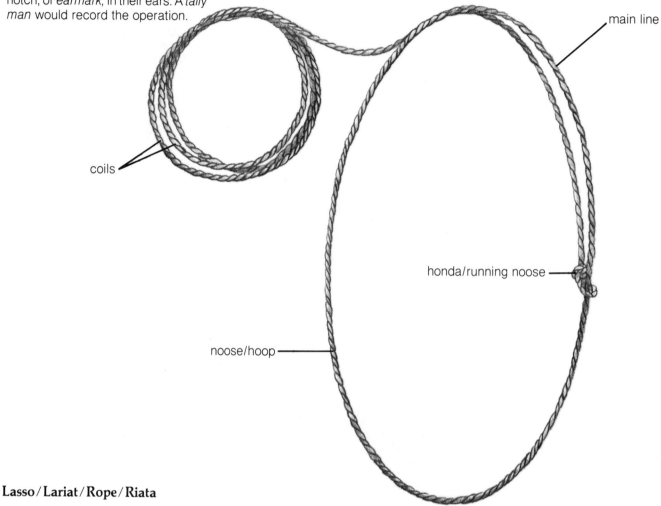

main line

coils

honda/running noose

noose/hoop

Lasso/Lariat/Rope/Riata

Barbed Wire

barb

wire strands

ironplate

handle

brand

fork

Branding Iron

Traps

Enclosing traps catch animals without hurting them. *Arresting traps,* such as the bear trap shown here, catch and hold animals in their teeth. *Killing traps* destroy animals and rodents.

bait

base

pedal lip

spring

locking bar

bow

Mousetrap

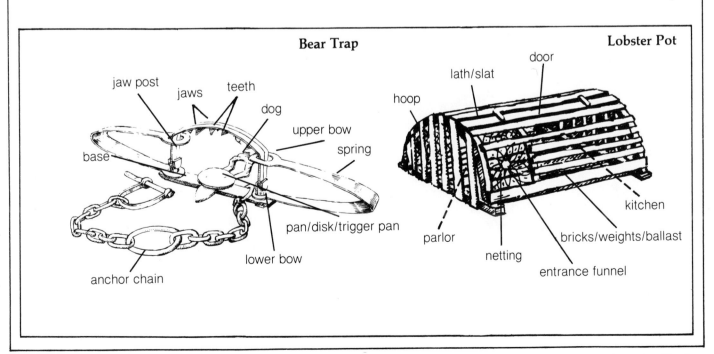

Bear Trap

jaw post

jaws

teeth

dog

upper bow

spring

base

pan/disk/trigger pan

lower bow

anchor chain

Lobster Pot

door

lath/slat

hoop

kitchen

bricks/weights/ballast

parlor

netting

entrance funnel

Trapping Devices

Tractor

Plows, reapers, cultivators, like the harrow seen here, and various *planting machines* are coupled to a tractor to work the land. The operating speed of attachments is controlled by a *power takeoff*. Optional *outboard planetaries* with *adjustable wheel treads* and *add-on segment weights* help boost traction.

front windows

cab

muffler

warning light

headlamp/headlight

hood

air filter

grille

fender

front-end weights

rear axle

adapter plate

frame

side panel

steps

wide tire

Hitch and Harrow

parking stand

SMV (slow-moving vehicle) symbol

lift link

top link

lower links

universal drive joint

flywheel

drive yoke and rocker

tine bars

tines

crumble roller

depth adjusting screw

Bulldozer

A *dozer* consists of a *crawler tractor* and a front attachment used to push, cut or grade earth. The operator sits in the *cab*.

hydraulic filter breather

air cleaner

steering levers

rear light

rain cap

oil cap

canopy

muffler

engine enclosure

headlights

hydraulic fuel tank

radiator grille

lift cylinder

tool box

starter switch

blade eye hook

fender

track shoes

track

trunnion

push arm

cutting edge

sprocket drive housing

track roller

upper strut

bulldozer blade

track frame

track idler roller

Instruments and Controls

left-hand steering lever

right-hand steering lever

brake pedal

instrument panel

decelerator pedal

transmission shift lever

engine-speed control lever

blade control lever

Construction Equipment

Transit and Jackhammer

A transit is used by *engineers* and *surveyors* to determine *angles, bearings* and *levels.* It is mounted on a three-legged stand called a *tripod.* A weight, known as a *plumb* or *plumb bob,* is suspended directly below the telescope to determine *true vertical.*

focusing knob

telescope clamp

diaphragm adjusting screw

stadia circle/ horizontal reduction

eyepiece

stadia circle/ vertical reduction

outside guard

vertical circle

vertical circle vernier

upright standard

horizontal circle

upper plate/vernier plate

clamp screws

leveling screws

leveling plate & shifting head

center/limb

telescope

telescope objective end

telescope vial

compass

plate vial/ leveling bubble

dustproof screw cover

Theodolite

Jackhammer/Breaker Hammer

motor housing

guide

housing cover

tool holder

switch cover

insert steel

operating lever

cord sleeve

handle

adjustable clip

Voting Booth

Voting booths, or *mechanized voting machines,* are located at *polling places,* or *polls.* An *x-indication* appears next to a candidate's name when a lever is pressed. When a *voter* presses levers for every candidate of a single political party, it is called voting a *straight ticket.* Any variation is a *split ballot.*

light

question index column

office index column

candidate's name column

R. F. Shoup corp. 10-35

selection levers/ individual voting levers

ballot/face

curtain

personal choice/ write-in

voter handle

custodian's seal

officer's lock & seal

poll's open & closed indicator

Sealed Booth

2046

serial number

split column control

protective counter

primary selector control

front door seal

front doors

public counter

officer's control

paper roll compartment

Computing Tools

Key Punch

A key punch or *card punch* codes data by punching holes in cards in a sequence of instructions designed by a *programmer.*

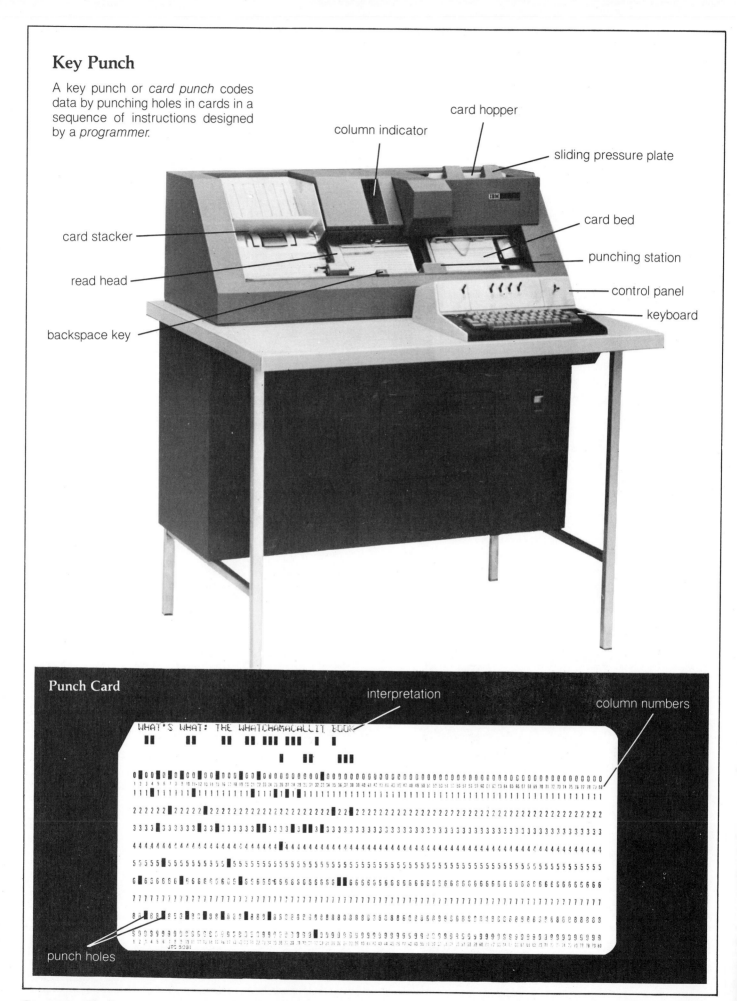

column indicator

card hopper

sliding pressure plate

card stacker

card bed

punching station

read head

control panel

keyboard

backspace key

Punch Card

interpretation

column numbers

WHAT'S WHAT: THE WHATCHAMACALLIT BOOK

punch holes

Computer

The heart of computer *hardware* is a *processing unit* containing an *arithmetic and logic unit* and a *memory unit*. *Software* consists of *procedures* or *programs* and information contained on *magnetic tape* or *disks, drums, cards, data cells* or *photodisks*.

monitor

on/off switch

reset switch

disk drive unit

video display

readout/printout

printer controls

line printer/ word processor

keyboard/console

disk expansion system

expansion unit control

system desk

blank panel

key pad & cursor positioning keys

storage drawer

external disk drive units

Home Computer/Word Processor

Diskette/Floppy Disk

label

spindle hole

index hole

DISKETTE

Do not bend or fold diskette.
Return diskette to envelope after use.
Write in label area only with a felt tip pen.
Do not touch exposed areas of magnetic disk.

PART NO. 34700

THIS END UP

read-write window

write-protect notch

jacket

Cash Register

The money drawer of a cash register is the *cash box,* or *till.* A roll of coins put up in paper is a *rouleau.* A *checkout center,* such as the one shown here, is sometimes equipped with a penlike optical *scanner* that translates information on the Universal Product Code, or *UPC label,* into a *cash register receipt* or *item-by-item tape.* It can also feed data to a *central inventory control unit.*

paper tape

journal printer

advance control

receipt printer

function keys

slip printer

display panel

keyboard & display module

on/off control

power supply module

numeric pad

printer & keyboard tray

drawer lock

cash drawer

Universal Product Code

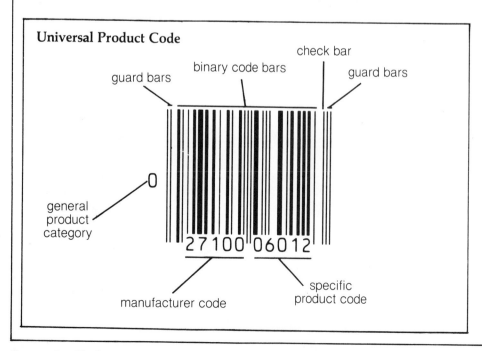

guard bars

binary code bars

check bar

guard bars

general product category

27100 06012

manufacturer code

specific product code

Calculators

The electronic calculator has generally replaced the *adding machine* today. The linear slide rule seen here often has scales on both sides. A *cylindrical slide rule* can only be used for *multiplication* and *division*. A *circular slide rule* is a series of long scales wound around a cylinder like a screw thread. The abacus is an ancient calculator used for solving problems of *addition, subtraction, multiplication* and *division,* all by the movement of beads. Other early devices include *counting rods,* or *"bones."*

casing

on/off switch

display

memory function keys

number entry keys

clear key

clear entry key

square root key

equals key

arithmetic function keys

decimal key

percent key

Electronic Calculator

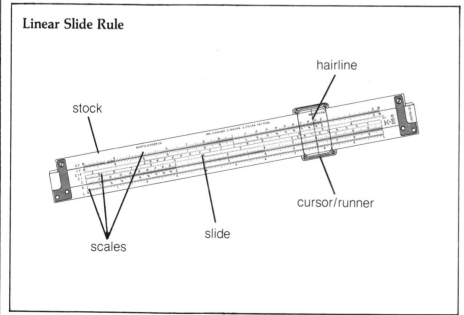

Linear Slide Rule

hairline

stock

cursor/runner

slide

scales

Abacus

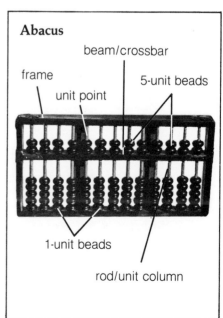

beam/crossbar

frame

5-unit beads

unit point

1-unit beads

rod/unit column

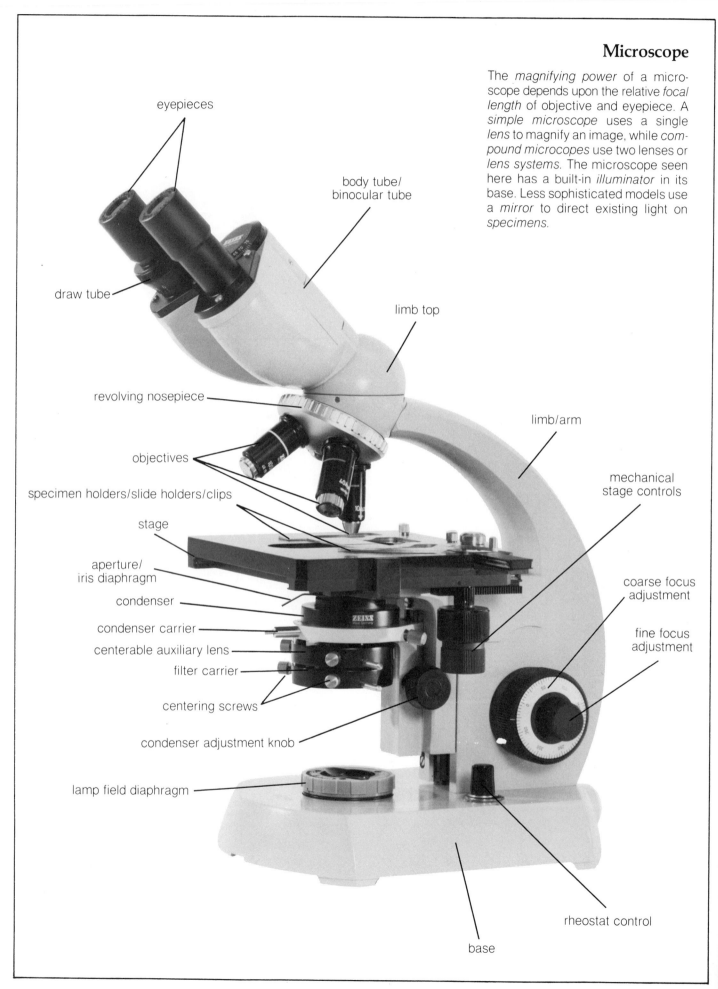

Microscope

The *magnifying power* of a microscope depends upon the relative *focal length* of objective and eyepiece. A *simple microscope* uses a single *lens* to magnify an image, while *compound microcopes* use two lenses or *lens systems*. The microscope seen here has a built-in *illuminator* in its base. Less sophisticated models use a *mirror* to direct existing light on *specimens*.

eyepieces

body tube/
binocular tube

draw tube

limb top

revolving nosepiece

limb/arm

objectives

specimen holders/slide holders/clips

mechanical
stage controls

stage

aperture/
iris diaphragm

coarse focus
adjustment

condenser

fine focus
adjustment

condenser carrier

centerable auxiliary lens

filter carrier

centering screws

condenser adjustment knob

lamp field diaphragm

rheostat control

base

Telescope & Binoculars

A *refracting telescope*, such as the one seen here, relies on the objective lens to concentrate incoming light. A *reflecting telescope* employs a *concave mirror* to do the same task. Binoculars are composed of two similar telescopes, one for each eye. *Field glasses* are lightweight binoculars that employ *erecting telescopes* of the *spyglass* type, while *opera glasses,* designed for use inside, use *Galilean telescopes.*

objective outer cell

objective lens

telescope maintube

dewcap/sunshade

cradle

altitude coarse-motion clamp

viewfinder/guide scope

slow-motion control knobs

viewfinder collimating screw

azimuth coarse-motion clamp

eyepiece

altazimuth mounting

focus knob

star diagonal

fine focus sleeve

drawtube

eyepiece holder

tripod leg

tripod accessories shelf

shelf mount

Binoculars   central focusing drive

eyecup

eyepiece

ocular lens

hinge

body/frame

objective lens

Telescope

Scientific Tools

Radar and Sonar

The cursor on a radar display unit is used to determine the *relative bearings* of *targets*. Most units come with a *viewing hood* and *magnifying lens*. Sonar, formerly known as *asdic*, uses a trainable *transducer* housed in a *soundome* beneath a vessel's hull.

variable range marker (VRM) display

VRM range-intensity control

tuning indicator

tuning control

heading alignment control

heading flash control

heading flash

range selector

cathode-ray tube screen

dimmer control

sea clutter control

interference rejector

bearing ring

rain-snow clutter control

cursor control

intensity/ brilliance control

vertical centering

horizontal centering

scanner switch

fuses

power switch

Radar Display Unit

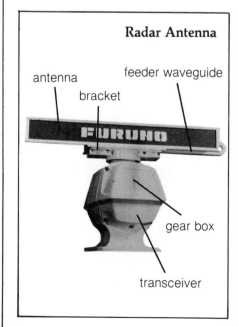

Radar Antenna

antenna

feeder waveguide

bracket

gear box

transceiver

Sonar Display Unit

power control

variable range marker control

cathode-ray tube screen

brightness control

range selector

display centering control

gain

presentation mode selector

speaker volume control

target lock

transducer tilt control

transducer position indicator

Detectors

A *metal locator* works by subtracting a frequency produced by an *oscillator* from a frequency produced by internal circuitry. When the *search coil* is near a metal object, this produces an audio frequency in the speaker or headphones.

search loop/coil/detection head

signal intensity & battery check meter

push-button tuner

discriminator adjustment

handle

on-off button & volume control

mode selector

rod

fine tuner

depth discriminator switch

speaker

ground control

battery door

headphone jack

Metal and Mineral Detector

Geiger Counter/Spectrometer/ Scintillometer

liquid crystal display

continuous battery monitor

fine calibrate

mode switch

audio knob

calibration source receptacle

coarse calibrate

audio port

Sensing Devices

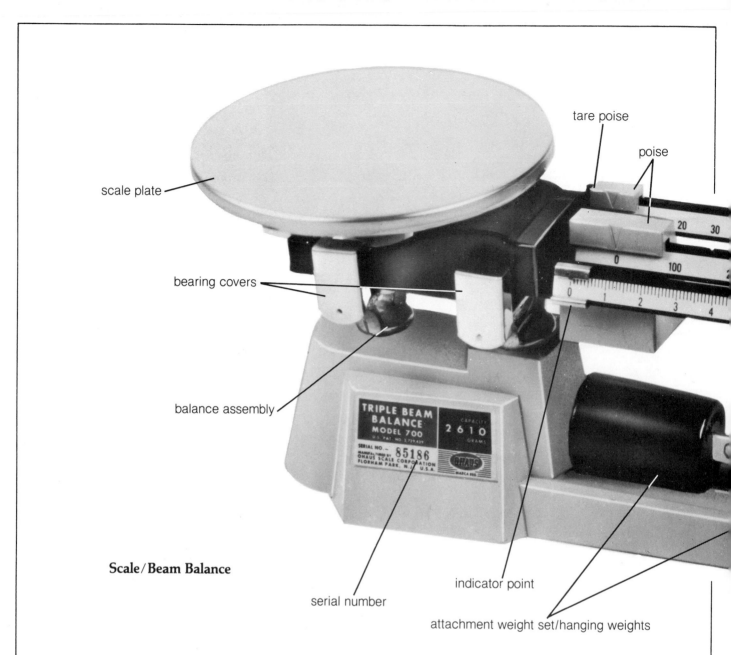

scale plate

tare poise

poise

20 30

0

100

bearing covers

0 1 2 3 4

balance assembly

**TRIPLE BEAM
BALANCE
MODEL 700**
U.S. PAT. NO. 3,729,439

CAPACITY
2 6 1 0
GRAMS

SERIAL NO.— **85186**
MANUFACTURED BY
OHAUS SCALE CORPORATION
FLORHAM PARK, N.J. U.S.A.

OHAUS
MARCA REG.

Scale/Beam Balance

indicator point

serial number

attachment weight set/hanging weights

Clamp/Holder

thumbscrew

tube

finger

rivet

clamp housing

Laboratory Equipment

Other laboratory equipment includes *ring stands*, to hold various cylinders, *flasks*, *laboratory thermometers*, *burettes*, for measuring the volume of liquids, *hydrometers*, *vacuum jars*, *microscopes* and *slides*, *adjustable stands* and *distilling equipment*.

poise notch

rear beam

center beam/coarse-adjustment beam

front beam/fine-adjustment beam

suspension pivot

pointer

60 70 80 90 100 g

400 500 g

7 8 9 10 g

0

trig-loop post

hanger

weight storage channel

base

Burner

top

tube

rib

shutter/ air regulator

spud/gas inlet

base

valve stem/gas regulator

Test Tube/Culture Tube

screw cap

neck

Beaker

mouth

bead

spout

900 ml ±5%

1000 ml PYREX

800

700

600

500

400

300

200

100

volume graduations

Sensing Devices

Examination Equipment

The scopes seen below are used by *Eye, Ear, Nose and Throat Doctors,* or *EENT specialists.* The speculum is used by *gynecologists* and *obstetricians. Headlights* mounted on headbands provide a light source for doctors.

pneumoscopy port

sliding eyepiece

ear speculum

brow rest

eyepiece

lens

housing

body

diopter value

lens-selection disc

neck

rechargeable power handle

battery charger

Ear Scope/Otoscope

Eye Scope/Ophthalmoscope

Speculum

angular adjustment

vertical adjustment

blades

light guide

lamp

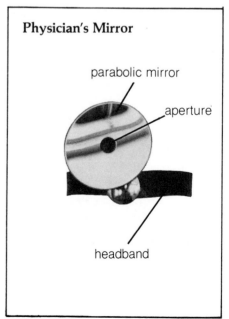

Physician's Mirror

parabolic mirror

aperture

headband

Examination Equipment

In addition to the examination equipment shown here, doctors use *tongue depressors,* or *tongue blades,* and a *hammer* to test reflexes. Thermometers have *opaque backgrounds* and *centigrade* and *fahrenheit scales.*

gauge

protective case

manometer/calibrated tube

scale markings

tube cap

mercury reservoir

tube

pressure cuff & bag

pressure control valve

thumbscrew

inflation bulb/ hand pump

Blood Pressure Gauge/Mercury Sphygmomanometer

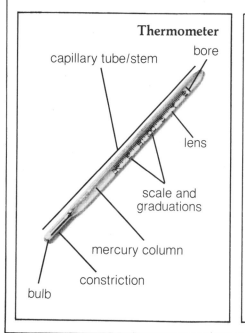

Thermometer

capillary tube/stem

bore

lens

scale and graduations

mercury column

constriction

bulb

Stethoscope

binaurals

ear tips

tubing

tube clip

corrugated diaphragm chest piece

flat diaphragm chest piece

diaphragm

turret

spindle

bell chest piece

Medical Tools

Medical Tables

Surgical, or *operating room*, *tables*, have built-in *channels* for holding *x-ray cassettes*. Among the accessories that can be attached to them are *intravenous*, or *IV*, *equipment*, *arm-* and *footboard extensions*, *crutch sockets* for holding legs in position, and buckle-type *body-restraint straps*.

sanitary paper

padded top

retractable footrest

stirrup/footrest

adjustment knobs

drawers

base/frame

retractable step

leg

Examination Table

Surgical Table / Operating Table

radio-translucent pad

headrest/footrest

multi-position table

model & serial number

side rail/accessory rail

table-position selector

lifting column/pedestal

mode lever

movable control-arm

manual-pump pedal

floor-locking system pedal

air inlet

air-motor power pedal

glide/adjustable foot

A hypodermic needle is protected by a *needle sheath* when not in use. *Injections* can also be administered painlessly with a jet-spray method called *hypospray*. A *bandage* is generally a strip of fabric used to bind up a wound or to keep a *dressing* or *compress* in place. A *splint* is any rigid material used in conjunction with *adhesive tape* to hold a bone or limb in a fixed position.

thumb rest

plunger

finger flange

scale markings

stopper

barrel

locking tip

needle hub

needle cannula

Hypodermic Syringe/Needle

Band-Aid®/Adhesive Bandage

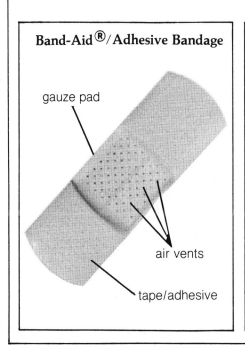

gauze pad

air vents

tape/adhesive

Eyedropper/Medicine Dropper

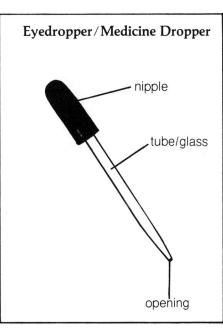

nipple

tube/glass

opening

Pill/Tablet and Capsule

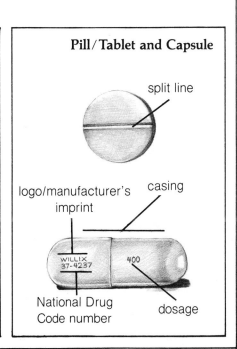

split line

logo/manufacturer's imprint

casing

WILLIX
37-4237

400

National Drug
Code number

dosage

Supportive Devices

Battery-powered *electric chairs* provide mobility for totally handicapped people. For minor leg and foot injuries, a *cane*, or *walking stick*, is used. Other supportive devices include *dialysis machines, iron lungs, oxygen tents, decompression chambers,* and *braces* of various kinds.

handgrip

back upholstery

back

spacer

large wheel

push rim

wheel lock

hub

tipping lever

cross brace

caster

axle bolt

armrest

arm

clothing guard

seat rail

seat upholstery

hanger bracket

bumper

heel loop

footplate

Wheelchair

Crutch

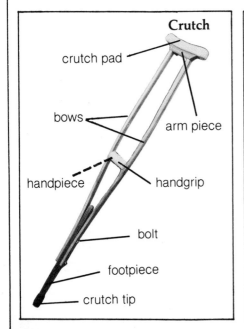

crutch pad

bows

handpiece

arm piece

handgrip

bolt

footpiece

crutch tip

Pacemaker

pulse generation

lead connectors

feed-through

ALPHA 28

can/casing

battery

Hearing Aid

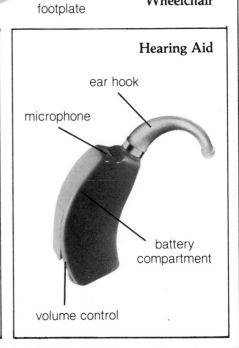

ear hook

microphone

battery compartment

volume control

Dental Corrective Devices

A *bridge* consists of one or more false teeth anchored between abutment teeth. The portion of the bridge that actually replaces the missing tooth or teeth is the *pontic*. A *crown* or *jacket crown* covers that part of the tooth normally protected by enamel. In *orthodontia*, the correction of the position of teeth, a *band* or *wire* is inserted in the slot and held in place by *rubber bands* looped over the tie wings.

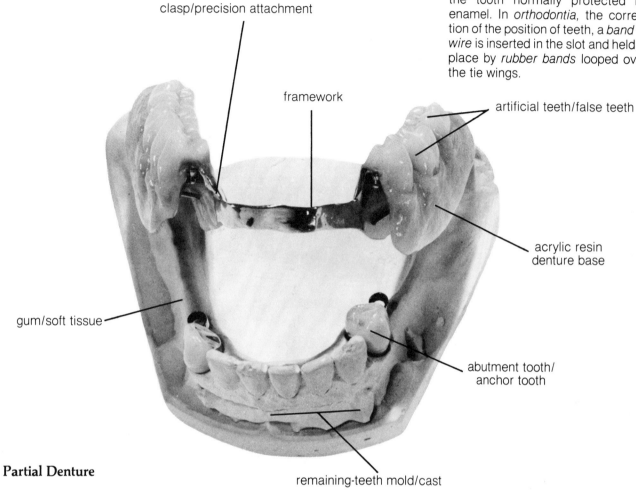

clasp/precision attachment

framework

artificial teeth/false teeth

acrylic resin denture base

gum/soft tissue

abutment tooth/ anchor tooth

remaining-teeth mold/cast

Partial Denture

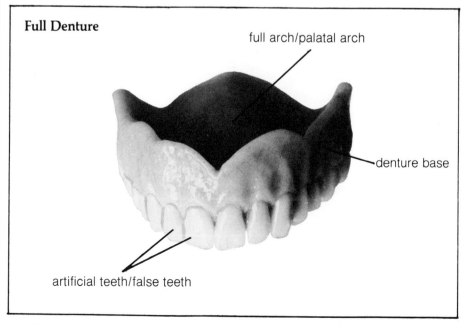

Full Denture

full arch/palatal arch

denture base

artificial teeth/false teeth

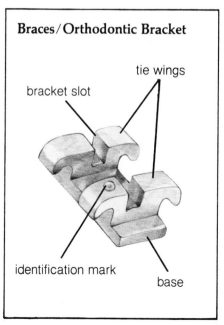

Braces/Orthodontic Bracket

tie wings

bracket slot

identification mark

base

Medical Tools

Dental Unit

A high-intensity *dental light* is usually attached to a dental unit, or *dental island.* Instrument trays may be attached to a *drift-free arm,* such as the one shown here, or to a *post-mounted arm.*

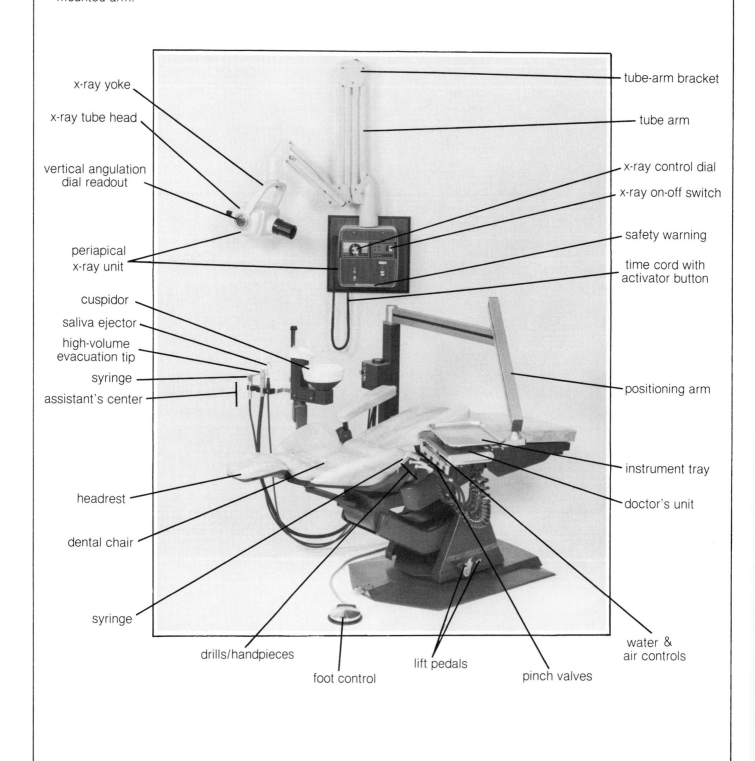

x-ray yoke

x-ray tube head

vertical angulation
dial readout

periapical
x-ray unit

cuspidor

saliva ejector

high-volume
evacuation tip

syringe

assistant's center

headrest

dental chair

syringe

drills/handpieces

foot control

lift pedals

pinch valves

tube-arm bracket

tube arm

x-ray control dial

x-ray on-off switch

safety warning

time cord with
activator button

positioning arm

instrument tray

doctor's unit

water &
air controls

Dental Equipment

Fillings of *silver amalgam* or *inlays*, *cast restorations* of *gold, synthetic porcelain* or *acrylic resins*, are used to fill *cavities*. Teeth can also be fitted with *crowns* or *caps*.

gas sterilizing flame

bracket table arm

needle/
anesthetic syringe

anti-fog liquid

cotton pellets

waste disposal

drill/
high-speed handpiece

3-way syringe/
water and air regulator

bracket table

cotton pad

gauze pad

alligator
towel clip

wedge

matrix

matrix holder

tubing

amalgam carrier

mirror

hand excavator

explorer

college pliers

steel burr

chuck tightener

diamond burr

drill bits

Teeth

Each tooth has one or two *neighbors* and a biting *partner* in the opposite jaw. Teeth fit into *sockets*. The first set of teeth are *baby teeth*, or *milk teeth*, replaced in time by permanent teeth. A person with a fondness for sugary edibles is said to have a *sweet tooth*.

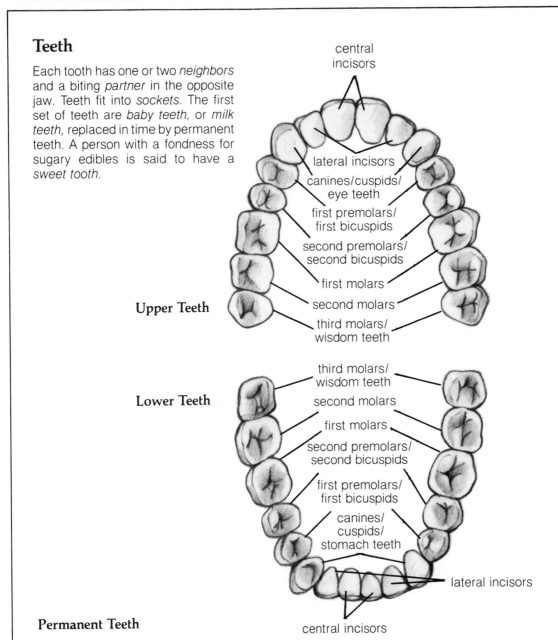

Upper Teeth

central incisors

lateral incisors

canines/cuspids/eye teeth

first premolars/first bicuspids

second premolars/second bicuspids

first molars

second molars

third molars/wisdom teeth

Lower Teeth

third molars/wisdom teeth

second molars

first molars

second premolars/second bicuspids

first premolars/first bicuspids

canines/cuspids/stomach teeth

lateral incisors

central incisors

Permanent Teeth

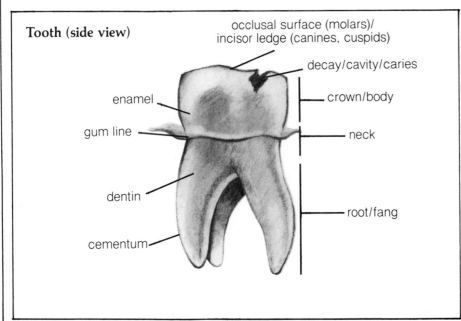

Tooth (side view)

occlusal surface (molars)/incisor ledge (canines, cuspids)

decay/cavity/caries

enamel

crown/body

gum line

neck

dentin

root/fang

cementum

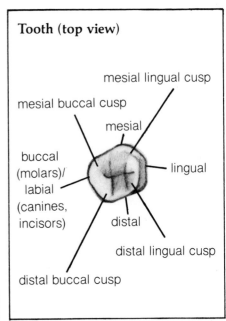

Tooth (top view)

mesial lingual cusp

mesial buccal cusp

mesial

buccal (molars)/labial (canines, incisors)

lingual

distal

distal lingual cusp

distal buccal cusp

Vault and Safe

Vaults are connected to *alarm systems*, which include *bells* and *silent alarms*. *Time locks* open safes or vaults at a predetermined time and prevent their being opened otherwise. A *strongbox* is a stoutly made box or chest for preserving valuable possessions. Most safes are insulated to protect against fire as well as theft. A home *money box, coin bank* or *piggy bank* is opened at the bottom or with a hammer.

door jamb

architrave

door hinge

bolt-retracting gears

primary combination dial

vault door

locking bolts

safe deposit boxes

door handle

bolt-activating gear rings

day gate

bolt guide ring

bolt holes

dust cover/ bolt cover

vestibule

Vault

bridge

timelock/movement dial

bolt linkage

recessed door

body wall

Safe

escutcheon plate

hinge

handle

combination lock

serial number

Security Devices

Door Locks

Many mortise locks have two *buttons* below the latch bolt which allow the *outside knob* to be independently locked or unlocked. Bolts fit into a *striker plate,* attached to the door frame. A *latch* is a device which holds a door closed, but cannot be locked. A *catch* holds lightweight doors, such as cabinet doors, closed. A *lockset* has the features of a lock and a catch.

latch assembly

spanner screw

cylinder

plug/core

keyhole/keyway

escutcheon

doorknob

faceplate/scalp

dead bolt

latch bolt

frame plate

gain

Mortise Lock

Chain Lock / Door Bolt

door plate

jamb plate

retainer

slide bolt

chain

Inter-grip Rim Lock

cylinder

case

strike

bolt

bolt housing

Key and Padlock

A key is inserted into a lock's cylinder via a *keyway*. The angled serrations, or *cuts*, on a key blade correspond to different sized *pin-tumblers*, or *pins*, within the lock cylinder. A key that has not yet been configured to any particular lock is a *blank*. A key used to open many common locks is a *skeleton key*.

bow

shoulder

serrations

blade

warding

Key

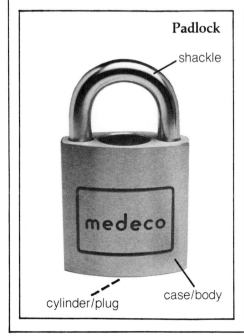

Padlock

shackle

medeco

cylinder/plug

case/body

Keychain

clasp

links

dumbbell

Security Devices

Hinge and Hasp

In addition to the *butt hinge,* seen here, there are *pivot hinges, full-surface hinges, half-surface hinges, spring hinges, strap hinges* and *continuous hinges.* Hinge pivot pins or *fixed pins,* used on smaller hinges, are available in a variety of ornamental *heads,* or *caps,* such as the ball tip seen here. A *safety hasp* is secured with a padlock or pin.

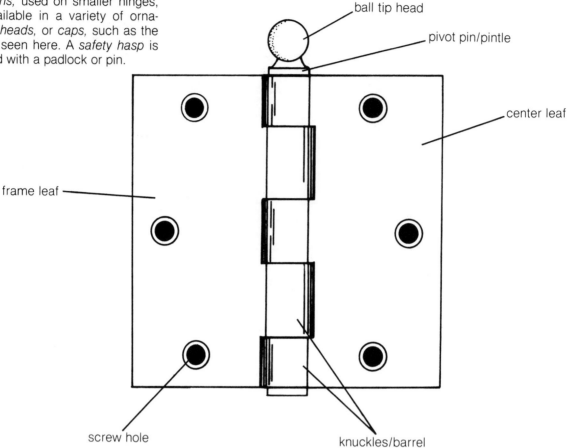

ball tip head

pivot pin/pintle

center leaf

frame leaf

screw hole

knuckles/barrel

Hinge

Hasp

strap/slotted flap/latch

slot

joint

swivel eye

pin

hinge portion

swivel plate/staple

Chain and Pulley

When a rope is reeved, or passed through the block, it fits into a narrow groove, or *score,* around the circumference of the sheave. That part of the rope used to apply power or hoist is the *fall.* The lower, or *choke,end* of a common wood block is the *arse.*

upper bolt

sidebar

center pin

swivel bolt

lower bolt

side plate/cheek

pulley/sheave

hook-thrust bearing assembly

latch support

hook

Pulley Block

shackle

link straps

side shell

sheave

Block and Tackle

becket

rope/line

hook

Chains

links

welds

Link Chain

rollers

roller link plate

pin link plate

chain pins

bushing

cotter pins

Roller Chain

Execution Devices

The blade on the guillotine is released by a *release cord* or *release button*. The Italian *mannaia* and the Scottish *maiden* were variations of the French guillotine. A *gibbet,* similar to a gallows, has a single, horizontal arm from which the noose was hung. On an electric chair, electrodes are attached to the prisoner's head and leg to complete the circuit. A *tumbrel* is any vehicle used to bring condemned people to the place of execution.

crossbeam

weight

blade/knife/ax

groove

post/upright

lunette

woven basket

trestle

ground beam

Guillotine

Gallows

gallows pin/crossbeam

running knot

noose

frame

scaffold

trap

steps

Electric Chair

back

straps

arm buckle

seat

electrode

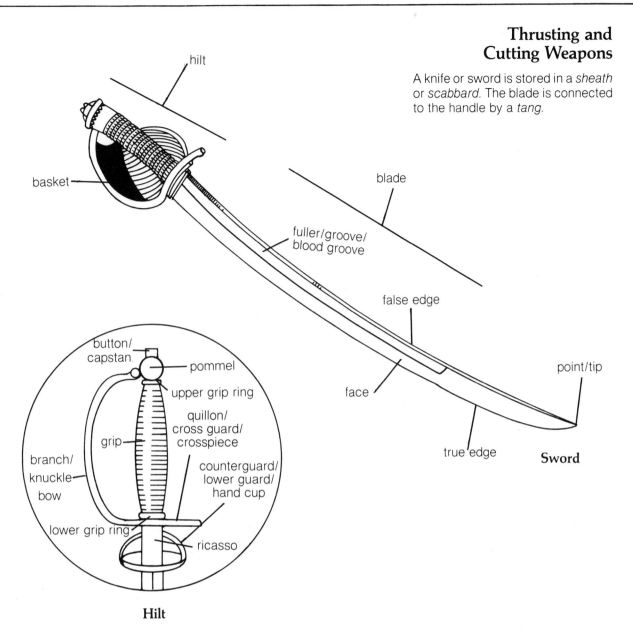

Thrusting and Cutting Weapons

A knife or sword is stored in a *sheath* or *scabbard*. The blade is connected to the handle by a *tang*.

hilt

basket

blade

fuller/groove/
blood groove

false edge

face

point/tip

true edge

Sword

button/
capstan

pommel

upper grip ring

grip

quillon/
cross guard/
crosspiece

branch/
knuckle
bow

counterguard/
lower guard/
hand cup

lower grip ring

ricasso

Hilt

hilt/handle   guard   blade

quillon/
cross guard

fuller   back

false edge   point/tip

Knife

pommel

grip/scale

ricasso   choil

concave

true edge

hilt/socket

edge

barrel ring

sight cut   locking system

Bayonet

Weapons

Medieval Arms

A round shield held at arm's length is called a *buckler*, while a shield held across the body by straps or handles called *enarmes* is a *target*. A shield offering protection during a siege is a *pavise*. Cutouts on the sides of a shield for holding spears to be thrown are called *bouches*. A shafted weapon having a *spear blade* and a pair of curved *lobes* at the base of the *spearhead* is a *partisan*.

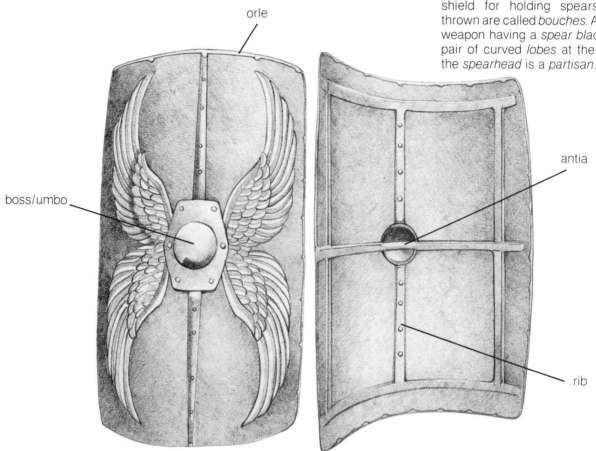

orle

boss/umbo

antia

rib

Shield

Striking Weapons

poll

eye

ear

leading edge

head

flange/spike

handle/haft/helve

face

blade

head

butt

handle

hilt

Axe

Mace

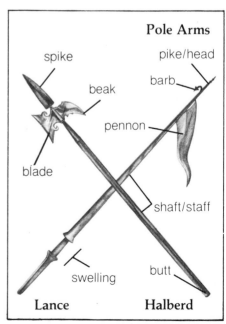

Pole Arms

spike

pike/head

beak

barb

pennon

blade

shaft/staff

swelling

butt

Lance

Halberd

Armor

Body armor, *protective clothing* and *headgear*, was usually made of iron or thick leather. It was often adorned with *decorative inlays*.

plume/comb

helmet

skull

visor

ocularium sight

beaver/chin piece

pauldron

gorget

rondel/
lance guard

standard/
neck guard

rerebrace

cuirie

breastplate

mail gusset

couter/
elbow cup

tace

tasset

codpiece

cuish

poleyn/knee cop

greave/jamb

solleret

plume holder

backplate

vambrace

loin guard

gauntlet

chain mail

fan plates

Weapons

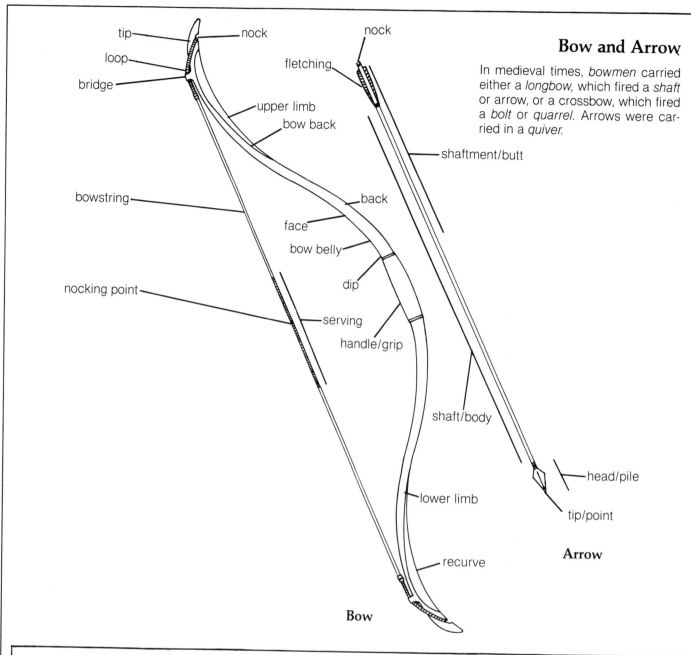

tip

nock

nock

loop

fletching

bridge

upper limb

bow back

shaftment/butt

bowstring

back

face

bow belly

nocking point

dip

serving

handle/grip

shaft/body

head/pile

lower limb

tip/point

recurve

Bow and Arrow

In medieval times, *bowmen* carried either a *longbow*, which fired a *shaft* or arrow, or a crossbow, which fired a *bolt* or *quarrel*. Arrows were carried in a *quiver*.

Arrow

Bow

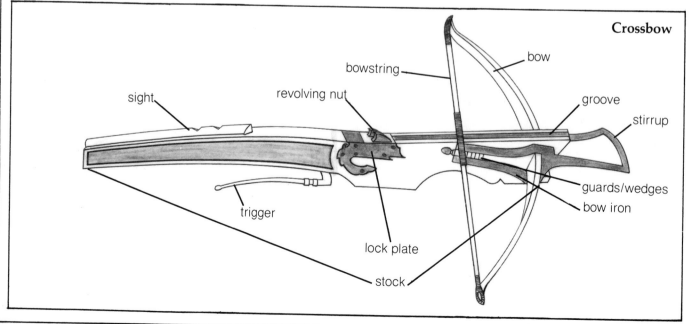

Crossbow

bowstring

bow

sight

revolving nut

groove

stirrup

trigger

guards/wedges

bow iron

lock plate

stock

Cannon and Catapult

Cannonballs fired by *muzzle-loaders* were transported in *caissons* and stacked in trays called *monkeys*. *Loaders* used a *swab* or *sponge* to get rid of residue, a *worm* to remove obstructions, and a *rammer* to drive the *projectile* into the *bore* at the muzzle, or *mouth*, of the cannon. Catapults were used to fire javelinlike shafts a quarter of a mile or more. Ballistas, using the same system of hurling, were employed to heave heavy stones short distances.

muzzle moldings

muzzle astragal & filets

second reinforce ring & ogee

dolphin

trunnion

first reinforce ring

first reinforce/ vent field astragal & filets

firing vent

base ring

breech

button/knob

muzzle

chase

second reinforce

first reinforce

cascabel/gunlock

Cannon Barrel

Carriage

cap square

steps

wedge

cheek

stool bed

truck/wheel

Ballista

cup

pad

crossbeam

arm

pulley rope

skein of cord

winding wheel

roller

windlass control

release cord

Shotgun and Rifle

A shotgun fires small *pellets* through a *smooth bore*, while a rifle fires *bullets* through a *rifled barrel*. Shotgun barrels are usually tapered, or *choked*, to constrict the *shot pattern*. Rifles may be carried across the shoulder on a beltlike *sling* connected to the weapon by *sling swivels* and adjusted with bucklelike *claws*.

Shotgun

extractor

breechblock

small of stock/pistol grip

receiver

comb/forecomb

stock/buttstock

loading gate

butt plate

heel

safety

forearm/fore-end/ slide handle

trigger guard

trigger

checkering

stock grip cap

toe

scope mount bases

bolt

bolt handle

safety

flat of stock

recoil pad

magazine floor plate

magazine release

swivel pin

Rifle

rear bead

barrel ring

ventilated rib

front bead

bore

magazine cap

barrel

magazine tube

open rear sight

front sight

swivel pin

Scope / Telescopic Sight

windage & elevation
adjustment knobs

objective lens

locking ring

ocular lens

scope rings

base

focusing ring

459

Weapons

Handguns

A *gun,* or *side arm,* is *fired* when a *firing pin* in the *breech* strikes the cartridge primer. A *silencer* dampens the sound of a gun's *discharge.* Grooves in the barrel, called *rifling,* cause a fired bullet to spiral for stability in flight. Cartridges are measured in *calibers,* their diameters in hundredths or thousandths of an inch written in a decimal fraction, or in *millimeters.* Handguns are carried in *holsters.*

rear sight
top strap
front sight/front sight blade
barrel
bore
hammer spur
hammer
loading gate
side plate
cylinder latch
ejector tube
muzzle
frame
chamber
ejector rod
cylinder
backstrap
trigger guard
trigger
butt
handle/grip

Revolver

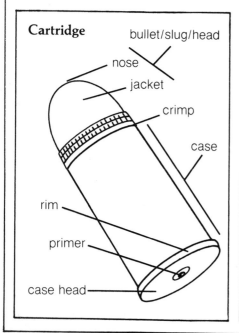

Cartridge

bullet/slug/head
nose
jacket
crimp
case
rim
primer
case head

Magazine/Clip

Automatic Pistol

front sight
slide
grip safety
barrel
safety/safety lever
recoil spring guide
rear sight
cartridge
frame/receiver
magazine follower
trigger
magazine spring
magazine release catch

Automatic Weapons

Multi-shot automatic weapons are grouped by weight: light, medium and heavy. The *air-cooled,* medium-weight machine gun shown here can be handled by one man on the ground or on a vehicle when mounted on *pintle mounts.* The light, hand-held automatic rifle is also able to deliver a rapid burst of continuous fire as long as the trigger is depressed. *Ammunition* is fed to it from *handle clips* or *banana clips.*

flash suppressor

front sight

forearm

barrel

cocking handle

chassis plate

carrying handle

rear sight

grips

feed plate

trigger/firing lever

operating rod

height adjustment control

tripod/tripod mount

cartridge

feed belt

cartridge box

Machine Gun

Ammunition Can

Automatic Rifle

rear sight/ receiver sight

receiver

carrying handle/ upper receiver

front sight housing

cocking piece

bolt

breech

handguard liner

barrel

heel

comb

flash suppressor

butt

barrel extension

handguard

slip ring

muzzle

butt plate

stock

safety

handguard cap

barrel nut

pistol grip

trigger

magazine/cartridge clip

trigger guard

461

Mortar and Bazooka

A mortar is a *muzzle-loading cannon,* or *midget howitzer,* used to throw *finned projectiles* at high angles. A bazooka is a portable shoulder weapon with an *open-breech smoothbore firing tube* that fires several types of *rockets.*

muzzle

traversing gear

sight bracket

elevating gear

elevating tube

tube

base cap

baseplate/bedplate

firing pin

swivel/pivot

bipod leg

Mortar

Bazooka/Rocket Launcher

ignition cable

infrared night scope

arming mechanism

sight

launcher tube

muzzle

shoulder rest

web sling

butt

handgrip

trigger mechanism

muzzle rest

Grenade and Mine

When the type of grenade shown here is detonated, it bursts into numerous metal fragments called *shrapnel.* Other types of grenades include *smoke grenades* and *concussion grenades.* Streamlined *rifle grenades* have rear *fins* to provide stability in flight. A *"Molotov cocktail,"* a crude grenade often thrown at tanks to set them on fire, consists of a gasoline-filled bottle with a lighted *wick* at the top.

lug

safety pin

primer

fuse

TNT

cast-iron casing/serrated body

pull ring

safety lever/spoon

Hand Grenade/"Pineapple"/Fragmentation Grenade

Land Mine/Antitank Mine

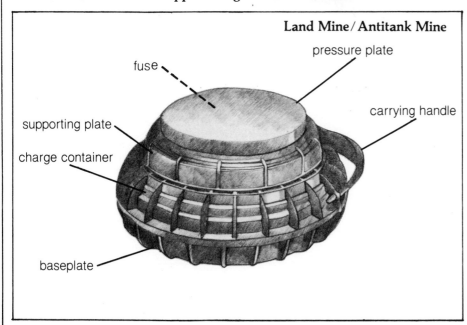

fuse

pressure plate

carrying handle

supporting plate

charge container

baseplate

Weapons

commander's hatch

commander's machine gun

cupola

searchlight

loader's hatch

sight

external fuel tank

gunner's sight

stowage rack

turret bustle

engine louvers

antenna

pistol port

transmission
louvers

stowage bin

U.S. ARMY
0·19510

muffler

exhaust pipe

drive wheel

track/crawler track/
caterpillar track

track links

track link pins

equipment
stowage box

bazooka plate

tracker roller/road wheel

Tank

A tank, such as the composite shown here, is an *armor-plated* vehicle consisting of a revolving *turret* set atop a tracked *hull*. Track links are sometimes covered with vulcanized rubber *pads*.

smoke bomb discharger

ventilator

gunner's telescope

mantlet

co-axial machine gun

front gunner's periscope

driver's periscope

bore evacuator/ fume extractor

gun/cannon

hatches

tube/barrel

muzzle brake

muzzle

headlight

driver's observation window

glacis plate

tow bar

hull machine gun

mud shield

idling wheel

drive wheel teeth

Missile and Torpedo

Unlike the rocket-propelled *anti-ballistic missile*, or *ABM*, seen here, *intercontinental ballistic missiles*, or *ICBMs*, fly outside earth's atmosphere and have no stabilizing fins. *Multiple independently targeted reentry vehicles*, or *MIRVs*, have several warheads which disperse as the missile nears the target. Modern torpedoes, fired from *torpedo tubes* inside submarines, home in on targets acoustically or are guided by wire.

nose

nose cone

stabilizing fins

warhead/payload

vanes

third stage

second stage

U S A F

stabilizing fin

thrust ring

first stage

stabilizing fin

rear skirt

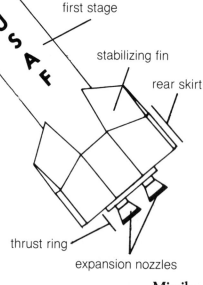

U S A F

thrust ring

expansion nozzles

Missile

tail section

afterbody/engine chamber

Torpedo

fuel & guidance chamber

propeller

warhead

control fin/rudder

firing pin/plunger

Uniforms, Costumes and Ceremonial Attire

The attire presented in this section ranges from vestments and formal dress used on special occasions to dress of distinctive design or fashion worn by members of particular groups. The parts of military or municipal attire, for example, serve to identify not only branch of service but rank and distinction as well.

Garb can be highly stylized or informal. Manchu Court dress, for example, was worn only on formal occasions, whereas the clothes commonly worn by cowboys, dictated by the demands of the profession, was casual.

In addition to the trappings that have come to typify characters in history— a general, pirate, miser, magician—this section also includes clothing used by performers such as clowns, ballet dancers and drum majorettes.

Beefeater / Yeoman Warder

halberd
tassel
flat hat
ruff
ornament
tunic
crossbelt
knee breeches
stocking
rosette
®

Royal Regalia

In coronations and investitures, a king wears a blunted sword called a *curtein* on his sash. Among a queen's foundation garments, or *underpinnings*, are a *corset, corselet, chemise* and *pantaloons*.

tiara/coronet

drop earrings/pendant

rosette

morse/clasp

choker

puff sleeve

lace front/chemisette/tucker

bodice

armilla/sash & star of order

pointed waist/V-waist

evening handkerchief/ handruff

overskirt

gown

flounce/furbelow

trim

embroidery

imperial mantle

turnover collar/military collar

morse/clasp

parure/medals of order/trophies

capelet

cordon/neckties

chain

belt/sash

tunic jacket

silver-bullion embroidered cuffs

trousers

dress shoes

tassels

imperial mantle/robe of state/coronation mantle

Queen

King

Royal Regalia

A *coronet* is a small crown worn by royalty ranking below the reigning monarch. A *tiara* is a royal headpiece, usually consisting of a *diadem,* or band, tied around the forehead, supporting several tiers of ornaments. A wreath, or circlet of leaves, worn as a crown or collar is a *garland.*

pearl

arms

bracket

cross patée

pendant pearl

arch

orb/mound/globe

fillet

imperial arches

velvet cap

cross patée

fleur-de-lis

gold balls of rank

circlet/rim

rosette

miniver

Crown

Scepter

cross patée

fillet

mound/orb/globe

foot

diamond

curves

staff/rod

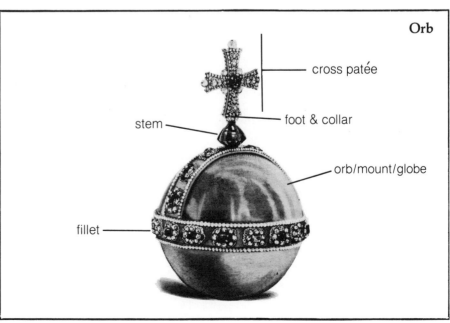

Orb

cross patée

foot & collar

stem

orb/mount/globe

fillet

Jewish Ritual Items

During regular service in a *Temple,* or *Synagogue,* excerpts are read by the *Rabbi,* who is assisted in leading the service by a *Cantor,* who sings the liturgy. Their vestments are the same as the rest of the congregation. During morning prayer, a *shel rosh,* similar to the tefillin, is worn on the forehead. Some Jews hang a *mezuzah,* a decorative box containing passages from the Torah, on the doorpost of their homes.

yarmulke/skullcap

tallith/prayer shawl

zecher lechurban/temple memorial bands

sepher/prayer book

zizith/fringes

Prayer Vestments

Ner Tamid/eternal light

Torah

ark

ark liner

yad/pointer

parocheth/ ark curtain

mantle

rimmon/headpiece

tree of life

crown

tzit/breastplate

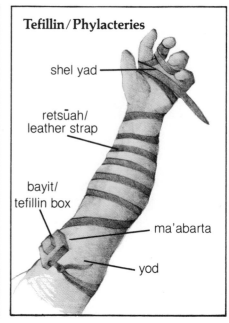

Tefillin/Phylacteries

shel yad

retsūah/ leather strap

bayit/ tefillin box

ma'abarta

yod

Religious Vestments

The small square cap with three corners worn by Roman Catholic clergy is a *biretta*. Ropes, belts or sashes used to keep vestments closed are *cinctures*. Traditionally, the white band worn by nuns to encircle their faces is a *wimple*, while the wide cloth worn below it to cover their necks and shoulders is a *guimpe*. The ring worn by the Pope is the *Ring of the Fisherman*.

simple miter

precious miter

lappet

Roman collar

crosier/pastoral staff

pectoral cross

dalmatic

stole

Episcopal ring

cope

chasuble

cope piping

alb

rochet

cassock

cassock

Bishop   **Cardinal**

Minister

clerical collar

academic hood

tippet

surplice

symbolic decoration

cassock

Nun

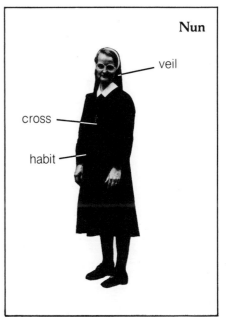

veil

cross

habit

Religious Attire

Bride and Groom

The bride, wearing white to symbolize purity, and a veil, symbol of modesty, is carrying a fan rather than the more traditional *wedding,* or *bridal, bouquet,* or *nosegay.* Some grooms wear semiformal evening dress at weddings: *tuxedos,* or *tuxes,* which are worn with *cummerbunds,* broad *waistbands, pleated* or *ruffled shirts* with *studs,* and *bow ties.*

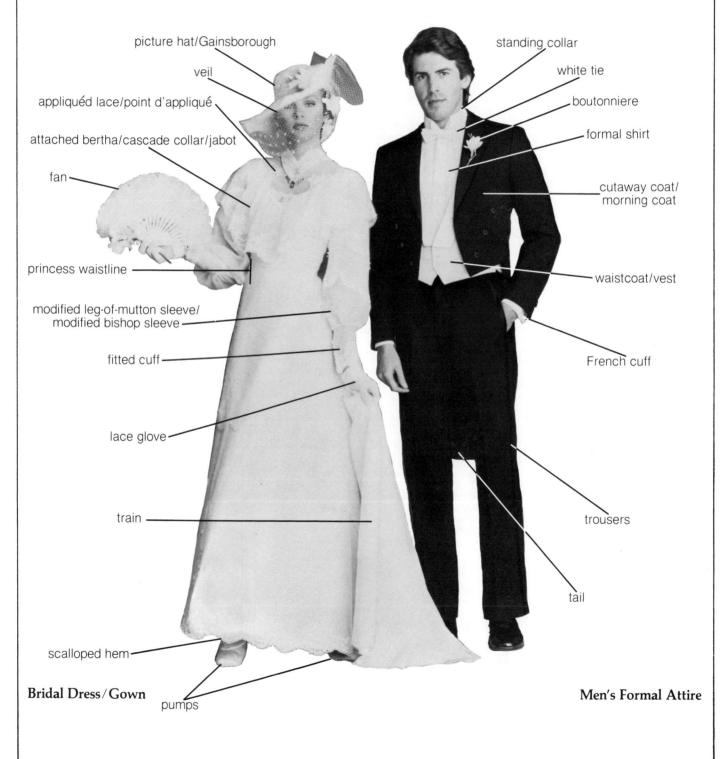

picture hat/Gainsborough

veil

appliquéd lace/point d'appliqué

attached bertha/cascade collar/jabot

fan

princess waistline

modified leg-of-mutton sleeve/
modified bishop sleeve

fitted cuff

lace glove

train

scalloped hem

standing collar

white tie

boutonniere

formal shirt

cutaway coat/
morning coat

waistcoat/vest

French cuff

trousers

tail

Bridal Dress/Gown

pumps

Men's Formal Attire

Maid and Butler

Attire worn by male servants is called *livery.* Maids often wear a *bib,* an inverted triangular piece of white linen attached at the neck and descending to just above the waist, as well as a knee-length or ankle-length *apron.*

bow

bow tie

ecru net/serving cap

studs

piquot front, wing-tip collared shirt

replaceable collar/ detachable collar

cutaway coat/ morning coat

puffed sleeve

lace cuff

roll-collar waistcoat/ morning vest

bodice

serving apron

French cuff

gathered skirt

gentleman's white glove

petticoat/crinoline

striped morning trousers

pumps

round-toed brogues

Butler

Maid

Servants' Attire

Cowboy and Indian

On the range, cowboys, *cow punchers,* or *buckaroos,* carried *oilskin slickers,* a *tarp,* and heavy cotton or wool quilts to make up a *bedroll, crumb incubator, shakedown,* or *fleatrap.* Bullets, carried in *loops* on *cartridge belts,* were known as *blue whistlers* or *lead plums.* A cowboy's *ten-gallon hat* was held in place in a wind by buckskin thongs known as *bonnet strings.*

Members of most Indian tribes wore *leggings* and *moccasins.* Many decorated their faces with *war paint* prior to battle. Indians in the East shaved their heads except for a ridge of hair in the middle called a *roach.*

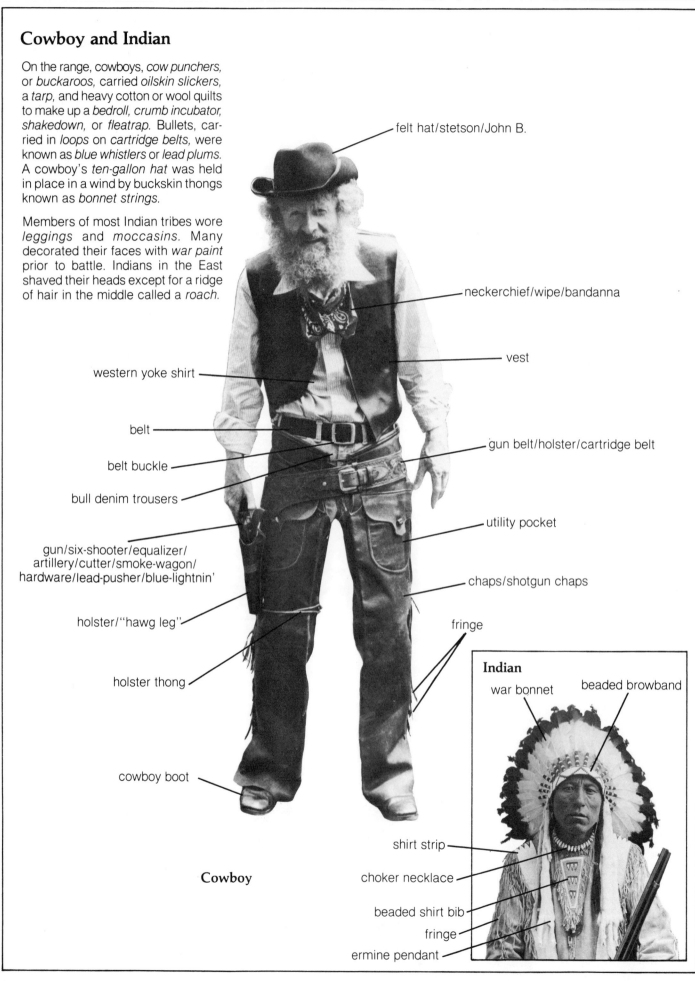

felt hat/stetson/John B.

neckerchief/wipe/bandanna

vest

western yoke shirt

belt

gun belt/holster/cartridge belt

belt buckle

bull denim trousers

utility pocket

gun/six-shooter/equalizer/
artillery/cutter/smoke-wagon/
hardware/lead-pusher/blue-lightnin'

chaps/shotgun chaps

holster/"hawg leg"

fringe

holster thong

cowboy boot

Cowboy

Indian

war bonnet

beaded browband

shirt strip

choker necklace

beaded shirt bib

fringe

ermine pendant

Native Dress

Romans wore full-length, loose-fitting robes called *togas*. East Indian women wear *sarongs*, but Indian (Hindu) women wear *saris*. An ankle-length Middle East garment with long sleeves and a waist sash is called a *caftan*. The loose-fitting, sleeveless robes worn by Arabs are called *abas*.

peacock-feather tassel

winter cap/Mandarin cap

ling-t'ou/court-robe collar

su-tshu/long necklace

p'u fang/mandarin square/ coat of arms & badge of rank

p'u-fu jacket

ma-ti hsiu/horse-hoof cuffs

trim

cheng-lung/facing dragon

mang-p'ao/dragon robe

li-shui portion of dragon robe

Formal Mandarin Attire

Arab Dress

akal

keffiyeh

brussa shirt

jellaba/thobe/abayeh

Bill Ashe photo

Native Attire

Historical Costumes

Many characters in popular lore and history have become identified or associated with the clothing they wear. Other military attire worn by *Revolutionary* officers included a tunic, a plain jacket with a stiff collar, and a particularly heavy overcoat called a *greatcoat*.

cockade

cocked hat

epaulette

infantry button

lapel

frock coat

button-down cuff

sword

scabbard

coat skirt

wig

crossbelt

embroidered buttonholes

waistcoat

gloves

knee britches

boot

Revolutionary War General

eyepatch

tricorne

crossbelt

scarf

petronel/revolver

Pirate

photo by BODI

top hat

Franklin glasses

muffler

fingerless glove

purse

Miser

Jim Vaum

steeple-crowned hat

magic wand

robe

Wizard

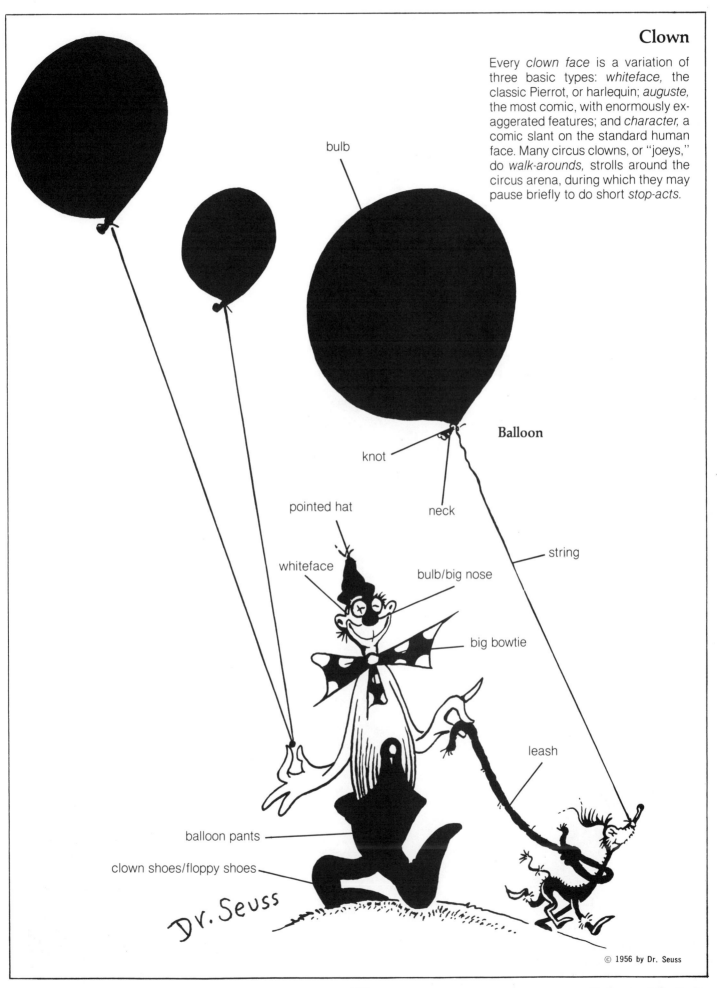

Clown

Every *clown face* is a variation of three basic types: *whiteface,* the classic Pierrot, or harlequin; *auguste,* the most comic, with enormously exaggerated features; and *character,* a comic slant on the standard human face. Many circus clowns, or "joeys," do *walk-arounds,* strolls around the circus arena, during which they may pause briefly to do short *stop-acts.*

bulb

Balloon

knot

neck

pointed hat

whiteface

bulb/big nose

big bowtie

string

leash

balloon pants

clown shoes/floppy shoes

Dr. Seuss

© 1956 by Dr. Seuss

Performers' Costumes

Ballet Dancer

The toeshoes worn by this *ballerina* are satin covered. Cloth mache has replaced wooden box toes. A short skirt of layered net often worn by female dancers is called a *tutu*.

leotard

tights

ribbon

knot

drawstring

box toe

Toeshoes

toeshoes

drawstring

sole

pleated toes/pleats

Slippers

plume

accessory cords

tip

busby

Drum Major

signal baton

Instead of busbies, some *marching bands* wear rounded, high-crowned box hats called *shakos*. Uniform accessories may include *gauntlets*, decorative glove extensions that cover the wrist, *spats*, cloth or plastic *gaiters* that cover the instep and ankle, *sashes* which cross the chest diagonally, and *streamers* with tassels that hang from waist *sashes* or *cummerbunds*.

shaft

visor

chin strap

standing collar

ball

epaulet

emblem/insignia

shield

tail coat

trefoil trim

trim

glove

riding breeches

boot top

trim

tassel

shoe

479

Performers' Costumes

Military Uniforms

The *uniform of the day* is worn for the season, day or occasion. A cloth band worn around the arm above the elbow, such as the one worn by *Military Police*, or *MPs*, is a *brassard*. A leather belt for a dress uniform is a *Sam Browne, or garrison, belt*. Service ribbons are worn on a *ribbon bar*. The only *neck decoration* awarded to members of the armed services is the *Medal of Honor*.

infantry rope/fourragère/ aiguillette/unit citation

branch insignia

US insignia

combat infantry badge

service ribbons & decorations

parachutist's badge

dress shirt

black tie

shoulder board/rank

nameplate

blouse/ dress-blue jacket

brass buttons

rank insignia

dress trousers

combat stripes/ overseas bars

officer's braid

dress shoe

garrison cap/ overseas cap/ service cap

unit crest

branch insignia

unit crest

current unit patch

service ribbons & decorations

rank insignia/grade

marksmanship badge

blouse

hash marks/ service time

trousers

Dress Uniform

Enlisted Man's Uniform

Military Uniforms

An *infantryman,* or "grunt," carries a *rain poncho* on his ammunition belt. A sailor, "swab," or "gob," may wear a *watch cap, leggings* and a *jersey* instead of a jumper. Sailors aboard ship keep their clothing in *seabags.*

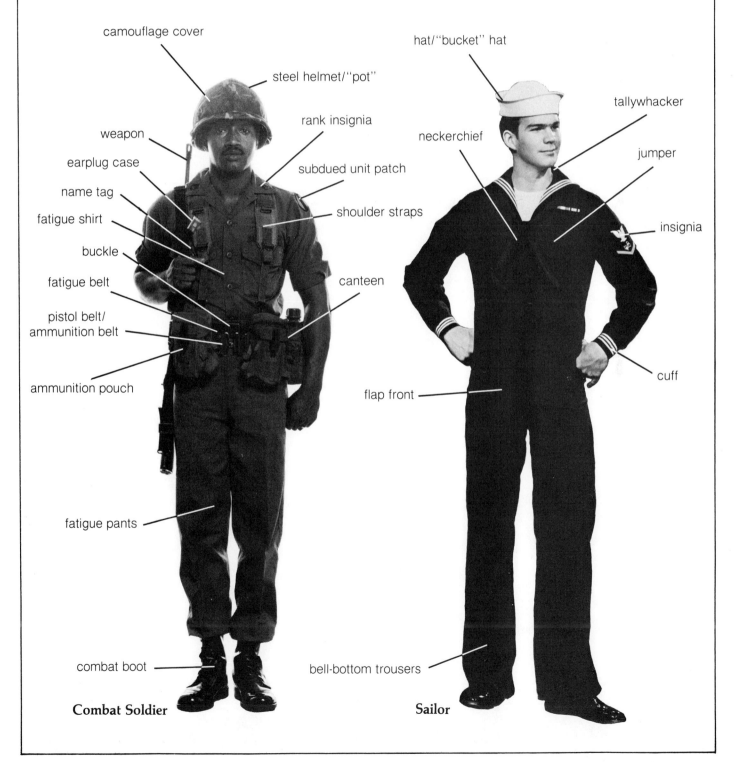

camouflage cover

steel helmet/"pot"

weapon

rank insignia

earplug case

subdued unit patch

name tag

shoulder straps

fatigue shirt

buckle

fatigue belt

canteen

pistol belt/
ammunition belt

ammunition pouch

fatigue pants

combat boot

Combat Soldier

hat/"bucket" hat

tallywhacker

neckerchief

jumper

insignia

cuff

flap front

bell-bottom trousers

Sailor

Military Attire

Police Officer

When walking a daylight *beat,* or *patrol,* wearing a uniform, or "in the bag," an *officer,* or *cop,* may carry a short rubber *daystick* rather than a nightstick. *Patrolmen* who work undercover, or *in mufti,* are said to work in "plainclothes," or "civvies." *Traffic officers* carry a *summons pouch* with *traffic tickets.*

riot helmet

hat device

winter hat

face shield

precinct number

medals/citations

badge/shield

nameplate

brass button

department patch

winter shirt

winter overcoat

gun belt/utility belt

thong

nightstick/"billy club"/baton

trousers

handcuffs

double lock

mace canister

shoe

Gun Belt/Utility Belt

buckle

bullets/rounds

bullet pouch/dump

mace holder

handcuff case

Police Officer

motor scooter helmet

summer hat

chin strap

In addition to the equipment shown below, officers may also carry a *flashlight* in a *holder* and *handcuff keys* on their belt. Some policemen carry six-shot ammunition *clips,* or "speedloaders," rather than individual bullets.

tie

bulletproof vest

summer blouse

summer shirt

uniform belt

key chain/key holder

gun/service revolver

swivel holster

whistle

pen holder

Municipal Uniforms

Fireman

A fireman's working uniform is called his *turnouts*.

helmet

unit number

badge number

frontpiece

visor/eye guards

turnout coat

reflective stripe/safety stripe

hook/pike pole

snap fastener

glove

fireboot

Signs and Symbols

While signs and symbols take the place of language or are used to represent meaning, either by suggestion, relationship or association, many have parts for which there are proper names. A flag is used as a sign of a nation, for example, or as a symbol of patriotism, yet it has distinctive components which are identifiable.

Other signs, such as editing and proofreading marks, also included in this section, are used to convey instructions, while sign language is a set of gestures used as a substitute for words or letters.

The fields of science, business and industry have all devised signs whose meanings have legal as well as instructional implications, and the world of transportation is largely controlled by traffic signs. Even hobos, whose pictographs appear here, use pictorial signs instead of written language to communicate messages.

Medal

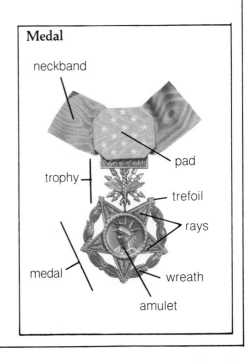

neckband

pad

trophy

trefoil

rays

medal

wreath

amulet

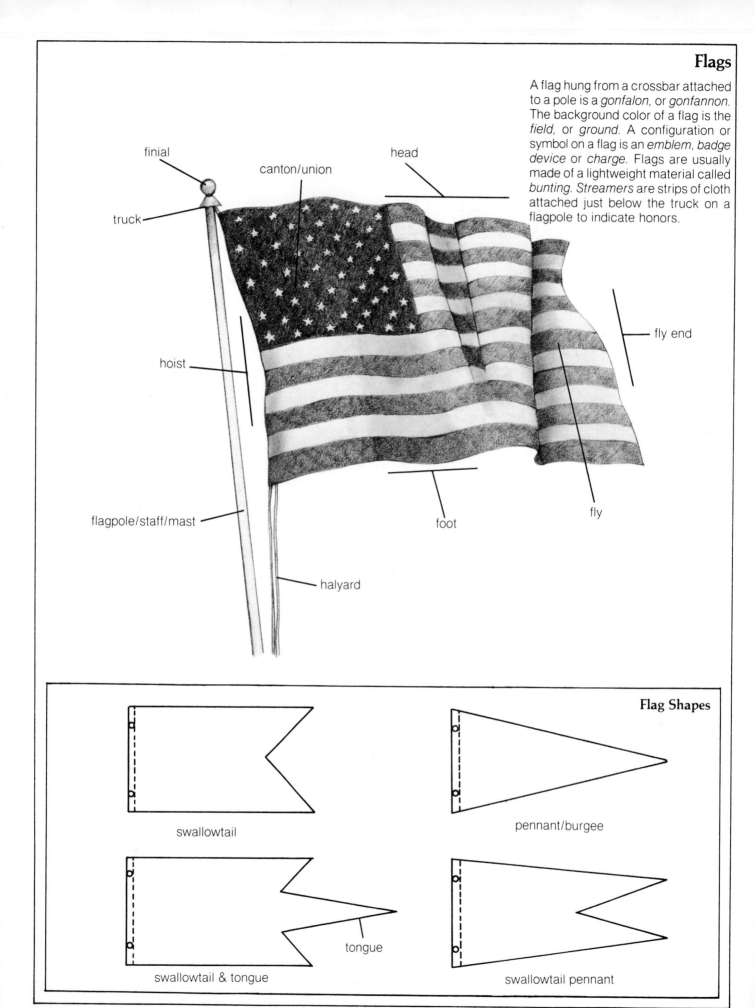

Flags

A flag hung from a crossbar attached to a pole is a *gonfalon*, or *gonfannon*. The background color of a flag is the *field*, or *ground*. A configuration or symbol on a flag is an *emblem, badge device* or *charge*. Flags are usually made of a lightweight material called *bunting*. *Streamers* are strips of cloth attached just below the truck on a flagpole to indicate honors.

finial

truck

canton/union

head

hoist

flagpole/staff/mast

halyard

foot

fly

fly end

Flag Shapes

swallowtail

pennant/burgee

swallowtail & tongue

tongue

swallowtail pennant

Coat of Arms

Technically, a coat of arms, or *achievement of arms*, consists only of a shield, the surface of which is called the *field*. Everything surrounding a shield is *exterior decoration*. The entire grouping is known as *armorial achievement*. To the wearer's left but the viewer's right is the *sinister side*. The opposite side is the *dexter side*.

crown

crest

torse

helmet/helm

mantling/lambrequin

arms/quarter shields

sinister supporter

dexter supporter

chief

shield
escutcheon

fess

base

scroll/escroll/
motto tape

motto/slogan

badge

compartment/mount

A MARI

AD MARE

USQUE

stop	yield	one way	one-way traffic/ do not enter	railroad crossing

no bicycles	no trucks	no U turn	no right turn	no left turn

interstate route	U.S. route	state route	trail	bike route

picnic area	camping	camping	hospital	telephone

Road Signs

With the exception of *route signs,* which are different shapes and colors, road signs are color-coded: red signs are *prohibit movement signs;* yellow are *warning signs;* white are *regulatory signs;* orange are *construction signs;* blue are *service signs;* green are *guide signs.* Octagonal red signs are used exclusively for *stop signs.* Rectangular signs with white letters on a green background are *destination signs.*

signal ahead	two-way traffic	no-passing zone	divided highway ends	merge
merge left	winding road	slippery when wet	hill	school crossing
pedestrian crossing	bicycle crossing	farm machinery	cattle crossing	deer crossing

Signs and Symbols

Public Signs

Pasigraphy is a universal written language that uses signs and symbols rather than words, whereas *pictographs* can represent an object as well as a thought. A symbol or character that represents a word, syllable or phoneme is a *phonogram*. A symbolic representation of an idea rather than a word is an *ideogram* or *ideograph*.

gift shop

hotel information

restaurant

mail

first aid

baggage lockers

men's toilets

women's toilets

nursery

information

taxi stand

bus transportation

air transportation

car rental

rail transportation

coffee shop

bar

no smoking

no parking

parking

baggage check-in

 baggage claim

 customs

 lost and found

 currency exchange

 falling rocks

 drinking water

 mechanic

 handicapped

 gas station

 viewing area

 campfires

 picnic area

 launching ramp

 horse trail

 bicycle trail

 hiking trail

 playground

 no entry

 elevator

Signs and Symbols

Religious Symbols

The symbols shown here represent beliefs and religions such as Christianity, Judaism, Islam, Shinto, as well as Chinese philosophy. The ankh was an ancient Egyptian *symbol of life,* and the gammadion was an eon-old Oriental and Indian *good luck symbol.*

Latin cross

St. Anthony's cross/ tau cross

Celtic cross

Patriarchal cross

Papal cross

Russian cross

Jerusalem cross

Maltese cross

botonée

moline

Greek cross

torii

crescent and star

Star of David/Magen David/ Shield of David

menorah

ankh

Yin-Yang/female-male

gammadion/swastika

Signs of the Zodiac

The *zodiac* is an imaginary belt in the heavens divided into twelve parts named for constellations, called *houses*. A *horoscope*, drawn by an *astrologer,* foretells the influence of these heavenly bodies on human affairs.

Spring Signs

Aries   The Ram   Taurus   The Bull   Gemini   The Twins

March 21—April 20   April 21—May 21   May 22—June 21

Summer Signs

Cancer   The Crab   Leo   The Lion   Virgo   The Virgin

June 22—July 22   July 23—August 23   August 24—September 23

Autumn Signs

Libra   The Balance   Scorpio   The Scorpion   Sagittarius   The Archer

September 24—October 23   October 24—November 22   November 23—December 21

Winter Signs

Capricorn   The Goat   Aquarius   The Water Bearer   Pisces   The Fish

December 22—January 20   January 21—February 19   February 20—March 20

Signs and Symbols

Symbols of Science, Business and Commerce

The symbols shown here are used in the medical and pharmaceutical fields, in chemistry, engineering and electronics, in mathematics and business, and by currency-exchange centers and banks. Also included are miscellaneous symbols used in other walks of life.

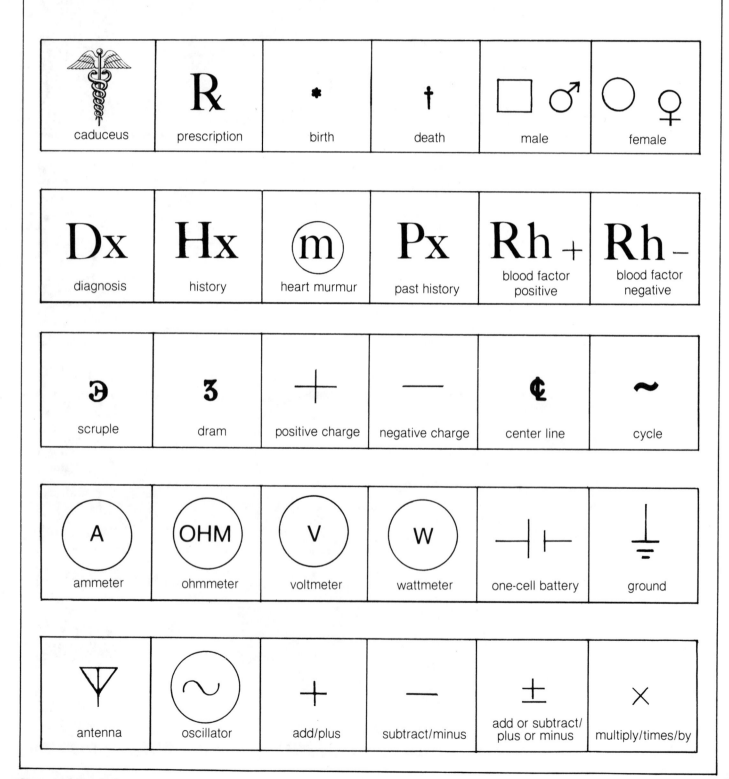

caduceus	prescription	birth	death	male	female
diagnosis	history	heart murmur	past history	blood factor positive	blood factor negative
scruple	dram	positive charge	negative charge	center line	cycle
ammeter	ohmmeter	voltmeter	wattmeter	one-cell battery	ground
antenna	oscillator	add/plus	subtract/minus	add or subtract/ plus or minus	multiply/times/by

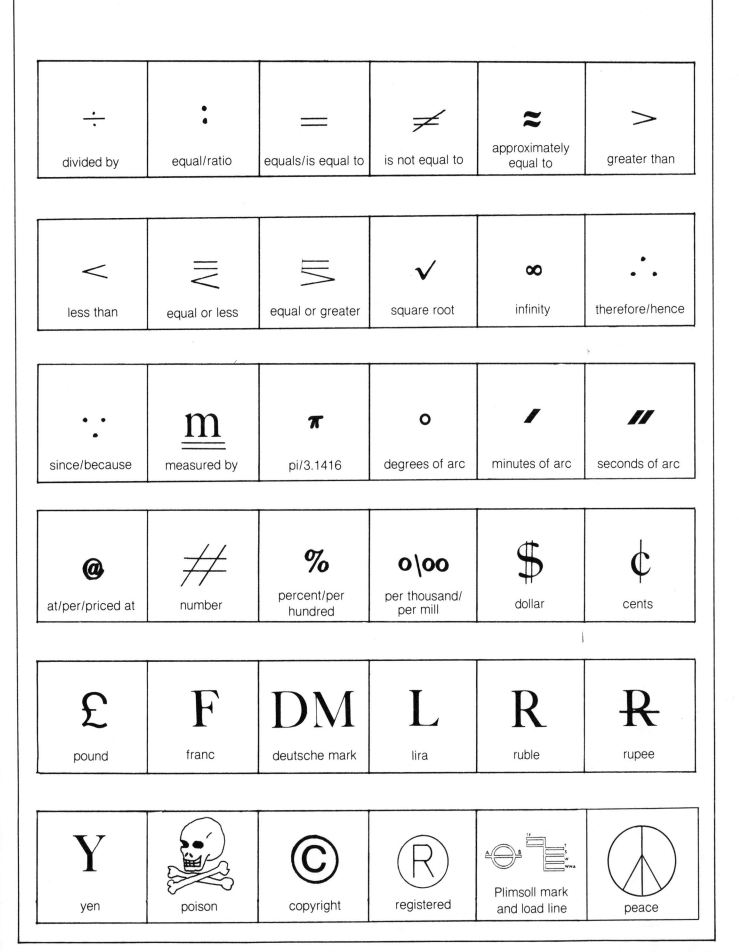

÷	:	=	≠	≈	>
divided by	equal/ratio	equals/is equal to	is not equal to	approximately equal to	greater than
<	≦	≧	✓	∞	∴
less than	equal or less	equal or greater	square root	infinity	therefore/hence
∵	m	π	°	′	″
since/because	measured by	pi/3.1416	degrees of arc	minutes of arc	seconds of arc
@	#	%	o\oo	$	¢
at/per/priced at	number	percent/per hundred	per thousand/ per mill	dollar	cents
£	F	DM	L	R	R̶
pound	franc	deutsche mark	lira	ruble	rupee
Y		©	®		
yen	poison	copyright	registered	Plimsoll mark and load line	peace

Symbolic Language

Sign language, used by deaf-mutes, substitutes *gestures* for spoken words. Embossed *dots* are used by blind people to read by touch. *Semaphore* and *wigwag* are systems of signalling by hand-held flags.

Sign Language

Braille

a	b	c	d	e	f	g	h	i	j	k	l	m

n	o	p	q	r	s	t	u	v	w	x	y	z

Grammatical Symbols

In addition to these *punctuation*, *diacritic* and *pronunciation symbols*, there are *phonetic symbols, abbreviations* and *contractions*.

'a' single quotation marks	**"a"** quotation marks	**'** foot/minute/prime	**"** inch/second/ double prime	**a'** apostrophe
(a) parentheses	**[a]** brackets/crotchets	**a-a** hyphen	**a—a** dash	
a/a virgule/ slant/slash	**,** comma	**;** semicolon	**:** colon	**&** ampersand
* asterisk	**•** period/full point	**• • •** ellipsis/marks of omission	**!** exclamation point/ bang/ecphoneme	**?** question mark/ eroteme
a̲ underline/ underscore	**ff** ligature	**é** acute accent	**à** grave accent	**â** circumflex accent/ doghouse
ñ tilde	**ç** cedilla	**ā** macron	**ă** breve	**äi** dieresis/umlaut

Proofreader's Marks

The marks illustrated below are used for the purpose of standardizing the transmittal of corrections and queries between *editors* and/or *proofreaders* and *typesetters* and/or *printers*. When the corrected *copy* is set in *type* it is *proved,* or *proofed,* and additional marks are then made on the *galley proofs.* The first *impressions* of the corrected galleys are called *page proofs.*

Mark

Enter HAMLET.

Ham. To be, or not to be: that is the question:

Whether 't is nobler in the mind to suffer

The slings and arrows of outrageous fortune

Or to take arms against a sea of troubles,

And end by opposing them? To die: to sleep:

No More; and by a sleep to say we end

The heart-ache and the 1000 natural shocks

That flesh is heir to 't is a consummation

Devoutly to be wish'd. To die, to sleep;

To sleep: perchance to dream: ay, there's

□□□ ⟵ the rub;

For in that sleep of death what dreams may come

When we have shuffled off this mortal coil,

Must give us pause. There's the respect

That makes calamity of so long life;

For who would bear the whips and scorns of time,

The oppressor's wrong, the proud man's contumely,

The pangs of disprized love, the law's delay,

The insolence of office, and the spurns

That patient merit of the unworthy takes,

When he himself might his quietus make

With a bare bodkin who would fardels bear,

to grunt and sweat under a weary life,

But that the dread of something death,

Symbol — Meaning

Symbol	Meaning
ital	set in italics
¶	begin a paragraph
G ?	grammar?
⌗	close up partly/less space/take out space
]	move right/flush left
tr	transpose
lc	set in lower case
sp	spell out
⌢	insert comma
eq #	equalize space
[	move left/square up
[	move left–indent 3 ems
⊔	move down
au ?	query author
⌒	close up completely/take out space
⟍	delete
#	insert space/insert lead
⟋	insert apostrophe
a/	substitute letter
=	straighten type horizontally
rom	set in roman type
stet	let it stand
?	insert question mark
cap	set in capitals
after	insert/insert omitted matter

Hobo Signs

Symbols, inscriptions, phrases and signatures drawn in public places are collectively called graffiti. Those shown here are used among tramps and vagrants.

kindhearted lady	dishonest man	town asleep, cops inactive	town awake, cops active
housewife feeds for chores	tell pitiful story	town allows alcohol	town dislikes alcohol
dog	doctor	judge	chain gang
danger	man with gun	don't give up	be quiet
go	unsafe place	good for handout	officer

Tombstone and Coffin

A stone placed at the foot of a grave is a *footstone. Crypts,* or *vaults,* are wholly or partly underground *burial chambers. Mausoleums* are large aboveground *tombs.*

ornament/carving

floral carving

inscription

year of birth

epitaph

base

tombstone/memorial/ monument/tablet/ gravestone/headstone

year of death

wreath

easel

grave/plot

J.SMITH

1803 – 1875

I TOLD THE DOCTOR I WAS SICK

MORT WALKER

Coffin/Casket

interior panel

pillow

drop

bed/mattress

arm

handle

lug

bridge

overlay

lid panel

fishtail

end handle

Index

504

505

507

508

511

521

523

551

upper header, solar
collector panel, 383
upper housing,
sander, 411
upper jaw, fish, 43
upper joint,
clarinet, 351
upper limb, bow, 456
upper lounge, jumbo
jet, 148
upper mandible, bird, 37
upper panel, piano, 355
upper plate,
theodolite, 426
upper spray arm,
dishwasher, 246
upper tail crest,
tadpole, 42
upper teeth, 446
upper thigh, dog, 34
upper pool, canal
lock, 97
upper rack,
dishwasher, 246
upper rail,
balustrade, 71
upper receiver,
rifle, 461
upper rudder, jumbo jet, 149
upper sash, window, 63
upper shell, turtle, 40
upper side-rail,
truck van, 117
upper windshield,
bus, 114
upright: basketball
backstop, 292;
croquet wicket, 312;
easel, 364; etching
press, 371; football, 289;
guillotine, 452; hand
loom, 379; horizontal
bar, 300; hurdle, 298;
lithographic press,
370; parallel bars,
300; pole vault, 299;
pommel horse, 301; roller
coaster, 90; tow
truck, 122
upright handlebar,
bicycle, 124
upright piano, 355
upright pole, tent, 336
upright standard,
theodolite, 426
upright vacuum
cleaner, 279
uprush, wave, 14
upstop wheel, roller
coaster, 90
upstream, river, 13
upstream gate, canal
lock, 97
Uranus, planet, 3
urine transfer
connector,
spacesuit, 157
urn, bed finial, 266
uropod, lobster, 45
usage register,
electric meter, 389
use, label, 264
used-blade box, razor
blade injector, 206
utility belt, police,
482-483
utility pocket: cowboy,
474; spacesuit, 157
uvula, 28

V

V: braille, 496; sign
language, 496
VAC scale, volt-ohm
meter, 413
vacuum cleaner, 279
vacuum hose,
automobile
engine, 107
vacuum jar,
laboratory, 437

vacuum mount, pencil
sharpener, 273
vacuum relief valve,
tanker, 136, 137
vacuum tube, 386
valance: curtain,
236; stage, 344
validation, postal
money order, 223
valley, 7; house roof, 61;
non-glaciated, 12;
river, 13
valley glacier, 12
value: coin, 221;
thematic map, 21
value range,
isarithmic map, 21
valve: automobile
engine, 107;
bicycle, 124; blood
pressure gauge, 439;
camper, 126; camp
stove, 336; clam, 45;
cornet, 353; drag
racing dragster,
333; dental unit, 444;
faucet, 269; football,
288; French horn, 352;
furnace, 390; hot air
balloon, 326;
inflatable, 129;
laboratory burner, 437;
lantern, 336;
motorcycle, 125;
nuclear reactor,
384; playing cards,
342; plumber's torch,
412; radiator, 390;
scallop, 45; skin
diving, 325; solar
heating system, 383;
standpipe, 57; steam
engine, 395; subway
motorman's cab, 115;
tanker, 136, 137;
toilet, 271; trumpet, 353;
water heater, 391
vambrace, armor, 455
vamp: boot, 202; man's
shoe, 200; running
shoe, 296; sandal, 202;
woman's shoe, 201
van, truck, 117
Vandyke beard, 207
vane: barn, 100; bird
feather, 37; missile,
466; weather, 18, 19;
windmill, 382
vanishing point,
perspective, 362
vanity, dresser, 268
varashield, truck
cab, 116
variable range
marker, radar and
sonar, 434
variable spacer,
typewriter, 162
variable-speed
control, saw, 407
variable sweep wing,
jet fighter, 152
vase, church, 85
VASI, airport runway, 92
vastus medialis,
human, 26
vault: bank, 447;
burial chamber, 500;
dome, 83; parking
meter, 109; pay
telephone, 178; pole,
294, 299
vaulter: gymnastics,
301; pole vault, 299
vaulting board, 301
vaulting horse, 301
V-berth, sailboat, 131
V-bottom hull,
powerboat, 134
VDC scale, volt-ohm
meter, 413
vegetable, 52, 53, 258;

juice extractor,
251; refrigerator
compartment, 245
vegetable organ,
grass, 56
vegetable slicer, 257
vehicle: airport, 93;
armor-plated, 464-465
V-8 automobile
engine, 107
veil: bride's, 472; nun's,
471; remnants of
universal, mushroom,
55; woman's hat, 199
vein: human, 27; leaf, 50
Velcro closure, 205;
football helmet, 288;
parka cuff, 197
velocity indicator:
pilot's instrument
panel, 153; space
shuttle, 155
velocity stack,
racing car, 332
velvet cap, royal
crown, 469
venetian blind, 237
venom, snake, 40
vent: automobile, 103;
Band-Aid, 441;
battery, 387; bus, 114;
cannon barrel, 457;
furnace, 390; hair dryer,
208; hot air balloon,
326; house gable, 61;
jacket, 184; paint
spray gun, 415;
radiator, 390; shoe
tree, 203; skin
diving fin, 325;
stove, 244; truck van,
117; volcano, 10; water
heater, 391
vent field astragal
and filets, cannon
barrel, 457
ventilated rib,
shotgun, 459
ventilation
building, underwater
tunnel, 96
ventilation hatch,
bus, 114
ventilation-heating
controls, car, 106
ventilation pack,
hovercraft, 145
ventilation
umbilical,
spacesuit, 157
ventilator: barn, 100;
lantern, 336;
locomotive, 113;
subway car, 115;
tank, 465
venting arm, launch
pad, 154
vent pipe: house, 60;
pressure cooker, 253
vent port, drag
racing driver's
fire suit, 333
ventral fin: fish, 43; jet
fighter, 152
ventral scale,
snake, 41
vent screw, outboard
engine, 133
venturi windshield,
powerboat, 135
Venus, planet, 3
veranda, house, 61
verge, barn, 100
vergeboard, house, 61
Vermeil Room, White
House, 73
vernier, theodolite, 426
verso, book page, 165
vertebral column,
human, 26
vertebral shield,
turtle, 40
vertex, pyramid, 69
vertical, transit, 426

vertical adjustment,
speculum, 438
vertical aerial,
volleyball net, 313
vertical angulation
dial readout, dental
x-ray unit, 444
vertical brace:
bridge, 95; oil
drilling platform, 99
vertical centering,
radar, 434
vertical circle,
theodolite, 426
vertical exhaust,
truck tractor, 116
vertical fin: blimp,
158; glider, 147;
single engine
airplane, 147
vertical gauge,
carpenter's level, 414
vertical reduction,
theodolite, 426
vertical speed
indicator,
747 cockpit, 150
vertical stabilizer,
jumbo jet, 149
vertical tail fin, jet
fighter, 152
vertical updraft,
tornado, 17
vertical velocity
indicator, pilot's
instrument panel, 153
very high frequency
antenna,
destroyer, 140
very high frequency
signal,
television, 181
very soft, music
notation, 347
vessel, 128
vest, 184; butler, 473;
cowboy, 474; man's
formal attire, 472;
police, 483; ski
clothes, 321, 323;
sweater, 195
vestibule, vault, 447
vestment, Jewish
ritual, 470
vestry, church, 85
V-gouge, 368
VHF aerial, jumbo
jet, 148
VHF antenna:
destroyer, 140, 141;
helicopter, 146; lunar
lander, 156
VHF radio,
747 cockpit, 151
vial: carpenter's
level, 414;
theodolite, 426
vibration damper
pulley, automobile
engine, 107
vibrissa: cat, 35;
ultimate beast, 46
vice president,
Senate, 72
video camera, 180
video cassette
tape, 180
video display,
computer, 429
video recorder, 180
viewer, television
LaserDisc
player, 181
viewfinder: camera,
170, 171; telescope, 433
viewing area,
public sign, 491
viewing hood,
radar, 434
vignette: book, 165;
label, 264
viola, 348, 349
violation flag,
parking meter, 109

560

Credits

pages **2-3**, illustration by Neal Adams; **5**, Time Zone map courtesy of Hammond Incorporated, Maplewood, NJ; **8-9**, illustration by Dee Molenaar; **18**, photo courtesy of Science Associates Inc.; **21**, thematic map of "Number of Irish Foreign Born 1930" courtesy of Carnegie Institution of Washington; **22**, photography by Color Lab, Hawthorne, NY; **58-59**, illustrations courtesy of American Plywood Association; **60**, illustration by Charles Addams, blueprint by Carl Hribar; **72-73**, photos by David Burnett, courtesy of Contact Press Images, Inc.; **74**, photo courtesy of State of N.Y. Department of Correctional Services; **75**, top photo courtesy of The Port Authority of New York & New Jersey, lower photo courtesy of Empire State Building; **76**, elevator shaft illustration courtesy of Westinghouse Elevator, elevator car illustration courtesy of Williamsburg Steel Products, Co.; **78**, photograph courtesy of British Information Service; **84-85**, illustrations courtesy of Cathedral Church of St. John the Divine, New York, NY; **86**, courtesy of Temple Emanuel, New York, NY; **88-89**, courtesy of Ringling Brothers and Barnum & Bailey; **90-91**, roller coaster courtesy of Magic Mountain Amusement Park, ferris wheel and merry-go-round courtesy of Rye Playland; **92-93**, airport photo courtesy of American Airlines; **94**, photo courtesy of Association of American Railroads; **95**, photos courtesy of Triborough Bridge and Tunnel Authority; **99**, photograph by Carroll S. Grevemberg, Grevy Photography, New Orleans, LA; **102-103**, AnyCar photos courtesy of Manufacturers Hanover Trust, New York, NY; **104-105**, photo courtesy of Buick Division, General Motors Corp.; **106**, photo courtesy of Alfa Romeo; **107**, photo courtesy of Bradford La Riviera Inc.; **110**, courtesy of Triborough Bridge & Tunnel Authority; **112-113**, steam locomotive photo courtesy of Association of American Railroads, turbine engine photo courtesy of National Railroad Passenger Corporation, panels courtesy of The Train Shop, Ltd.; **114**, coach courtesy of American Eagle, commuter bus interior courtesy of NY Metropolitan Transit Authority; **115**, courtesy of NY Metropolitan Transit Authority Museum; **116-117**, photos courtesy of Mack Trucks Corporation; **120-121**, photos courtesy of New York City Fire Department; **122**, tow truck courtesy of LST Towing, New York, NY; **123**, courtesy of NYC Department of Sanitation; **125**, photo courtesy of Kawasaki Motorcycles; **126**, camper photo courtesy of Winnebago Industries, Inc., snowmobile photo courtesy of Yamaha Motor Corporation; **127**, stagecoach courtesy of Wells Fargo Bank History Department, hansom cab courtesy of The New York Historic Society; **129**, photo courtesy of Dyer Jones, Warren, RI; **130-131**, illustrations courtesy of CSY Yacht Corporation, Tampa, FL; **132**, compass photo courtesy of Aqua Meter Instrument Corporation, Roseland, NJ; **133**, sextant photo courtesy of Weems & Plath, Annapolis, MD, outboard photo courtesy of Mariner Outboards, Fond du Lac, WI; **134-135**, illustration courtesy of Bertram Yachts, Miami, FL; **138-139**, illustration courtesy of Cunard Line Limited, New York, NY; **140-141**, courtesy of the officers and men of *USS Thomas C. Hart* (DE 1092); **142-143**, photos courtesy of US Navy Department; **144**, tugboat courtesy of Moran, fireboat courtesy of NYC Fire Department; **145**, hovercraft photo courtesy of British Hovercraft Corp. Ltd.; **146**, photo courtesy of Sikorsky; **147**, airplane photo courtesy of Piper Aircraft Corp.; **148-149**, illustration courtesy of Boeing; **150-151**, photo courtesy of Boeing; **152-153**, photo and illustrations courtesy of Grumman; **154-155**, photograph and illustration courtesy of NASA; **156-157**, illustrations courtesy of NASA; **158**, photo courtesy of Goodyear; **161**, caligraphy by Melissa, text by Sean Kelly; **162**, manual typewriter photo courtesy of Royal Business Machines, Inc.; **164**, illustrations courtesy of International Paper Company; **167**, *TIME* cover reprinted by permission from *TIME,* The Weekly Newsmagazine, copyright Time Inc., 1980, contents page reprinted courtesy of *SPORTS ILLUSTRATED,* from the March 3, 1980 issue. Copyright (c) 1980, Time, Inc.; **166**, courtesy of *The New York Times,* New York, NY; **168-169**, prepared by *New York Magazine,* New York, NY; **170**, top photo courtesy of Poloroid Corp., panel photo courtesy of Vivitar; **171**, camera photo courtesy of Minolta Camera Co., Ltd.; **172**, photo courtesy of Minolta Camera Co., Ltd.; **173**, movie photo projector courtesy of Minolta, slide projector photo courtesy of Kodak, screen courtesy of Da-Lite Screen Company; **174**, light meter courtesy of Gossen-Luna Pro, electronic flash courtesy of Vivitar Corp., tripod courtesy of E. Leitz Inc.; **175**, reel-to-reel recorder photo courtesy of Pioneer Electronics, cassette tape photo courtesy of Sony; **176-177**, photographs courtesy of Pioneer Electronics Corp., NJ, and Executive Recording Limited, N.Y.; **179**, photo courtesy of Radio Shack; **180**, video recorder courtesy of U.S. JVC Corp.; **181**, television photo courtesy of Sony, LasarDisc courtesy of Pioneer; **182**, illustration courtesy of NASA; **191**, panty hose photo courtesy of Hanes Corp.; **192-193**, illustrations by Calvin Klein; **197**, fur photo courtesy of Rosette, NY; **201**, courtesy of Andy Warhol; **203**, sock photo courtesy of Alexander Lee Wallan Inc.; **205**, photo courtesy of Velcro USA; **206**, electric razor photo courtesy of Sunbeam Corp.; **208**, hair dryer photo courtesy of Conair; **210**, curling iron photo courtesy of Conair; **212-213**, products courtesy of Avon Products, Inc., make-up by Tom Gearhard; **214-215**, ring and pendant illustrations courtesy of Jane Evans; **216**, wristwatch courtesy of Chronosport Inc., Rowayton, CT; **222**, check courtesy of Rudco Corp., credit card courtesy of Visa; **223**, traveler's check courtesy of Barclay's Bank, New York, NY, money order courtesy of U.S. Postal Service; **233**, candle snuffer courtesy of Fortunoff Department Store, New York, NY; **240**, place setting courtesy of Rosenthal China Co.; **241**, desert setting courtesy of Rosenthal China, panels courtesy of Gorham Division of Textron Inc.; **243**, sink courtesy of Elkay Manufacturing Company, disposal unit courtesy of Hobart Corporation; **247**, electric opener courtesy of Oster Corp., can piercer courtesy of Ekco Industries; **251**, vegetable juicer courtesy of Hamilton Beach, automatic juicer courtesy of Oster Corp., manual juicer courtesy of Acme Juicer Manufacture Corp.; **253**, pressure cooker courtesy of National Presto Industries, electric wok courtesy of Faberware; **254-257**, courtesy of H&P Mayer Corp.; **263**, pump dispenser courtesy of Calmar Division/Diamond International; **264-265**, illustration by The Schecter Group; **274**, courtesy of Viking Sewing Machine Co.; **275**, courtesy Proctor-Silex; **277**, dryer courtesy of General Electric; **279**, vacuum cleaner courtesy of Hoover Co.; **280**, fire extinguisher courtesy of Amerex Corp., smoke alarm courtesy of General Electric; **282**, stroller courtesy of Perego/Pines, Milan, Italy, playpen and car seat courtesy of Century Products, Los Angeles, CA; **283**, wagon illustration courtesy of Flexible Flyer; **284**, barbecue courtesy of King Seeley Company; **287**, glove courtesy of Rawlings Sporting Goods, models: Rod Carew, California Angels (batter), Ossie Virgil Jr., Philadelphia Phillies (catcher); **288**, helmet courtesy of Bike Athletic Company, model: Bruce Harper, New York Jets; **290-291**, models: Ken Morrow (defenseman) and Billy Smith (goalie), New York Islanders; **292**, model: Mike Glenn, New York Knickerbockers; **296**, running show courtesy of Adidas; **300**, photos courtesy of Nissen/Walter Kidde & Company; **301**, photos courtesy of Nissen/Walter Kidde & Company; **303**, model: Wendal Newton; **304-305**, equipment photos courtesy of Northwestern Golf Company; **308**, courtesy of Bridgeport, Conn. Jai Alai, model: Donald Mazza; **309**, piste courtesy of George Santelli Fencing School, NYC; **314**, photo courtesy of Brunswick Corp.; **318**, photo courtesy of Chicago Roller Skates Inc.; **316**, courtesy of Darts Unlimited, New York, NY; **320**, equipment courtesy of Scandinavian Ski Shop; **321**, cross-country equipment courtesy of Scandinavian Ski Shop, snowshoe courtesy of The Snowcraft Corp.; **323**, ski courtesy of Connelly Skis, Inc.; **325**, equipment courtesy of Atlantic Divers World, NY; **326**, photo courtesy of The Balloon Works, Statesville, NC; **327**, parachute courtesy of Para-Flite Inc., US Parachuting Assoc., hang glider courtesy of United States Hang Gliding Assoc.; **328**, photos courtesy of George Willig, Topanga, CA; **329**, Western saddle courtesy of H. Kauffman and Sons, Inc., English saddle by Crosby, courtesy of Millers, NY; **330**, program entry courtesy of Pimlico Race Track; **331**, Meadowlands Racetrack, East Rutherford, NJ, model: Courtney Foos; **332**, illustration by Jack Lane, courtesy of L'Art et L'Automobile Gallery, 354 E. 66 Street, New York, NY, Jacques Vaucher; **333**, photos courtesy of National Hot Rod Association; **334-335**, fishing reel photo courtesy of Penn Reels, rod photo courtesy of Shakespeare Fishing Rods; **336**, photos courtesy of Coleman Co.; **337**, backpack photo courtesy of Johnson/Camp Trails; **338**, universal gym photo courtesy of Nissen; **340-341**, courtesy of Mr. Lucky Equipment, Rosedale, NY; **343**, ticket courtesy of Globe Ticket Company **345**, photo of the Bardavon Theatre courtesy of Robert Paul Molay; **346**, *Theme From What's What Book* written by John Hill, John Hill Music Inc.; **348**, illustration and photo courtesy of Chicago Symphony Orchestra; **354**, photo courtesy of Rodgers Organ, New York, NY; **359**, bagpipes courtesy of Larry Cole; **360**, accordion courtesy Stuyvesant Music; **363**, painting courtesy of the Metropolitan Museum of Art, New York, NY; **364-365**, painting equipment courtesy of Grumbacher; **366**, Sculpture House, New York, NY; **368**, equipment courtesy of Rembrant Graphic Arts, NJ; **370**, courtesy of Rembrant Graphic Arts, NJ and Charles Brand Machinery Inc., NY; **371**, Rembrant Graphic Arts, NJ and Charles Brand Machinery, Inc., NY; **372**, equipment courtesy of Glassmaster Guild; **374-375**, cartoon by Mike Witte, comic strip by Mort Walker, copyright 1978 King Features Syndicate, Inc.; **377**, quilt courtesy of Fairfield Processing; **378**, shuttle courtesy of C.J. Bates & Son, Inc.; **379**, loom courtesy of LaClerc Weaving Looms; **382**, wind turbine photo courtesy of Grumman Corp.; **386**, transistor photo courtesy Bell Laboratories; **392**, courtesy of Hampton Sales; **396**, courtesy of Teledyne Wisconsin Motor; **399**, photos courtesy of Adjustable Clamp Company; **407**, table saw photo courtesy of ToolKraft, circular saw photo courtesy of Skil, saber saw photo courtesy of Rockwell International; **411**, sander photo courtesy of Rockwell International; **413**, voltmeter courtesy of Amprobe Instruments; **414**, folding rule courtesy of Stanley Tools, carpenter's level courtesy of Toolkraft; **415**, spray painter courtesy of Spray Tech Corp.; **416**, photo courtesy of Hoffritz; **417**, courtesy of Douglas Products; **418**, photos courtesy of L.R. Nelson Corp.; **419**, photo courtesy of Sears, Roebuck & Company; **420**, wheelbarrow courtesy of Jackson Manufacturing Company, seeder courtesy of Cyclone Seeder Company, Inc.; **421**, chainsaw photo courtesy of Skil Corporation; **424**, tractor photo courtesy of J.I. Case; **426**, theodolite courtesy of Dietzgen Corp., jackhammer courtesy of Bosch Power Tools; **427**, photos courtesy of R.F. Shoup Corp., Bryn Mawr, PA; **428**, courtesy of International Business Machine; **429**, computer photo courtesy of Radio Shack; **430**, courtesy of NCR Corporation; **432**, photo courtesy of Carl Zeiss Inc.; **433**, telescope photo courtesy of Unitron Instruments Inc., binoculars photo courtesy of Minolta Camera Co., Ltd.; **434**, photos courtesy of Furuno U.S.A., Inc.; **435**, metal detector photo courtesy of White Electronics Inc., geiger counter photo courtesy of EDA Instruments; **436-437**, burner courtesy of Fisher Scientific Company, scale courtesy of Ohaus Scale Corporation; **438**, photos courtesy of Welch Allyn, Skaneateles Falls, NY; **439**, photos courtesy of Sybron Corp.; **440**, courtesy of Affiliated Hospital Products; **442**, wheelchair photo courtesy of Invacare Corporation, hearing aid photo courtesy of Dahlberg Electronics, pacemaker photo courtesy of Medtronic, Inc.; **443**, denture photo courtesy of Sterndent Corporation, braces bracket photo courtesy of 'A' Company, Inc.; **444**, courtesy of Ritter Dental Corp.; **445**, courtesy of Dr. Herbert Spasser; **447**, photographs courtesy of Mosler Safe Company; **448**, Safe Hardware Corporation, Emhart Industries Inc.; **449**, lock photo courtesy of Medico Security Locks Inc.; **450**, hasp photo courtesy of Lawrence Brothers, Inc.; **451**, chains courtesy of Diamond Chain Co., block and pulley courtesy of The Crosby Group; **467**, illustration courtesy of James Burrough Limited, New York, NY; **468**, costumes courtesy of Eaves-Brooks Costume Company; **470**, photograph courtesy of Irving Fisher; **471**, minister photo courtesy of The Very Reverend Francis B. Sayre; **472**, photo courtesy of After Six Formal Wear; **473**, costumes courtesy of Eaves-Brooks Costume Company; **474**, costume courtesy of Eaves-Brookes Costume Company, Indian courtesy of the Museum of the American Indian, Bronx, NY; **475**, Manchu Court Dress courtesy of Reginald Bragonier, Arab courtesy of Bill Ashe, model: Jan Leighton; **476**, model: Jan Leighton, pirate photograph by BODI, mizer photograph by Michael Weiss; **477**, illustration by Ted Geisel; **478**, photo courtesy of Lois Greenfield/Capezio Ballet Makers; **480-481**, photographs courtesy of Phil Koenig, soldiers courtesy of US Army, sailor courtesy of US Navy; **487**, courtesy of Government of Canada; **484**, photo courtesy of New York Fire Department; **490-491**, symbols courtesy of Handbook of Pictorial Symbols, Rudolph Modley, Dover Publications, Inc., New York, NY; **498**, courtesy of Mary Grace and Maria Maggi; **500**, casket courtesy of Simmons Casket Company/Gulf and Western Casket Co.

Acknowledgements

Harold Adler, Adler Monument and Granite Works; Roslyn Alexander, librarian Charles Evans Hughes High School; Jack Arnoff; Dave Lipsky, Juana Torres and Frank Coppinger, Army Corps of Engineers; Martin Bacheller, Hammond, Inc.; Sandy Bartram; Susan Bates Inc.; Roberta Baker, LIFE Magazine; Barney's Clothing Store; David Baxley, Triborough Bridge & Tunnel Authority; Mitch Becker, Globe Ticket Corp.; Paul Berkovitz, Algoma Net Company; Randy Black, Bike Athletic Corp.; Mitchell and George Tepper, Bond Street Suspender Inc.; Bonny Products; Carol Boswell and Gina Frantz, Boswell-Frantz Public Relations; Jerry Boxer, Abraham Boxer and Sons; Lee Bracy, Westinghouse Elevator Inc.; Benjamin Bragonier; Dana Bragonier; queen model Penelope Bragonier; Bill and Betty Brennan; Andreas Brown, Gotham Book Store; Cadillac Meat Company; Camrod Motorcycles; Carez Health Care Corp.; Zack Carr, Calvin Klein Ltd.; cross-country skiing model Catherine Carlen; Robert E. Lewis and William S. DeArment, Channellock Corp.; Betty Charak, Personality Hanger Inc.; Jerry Charles, Hollco Tools; Coats and Clark, Inc.; accordion supplied by Larry Cole; Phil Colicchio, Oreo Cookies; Dita Comacho; Nancy Conforti, H & P-Mayer Inc.; H.C. Cook, Inc., Division of Gem Products; Ron Coplon, Rubin Gloves Inc.; Richard Curtis, Richard Curtis Associates; Elmer Danch and Elaine Harr, DaLite Movie Screen Company; Frank Davis; John and Jessica Dorfman; Rose Dreger; Alfred Dunhill Inc.; Ernest DuPuy, Hammond Inc.; Ken Durst, Rawlings Inc.; John Edelmann; EKCO Housewares Corp.; Lt. Juan Torres and Ray Florida, NYC Emergency Medical Service; Lee Entwhistle, Eves-Brooks Costumes Inc.; Herbert Eskelson, Para-Flite Inc.; Eye Center Inc.; Penny Farber, Foxmore Inc.; staff of Fashion Institute of Technology library; Arthur Ferguson, Metropolian Transit Authority; Steve Fineberg, Feinberg Associates; Ira Finke, Ira Finke Photography; Nini Finkelstein, Ringling Brothers & Barnum and Bailey Circus; Irving and Sylvia Fisher; butler model Jim Fitzgerald; Anthony Forgione, Consolidated Wafer and Cone Corp.; Joann Forster, International School of Harness Racing at Roosevelt Raceway; William Free Advertising Agency; Bill Freeman, The Gill Track and Field Equipment Company; Steve Friedman; Lois Fry, Shakespeare Fishing Equipment; Fuller Brush Corp.; Louise Gaither, Executive Services Advertising; Gary Galante, Museum of American Indian; cosmetic model make-up by Tom Gerhart; Irv Goldfinger, Forsyth Monument Works; Matthew Goldman; Bob Goldstein, M & F Hanger; Brian Goodman; Mary Grace: Kathy Graham, Bridgeport, Conn, Jai Alai; J.F. Grgula, Structo Division, King-Seeley Thermos Comp.; John Growth, School of Visual Arts; Mike Gue, Ethics Automobile Racing; Walter Guslawski, Williamsberg Steel Products; Stephen A. Hallis, Jr., Digital Equipment Corp.; Dana Hammond, Hammond Inc.; Dean Hammond, Hammond Inc.; Stuart Hammond, President, Hammond Inc.; management and staff of Hampton Sales; Harvey Sound Corp.; Irving Heiberger, Marshall Clark Inc.; Joyce Heiberger, JBH Advertising; Kenneth Heinz, Welch-Allyn Corporation; Paul Heller, International Creative Management; Katharine Hill; Hoffritz Inc.; Edward Irrizarry; PO Ken Kaufman, NYPD co-author of *The Incredible Scooter Cops*; Scrooge's letter by Sean Kelly, former editor of THE NATIONAL LAMPOON; Chris Kelly; cowboy model by William Ketchum Jr., author of *Western Memorabilia*; George Klauber, George Klauber Graphic Arts Studio; Morris and Ruth Kleinman; Drew Kuber, Hammond Inc.; Richard and Elyse Langsam; Larry Letizia, Joyson Motors; Leaf Tent and Sail Inc.; Charles Leib; Leland-Penn; Patricia Lewis; Robert Lewis, Chrysler Corporation; Teresa Longhitano; Mel and Cheryl London, authors of *Bread Winners*; Lionel V. Lorona, New York Public Library; Candace Lovell; Donald A. Macaulay; Joseph W. Maresca, Jr., SRI Institute; Daniel Mazzarella, Science Associates Inc.; Ken McAdams; Kay McDowell, US Postal Data Center; Frank 'Tug' McGraw, Philadelphia Phillies; Dave McNamara, Wilson Sporting Goods, Inc.; The Meadowlands Racetrack management; John Meyers, Fisher Scientific Company; Ray Miller, VISA; Mr. Lucky School of Gambling; Macmillan Publishing Corp.; Captain Don Mitchell, Eastern Airlines; Jenny Moradfar; Ruth Grevey and Larry Osterman, Mosler Safe Corp.; Edward J. Murphy, Edward J. Murphy Corp.; Neckwear Association of America; Steve Nesbitt, Mark Hess, Tom Jacqua, NASA; New York Jets; New York Knickerbockers; New York Yankees; Don Morris and Suzanne Eagle, NEW YORK Magazine; PO George Legas and Steve Berenhaus, NYPD; John Nicholson; C. Michael Oldenberg, Centennial Management Corp.; Joan Rubin and Christine Martorana, Omega Fashions Ltd.; John Pace, National Cash Register; Rolando Pena; Arthur and Lois Perschetz; LTC Gerald Perschetz U.S. Army (Ret.); Clarence Peskac, Dietzgen Corp.; Allen Petersen, Petersen Manufacturing Co., Inc.; Robert Pledge, Contact Press Images; Brigit Polk, The Factory; Marian Powers, TIME Magazine; Donald Quest, Southwest Texas Drilling Co.; Jim Ramsey, Rodgers Organ Corp.; Mark Resnick, Hammond Inc.; Rock of Ages Corp.; Rosemary Rodgers, John Hill Music, Inc.; Linda Rosenblatt, R.D.H.; Joan Evanish, Judith Johnson and Canon West, St. John the Divine; Teddi Sann, Avon Products, Inc.; Gene Sayet, Executive Recording Ltd.; Frank and Harriet Sayre; Rosette Schecter, Furs by Rosette; Deputy Police Commissioner 'Mickey' Schwartz, NYPD; Ann Scott, SPORTS ILLUSTRATED; Elizabeth Scott, Chicago Symphony Orchestra; Ray Scroggins, Wisconsin-Teledyne; Dr. John H. Seward, MD EENT; Joel Shaffer, Hammond Inc.; J. Ronald Shumate, Association of American Railroads; Craig Siebert; Harold Silver, Caldwell Button Corp.; Robert Simon, Wallin, Simon and Black; Robert Smith; NY-NJ Port Authority; Dr. Herbert Spasser, D.D.S.; cosmetics model Tina Stahle; Stappers Equipment Corp.; Stuyvesant Music; Tom Szobe, Paragon Sporting Goods; Bob Taylor, Hedstrom Baby Furniture; Technigraph Studio; Marilyn Tempkins, Vivitar Inc.; caligraphy letterhead on Scrooge's letter by Melissa Topping; Tower Manufacturing; Paul Schulhaus, Russ Levin, Train Shop Ltd.; Bobbie Tupper, Park West Chapel; Helen Turi, General Motors Corp.; Helen Tutt, American Eagle; Universal Fastenings Inc.; Anna Urband, US Navy Public Relations; officers and men of the *USS Thomas C. Hart* (DE 1092); Jaques Vaucher, L'Art et L'Automobile Gallery; Ossie Virgil Jr., Philadelphia Phillies; Dan Walden, Consolidated Edison Corp.; John Wanamaker; Sam Weinstein, Color Group; Western Union Corp.; George Willig; king model Robert Wills; PO 'Scooter' Joe Willins, NYPD, co-author of *The Incredible Scooter Cops*; John Wisdom; Laurie Wolford; Janet Wygall; Will Yolin, author of *The Complete Book of Kites and Kite Flying*; Richard Ziskin, American Umbrella Co.; Roger Zissu, Cowan, Liebowitz & Latman; Nell Znamierowski, Fashion Institute of Technology; and special thanks to the Hammond staff, both in Maplewood, NJ, and New York City, for their numerous contributions and assistance in producing this book.

Afterword

Creating and executing an imaginative new concept is a
rewarding task. In that respect, WHAT'S WHAT has
been no exception. We have been inordinately lucky in
having been able to attract like-minded people with
vision and imagination who have helped make this book
what it is. They, like us, have made every effort to make
the information and its presentation as useful and
accurate as possible. But, as with any major new
undertaking, errors are bound to creep in. If you found
the book engaging and informative, if it has given
you some of the pleasure it has given us, we ask that
you help make future editions of WHAT'S WHAT even
more complete and accurate by sharing your special
knowledge and observations with us in writing.

David Fisher
Reginald Bragonier Jr.
Post Office Box 1
Chappaqua, NY 10514